ARMY BOWL GAMES

VOLUME 1: 1890-2010

BY
MIKE BELTER

Army Bowl Games, Volume 1: 1890-2010

By Mike Belter

Published by Mike Belter

Copyright 2022 Mike Belter

License Notes

Thank you for downloading this eBook. You are welcome to share it with your friends. This book may be reproduced, copied, and distributed for non-commercial purposes, provided the book remains in its complete original form. If you enjoyed this book, please return to your favorite eBook retailer to discover other works from this author. Thank you for your support.

This paperback is licensed for your personal enjoyment only. If you would like to share this paperback with another person, please purchase an additional copy for each recipient. If you're reading this paperback and did not purchase it, or it was not purchased for your use only, then please return to your favorite paperback retailer and purchase your own copy. Thank you for respecting the hard work of this author.

Prologue

Go Army!!! Beat Navy!!!

Go Army!!! Win the Bowl Game!!!

Living for two decades in a large city hosting a major college football team in a Power Five conference that routinely completes for national championships, my friends are often startled when they hear about me traveling in late December to cheer my Black Knights in a college football bowl game, given that most of them grew up in times when Army Football was not very competitive. When I tell them how few bowl games West Point has played in, they are very surprised.

I published my first Army Football book in 2016 about the 2014 national championship team in hopes to eventually get this team and the 1916 national championship team recognized on the walls of Michie Stadium someday. I point out that even the NCAA recognizes these national championships in the same manner as the 1944, 1945, and 1946 Army Football Teams. These men, long gone, deserve the recognition by my alma mater; hopefully someday they will receive it.

After publishing my first book, I was talking one day with a classmate, and we came to the realization that someone in 2077 might be just like me, wanting to recognize the members of the 1977 Army Football Team for what they did on the field, but they would be like the 1914 team, all dead and gone by then. That prompted me to write and publish my second Army Football book in 2018 about my friends, who received an invitation to play in the 1977 Independence Bowl, which was quickly dismissed by the West Point leadership.

I took a break for a year, planning to work on the next Army Football book in 2020 about my next favorite Army Football Team, the 1984 edition which actually went to the first bowl game.

The Covid-19 pandemic disrupted those plans for the next two years, but I began researching and gathering information in the last half of 2021.

As was my practice for the two prior books, I planned to spend a week at West Point digging into the records. There was a change in administration in the Army West Point athletic organization, and it took a while to get their attention on my questions as to when would be a good time to visit, given the pandemic situation.

It appears the annual sports records kept at West Point that I used in my previous books are now either in storage or have been lost by the new athletic administration; and it would be difficult to schedule a visit anytime in 2022 to view whatever might be still available. So I took a step back and thought things out.

In my researching of the 1984 team, I accidently discovered that several colleges have had books written about their bowl teams; and was impressed by the book written about Louisiana State's and Penn State's bowl games. I searched the internet, but could not find any Army books that directly touch on our bowl games. By the end of 2021, I had attended seven of the ten Army West Point bowl games.

Due to the pandemic, I did not attend the 2020 Liberty Bowl game, missing my first Army bowls since the 1985 and 1988 games. I certainly attended the 2021 Armed Forces Bowl in person and was thrilled with our team's comeback victory. On the trip back home, I decided that having a book on Army's bowl experiences might not be a bad idea. So in January 2022, I started sketching this out; with a very aggressive objective to publish the book prior to the beginning of the 2022 football season.

I decided that I would have a chapter that briefly described the team's regular season, and another chapter on the bowl game. I had lots of electronic information on our Army Football since the 2005 season, and had a number of media guides, game programs, and other materials, including videos of all ten games.

Dedication

This book is dedicated to everyone who has ever attended the United States Military Academy at West Point, as well as to anyone who has died in the service to our country, including my father.

Chapter 1

The First Army Post-Season Games

Army's Richard Hutchinson kicked off from the twenty yard line, and Stanford's Lud Frentrup fielded the football and returned it down the field before being tackled by the Cadets. The crowd of 70,000 in Stanford Stadium roared to life as their team lined up to hike the ball on this Saturday afternoon in Palo Alto CA on December 28, 1929.

After a request was made to the President of the United States, Army scheduled an exhibition football game two weeks after the end of the 1930 season with the Navy Midshipmen, and played a charity game to raise money for unemployment relief on December 13, 1930. The Cadets did it again on December 12, 1931, two weeks after they ended their regular season with a 12-0 victory over Notre Dame at Yankee Stadium.

What? Are you telling me some made up story? Is this Earth 2, or some kind of Bizarro World? Nope, these three games actually happened (Google them). They were the Army Football Team's first postseason games; as they were played weeks after the end of the regular college football season. Only the annual Rose Bowl game was played later than these.

Army-Navy Game Interrupted

Our story began after the 1927 Army-Navy game was over, another 24-9 victory by West Point over their Annapolis rivals. At the time, a number of colleges actively recruited former college players to play for them by offering them "inducements," while other schools became wary of rivals trying to poach the best players off their rosters as "tramp athletes."

The United States Naval Academy (USNA) had decided to establish a new policy which a player only allowed three years of varsity eligibility in total at one or more colleges. Navy intended to play football only with opponents who adhered to a similar policy. Generally, these colleges did not allow freshman to play in varsity games. Harvard had done this since at least 1897, as Charles Daly only was allowed to play his last three years there for the Crimson. And Daly became a "tramp athlete" when he was appointed as a Cadet in 1900 and played football over the next two seasons. He was also an All-American each of those five seasons.

The United States Military Academy at West Point (USMA) policy in late 1927 was to allow any student-athlete, even those who have participated or even graduated from another college, to participate in varsity athletics so as long as they were in good standing with the academy. And West Point said they did not need a three-year rule to prevent transfers, given their rigorous admission standards. Army also argued that given that USMA was half the size of USNA's student body, having the three-year rule would hurt it disproportionately.

Navy's complaints were partly due to not beaten Army since the 1921 game. Other football coaches, such as Frank Cavanaugh (Fordham), Henry Schulte (Nebraska), and Fielding Yost (Michigan) supported Navy's position that each team should use the same eligibility playing rules.

Another area of dispute between the two service academies was differences in the federal law regarding admissions of individuals. USNA eligibility requirements at the time only admitted individuals aged 16 to 20, while USMA admitted individuals between 17 and 22 years old. Complaints were made by Navy that Army's older athletes gave the Cadets an unfair competitive advantage. West Point's response was to suggest USNA talk to Congress about this issue, but USMA preferred its current age restrictions.

On December 7, 1927, the *Associated Press* reported that "Dissatisfaction had arisen among naval authorities over the Army eligibility rules which allow stars of college football teams to continue their athletic careers at West Point." A week later, Army fired back, "Rules governing eligibility of Cadets for membership on athletic teams of USMA will undergo no changes."

The two service academies had signed a contract in October 1926 to play football games for four years from 1927 through 1930. USNA Superintendent Rear Admiral Louis Nulton sent an individual contract for the 1928 game to USMA with a clause that said "no contestant shall take part in this game on either team who has had more than three years' experience in intercollegiate football" with a refusal to accede to this request would be considered a 'rejection' of the contract and USNA will consider itself free to schedule another game on November 24, 1928. USMA Superintendent Major General Edwin Winans returned the contract, unsigned, on December 16th.

Scheduling the 1928 Army Football Season

This dispute resulted in the cancellation of the 1928 Army-Navy game and no games planned for the next four years. Graduate athletic manager Major Philip Fleming had been appointed to his job two months before the break with Navy. To compensate for the loss of the Navy game, Fleming worked to finalize opponents for the 1928 schedule. Fleming signed a four year deal with Harvard, persuaded powerhouse Southern Methodist to come to West Point, and signed a home and home agreement with Illinois that started with an away game in 1929.

Both service academies shortly announced replacement games for the November 24th Army-Navy game date. Navy would play Princeton in Philadelphia, while Army would host the University of Nebraska at Michie Stadium. On June 11th, the War Department announced that Army would play at Stanford in 1928 and at West Point in 1929. It seems that Fleming had worked a deal with the visiting Stanford graduate manager Alfred Masters for these games.

The word that that Army would be traveling across the country must have caused a mild shock at USMA. Within a day, a correction was made by both Stanford and USMA that the first game would be played in 1928 at Yankee Stadium, while the 1929 game would be played in 1929 in Palo Alto. It was later revealed that the 1929 game would be on December 28, 1929, to give the Cadets time to cross the continent after term-end examinations (finals) ended.

There was also a bit of shock at the Lincoln campus of the University of Nebraska. The Cornhuskers had lobbied hard to have the Army game at Lincoln, but USMA pointed out the Cadets were already playing three away games from West Point, and persuaded Nebraska to play at West Point. I'm sure there were a few words said when the Cornhuskers arrived at West Point, given that the Army team, the Corps of Cadets, and most of the staff and faculty would leave post for a fourth time that season to play Stanford the next weekend in New York City.

Early Army Football History - Restrictions on Away Games

In 1928, and even in the days before Army started playing football in 1890, the USMA Academic Board fully scheduled the Cadets day from Reveille to Taps, with a few hours off on Saturday and Sunday, if they had no demerits. The staff and faculty felt that Cadets being away from West Point would distract from their academic and military preparations to become officers in the United States Army.

These were the days at West Point where Cadets arrived in July for their first year, and except for certain events, did not leave the post until graduation. The typical exceptions were that Cadets were allowed to take leave during the summer between their second and third year and members of the Corps of Cadets attended Presidential Inaugurations and funerals of national leaders. Also, those proficient in academics, with no demerits and a little bit saved up might take a four or six day Christmas Leave from Christmas Eve until New Year's Eve. Weekend leaves were years into the future.

I suspect that if Army had beaten Navy in 1890, the members of the Academic Board would have clapped and said that is that, let's get back to going to classes, and it would have been decades later before West Point would have fielded a football (or any other sport) team to play other colleges. But losing 24-0 called for a rematch, and in those sometimes gentlemanly times, it would be played in Annapolis.

Seeing that only a few Cadets knew how to play football, called for a few practice games to prepare for the Midshipmen and some professional advice. Five games were scheduled for the 1891 season. Former Yale football player Dr. Harry Williams was just up the road in Newburgh teaching, and was hired to come down a few hours per week. The team, a few substitutes, and the head coach were allowed to leave post by train to go to the game. Williams originally did not even have a seat, but a Cadet sub gave it up and stayed in the barracks.

Lucky for Army, it could find teams to come to West Point each season, including some of the top ones in the nation. The Academic Board relented again when the University of Pennsylvania invited both the Corps of Cadets and the Brigade of Midshipmen to attend the first game in Philadelphia in 1899, especially when USNA immediately said yes.

Harvard, Yale, and other teams began to ask Army to come play at their places, but USMA officials would not allow that. Harvard stopped playing Army after the 1910 game, and Yale did after 1912. Football games continued to be played on The Plain in temporary stands that seated around 7,000 fans, with other spectators standing around the sidelines. Except for Navy, there were no away games.

Army Football Starts to Play at Away & Neutral Sites

Brigadier General Douglas MacArthur became USMA Superintendent in 1919. MacArthur wanted to build a big stadium seating 50,000 along the Hudson River at Target Hill Field and he wanted Army to play away football games. Army played in the Yale Bowl in 1921 and Notre Dame at Ebbets Field in 1923. Michie Stadium opened in 1924 with a capacity of 16,000. The Academic Board relented again to allow the Corps of Cadets to attend at Yale and New York City games.

In 1922, Chicago began building a large stadium that opened in 1924 as Municipal Grant Park Stadium with several events in September, plus the first college football game with Notre Dame beating Northwestern, 13-6, on November 22nd. Navy was responsible for obtaining bids from interested parties to host the 1925 Army-Navy game, and Chicago officials lobbied hard, but USNA selected the Polo Grounds over the new and larger Yankee Stadium.

USMA would be in charge of selecting the site for the 1926 Army-Navy game, and lobbying was intense from Chicago officials and Illinois Congressmen. They offered to play for the travel of the Cadets and Midshipmen to the game and offered each athletic association an additional $100,000. The clincher was the renaming of the stadium to Soldier Field, in dedication to US soldiers who had died in combat during World War I.

USMA finally agreed. Each service academy came by train to Chicago, arriving Friday morning to much pre-game activity, including the formal dedication of Soldier Field. On Saturday, the teams played to a memorable 21-21 tie. I'm sure some USMA professors were up in arms over the loss of two days of class time.

1928 Army Football Season

Army's 1928 schedule now consisted of ten games beginning with two home tilts versus Boston University on September 29th followed the next Saturday with Southern Methodist; October games at Harvard and Yale; the annual meeting with Notre Dame on November 10th in Yankee Stadium; and ending with the Nebraska and Stanford contests on November 24th and December 1st. The Harvard game was the third away game Army ever scheduled, after Navy and Yale.

The 1928 Army football schedule was considered at the time, the "most strenuous program ever attempted by an Army team." Earl Blaik wrote years later about this, calling Fleming "reckless" for what he did regarding the 1928 schedule. Even former head coach Charles Daly voiced concerns.

Despite being the hardest schedule in years, Army Football had a really good season in 1928. The Black Knights won their first six games, including beating Southern Methodist (14-13), at Harvard (15-0), and at favored Yale (18-6). The Fighting Irish eked out a win, 12-6. Army beat Nebraska (13-3). At Yankee Stadium, the Cadets went scoreless and clearly were beaten bad, 0-26, by #4 Stanford to end the 1928 season at 8-2; a step back from 1927's overall record of 9-1. The Cadets were ranked 9th in the nation by the Dickinson System ratings announced on December 9th, 1928.

1929 Army Football Season

Still, the scheduling of a 1929 trip to California seemed quite a shift for USMA. My theory is that you can blame this on three head football coaches talking to each other, Notre Dame's Knute Rockne, Stanford's Glenn "Pop" Warner, and Army's Biff Jones. First, Notre Dame had been coming to/from West Point since 1913 by train, with the exceptions of the war years (1917-1918), as well as other eastern foes.

Second, Notre Dame traveled by train to/from Pasadena and beat Stanford in the 1925 Rose Bowl (27-10). Third, Rockne then scheduled games in 1926 and 1928 at Southern California. Fourth, was Army's own train rides to/from Chicago for the 1926 Army-Navy Game might have changed a few USMA minds about away football games, though probably not. Finally, Stanford played at California on November 24th, then traveled across the country to play Army on December 1st in New York City; and won big.

Still, the 1920s were different in America. Earl "Red" Blaik, who was then a volunteer coach on the Army staff, wrote years later, "If the Army Athletic Association was making a lot of money, it was also spending it freely. The spirit of the times was freewheeling. The times, to repeat, were liberal and comfortable, even though traditionalists were shaking their heads over Phil Fleming and muttering about commitment papers to some suitable institution."

In early September, the 1929 season was considered even harder than the prior one. Instead of wearing black jerseys with a band of gold and gray as they had in past yards, the Cadets would wear gold jerseys with a band of black and gray during the 1929 season.

Army began the season with three straight home wins over Boston University (26-0), Gettysburg College (33-7), and Davidson College (23-7). At Harvard, the Cadets comeback from a Crimson 13-0 halftime lead was dwarfed by their opponent's 50 yard touchdown pass with less than two minutes left in the game for a 20-20 tie. Army was ahead 13-7 at halftime at Yale, but the Bulldogs rallied for a 21-13 victory on October 26th.

Army then beat South Dakota, 33-6, before traveling to Champaign IL for their first meeting with Illinois. The Fighting Illini took a 17-7 lead at halftime on an 80 yard punt return and an 80 yard fumble return, and held on to win, 17-7. On the next two Saturdays, the Cadets handily beat Dickinson College (89-7) and the Cadets reserves edged Ohio Wesleyan University (19-6).

In the annual game with Notre Dame at Yankee Stadium, Jack Elder intercepted an Army pass on his goal line and took it back 100 yards for the only score of the game, 7-0. Notre Dame was named national champion for the 1929 season. WP-6-3-1 Cadets squad then had 28 days to prepare for Stanford.

Army at Stanford - the First Post-Season Game

Stanford began the 1929 season with five straight victories over West Coast Army (45-0), Olympic Club (6-0), Oregon (33-7), at UCLA (57-0), and Oregon State (40-7) before losing to eventual national champion Southern California, 0-7. Wins versus Cal Tech (39-0) and at Washington followed (6-0) before Santa Clara upset Stanford, 7-13. Stanford then beat California (21-6) and finished second in the Pacific Coast Conference with a 5-1 record and 8-2 overall record before the Army game.

On Wednesday, December 18th, there was a noontime rally by all the Cadets for their football team prior to the team's departure for the Stanford game. An hour practice and signal rehearsal followed on The Plain directed by head coach Biff Jones. Despite the pouring rain, about half of the Corps of Cadets saw their team off at the railroad station, probably missing class or drill.

At 3 pm ET, proceeding under USMA Special Orders Number 285; seven Pullman cars packed with 109 members of the varsity, "B", and plebe squads and their managers; with about forty coaches, trainers, official party, and newspapermen; left West Point for San Francisco.

The special train consisted of 13 dining, sleeping, and baggage cars. The baggage cars contained showers, electrical contrivances, and lockers for the convenience and training for the athletics in route. Stops were planned in Galesburg IL, Syracuse KS, and Needles CA for practices, with arrival expected in Palo Alto by December 22nd.

The train stopped briefly at South Bend and were met by Notre Dame Football players who wished the Cadets luck in their upcoming game with Stanford. A snowstorm outside Chicago on Thursday, December 19th held the train for between three and twelve hours.

Upon arrival at Galesburg at 3 pm, the train was met by the Mayor, members of the Chamber of Commerce, and the Presidents of Knox and Lombard Colleges. The team was then escorted to Knox field for a practice. However, other reports said they did not stop for practice in Galesburg.

Unable to make it to Syracuse KS before later that evening, a stop was made at Hutchinson KS on late Friday afternoon, December 20th. The team practiced at the local high school field, escorted by a "committee of senators." Another report said that Army center Aaron Lazar, who was left behind at West Point due to scholastic difficulties, would fly by airplane to rejoin the team.

A report said that stops and receptions along the route had been cancelled in order to make up for time lost due to the blizzard and the special train was speeding across Colorado on Saturday. The train stopped at Canyon Diablo, halfway between Flagstaff AZ and Winslow AZ on Saturday, December 21st, to have a twenty minute workout in the desert.

Earl Blaik wrote briefly about the trip that he attended. He mentioned that Red Cagle almost disappeared chasing a jack rabbit during the desert practice and that Cadets were observed during the practice by Native Americans that he surmised were likely Pop Warner scouts.

Blaik told that one of the assistant coaches, Ralph Sasse, had the porter hide the shoes of everyone in the last two cars on the last night on the train. The USMA Superintendent, Major General William R. Smith, had a brief inspection upon arrival in Palo Alto, and assistant coach Red Reeder stood proudly in his beaded moccasins and received a glacial stare from the Supe.

The train arrived at Palo Alto shortly before midnight on Sunday, December 22nd, and were met by several hundred Stanford students and their head football coach Glenn "Pop" Warner at the station. The team was taken immediately to Branner Hall on the campus where it would have exclusive use of the facilities.

Head coach Biff Jones planned a stiff workout later on Monday at Stanford Stadium and two practices a day before the game. There were reports of intense heat leading up to and during the game. There may have been a visit to San Francisco and Chinatown prior to the game.

The officials for the 1929 Army-Stanford game were referee Herb Dana, umpire Tom Loutitt, field judge Bill Mulligan, and head linesman Tom Fitzpatrick.

The starting lineup for Stanford was left end Donald Muller, left tackle Ray Tandy, left guard William Bardin, center Perry Taylor, right guard Thomas Driscoll, right tackle James Thompson, right end John Preston, left halfback Harlow Rothert, right halfback Lud Frentrup, fullback Charles Smalling, and quarterback Herbert Fleishhacker.

The starting lineup for Army was left end Carl Carlmark, left tackle John Price, left guard Charles Humber, center Paul Miller, right guard Loren Hillsinger, right tackle George Perry, right end Ed Messinger, left halfback Richard Hutchinson, right halfback Christian "Red" Cagle, fullback John Murrell, and quarterback Bob Carver.

Substitutes for Army were George Fletcher, Frederick Crabb, Joe Golden, John Gordon, Harley Trice, Aaron Lazar, Edward Suarez, Allan McLean, John Malloy, Herbert Gibner, Wendell Bowman, and Ray Stecker.

Substitutes for Stanford were Philip Neill, Sherman Crary, Theodore Klabau, Elwood Wilson, Macellus Albertson, Raymond Dawson, Harris Bogue, Clarence Bush, Philip Moffatt, Harry Hillman, William Clark, Guido Caglieri, and Phil Winnek.

During the first period, Stanford's Perry Taylor recovered a fumbled on a punt return by Bob Carver at midfield .Paul Miller then intercepted a Stanford pass and returned it to the WP-40. Red Cagle rushed off tackle for seven yards. Murrell went up the middle for 13 yards. John Murrell gained five yards.

Cagle completed a 16 yard pass to Carl Carlmark to the S-19. Murrell and Cagle gained twelve yards in two rushes to the S-7. Cagle then gained one yard. John Murrell rushed for six yards for a touchdown over the guard. Richard Hutchinson's point after touchdown was blocked by Stanford's Donald Muller, making the score 6-0 in favor of the Cadets.

Murrell punted to the S-40. Stanford's Lud Frentrup rushed 26 yards on a double reverse. Charles Smalling completed a 24 yard pass to Muller to the WP-10. Herbert Fleishhacker rushed for four yards. Frentrup rushed around the end for a gain of five yards. Herbert Fleishhacker ran for one yard and a touchdown. Ed Messinger blocked the try for goal to make the score, 6-6, at the end of the first period.

Harlow Rothert punted out of bounds to the WP-2. Murrell punted back to the WP-31. The Black Knights forced a punt which went out of bounds at the WP-1. John Murrell fumbled a low snap in the end zone and was tackled by Stanford's Donald Muller for a safety. Stanford led, 8-6.

Hutchinson kicked off after the safety, and Frentrup returned it 37 yards. Frentrup rushed for twelve yards over tackle. Smalling rushed for eight yards to the WP-11. Army was penalized ten yards for holding to the WP-1. Stanford was penalized five yards for the backfield in motion. Fleishhacker rushed for four yards. Charles Smalling ran for two yards for a touchdown. Harlow Rothert missed the kick, making the score 14-6 in favor of Stanford in the second quarter.

Cagle returned a punt 18 yards to the S-44. Cagle completed a 19 yard pass to Hutchinson. Richard Hutchinson rushed for 25 yards for a touchdown. Hutchinson kicked the extra point kick to make the score, 14-13, in favor of Stanford. Smelling rushed 46 yards to the WP-37, tackled by John Malloy from behind potentially saving a touchdown. Edward Suarez then intercepted a pass by Smalling to end the first half.

In the third quarter, Cagle returned a kickoff 30 yards to midfield. Cagle rushed around the left end for 16 yards. Cagle's touchdown pass attempt was intercepted by Guido Caglieri, who returned it to the S-26. Army's defense forced a punt.

A few plays later, Cagle fumbled the football and Thomas Driscoll recovered it for Stanford at the WP-17. Charles Smalling rushed several times before scoring a touchdown. The extra point kick was no good, making it 20-13 in favor of Stanford.

A series of punts put the football around the fifty yard line in the fourth quarter. Smalling rushed several times to move the ball to the WP-33. Caglieri rushed 18 yards to the WP-15. From there, Charles Smalling rushed several times until he crossed the goal line. Philip Moffatt made the extra point kick to extend the score to 27-13, Stanford.

Cagle and Murrell ran the football on successive attempts to midfield. A Cagle pass attempt was intercepted by Rothert to end the Army possession. Stanford moved down the field. Moffatt made a diving catch on a pass to the WP-2. On fourth down, Hebert Fleishhacker went over the goal line. Philip Moffatt converted the extra point to make the final score, 34-13 Stanford.

Army made a contest of this game for one half. The dazzling reverses, fake reverses, spinners, and deceptive passes that Coach Pop Warner had installed for his Stanford team was too much for Army. *The 1930 Howitzer* concluded, "Army could not cope with the deception and power of the Westerners, and the second half approached a walk-away. Perhaps the intense heat had something to do with our showing, but the fact remains that we took one sweet lacing."

Army had six first downs (five rushing), 97 yards rushing, 62 yards passing (3-6-1), three out of four fumbles lost; punted nine times for a 32.4 yard average, had three penalties for 20 yards, intercepted four passes, returned one punt for 17 yards, and returned six kickoffs for 86 yards. Cagle rushed for 48 yards, while Murrell gained 43 yards.

Stanford had 15 first downs (13 rushing), 247 rushing yards, 35 yards passing (2-2-4), no fumbles, punted nine times for a 42.0 average, intercepted one pass, had five penalties for 35 yards, returned two punts for 18 yards, and returned three kickoffs for 76 yards. Smalling rushed for 162 yards, while Frentrup gained 40 yards.

After the game, the team traveled and stayed overnight in San Francisco. They left on Sunday by train to Los Angeles on Sunday, December 29th, and toured several movie studios. Based upon pictures in *The 1930 Howitzer*, the train stopped at the Surf CA beach in southern California, the Grand Canyon, and near Albuquerque NM where Cadets bought Native American pottery, moccasins, and other items. The train returned to West Point around January 4th.

Afterwards, USMA Superintendent Major General William R. Smith, who went on the train trip to Stanford, considered the trip a disaster because it interfered with academics. Army officials put into place policies to not play post-season games, potentially because of this experience.

1930 Army Football Season

On December 7, 1929, the 1930 football schedule was announced with ten games, beginning with Boston University on September 27th and ending with Notre Dame in New York City on November 29th. Navy was not on the schedule. On February 11th, USMA and Notre Dame agreed to move their game to Chicago's Soldier Field as the Fighting Irish had an away game scheduled the next Saturday at Southern California and avoid having the squad miss two days of classes.

Army opened its 1930 football season with four straight shutouts, versus Boston University (39-0), versus Furman University (54-0), versus Swarthmore College (39-0), and at Harvard (6-0) in Ralph Sasse's first season as the head football coach. On October 25th at the Yale Bowl, the Cadets tied the Bulldogs, 7-7, in the pouring rain. The University of North Dakota arrived at Michie Stadium, but left in a 33-6 defeat to the 5-0-1 Cadets.

A Charity Game?

On November 2nd, the *New York Daily News* wrote an open letter to President Herbert Hoover about the possibilities of an Army-Navy post-season charity game. Two days later, Alan Gould of the *Associated Press* reported, "Proposals for post-season college football games for the benefit of unemployment relief, fast accumulating every day, have attracted widespread support and interest, especially in so far as they involve the possibility of Army and Navy patching up their differences for a common cause."

Reports of potential bids from Chicago, New York, and Philadelphia surfaced over the next few days. On November 5th, reports said Navy was fully in favor of the idea for a charity game, but West Point flatly rejected it. Charles Egan of *United Press* reported on November 7th that the two sides have ironed out all their differences but the charity game rested in the hands of the President and his subordinates, the Secretary of War Patrick Hurley and the Secretary of the Navy Charles Adams.

Reports the next day said West Point was surprised of any agreement being made, while Annapolis was willing to play Maryland or George Washington for the benefit of the unemployed. Army beat the University of Illinois, 13-0, at Yankee Stadium that afternoon. There were no news over the next week, though there were suggestions of behind-the-scenes negotiations happening.

On November 13th, the *Associated Press* reported, "All efforts to bring about a football clash between the Army and Navy this year has apparently failed. While both institutions willing to forget their difference over eligibility rules long enough to meet for charity, negotiations for the game seemed to have floundered because no date, agreeable or convenient to both, could be found."

West Point wanted the game on December 6th at Yankee Stadium, but Navy already had a game scheduled that day with the University of Pennsylvania at Franklin Field in Philadelphia. Navy offed two dates, November 29th and December 13th. West Point rejected both dates, as they already had their game in Chicago with Notre Dame at Soldier Field on November 29th; and December 13th was in the middle of semi-annual examinations and it would be "embarrassing to the academy to be playing football during this period." Navy countered that they also had examinations that would be embarrassing.

Suddenly, divine intervention from Washington occurred, and on November 15th, it became official, a charity post-season game would be played on December 13th at Yankee Stadium between the two teams. Annapolis and West Point officials then began to immediately meet with Colonel Edward Underwood and Adjutant L.E. Cowan of the Salvation Army to work out all the details for the game.

Army finished its season by beating Kentucky Wesleyan College (47-2) and Ursinus College (18-0); and losing to 1930 national champion Notre Dame. 6-7, in Knute Rockne's last game as head football coach before his untimely plane crash. Army entered the game with Annapolis with an 8-1-1 record and favored by a touchdown.

Army-Navy Game - the second Post-Season Game

Navy opened its 1930 season on October 4th beating William & Mary University at home in Thompson Stadium, 19-6. The Midshipmen lost the next two games at South Bend (2-26) and at home versus Duke University (0-18). Navy was victorious in its two next outings, at Princeton University (31-0) and versus West Virginia Wesleyan College (37-14).

The Midshipmen played back-to-back games at Municipal Stadium in Baltimore, losing both to Ohio State University (0-27) and Southern Methodist University (7-20). Navy finished its regular season with three victories versus University of Maryland (6-0), versus George Washington University (20-0), and at Penn (26-0) to finish with a 6-4 record in head football Coach Bill Ingram's sixth season.

The officials for the 1930 Army-Navy Game were referee Eddie O'Brien, umpire William Crowley, field judge A.W. Palmer, and linesman D.W. Very.

The starting lineup for Navy were left end Edward Steffanides, left tackle Robert Bowstrom, left guard Gordon Underwood, center Magruder Tuttle, right guard Albert Gray, right tackle Louis Bryan, right end John Byng, left halfback John Gannon, right halfback Louis Kirn, fullback Oscar Hagberg, and quarterback Dale Bauer.

The starting lineup for Army were left end Carl Carlmark, left tackle John Price, left guard Charles Humber, center Paul Miller, right guard Harley Trice, right tackle Edward Suarez, right end Ed Messinger, left halfback Ray Stecker, right halfback William

Frentzel, fullback Thomas Kilday, and quarterback Wendell Bowman.

Substitutes for the Midshipmen were Theodore Torgeson, James Reedy, Orrin Black, Willis Johnson, Lynn Elliott, Russell (or Richard) Williams, Harvey Tschirgi, Thomas Hurley, Forest Thompson, and Richard Antrirn.

Substitutes for the Cadets were Richard King, Milton Summerfelt, Aaron Lazar, John Armstrong, John Malloy, Joe MacWilliam, Kenneth Fields, James Glattly, Ed Herb, Roy Evans, Charles Broshous, Bob Carver, and David Crickette.

The two teams met in fabulous weather, with bright sun and cool temperatures; with 70,000 fans in the Bronx in what was called a long line of vicious hitting, low scoring affair. The Navy's Robert Bowstrom kicked off to Army's Thomas Kilday to open the 31st meeting between the two arch rivals.

The Cadets made a first down but then were forced to punt. A wild Midshipmen snap pushed the football back to the N-1. Bowstrom was able to punt from the end zone 42 yards before Ray Stecker returned it for the Cadets to the N-34. On third and six, Stecker completed a swing pass to Wendell Bowman who gained 16 yards to the N-14. Navy prevented a first down and a score. Each team next had four possessions that ended with each punting, making it scoreless at halftime.

The punting continued in the third quarter, interrupted by a Stecker fumble recovered by Theodore Torgeson at the N-42 and a Midshipmen fumble by Dale Bauer, recovered by Ed Messinger on the WP-46. Navy's Bowstrom punted and Bowman returned it to the WP-44 with ten minutes left in the scoreless game.

On the next play, Ray Stecker, playing deep, faked to another back, ran through the defensive line over left tackle, cut to his left and ran down the sideline for a 56 yard touchdown run. Charles Broshous missed the extra point kick, but it was 6-0 in favor of Army. Navy punted after receiving the kickoff, and the Cadets punted back.

Army held Navy and forced a punt. Bowman muffed the punt, and Midshipman John Byng recovered the football at the WP-37. After a two yard rush by Louis Kirn, John Gannon completed a ten yard pass to Byng for a first down at the WP-25. Navy rushed once, and tried three passes, having a turnover on downs. Army then drove down the field to the N-7 as time ran out and the gun sounded. Final score, Army 6, Navy 0. "Army earned its victory but never had a harder fight," said *The 1931 Howitzer*.

Army had twelve first downs, rushed 182 yards, passed for 56 yards (7-18-1), and lost one fumble. Navy had three first downs, had 63 yards rushing in 27 attempts, passed for 23 yards (3-14-0), and lost one fumble. A total of 23 Cadets and 22 Midshipmen played in the game. Army then led the series with a 16-12-3 record. Army was ranked 9th in the Dickinson System for the 1930 season. The Salvation Army raised $600,000 in the game, worth $10.9 million in 2022.

A review of 1927-1931 college football game results showed that it was common practice back then to end the regular season Thanksgiving weekend with a handful of games played on the first Saturday in December. Any games after that were generally considered post-season or exhibitions in the press.

In the 1930 season, there were ten games played on December 6th that ended the regular season. There were six post-season games played, including the 1931 Rose Bowl between Alabama and Washington State on January 1st and the Army-Navy game. The other post-season games were December 10th (Brigham Young at Hawai'i), December 13th (Oklahoma State at Tulsa), December 25th (Idaho at St Louis Alumni Hawai'i), and January 1st (Idaho at Hawai'i).

<u>1931 Army Football Season</u>

On December 20, 1930, USMA announced its 1931 football schedule, without Navy on it. Army would play seven of their games in Michie Stadium, beginning with an opening game on September 26th with Ohio Northern University. There were two away games at Yale and Pittsburgh, with the season ending on November 28th versus Notre Dame in New York City.

USMA and USNA officials had meetings in May to try to resolve the eligibility issues that have prevented the resumption of the Army-Navy game, with no resolution. On October 2nd, the Salvation Army sent requests to each service department and academy requesting a charity game in December. On October 6th, the service secretaries announced that there would be a charity game on December 12th, with the location to be decided by the two academy superintendents. The service academies agreed to have the 1931 Army-Navy Charity Game at Yankee Stadium.

Army won its first three games versus Ohio Northern (60-0), versus Knox College (67-6), and versus Michigan State College (20-7) to open Ralph Sasse's second season. Hosting Harvard University at West Point for the first time since 1910, the Cadets jumped out to a 13-0 lead in the first quarter. But the Crimson, which would finish the season with a 7-1 record after losing to Yale, scored two touchdowns in the second quarter for a 14-13 victory over Army.

Seven point favorite Army traveled to New Haven on October 24th and played a scoreless tie through three quarters. The Cadets drove 66 yards down to the Y-2 as time expired in the third period. Two plays later, Ray Stecker went over the goal line, but the extra point kick was missed, making it 6-0, in favor of Army. Yale's Bud Parker ran the kickoff back 88 yards for a touchdown, but the extra point kick went wide, tying the game at six.

In those days, the team scoring the touchdown could elect to receive the kickoff. Army kicked off to Robert Lassiter, who returned it to the Y-22 where he was tackled by Army end Richard Sheridan, with several players piling on. Sheridan remained on the ground, unconscious. He was taken by ambulance to New Haven Hospital, accompanied by Yale and Army doctors and head coach Ralph Sasse. The game ended in a tie.

Doctors discovered that Sheridan had broken his neck, and he passed away two days later. Cadet Richard Brinsley Sheridan Jr.,

21 years of age, USMA Class of 1933, was buried with honors at West Point Cemetery on October 27th. Yale, Harvard, and Notre Dame Football players were present to pay their respects. USMA Superintendent, Major General William R. Smith, announced that the season would continue based on the expressed desires of Sheridan's mother, the Army Football Team, and the Corps of Cadets.

Army continued its season on October 31st with a victory over Colorado College (27-0) followed by another win at home versus Louisiana State University (20-0). The Corps of Cadets traveled to Pittsburgh to cheer on the Army team, only to be met with an impressive passing attack of ten out of 18 completed passes for 290 yards with four touchdowns; and a 0-26 shutout to the eventual co-national and eastern champion Panthers.

Returning to Michie Stadium, Army slammed Ursinus College, 54-6. The Cadets continued their great defensive efforts by upsetting Notre Dame in front of 78,000 fans at Yankee Stadium on November 28th, 12-0. The Army players returned to West Point for further practices and preparation work for their semi-annual examinations.

1931 Army-Navy Game - the Third Post-Season Game

Navy began the 1931 season with a victory at home in Thompson Stadium over the College of William & Mary, 13-6, on October 3rd. The Midshipmen lost, 0-6, to the University of Maryland in a game played in Griffith Stadium in Washington DC. Two wins followed versus the University of Delaware (12-7) and at Princeton University (15-0). The Midshipmen played to a scoreless tie at home against West Virginia Wesleyan College on October 31st.

Navy lost their next three games at Ohio State University (0-20), University of Notre Dame (0-20) at Baltimore's Municipal Stadium, and versus Southern Methodist University (6-13) at home. The Midshipmen then beat the College of Wooster (Ohio) (19-6) and the University of Pennsylvania (6-0) at Philadelphia's Franklin Field to finish its regular season with a 5-4-1 record.

The officials for the 1931 Army-Navy Game were referee Tom Thorpe, umpire J.P. Egan, field judge E.E. Miller, and linesman W.M. Hollenbeck of Penn.

The starting lineup for Navy were left end Lawrence Smith, left tackle George James, left guard James Reedy, center Magruder Tuttle, right guard Gordon Underwood, right tackle Louis Bryan, right end Lynn Elliott, left halfback Harvey Tschirgi, right halfback Louis Kirn, fullback Thomas Hurley, and quarterback Samuel Moncure.

The starting lineup for Army were left end Richard King, left tackle John Price, left guard Milton Summerfelt, center Roy Evans, right guard Harley Trice, right tackle Edward Suarez, right end Peter Koczak, left halfback Ray Stecker, right halfback Travis Brown, fullback Thomas Kilday, and quarterback Bob Carver.

Substitutes for the Midshipmen were Hugh Murray, Thomas Chambers, Forest Thompson, James Denny, Lawrence Becht, Ralph Pray, James Campbell, Nelson Samuels, and John Waybright.

Substitutes for the Cadets were Norman Lankenau, Lawrence Lincoln, Lauri Hilberg, William Senter, Harvey Jablonsky, Edwin Simenson, John Lawlor, Joe MacWilliam, Kenneth Fields, Paul Johnson, and Ed Herb.

The teams arrived in New York City on Thursday and made their final preparations in seclusion. Heavy rains on Wednesday with a charity event forced the grounds crew to do constant repairs and keep the field covered until Saturday morning, when the field was declared a "heavy track." Weather conditions were sunny with clear skies.

It was a scoreless first quarter. In the second period, the Cadets drove 63 yards in 14 plays (sounds like option football) but were finally stopped by the Midshipmen at the N-7. After a Navy punt out of their end zone, Army started on the N-38. On second and seven, Ray Stecker completed a 25 yard pass to Bob Carver to the N-10. Navy's defense held again, and Travis Brown made a field goal for a 3-0 Army lead.

After an exchange of punts by both teams, Army had the ball at the N-43. Head football coach Ralph Sasse then decided to substitute the entire backfield. Kenneth Fields rushed for eight yards. Fields completed a 34 yard pass to Peter Koczak to the N-1. Ed Herb plunged over the goal line and made the conversion to make it 10-0 at halftime.

Late in the third quarter, Navy returned a punt to the N-35. Louis Kirn ran for ten yards and a first down. Kirn then completed a long pass down the middle into the hands of Harvey Tschirgi for a 55 yard touchdown pass. Lawrence Becht made the extra point kick to close the score to 10-7. Army received the kickoff, made a first down, and were then forced to punt to end the third period, with the football at the N-33.

On third and 13, Kirn completed a 20 yard pass to Hugh Murray to midfield. Kirn ran to the right side, reversed himself, and was thrown for a loss of ten yards. On the next play, Kirn's attempted pass to Murray was intercepted by Joe MacWilliam and returned 16 yards to the WP-43. The teams exchanged punts, with the Cadets changing field position with the football at the N-35.

Stecker ran for 16 yards to the N-24. Stecker, Brown, Herb, and then Stecker completed runs to move the football to the N-12 and a first and ten. Stecker rushed for a gain of two yards, then ran nine yards to the N-1 and a first down. Herb rushed twice for no gain. On his third try, Ed Herb plunged over the goal line for the touchdown. Herb also converted the extra point, making it 17-7 in favor of Army. The remainder of the game consisted of Navy's passing attempts and Army punting to shift field position. Final score, Army 17, Navy 7.

Army had 13 first downs, 235 yards rushing, 74 yards passing (6-12-0), two lost fumbles, punted 14 times, and was penalized 45 yards. Navy had 5 first downs, rushed for 28 yards, had 135 yards passing (6-17-3), lost one fumble, punted ten times, and was penalized 35 yards.

Navy's losing streak over the last ten years was 0-6-2 and Army's series record stood at 17-12-3. As *The 1932 Howitzer* reported, "Navy's Chinese Victory Bell has not been rung in eleven years. You glorious Army teams of a future day, may it never ring again."

Army finished the 1931 season with an 8-2-1 record, while Navy was 5-5-1. The Charity Game raised $350,000 for the Salvation Army for unemployment relief. This was the last of eleven Army-Navy games played in New York City in the twentieth century.

In the 1931 season, most teams finished their regular season on November 28th with 18 games played on December 2nd, 5th, or 6th. Some of these were charity games to help the nation's unemployed, identified by Bill Cromartie as Nebraska versus Colorado State at Denver, Carnegie Tech at Duquesne, Centre College at South Carolina, and Tennessee versus New York University at Yankee Stadium.

A unique All-Star charity game was pulled off among the Big Five schools of North Carolina (Duke, Davidson, North Carolina, North Carolina State, and Wake Forest) on December 5th in Durham. The Blue Devils and Tar Hills combined to play the other three teams, billed as DUKOLINA versus WAKIDSON STATE according to Cromartie, with the Duke-UNC team winning, 14-0.

There were six post-season games, other than Army-Navy and the 1932 Rose Bowl games. These included Oklahoma at Tulsa and Georgia at Southern California, both on December 12th; Oklahoma at Hawai'i All-Stars on Christmas Day; California at Georgia State on December 26th; Oklahoma at Hawai'i on January 1st; and undefeated Tulane versus Southern California in the Rose Bowl on January 1st. USC won, 21-12.

Conclusion

In 1932, USMA and USNA agreed to a new contract to play each other in football every season. The contract allowed each service academy to make their own eligibility rules. They went back to the way things had been before the breakup.

West Point's unexpected experiment in have post-season games in the 1929, 1930, and 1931 seasons ended with the restoration of the annual Army-Navy Games in 1932; with all football seasons ending either the weekend of Thanksgiving or the first couple days in December for more than five decades.

I believe that many in USMA leadership felt that these football seasons played havoc with the orderly structure of USMA; interfering with semi-annual or term end examinations, extending the football team activities by several weeks, and taking Cadets away from more important academic and military activities. Memories were long, and I believe these three seasons had a negative impact when there were opportunities for the Cadets to go to bowl games in future seasons.

Chapter 2

No Bowls for the Army Team, no sugar bowls for the Corps

The 1901 College Football Season

On October 5, 1901, Army kicked off its twelfth football season hosting Franklin & Marshall University on The Plain at West Point, winning the game 20-0, under the watchful eyes of new head coach Lieutenant Leon Kromer. The Cadets would go on to host six more games that season, beating Trinity, Williams, and Penn; losing only to Eastern power Harvard, 0-6, and tying two other Eastern powerhouses, Yale and Princeton. Army went to Philadelphia's Franklin Field and beat Navy, 11-5, on November 30th, finished the season with a 5-1-2 record. Quarterback Charlies Daly and tackle Paul Bunker were consensus All-Americans.

Three thousand miles away during that season, a committee consisting of civic leaders in the town of Pasadena CA, population 9,017 in the 1900 Census, was considering how to entice more people from colder climes to California. Newly elected president James Wagner of the Tournament of Roses committee reviewed the prior events held since 1890, such as an annual parade, polo matches, foot races, tug-of-war matches, jousts, and a game called tourney of the rings; and suggested holding a football game, with a team from the West taking on a team from another part of the country. Wager made arguments that the team located in a cold climate would bring its fans to sunny Pasadena.

And so began what was later called the Rose Bowl, played on January 1, 1902 between Stanford University (3-1-2) and Fielding Yost's undefeated (10-0) University of Michigan (the point-a-minute team). The Wolverines won, 49-0, before a crowd of 8,000 spectators. Both teams were paid $3,500 for the exhibition game, and the Committee made a $3,161.86 profit (about $100,000 in 2022).

There were 64 FBS teams that played in the 1901 season, according to the *2005 ESPN College Football Encyclopedia*. At the beginning of the 1984 season, 62 of these institutions had played in one or more bowl game. The remaining two? Both the University of Virginia and the United States Military Academy at West Point had never played in a bowl game, until the 1984 season. I have no knowledge why the Cavaliers never played in one, but let me document the story of why Army had never went bowling for 83 years, using public sources. Complete with public outcries, confusion, a Congressional investigation, and one of the best Cadet pranks ever.

Early Rose Bowl History

As *ESPN* described in Todd Jones' article, "The Second Season, How the Rise of the Bowls Shaped College Football" in their Encyclopedia: "College bowl games came into being to serve one simple goal: entice people to take midwinter vacations. The promise of fun was at their core. Organizers figured fans would travel to the host town to cheer on their favorite team, and please the local chamber of commerce by spending money during the holiday season. Sure, fans would see a good football game. But bowl games were mainly about parties and parades and pageantry and - above all - fun." This idea was behind the first bowl game in 1902, and was behind almost all bowl games.

The Tournament of Roses committee did not want to invite the 11-0 Michigan team back for a 1903 bowl game to beat up on a West squad (probably 9-0 California or 6-1 Stanford), so it returned to having other events over the next twelve years, such as chariot races and even a race between an elephant and a camel. After the 1915 season, the football game would return to what would become an annual event, the Rose Bowl, or nicknamed "The Granddaddy of Them All" bowl games.

The committee would usually pick a team from the Pacific Coast Conference, sometimes the champion, sometimes not. That team picked often had influence on who from the East might be picked. In the early games, a telegram would be sent to that institution's president, inviting them. A team might turn the Rose Bowl down, most accepted. An example of that occurred when the Tulane faculty voted to not attend the 1926 Rose Bowl.

By the early 1930s, often a committee member would call the school's president or athletic director to feel them out on their interest in playing in the bowl. This avoided sending an official invitation and having it be rejected. This practiced continued for decades and was followed as other bowl games were established.

From 1915 until 1934, there was only one bowl game for major college teams to play in after the regular season, the Rose Bowl. *ESPN* lists several other minor bowls during this time period, such as the Dixie Classic in Dallas (1922, 1925, & 1934), the Fort Worth Classic (1921), the Los Angeles Christmas Festival (1924), and the San Diego East-West Christmas Classic (1921-1922).

There is little in the public record to indicate that the Rose Bowl selection ever considered Army to play in any games until the 1945 season. Only six teams selected from the eastern United States had lost one or more games for the 1920-1944 Rose Bowls; and 19 of the eastern teams selected had not lost any games (they may have had one or more tied games, quite common in that era).

It is quite possible that the committee in its deliberations considered Army as an opponent, especially given the outstanding records during this time period, particularly the 1922 (8-0-2), 1924, (5-1-2), 1926 (7-1-1), 1927 (9-1), 1930 (9-1-1), 1933 (9-1), and 1944 (9-0) teams, as well as nine seasons with only two losses.

In 1915, Army finished 5-3-1 under head football coach Charles Daly. The Rose Bowl selected Washington State (6-0) and Brown (5-3-1), The NCAA lists Cornell, Oklahoma, and Pittsburgh as being selected as national champions. Minnesota, Illinois, Nebraska, Colorado State, Columbia, and Georgia Tech were undefeated that season. Given that the committee was just returning to a football game after twelve years, the selection was probably made by who knew who.

In 1916, Army finished 9-0, beating both Navy and Notre Dame, again under Coach Daly. Oregon (6-0-1) and Penn (7-2-1) were selected for the Rose Bowl, ahead of national champions Pittsburgh and Army, as well as undefeated Ohio State, Washington, Colorado State, Tulsa, Georgia Tech, and Tennessee.

For Army and many schools, the 1917 season was cancelled due to the United States entering World War I in April. As football season approached, USMA decided to play football, and a new schedule was produced (excluding Navy but including Notre Dame) and Lieutenant Geoffrey Keyes became head football coach. Army went 7-1 that season. The Rose Bowl decided to have the Mare Island Marines play Great Lakes Naval Air Station in the 1918 Rose Bowl.

Army played one game in 1918 against the Mitchel Field Aviators and won, 20-0. The 1968 Congressional Hearings that investigated service academy bowl games mentioned several Rose Bowl games. There was testimony that Army had participated in a Rose Bowl, and it was partly true. During World War I, the Camp Lewis WA football team (5-2-1) lost to the Mare Island Marines (5-0), 19-7, in the 1918 Rose Bowl. So the United States Army had played in the Rose Bowl, not the Army Football Team.

Charles Daly returned as head football coach for the 1919 season, and Army went 6-3, losing to both Notre Dame and Navy. The bowl committee selected Oregon (5-1) to play Harvard (8-0-1). Good choice, as only Texas A&M, Notre Dame, and Tulsa were undefeated. In the 1920 and 1921 seasons, Army went 7-2 and 6-4, respectively. The bowl committee selected Ohio State (7-0) and Washington & Lee (10-0) to play California in the 1921-1922 bowl games. Sometime after that, the Western (Big Ten) Conference choose not to have any of its teams play in the Rose Bowl until 1947.

Charles Daly's last team in 1922 went undefeated (8-0-2), tying Yale and Notre Dame and beating Navy. The committee selected Southern California (9-1) against Penn State (6-3-1). USC came in fourth place, and champion California's players voted not to go. A vote by each team in the PCC (6-2) landed USC in the bowl, fair enough.

The Nittany Lions were 5-0 when they received the invitation on October 21st. They then went 1-1-1 in their next games. The bowl selection committee reaffirmed their choice, not once, but twice on November 7th and November 16th. Penn State then lost to Penn and Pitt. There were seven other undefeated teams besides Army the Rose Bowl could have taken. One, West Virginia (9-0-1), played in the San Diego East-West Christmas Classic against Gonzaga and won. In the first Rose Bowl played in the Rose Bowl Stadium, USC won 14-3.

In the 1923 season, Army went 6-2-1, losing to Yale and Notre Dame, and tying Navy, 0-0. Navy (5-1-2) was selected on November 30th to play the University of Washington (4-1-0), primarily at the insistence of the Huskies and despite more than 15 teams having better records. The Midshipmen upset the favored Huskies, 14-14.

Army went 5-1-2 and 7-2 over the 1924-1925 seasons, and the Rose Bowl selected national champion teams, Notre Dame (9-0) and Alabama (9-0) who beat their PCC opponents, Stanford and Washington. Army went 7-1-1, 9-1, and 8-2 in head football coach Biff Jones first three seasons in 1926-1928. In the Rose Bowl were Alabama (9-0), Pitt (8-0-1), and Georgia Tech (9-0); with only Pitt losing and the other two being named national champions that season.

In the 1926 season, undefeated Navy (9-0) played Army (7-1) at Chicago's Soldier Field. Before the game, there were some speculation that the winner would be considered for the 1927 Rose Bowl. The two teams tied, 21-21, and Alabama (9-0) was selected to play Stanford (10-0-1) in the bowl game.

We've talked more about the 1929-1931 Army seasons in Chapter 1. The Rose Bowl selections were Pitt (9-0), Alabama (9-0), and Tulane (11-0). Each season there were several undefeated squads available also for the bowl to choose from compared to one or two loss teams. In the 1932 season, Army went 8-2, losing only to Pitt and Notre Dame and beating Navy. Pittsburgh (8-0-2) went to the 1933 Rose Bowl and lost, 35-0 to undefeated national champion Southern California (9-0).

Late in the 1933 season, after Army (9-0) had beaten Navy, 12-7, there was a press article indicating West Point's desire to accept an invitation from the Rose Bowl. Instead, Columbia (7-1) was invited a few days later. Princeton, LSU, and Army were all undefeated in late November. The Black Knights ended its season with a close loss to Notre Dame, 12-13, on December 2nd, one of only two seasons where Army played Navy and then played another team during the regular season (2020, Air Force).

As demonstrated in the 1933 season, and maybe earlier, it appears that Army's policy was that it would play in the Rose Bowl if they were invited and they beat Navy. This policy continued through at least the 1946 season. It appears that initially the policy did not consider the newer bowl games as candidates for post-season play.

Starting in January 1935, the Orange, Sugar, and Sun Bowls came into existence, and there were opportunities for more than two teams to play in bowl games. The Cotton Bowl started in 1937; while the Gator (1946), Tangerine (1947), Liberty (1959), Bluebonnet (1959), Peach (1968), Fiesta (1971), and Independence (1976) Bowls followed.

While the records of Army Football were good from 1934 through the 1938 seasons, losing two or three games usually put the Black Knights out of the running for Rose Bowl selection. The 1939 and 1940 seasons were the first losing campaigns since 1906. This led to USMA hiring Earl Blaik from Dartmouth as Army's head football coach.

The Rose Bowl chose undefeated teams each season, except in 1936, when it chose #3 Pitt (7-1-1), and in 1940, when it chose #8 Nebraska (8-1). A side note, West Point graduates were the head coaches at Tennessee and Nebraska in the 1940-1941 Rose Bowls.

Blaik's Army team went 5-3-1 during the 1941 season, tying Notre Dame, and losing to Harvard, Penn, and Navy. #3 Duke (9-0) was selected for the 1942 Rose Bowl, and due to the concerns after Pearl Harbor, the game was played in Durham on January 1, 1942. In 1942, Army dropped out of the Top Twenty after losing back-to-back games to Notre Dame and Penn, and finished losing to the Midshipmen, 6-14, to end the season at 6-3. #2 Georgia (10-1) was selected for the 1943 Rose Bowl.

During the 1943 season, Army was tied by Penn and lost to Notre Dame, and was 7-1-1 and ranked seventh in the *Associate Press* Poll before meeting #6 Navy (7-1) on November 27th. The Mids blanked the Black Knights, 14-0; and the Rose Bowl decided to have two PCC teams play in the 1944 Rose Bowl, Southern California (7-2) and #12 Washington (4-0). There was little talk in the press for national champion Army (9-0) to go to any of the five bowls after the 1944 regular season. #12 Tennessee (7-0-1) was selected to play in the 1945 Rose Bowl.

The 1945-1946 Army Football Teams

During the 1945 season, a press article appeared on November 17th after #1 Army (8-0 at the time) had beaten #2 Notre Dame, 58-0, and #6 Penn, 61-0, in back-to-back Saturdays. USMA Superintendent Major General Maxwell Taylor was reported "considering" whether he would permit Army to play in the 1946 Rose Bowl. The article also reported that the Black Knights had not received any feelers to any post-season game.

There was likely some informal contact between Army and the Rose Bowl Committee around this time. Articles published contained three conditions that Army would have in order to play in the bowl game - first, Army could give no answer to an invitation until after the Navy game on December 1st; second, Army must beat #2 Navy (7-0-1); and three, the new Army Chief of Staff, General Dwight Eisenhower, had to approve going to the bowl game.

Back in the days prior to the 1934 season when the Orange and Sugar Bowls were formed, the Rose Bowl Committee could sit and wait. During the 1945 season, it appears that Army was their first pick for the Rose Bowl selection committee, while #3 Alabama (then 8-0, with a game with Mississippi State on December 1st) was their second choice.

But there was a problem, as the Sugar Bowl had invited Alabama to their game. The Crimson Tide wanted to play in the Rose Bowl. The Rose Bowl feared that it might lose both teams, with Army saying no and Alabama tired of waiting. So on November 23rd, the Committee invited Alabama to play against Southern California for the 1946 Rose Bowl.

The next day, November 24th, head football coach Earl Blaik reported that the players were disappointed in not receiving an invitation from the Rose Bowl and that the Cadets would not play in any bowl games after the Navy game. Army finished with a 9-0 record, a national championship for the second straight season, and fullback Doc Blanchard won the 1945 Heisman Trophy, with his teammate Glenn Davis finishing second.

#1 Army won its first seven games in the 1946 season, and on November 9th, faced #2 Notre Dame (5-0) at Yankee Stadium. The two teams played to a 0-0 tie. The Cadets rebounded the next Saturday to beat #5 Penn (5-1), 34-7. They would then play Navy (1-7) two weeks later on November 30th at Municipal Stadium in Philadelphia. It appears that informal conversations had gone out from USMA that Army would accept an invitation to the Rose Bowl. From November 18th to the 22nd, a number of events went on.

For the last eight years, there had been off and on negotiations between the Western (Big Ten) Conference and the Pacific Coast Conference to agree to have their champions play annually in the Rose Bowl. A meeting on November 19th was scheduled at Berkeley CA to discuss a potential agreement, attended by all institutions of both conferences.

On November 18th, more than 80 members of the Southern California chapter of the Football Writers Association unanimously adopted a vigorous resolution for the two conferences to issue a joint invitation to Army to play in the 1947 Rose Bowl. The writers suggested the new agreement go into effect for the 1948 Rose Bowl, with any Western Conference representative stepping aside this season in favor of Army. In another article, it stated that the Western Conference was in favor of stepping aside, and potential bowl opponents UCLA (8-1) and Southern California (5-2) were also in favor of playing Army instead.

Another article on November 19th reported that the Orange Bowl committee first choice was Army to play against Georgia (8-0), Georgia Tech (7-1), or Tennessee (7-1). Later that day, a press release announced that the Pacific Coast and Western Conferences signed a five-year agreement for each champion to play in the Rose Bowl, effective with the 1947 game. This would prevent Army from ever playing in the Rose Bowl. It was later revealed that the PCC vote was 6-2, with USC and UCLA voting against it taking effect immediately, as did Minnesota and Illinois for the Western Conference vote.

On November 21st, it was reported that the Sugar Bowl had immediately dispatched an invitation to Army after they heard about the Rose Bowl agreement. Army would play the winner of the Georgia - Georgia Tech game on November 30th. In the same report, the USMA public relations office stated that the Athletic Council was meeting later that day to provide a recommendation to the USMA Superintendent.

The Las Angeles city council announced a protest game in Memorial Coliseum between #1 Army and #2 Notre Dame a week before the Rose Bowl game. The Orange Bowl indicated that they were still interested in inviting Army. Portland OR businessmen wanted to arrange a "northwest bowl" game with Oregon State (then 5-1-1) on New Year's Day to benefit the Shrine Hospitals for crippled children.

The San Diego chamber of commerce wanted a "harbor bowl" game for Army against one of six other teams. UCLA made an offer to play Army in mid-December and then play in the Rose Bowl. USMA Superintendent Major General Taylor announced on November 23rd that Army would not play in any bowl game, and thanked the many invitations received.

On January 1, 1947, Illinois (8-2) beat UCLA (10-1), 45-14, in the Rose Bowl; Georgia (11-0) beat North Carolina (8-2-1), 20-10 in the Sugar Bowl; Rice (9-2) beat Tennessee (9-2), 8-0 in the Orange Bowl; and Arkansas (6-3-2) tied LSU (9-1-1), 0-0, in the Cotton Bowl. The top two teams in the nation, Notre Dame and Army, stayed home. Halfback Glenn Davis won the 1946 Heisman Trophy, fullback Doc Blanchard and quarterback Arnold Tucker finishing fourth and fifth.

The 1947-1958 Army Football Teams

#11 Army finished the 1947 season with a record of 5-2-2, but it appears to not have caught the attention of any of the eight bowl games played. #3 Army was undefeated (then 7-0) during the 1948 season, when Major General Taylor announced on November 9th that #3 Army was "not interested in post season games." Pressure continued to mount after the Cadets defeated #17 Penn, 26-20, the next Saturday.

The Secretary of the Army, Kenneth Royall, contacted Taylor to see if he had changed his mind, as Royall provided approval for Army to play in the Sugar Bowl to play against #16 North Carolina (9-0-1). The unexpected tie by Navy (0-8) on November 27th ended some of the bowl speculation during the 1948 season.

The 1968 Congressional Hearings showed that the Army Football Team voted to not accept the bid from the Sugar Bowl in 1948, according to head football coach Earl Blaik. Still, Army (8-0-1) finished #6 in the final *Associated Press* Poll on November 29th. The Tar Heels played and lost to #2 Oklahoma (11-0) in the 1949 Sugar Bowl.

Head Coach Blaik, while receiving the 1948 Lambert Trophy on December 3rd, denied receiving any bowl bid, though three were reported in the press, included one from the Sugar Bowl. Blaik explained to the crowd that he did not believe in bowl games, and had turned down a Rose Bowl bid while coaching at Dartmouth sometime in the 1930s. He also was worried that preparing for a bowl game would distract the players from their final examinations, "and a bowl game would not be worth it if it caused one Cadet to flunk out of the academy."

It was revealed in a 1957 article that USMA Superintendent Maxwell Taylor had established a bowl policy in 1948. The policy stated: "The Superintendent cannot view with favor any post-season games for the Army team under any condition. The regular nine-game schedule produces all the benefits which can be reasonably sought from the playing of inter-collegiate football and keeps the game within normal proportions. If we go beyond our regular schedule, the law of diminishing returns starts to apply at once, particularly in terms of loss of study time to the players. Hence, the Military Academy feels duty-bound to oppose any increase of Cadet playing commitments."

In late November 1949, it was reported that the Sugar Bowl committee wanted to make a bid to undefeated #4 Army (the 8-0, before beating Navy). Academy officials continued to tell the world that Army was not interested. In the final *Associated Press* Poll for the 1950 season on November 27th, Army was 8-0 and ranked second behind Oklahoma. Six days later, the Black Knights suffered its only defeat to Navy, 14-2, who won their third game of the season to finish 3-6. I could find no bowl speculation that season. The 1951 and 1952 Army Football Teams finished 2-7 and 4-4-1, affected by the 1951 honor scandal.

In 1953, Army finished the season beating Navy (4-3-2), 20-7, a #18 ranking in the *Associated Press* Poll, #19 in the *United Press* Coaches Poll, won the Lambert Trophy as best team in the East, and an overall record of 7-1-1. There was talk of bowl bids, but no press reports survive.

Sometime in 1953 or 1954, the United States Naval Academy established its policy on bowl games, according to the 1968 Congressional testimony of USNA Superintendent Draper Kauffman. The specific policy description is not in the hearing records, but from the testimony of the USNA Superintendent, an invitation to a bowl game could be accepted with the approval of the Secretary of the Navy, the USNA Superintendent, and the players provided Navy's attendance would benefit the United States Navy.

Prior to the 1954 Army-Navy game, rumors were flying that the Sugar Bowl would issue an invitation to the winner. Army (7-1) was ranked #5 in the nation in both polls, while Navy (6-2) was ranked sixth. Army officials again stated that they were not interested in a post season game. Navy upset the Cadets, 27-20, and the Secretary of the Navy, Charles Thomas, informed the Midshipmen players that they could vote to accept a bowl bid. #5 Navy accepted the bid from for the 1955 Sugar Bowl and went on to beat #6 Mississippi, 21-0. Army finished ranked seventh in both polls.

Navy's attendance and victory in the 1955 Sugar Bowl was credited in testimony at the 1968 Congressional hearings with increasing enlistment rates in the Navy, as well as increasing the number of applications to USNA. Navy's bowl game attendance likely led to some scrutiny of why Army was not attending bowl games.

Several Congressmen who were members of the USMA Board of Visitors were concerned about the unequal treatment of bowl games between West Point and Annapolis. A resolution was proposed and considered by the Board members, with the approvals of the Board Chairman General Lucius Clay, USMA Superintendent Blackshear Bryan, and Athletic Director Earl Blaik. On February 11, 1955, the Board report states that, "therefore approves participation by the Military Academy in intercollegiate athletics, including inter-sectional competition and recognized 'Bowl' games."

While the Congressional members of the Board of Visitors felt they had now established a policy for Army to at least consider going to bowl games, they found out 13 years later during the 1968 Congressional hearings that both the Department of the Army and USMA felt the Board's resolution was advisory and not mandatory. The USMA policy statement made around 1948 "which ends the Cadets' football after the final game of the regular season" remained in effect.

Rumors circulated before the 1955 Army-Navy game that either the Sugar or Cotton Bowls would invite the winner. Navy officials told the press that any invitation would have to be approved by "higher-ups." A press report out of the Army team doubted that their 5-3 record so far would get much interest from any of the bowls, but if they beat Navy and get a bowl bid, then "official approval would be speedy." Navy's head football coach Eddie Erdelatz described the Sugar Bowl as a "very pleasant experience" and indicated Navy's interest in going to the Cotton Bowl.

Army beat the #10 Midshipmen, 14-6, and the Cotton Bowl representative sought out Army officials. Not sure what happened to the Sugar Bowl rep. Head football coach Earl Blaik said after the game that he, "Had enough football for one season." Blaik would not say if Army had received a bowl bid and added, "Anything like that would be up to the Secretary of the Army. But I can tell you, I'm not interested in any post-season game."

The Cotton Bowl invited #10/#9 Mississippi (9-1) to play #6/#5 Texas Christian (9-1), while the Sugar Bowl invited #11 Pittsburgh (7-3) to play #7 Georgia Tech (8-1). The Orange Bowl had the national championship game, with #1 Oklahoma (10-0) versus #3 Maryland (10-0). Army finished 6-3, ranked #20 in the *Associated Press* Poll, and #15 in the *United Press* Coaches Poll. Navy finished #18/#20.

Navy had another successful season in 1956, and was ranked #13/#16 prior to the Army game with a 6-1-1 record. The Cotton Bowl had announced its intention to award Navy a bid to play #14 Texas Christian. The game ended in a 7-7 tie, and the Midshipmen players voted to accept the bid. The President of the Cotton Bowl committee, Robert Cullum, was in the Navy locker room to make the invitation, but the Navy officials decided to not accept it. The coaches and players were irked. Army finished the 1956 season with a 5-3-1 record, unsatisfied as they had beaten the Midshipmen throughout the game until the final quarter.

Talk began to surface in 1957 that the winner of the Army-Navy game would be invited to the Cotton Bowl, with some interest from the Gator Bowl. USMA Superintendent Lieutenant General Gar Davidson said on November 15th that Army's policy had not changed from the one written in 1948.

Another article noted that Navy was in the middle of a $3 million campaign to raise money for their new stadium. On November 19th, the Navy athletic director Slade Cutter announced that Navy would accept a bowl bid only if they beat Army and the players vote for it. #8/#7 Navy (7-1-1) won 14-0 over #10/#9 Army (7-1). The #5/#6 Midshipmen accepted a bid from the Cotton Bowl to play #8/#7 Rice (7-3). Navy beat the Owls 21-7 on New Year's Day.

There was a memorandum for record, subject Bowl Games, written on November 10, 1958, and signed by then USMA Superintendent, Lieutenant General Garrison Davidson; that was part of the 1968 Congressional hearings record. It states that the then current intercollegiate athletic policy in 1958 was "post-season contests, other than intercollegiate championships, are against our policy to accept."

The memorandum goes on to list three Pro's that participation in a bowl game would provide - additional publicity in the bowl game area and nationally; increased income to the Army Athletic Association; and provide a reward for coaches and players and an enjoyable trip.

The Con's were participation in a bowl game is contrary to current policy established in accordance of the USMA mission (loss of study time, upcoming term end examinations, loss of sleep, need for football players to catch up for time lost during regular season, and loss of Christmas Leave); and accepting one bowl game sets a precedent in needing to accept other postseason events in football and other sports.

The Con's continue - conflicts with other sports, seasons, and facilities by extending the football season; accepting a bowl bid prior to Navy might cause the Middies to try to "knock-us-off" or cause the team to look beyond the Navy game; practice conditions in December at West Point are poor and would hinder preparing for a larger and more qualified opponent; and bowl contests are commercial enterprises to exploit the teams selected and institutions involved. The memorandum then ends, with no conclusion or decision, just a signature block.

In early November 1958, #3 Army (6-0-1) received feelers from the Cotton and Orange Bowl committees regarding their interest in playing. Superintendent Davidson responded on November 13th that USMA still did not approve of playing post season games, and he felt he had a duty to address the two feelers. The #6/#8 Air Force, playing in its fourth season ever, took a 9-0-1 record to the Cotton Bowl and tied #10/#9 Texas Christian, 0-0. Army did beat Navy (6-3), 22-6, won the Lambert Trophy, and finished #3 in both polls, with halfback Pete Dawkins winning the Heisman Trophy.

Department of Defense Policy on Bowl Games?

Included in the 1968 Congressional hearings record was a letter by Congressman F. Edward Hebert of Louisiana on November 24, 1958 and an undated response from Superintendent Davidson. Hebert reminds the general of the 1955 USMA Board of Visitors Report, which was approved by President Eisenhower and sent to the Department of Defense to implement and accept bowl games. Davidson's response is that he is following the spirit of the Board's recommendation.

Hebert then wrote on February 10, 1959 to the Secretary of Defense, Neil McElroy, asking that DoD establish a consistent policy on accepting bowl bids, as each service academy has their own policy that conflicts with each other. Hebert also noted that four members of Army's 1958 football team were allowed to participate in postseason all-star games, contradicting Davidson's argument for the impact on Cadets' time. The Secretary then directed his Assistant Secretary of Defense, Stephen Jackson, to coordinate with the service departments to establish one policy.

The Air Force response on March 19th was to not have a DOD policy, and continue the USAFA policy that lets the Superintendent decide given the situation, with the approval of the Chief of Staff and/or the Secretary of the Air Force. It also contains the conditions that the USAFA Superintendent makes a decision - only going to major bowls; the Falcons team must be of high caliber to warrant an invitation and be a worthy representative; majority vote of the squad to go; and the Academy will not solicit an invitation or consider any action until an official invitation is received.

The Army's response on March 26th was there is a need for uniform DOD policy for post-season football bowl games for service academies that allows them to participate in them if in the opinion of the service academy's Superintendent, that it is in the best interests to allow the team to compete; that the USMA Superintendent and the Department of the Army feel that it is in the best interests of USMA not to participate in bowl games; that the participation of individuals in post-season football events is quite different from having a team compete in a bowl game and should be allowed to continue; and that the USMA Board of Visitors report is an advisory agency and the President does not approve the report, but merely passes on recommendations to the Department of Defense for further study and initiation of actions and that it is not a directive to the USMA Superintendent.

The response by the Navy was not found on this matter.

On April 14th, the Secretary of Defense, Neil McElroy, wrote Congressman Hebert a response to Hebert's February 10th letter asking for a uniformed policy regarding service academy bowl games. McElroy's summarized responses from the three services, felt that individual players in all-star games was a different issue from having a team attend a bowl, that the USMA Board of

Visitors is advisory and not directive, and said it was the Administration's position that each academy can best judge for itself which bowl bid to accept or whether participation is advisable. It is further believed that the continuation of the practice of decision by the individual academy is of the best interests to DoD. There were subsequent letters exchanged, but dealing with segregation issues with service academy bowl participation.

USMA did issue an updated memorandum on its intercollegiate athletic policy on June 20, 1960; as it is referenced in the July 2, 1964 updated policy. It is unclear what the 1960 policy actually said regarding bowl games; but the assumption is that it followed the language of the Department of Defense letter issued in 1959.

The Early 1960s Army Football Teams

Navy (5-4-1) beat Army (4-4-1) 43-12 at the end of the 1959 season, neither team receiving any interest from the nine bowl games. Army (6-3-1) lost again to #7 Navy in 1960, 12-17. #4/#6 Navy (9-1), with halfback Joe Bellino winning the Heisman Trophy, was invited to play in the 1961 Orange Bowl against #5/#4 Missouri (9-1). The Midshipmen lost, 21-14. In the 1961 season, Army (6-4) lost to Navy (7-3), 7-13; with neither team receiving any bowl interest.

On November 6, 1962, first year head football coach Paul Dietzel surprised everyone by announcing that Army had modified its stand on bowl games. Dietzel said "The academy's stand on the matter is unchanged. I have been told the authorities would agree to a bowl appearance on two conditions. First, Army must have a team that would do the academy credit. Second, the trip must be made without inconvenience to the players or the academy. Personally, I'd like to add a third condition of my own. I'd want the players to want to play in a bowl game. It should be a reward for a team, not a chore."

Riding on a 6-1 record, the loss being at Michigan (7-17), the Orange and Gator Bowl committees expressed interest in Army playing in their games. But a 7-12 upset by Oklahoma State, followed by a 6-7 loss to Pittsburgh, caused these interests to go away. Army (6-4) ended the season with 14-34 loss to Navy (5-5).

Army was 6-1 during the 1963 season and was receiving votes (the polls that season only ranked the first ten teams), with #8/#9 Pitt and #4 Navy remaining on the schedule. A November 4th article indicated interest by the Cotton, Orange, and Gator Bowls for Army. Dietzel revealed after the season was over that the Cotton Bowl was going to invite the winner of the Army-Navy game and that the Department of the Army had approved the trip if the players voted to accept it.

Army lost to Pittsburgh 0-28 and then ran out of time on the goal line to lose to Navy 15-21. #2 Navy (9-1) accepted the 1964 Cotton Bowl bid to play #1 Texas (10-0), losing 6-28 on New Year's Day. Air Force (7-4) lost to North Carolina (9-2) in the 1964 Gator Bowl, 35-0. Navy's quarterback Roger Staubach won the 1963 Heisman Trophy.

On July 2, 1964, USMA issued guidance on bowl games in its intercollegiate athletic policy. In the section *Postseason Football Bowl Games*, the policy now said, "The United States Military Academy does not have a firm policy concerning participation in postseason bowl games. Rather, each individual case is considered on its own merits. However, an Army Team will not participate in a postseason game unless the Athletic Board, the coaching staff, and a majority of the team members favor such participation."

In a battle of undefeated, 2-0, teams, #10 Army lost to #1 Texas in Austin, 6-17, during the 1964 season. The Black Knights (4-6) finished the season beating Navy (3-6-1), 11-8.

Army was 4-5-1 in the 1965 season, tying Navy (4-4-2), 7-7. Paul Dietzel unexpectedly resigned in spring 1966 to take the athletic director and head football coaching jobs at South Carolina. Plebe football coach Tom Cahill took over spring drills and in May was named head football coach.

Army was 5-2 going into November during the 1966 season, having lost to #3 Notre Dame and Tennessee. There did not seem to be any bowl interest that season, even though the Cadets won their last three games, including a 20-7 win over Navy (4-6), to improve their record to 8-2.

The 1967 Army Football Team

In mid-November 1967, Army was 7-1, having lost only to Duke, 10-7, with two games at Pitt (1-7) and with Navy (4-4) to go. Army officials indicated that they were in "a wait and see if they get a bowl bid." Newspaper accounts had the Cadets going to the Sugar, Cotton, Orange, or Gator Bowls.

On Tuesday, November 14th, the Sugar Bowl contacted USMA to gauge the Black Knights interest. USMA Superintendent Donald Bennett had his staff do a thorough review and he concluded that Army should accept, in accordance with the 1964 USMA policy. Bennett then called the Pentagon on Wednesday to seek approval from the Secretary of the Army. The Pentagon called back with a curt answer to the request, NO.

Late Thursday afternoon on November 16th, the Secretary of the Army, Stanley Resor, and the Army Chief of Staff, General Harold K. Johnson, had USMA issue a press release. It began with "It was concluded that accepting an invitation to play in a post season bowl game would tend to emphasize football to an extent not consistent with the basic mission of the Academy, which is to produce career Army officers."

The statement further said "that no bowl bids will be accepted this year for the Army football team. It was determined that it was not advisable for the Army team to participate." On Friday morning, all 324 heavy metal sugar bowls went missing from the Cadet Mess Hall, with a sign left behind "No Sugar Bowl for the Army team, no sugar bowls for the Corps." Sugar from the bowls were heaped on plates sitting on each table. The sugar bowls were returned later in the day.

Army struggled in its next game at Pittsburgh, ultimately scoring two touchdowns to beat the Panthers, 21-12. Navy (then 4-4-1) went out to a 19-0 lead until the Black Knights scored their first two touchdowns with nine and seven minutes to go in the game. Army was driving for another score when the Midshipmen recovered a lost fumble with 4:32 to go and ran out the clock to win, 19-14. Army finished the 1967 season with an 8-2 record.

The 1968 Congressional Investigation

The Special Subcommittee on Service Academies of the Committee of Armed Services, United States House of Representatives, conducted a series of hearings from September 29, 1967 through July 16, 1968 to discuss matters concerning the service academies. There were a total of eight hearings, one conducted at each service academy, and the remainder in Washington.

There were a number of subjects discussed, such as academics, admissions, separations, honor code, training, and postseason bowl games. Staff and faculty at each service academy testified, as well as Cadets and Midshipmen; plus in a few cases officials of the individual service departments.

Air Force Academy staff, faculty, and Cadets testified in Colorado Springs on February 5, 1968 while Department of the Air Force officials testified in Washington on March 5th. On the matter of postseason bowl games, the USAFA policy was for the Superintendent to consider any major bowl bids received, make a determination, and seek approval from the Air Chief of Staff and/or the Secretary of the Air Force; ensure that a majority of the squad wants to play; and make no solicitation of bowl bids or consideration on unofficial invitations. This was consistent with the policy adopted in 1958 around the time of the Falcons bowl bid to the Cotton Bowl.

Naval Academy staff, faculty, and Midshipmen with some Department of the Navy officials testified on February 2, 1968 in Annapolis. Regarding postseason bowl games, Navy had already been to all four of the major bowls (Rose, Sugar, Cotton twice), and Orange) and had a clear policy established in 1954 or 1955 to consider all bowl invitations, with the USNA Superintendent making a decision based on majority approval of the squad with the approval by the Secretary of the Navy. Navy had even demonstrated where they turned down bowl invitations for cause (losing to or tying Army).

Military Academy staff, faculty, and Cadets testified on February 4, 1968 at West Point on a number of matters. On the matter of postseason bowl games, USMA Superintendent Donald Bennett and athletic director Colonel Jerry Capka discussed the events of November 13-17 upon the receipt of the Sugar Bowl feeler through the Mess Hall incident, told above in this chapter. Bennett also discussed the 1964 USMA Intercollegiate Athletic policy, and the steps he took to consider the bowl feeler.

The subcommittee members found out that Bennett had only called and was called back by Lieutenant General Albert O. Connor, Deputy Chief of Staff for Personnel, in the Pentagon, and Bennett's immediate supervisor. In Bennett's testimony, he recalled that Connor called back and said, "in answer to your question, the answer is No." Connor did not explain any reason for the decision to Bennett, nor did Bennett ask for any rationale.

Bennett then directed Capka to contact head football coach Tom Cahill and have him tell the squad that they would not be going to the Sugar Bowl. Cahill spoke briefly at the West Point hearing, and said he notified the squad just before practice began, and then everyone left the locker room for the field. After practice, several Cadets talked to Cahill, asking questions why they could not go to a bowl game. When asked if he felt the team wanted to go to a bowl game, Cahill said he certainly felt they did.

After Bennett was told No by Connor, then USMA and the Department of the Army public affairs offices worked together in preparing the November 16th press release. The only things unexplained in the hearing was who did what regarding the contents of the press statement (USMA released it to the press, but any questions would have to asked to the Department of the Army) and why the Thursday 1 pm release was delayed until 5 pm.

On April 2, 1968, the Secretary of the Army, Stanley Resor, and the Army Chief of Staff, General Harold K. Johnson, testified in Washington. Lieutenant General Connor was sick and unavailable for this testimony. Johnson explained that Connor received the phone call from Bennett, and then Connor came to his office on Wednesday, November 15th, at 8:30 am.

Johnson and Connor discussed briefly the bowl bid over a five minute period. Johnson quickly decided that he would recommend to Resor that Army not go to a bowl game, and both officers went immediately to the Secretary's office. A discussion occurred for an unknown time period between the three men, and then Resor made his decision that Army could not accept any bowl bid. Resor then told Connor to call Bennett to inform him of the Secretary's decision.

Subsequent testimony by Resor revealed that Congressman Hebert and others called Resor later that day as word got out about the decision, pleading for Resor to reconsider, which Resor refused. As word spread of the Secretary's decision, it seems that several members of Congress called West Point, the Sugar and Cotton Bowl officials, and others in the Pentagon to try to get the decision reversed.

The subcommittee discovered that Resor and Johnson had no knowledge of the Defense Department guidance on bowl games or the 1964 USMA policy before making a decision; and the subcommittee members chided them for this, with Johnson admitting he failed to make an informed recommendation. Resor and Johnson made no effort to contact the USMA Superintendent.

Each considered the issue based on the history of Army never going to a bowl games and their personal opinions of what was best for the Army and USMA. Both gentlemen provided rationales; most of which paralleled the reasoning used in General Davidson's 1958 memorandum on football bowl games.

General Johnson slipped initially in the hearing by saying his recommendation was made almost immediately by the 1951 Honor Scandal in that the football players were being treated better than the rest of the Corps of Cadets. Resor admitted that afterward he read the Defense and USMA policies on bowl games and other information, but his decision to not accept a bowl bid would have been the same had he had more knowledge.

On July 16, 1968, Lieutenant General Albert O. Connor testified in Washington before the subcommittee. Connor admitted he had reviewed the testimonies of Resor, Johnson, and Bennett to the subcommittee. His testimony verified what Resor and Johnson had said to the subcommittee.

Bennett had testified that his call to Connor was to make a recommendation that Army go to the bowl game and obtain the approvals of the Secretary of the Army and the Chief of Staff. Connor's recollection of their phone call was quite different, that Bennett was merely calling to feel out the Chief and the Secretary as to their opinion of whether to go to a bowl game or not.

Connor admitted he should have discussed this further with Bennett and asked more questions. Connor disclosed that because of this misunderstanding, there was never a discussion of USMA's position on the matter in Connor's meeting with Johnson, or the later meeting with the Secretary. Thus, the subcommittee discovered that no one at the Pentagon knew that the USMA Superintendent was recommending attending the 1968 Sugar Bowl if Army had been invited.

Connor did admit he knew about all the Army's polices and guidelines regarding postseason bowl games; since he also served on the academy staff in a prior assignment. Connor stated that he never told Johnson in their five minute meeting or Resor and Johnson in the Secretary's office about the 1964 USMA bowl policy or the Defense policy. He admitted that he should have brought these into the discussion.

On October 8th, the subcommittee issued its report. Regarding bowl bids, it recommended that "that when the opportunity presents itself, athletic teams at the Academies should be encouraged to participate in post season intercollegiate athletic contests; and that the decision to participate in future recognized post-season intercollegiate athletic contests should, in accord with long established service and Department of Defense policy, be made at the Academy concerned."

The 1969 Army Football Team

On November 5, 1968, USMA Superintendent Major General Samuel Koster approved an updated intercollegiate athletic policy to allow for postseason play only "in the most prestigious bowls, i.e., Sugar Bowl, Orange Bowl, Cotton Bowl, or Gator Bowl." Participation would permit the football team to "be representative of the Academy's ideals."

Mid-November 1968 reports indicated that the "Department of the Army may let the Cadets bowl," based upon the support of the new Army Chief of Staff, GEN William Westmoreland. Army was 5-3 prior to its remaining games at Pitt (1-9) and versus Navy (2-8); with three close four-point losses to Vanderbilt (5-4-1), at #16 Missouri (8-3), and at #3 Penn State (10-0); and a victory over then #16 California (7-3-1). Articles reported that Army might receive a Gator Bowl bid if it won both games. Army (7-3) beat both Pitt and Navy to end its season. #16 Missouri (7-3) played #12 Alabama (8-3) in the Gator Bowl.

The 1969-1983 Army Football Teams

Army went 4-5-1 and 1-9-1 in the 1969 and 1970 seasons, beating Navy (1-9), 27-0, in 1969 while losing to the Midshipmen (2-9) in 1970, 7-11. #11 Air Force (9-2) was invited to the 1971 Sugar Bowl. The Falcons lost 34-13 to #4 Tennessee (11-1) and finished #16/#13 in the final polls after the bowl games. Army went 6-4 in both the 1971 and 1972 seasons, beating Navy (3-8 and 4-7) each year. Air Force also went 6-4 each season.

Head football coach Tom Cahill was fired after Army went 0-10 in the 1973 season. Homer Smith was hired as the Army head football coach. In his next three seasons, the Black Knights went 3-8, 2-9, and 5-6. During these four seasons, Navy went 4-7, 4-7, 7-4, and 4-7; while Air Force went 6-4, 2-9, 2-8-1, and 4-7.

Army was 6-4 in 1977 when reports surfaced that the Independence Bowl wanted to invite the Cadets to play Louisiana

Tech (then 7-0-2). Army officials did not view this as a favorable event given it was a minor bowl in its second year and the opponent was not considered a major college team. The USMA leadership told the football captains that West Point would not be accepting the bowl bid. On November 21st, the Independence Bowl invited Louisville (then 7-3-1). Army then beat Navy (5-6), 17-14 to finish the season with a 7-4 record.

Clearly in 1977, no one asked the football team if the players wanted to play in a bowl game. The 1977 Independence Bowl was on Saturday, December 17th, which was near the start of Cadets' Christmas Leave (with term end examinations in January). I would have found a way down to Shreveport LA, as would a number of Cadets. A fork in the road not traveled.

It is unclear what, if any, policy decisions were made at USMA regarding bowl games after the 1977 season. I'm guessing the bowl bid from a "minor" bowl game raised the question of whether Army's prior policies on considering only major bowl games should continue, especially with the rise of the number of bowl games. In 1945, there were six bowls games attended by major college football teams. In 1958, there were only eight bowls. There were ten bowls in 1968 and 13 in 1977. By the 1984 season, there were now 18 bowl games played by Division 1-A (FBS) teams.

From 1978 through the 1983 season, Army had losing seasons (4-6-1, 2-8-1, 3-7-1, 3-7-1, 4-7, and 2-9) under four head football coaches (Smith, Lou Saban, Ed Cavanaugh, and Jim Young). The Black Knights tied Navy in 1981, 3-3, and lost decisively in the other games. Army beat Air Force in 1978 (28-14) and 1980 (47-24), losing to the Falcons during the other seasons.

Navy had winning records from 1978 through 1982 (9-3, 7-4, 8-4, 7-4-1, and 6-5) and a losing record in 1983 (3-8). In 1978, the Midshipmen played in the Holiday Bowl on December 22nd and beat Brigham Young (9-4), 23-16. Navy finished #17 in the final *United Press International* Coaches Poll for the 1978 season. Navy played on December 14th in the 1980 Garden State Bowl, losing to Houston (7-5), 0-35. The Midshipmen lost a close game to #15/#14 Ohio State (then 8-3) on December 30th at the 1981 Liberty Bowl.

Air Force had four losing seasons from 1978 through 1981 (3-8, 2-9, 2-9-1, and 4-7). In the 1982 season, Air Force (8-5) played in the 1982 Hall of Fame Classic/All-American Bowl on December 31st against Vanderbilt (8-4), winning 36-28. The #16 Falcons (10-2) played in the 1983 Independence Bowl on December 10th, against Mississippi (6-5), winning 9-3. Air Force was ranked 13th in the final *Associated Press* Poll and 15th in the final *United Press International* Coaches Poll.

Lost Bowl Opportunities

My assessment is that if USMA had either adopted USNA's bowl game policy or a policy similar to the USMA Board of Visitors report in 1955, Army might have attended the 1956 Cotton Bowl, the 1959 Sugar Bowl, the December 1966 Sun Bowl, the December 1969 Gator Bowl, and the December 1977 Independence Bowl.

In addition, Army might have played in the 1946 Rose Bowl, the 1949 Sugar Bowl (bet the players would have voted for that if the '45 team had gone to Rose Bowl), and the 1950 Sugar Bowl.

I've excluded seasons where Army did not beat Navy, though the Black Knights might have gone to the either the January 1951 Sugar or Gator Bowls; the December 1963 Gator Bowl (having actually beaten bowl participant Air Force and were robbed in the Navy game); and either the December 1967 Gator Bowl or the January 1968 Sugar Bowl.

As history shows, Army went to no bowl games until the 1984 season.

The good news from my prospective is that Army football players since 1984 have had an opportunity to play in a bowl game, to have some postseason fun, and to be recognized for having a good season.

Chapter 3

Bowl Data

At the end of the 2021 season, Air Force had been to 28 bowl games, Navy to 24, Army to 10, Coast Guard to 7 postseason games, and Merchant Marine to 10 postseason games.

This chapter provides bowl game or postseason game history for all five service academies as of January 9, 2022:

ARMY WEST POINT - Bowl Games (7-3):

* 1984 Cherry Bowl, December 22nd, HC Jim Young, Michigan State, W, 10-6

* 1985 Peach Bowl, December 31st, HC Jim Young, Illinois, W, 31-29

* 1988 Sun Bowl, December 24th, HC Jim Young, Alabama, L, 28-29

* 1996 Independence Bowl, December 31st, HC Bob Sutton, Auburn, L, 29-32

* 2010 Armed Forces Bowl, December 30th, HC Rich Ellerson, Southern Methodist, W, 16-14

* 2016 Heart of Dallas Bowl, December 27th, HC Jeff Monken, North Texas, W, 38-31 OT

* 2017 Armed Forces Bowl, December 23rd, HC Jeff Monken, San Diego State, W, 42-35

* 2018 Armed Forces Bowl, December 22nd, HC Jeff Monken, Houston, W, 70-14

* 2019 Liberty Bowl, December 31st, HC Jeff Monken, West Virginia, L, 21-24

* 2021 Armed Forces Bowl, December 22nd, HC Jeff Monken, Missouri, W, 24-22

NAVY - Bowl Games (12-11-1):

1924 Rose Bowl, January 1st, HC Bob Folwell, Washington, T, 14-14

1955 Sugar Bowl, January 1st, HC Eddie Erdelatz, Mississippi, W, 21-0

1958 Cotton Bowl, January 1st, HC Eddie Erdelatz, Rice, W, 20-7

1961 Cotton Bowl, January 1st, HC Wayne Hardin, Missouri, L, 14-24

1964 Cotton Bowl, January 1st, HC Wayne Hardin, Texas, L, 6-28

1978 Holiday Bowl, December 22nd, HC George Welsh, Brigham Young, W, 23-16

1980 Garden State Bowl, December 14th, HC George Welsh, Houston, L, 0-35

1981 Liberty Bowl, December 30th, HC George Welsh, Ohio State, L, 28-31

* 1996 Aloha Bowl, December 25th, HC Charlie Weatherbie, California, W, 43-38

* 2003 Houston Bowl, December 30th, HC Paul Johnson, Texas Tech, L, 14-38

* 2004 Emerald Bowl, December 30th, HC Paul Johnson, New Mexico, W, 34-19

* 2005 Poinsettia Bowl, December 22nd, HC Paul Johnson, Colorado State, W, 51-30

* 2006 Meineke Car Care Bowl, December 30th, HC Paul Johnson, Boston College, L, 24-25

* 2007 Poinsettia Bowl, December 20th, HC Ken Niumatalolo, Utah, L, 32-35

* 2008 EagleBank Bowl, December 20th, HC Ken Niumatalolo, Wake Forest, L, 19-29

* 2009 Texas Bowl, December 31st, HC Ken Niumatalolo, Missouri, W, 35-13

* 2010 Poinsettia Bowl, December 23rd, HC Ken Niumatalolo, San Diego State, L, 14-35

* 2012 Kraft Fight Hunger Bowl, December 29th, HC Ken Niumatalolo, Arizona State, L, 28-62

* 2013 Armed Forces Bowl, December 30th, HC Ken Niumatalolo, Middle Tennessee, W, 24-6

* 2014 Poinsettia Bowl, December 23rd, HC Ken Niumatalolo, San Diego State, W, 17-16

* 2015 Military Bowl, December 28th, HC Ken Niumatalolo, Pittsburgh, W, 44-28

* 2016 Armed Forces Bowl, December 23rd, HC Ken Niumatalolo, Louisiana Tech, L, 45-48

* 2017 Military Bowl, December 28th, HC Ken Niumatalolo, Virginia, W, 49-7

* 2019 Liberty Bowl, December 31st, HC Ken Niumatalolo, Kansas State, W, 20-17

AIR FORCE - Bowl Games (14-13-1):

1958 Cotton Bowl, January 1st, HC Ben Martin, Texas Christian, T, 0-0

1963 Gator Bowl, December 28th, HC Ben Martin, North Carolina, L, 0-35

1970 Sugar Bowl, January 1st, HC Ben Martin, Tennessee, L, 13-34

* 1982 Hall of Fame Bowl, December 31st, HC Ken Hatfield, Vanderbilt, W, 38-28

* 1983 Independence Bowl, December 10th, HC Ken Hatfield, Mississippi, W, 9-3

* 1984 Independence Bowl, December 15th, HC Fisher DeBerry, Virginia Tech, W, 23-7

* 1985 Bluebonnet Bowl, December 31st, HC Fisher DeBerry, Texas, W, 24-16

* 1987 Freedom Bowl, December 30th, HC Fisher DeBerry, Arizona State, L, 28-33

* 1989 Liberty Bowl, December 28th, HC Fisher DeBerry, Mississippi, L, 29-42

* 1990 Liberty Bowl, December 27th, HC Fisher DeBerry, Ohio State, W, 23-11

* 1991 Liberty Bowl, December 29th, HC Fisher DeBerry, Mississippi State, W, 31-15

* 1992 Liberty Bowl, December 31st, HC Fisher DeBerry, Mississippi, L, 0-13

* 1995 Copper Bowl, December 27th, HC Fisher DeBerry, Texas Tech, L, 41-55

* 1997 Las Vegas Bowl, December 20th, HC Fisher DeBerry, Oregon, L, 13-41

* 1998 Oahu Bowl, December 25th, HC Fisher DeBerry, Washington, W, 43-25

* 2000 Silicon Valley Bowl, December 31st, HC Fisher DeBerry, Fresno State, W, 37-34

* 2002 San Francisco Bowl, December 31st, HC Fisher DeBerry, Virginia Tech, L, 13-20

* 2007 Armed Forces Bowl, December 31st, HC Troy Calhoun, California, L, 36-42

* 2008 Armed Forces Bowl, December 31st, HC Troy Calhoun, Houston, L, 28-34

* 2009 Armed Forces Bowl, December 31st, HC Troy Calhoun, Houston, W, 47-20

* 2010 Independence Bowl, December 27th, HC Troy Calhoun, Georgia Tech, W, 14-7

* 2011 Military Bowl, December 28th, HC Troy Calhoun, Toledo, L, 41-42

* 2012 Armed Forces Bowl, December 29th, HC Troy Calhoun, Rice, L, 14-33

* 2014 Idaho Potato Bowl, December 20th, HC Troy Calhoun, Western Michigan, W, 38-24

* 2015 Armed Forces Bowl, December 29th, HC Troy Calhoun, California, L, 36-55

* 2016 Arizona Bowl, December 30th, HC Troy Calhoun, South Alabama, W, 45-21

* 2019 Cheez-It Bowl, December 27th, HC Troy Calhoun, Washington State, W, 31-21

* 2021 First Responder Bowl, December 28th, HC Troy Calhoun, Louisville, W, 31-28

\# Bowl Games played with the academy offense not using an option running attack

* Bowl Games played with the academy offense using an option running attack

COAST GUARD - Bowl and Post-Season Games (1-6):

1963 Tangerine Bowl, December 28th, HC Otto Graham, Western Kentucky, L, 0-27

1988 ECAC North Championship, November 19th, HC Thomas Bell, Plymouth State, W, 28-19

1996 NCAA Division III Playoffs, November 23rd, HC Bill Schmitz, College of New Jersey, L, 16-17

1997 NCAA Division III Playoffs, November 22nd, HC Chuck Mills, Rowan, L, 0-43

2006 NEFC Championships, November 11th, HC Bill George, Curry, L, 28-34

2006 ECAC North Atlantic Bowl, November 18th, HC Bill George, Bridgewater State, L, 22-41

2007 NEFC Championship, November 10th, HC Bill George, Curry, L, 7-10

MERCHANT MARINE - Bowl and Post-Season Games (8-2)

1984 ECAC Bowl Game, November 17th, HC Dennis Barrett, Widener, W, 38-6

1985 ECAC Bowl Game, November 23rd, HC Dennis Barrett, Wagner, L, 7-9

1992 ECAC Bowl Game, November 21st, HC Charlie Pravata, Dickinson, W, 20-13 OT

1994 NCAA Division III Playoffs, November 19th, HC Charlie Pravata, Plymouth State, L, 18-19

1996 ECAC Bowl Game, November 23rd, HC Charlie Pravata, Franklin & Marshall, W, 20-0

1997 ECAC Bowl Game, November 22nd, HC Charlie Pravata, Grove City, W, 25-12

2002 ECAC Bowl Game, November 23rd, HC Charlie Pravata, Wilkes, W, 33-7

2017 ECAC Clayton Chapman Bowl, November 17th, HC Mike Toop, Buffalo State, W, 35-20

2018 New England Bowl, November 17th, HC Mike Toop, Endicott, W, 38-22

2021 New England Bowl, November 20th, HC Mike Toop, Western New England, W, 63-35

ARMY WEST POINT - Contractual Bowl Games not played due to Bowl Ineligibility and/or not winning Commander-in-Chief's Trophy for 1989-1992 Liberty Bowls, and the likely opponent the Black Knights would have played:

1989 Liberty Bowl, December 29th, Mississippi

1990 Liberty Bowl, December 27th, Ohio State

1991 Liberty Bowl, December 29th, Mississippi State

1992 Liberty Bowl, December 31st, Mississippi

2006 Poinsettia Bowl, December 19th, Texas Christian

2009 EagleBank Bowl, December 29th, Temple

2011 Kraft Fight Hunger Bowl, December 31st, UCLA

2012 Military Bowl, December 27th, Bowling Green

2013 Poinsettia Bowl, December 26th, Utah State

2015 Armed Forces Bowl, January 2nd, Houston

2015 Poinsettia Bowl, December 23rd, Boise State

2020 Independence Bowl, December 26th, no Pacific 12 Conference opponent available

ARMY WEST POINT - Seasons since 1983 where the team was bowl eligible but was not selected for a bowl game:

1986 Season (6-5), beat Air Force, 21-11, and beat Navy, 27-7

1989 Season (6-5), lost at Air Force, 3-29, and lost to Navy, 17-19

1990 Season (6-5), lost to Air Force, 3-15, and beat Navy, 30-20

1993 Season (6-5), lost at Air Force, 6-25, and beat Navy, 16-14

ARMY WEST POINT - Seasons since 1983 where the team was not bowl eligible due to not having a winning record:

1987 Season (5-6), lost at Air Force, 10-27, and beat Navy, 17-3

1991 Season (4-7), lost at Air Force, 0-25, and lost to Navy, 3-24

1992 Season (5-6), lost to Air Force, 3-7, and beat Navy, 25-24

1994 Season (4-7), lost to Air Force, 0-10, and beat Navy, 22-20

1995 Season (5-5-1), lost at Air Force, 20-38, and beat Navy, 14-13

1997 Season (4-7), lost at Air Force, 0-24, and lost to Navy, 7-39

1998 Season (3-8), lost to Air Force, 7-35, and beat Navy, 34-30

1999 Season (3-8), lost at Air Force, 0-28, and lost to Navy, 9-19

2000 Season (1-10), lost to Air Force, 27-41, and lost to Navy, 28-30

2001 Season (3-8), lost at Air Force, 24-34, and beat Navy, 26-17

2002 Season (1-11), lost to Air Force, 30-49, and lost to Navy, 12-58

2003 Season (0-13), lost at Air Force, 3-31, and lost to Navy, 6-34

2004 Season (2-9), lost to Air Force, 22-31, and lost to Navy, 13-42

2005 Season (4-7), won at Air Force, 27-24, and lost to Navy, 23-42

2006 Season (3-9). lost to Air Force, 7-43, and lost to Navy, 14-26

2007 Season (3-9), lost at Air Force, 10-30, and lost to Navy, 3-38

2008 Season (3-9), lost to Air Force, 7-16, and lost to Navy, 0-34

2009 Season (5-7), lost at Air Force, 7-35, and lost to Navy, 3-17

2011 Season (3-9), lost at Air Force, 14-24, and lost to Navy 21-27

2012 Season (2-10), beat Air Force, 41-21, and lost to Navy, 13-17

2013 Season (3-9), lost at Air Force, 28-42, and lost to Navy, 7-34

2014 Season (4-8), lost to Air Force, 6-23, and lost to Navy, 10-17

2015 Season (2-10), lost at Air Force, 3-20, and lost to Navy, 17-21

2019 Season (5-8), lost at Air Force, 13-17, and lost to Navy, 7-31

Chapter 4

The 1984 Football Season

Prior Army Seasons

The beginnings of the 1984 football season start with what happened seven seasons before. The 1977 Army Football Team achieved a 7-4 record, beating both Navy and Air Force while earning the Commander-in Chief's Trophy for only the second time, and receiving a bowl bid that USMA Superintendent Lieutenant General Andrew Goodpaster declined in 1977. This rebound from a 0-10 record in 1973 with four seasons under head coach Homer Smith led to higher expectations by USMA leadership and Army fans.

Smith lost a lot of starters and lettermen from that 1977 team, but began the 1978 season with a win over Lafayette, loss to Virginia and a tie against Washington State. Three straight losses hurt against Tennessee, Holy Cross, and Florida. But the team rebounded, with wins against Colgate, Air Force (28-14), and Boston College.

A loss to Pitt was not a surprise, but bowl-bound Navy blanked the Cadets, 28-0. Goodpaster had Homer Smith fired after the 4-6-1 season, and Army hired Lou Saban as Army's 28th head football coach. This was the 11th out of 21 coaching positions Saban held over his fifty year career.

Saban won his first two games against Connecticut and Stanford in the 1979 season. After a loss to North Carolina and a tie to Duke, the Cadets then lost seven straight games, including a 28-7 loss to Air Force and 31-7 loss to Navy for a 2-8-1 record. While Saban claimed he was going to stay at Army "until they put me out to pasture," in July 1980, he abruptly resigned and went to work for George Steinbrenner.

With the 1980 season rapidly approaching, USMA elevated offensive line coach Ed Cavanaugh as its head football coach. Cavanaugh lasted three losing seasons. He did beat Air Force in 1980, 47-24, and upset Navy by tying them, 3-3, in 1981. After watching the 1982 football season, USMA Superintendent Willard Scott, Jr. fired him.

A former head football coach was one of the first to apply for the vacant Army job, and met with Army Athletic Director Carl Ullrich at a Chicago airport hotel for an interview, impressing Ullrich "with his single-mindedness, football knowledge, and commitment to what has to be done."

In January 1983, Jim Young became Army's 30th head football coach. Young had had a long association with Bo Schembechler, serving as Michigan defensive coordinator during the 1969 through 1972 seasons. He became the head coach at Arizona for four years (1973-76) and Purdue for five (1977-1981), turning these programs around and achieving 69-32-1 record and three bowl games for the Boilermakers.

Jim Young was quick to project a winning season for the 1983 campaign, stating "he wasn't one to believe in rebuilding. Once you say it's going to take two or three years to rebuild a program, then that's what you wind up with." His coaching staff installed the I-formation and a pass oriented attack. It sputtered. The Cadets lost the home opener against Colgate, 13-15, before being whipped 7-31 at Louisville. Army barely beat Dartmouth, 13-12, before losing at Harvard, 21-24. After a win at home versus Rutgers (20-12), Army had a 2-3 record.

A 0-42 shutout by Notre Dame at Giants Stadium set the stage for the remaining games. Four straight losses followed, to Lehigh (12-13), at Air Force (20-41), Boston College (14-34), and at Pitt (7-38). Even with two weeks to prepare, Navy soundly beat Army, 13-42, in a game played for the first time west of the Mississippi River, at the Rose Bowl Stadium in Pasadena CA.

<u>The Big Decision to go to the Wishbone</u>

The season-ending loss to Navy was the final blow. Young realized that a change had to be made. "Jim did a little crying, I know that, just as I did," said Ullrich. "It took about an hour and then he got his old pad out and was working on what he had to do. I got list after list of things. Not that he was demanding, but they were simple suggestions on improving the program."

I have no idea what ideas Young was scratching out on his pad or when he did this, but my suspicion is that it came on the almost six hour flight back to West Point after the Navy game. This was the second long flight back east in a month, the other being from Colorado Springs to New York after the loss to Air Force.

There, Young was exposed to another service academy operating the wishbone offense. The Falcons ran 469 yards on 72 carries that day, a new single-game record. They did lose four out of five fumbles that day, but the Falcons quarterback Marty Louthan rushed for 142 yards in 20 attempts for three touchdowns. Air Force, which went to the option in the middle of the 1971 season, finished the 1983 season second in the nation with 346.5 yards rushing per game.

This was not the first time Young had coached against the option. As defensive coordinator for Michigan, his defense shut down the UCLA and Purdue wishbone offenses in Wolverine victories during the 1972 season. He also beat New Mexico's option in 1973 while head coach at Arizona, 22-14. There were probably other opponents who ran portions of the wishbone offense in games coached over Young's career.

It should be noted that UCLA option quarterback Mark Harmon (yes, the actor from the television series NCIS) was knocked out of the 1972 Michigan game in the first quarter, but UCLA did finish second in the nation in rushing with 346.4 yards per game, under their offensive coordinator, Homer Smith.

An article in the 1985 Army Football Annual on the Wishbone laid out several of Young's thinking. "We don't have the great size in the line or the great running tailbacks or passing quarterbacks, so it became obvious we had to make some changes. Air Force had great success with the wishbone, utilizing what I thought was similar personnel, so that's why we went to it. My assessment was we had tough, disciplined individuals trained to deliver perfection and revel in repetition."

I don't know if the wishbone decision was made during the long flight back from Pasadena. But it did offer Jim Young an opportunity for deep thinking about what needed to change for Army Football. We know that Coach Young made the decision, sometime during the late November to January time period, to switch to the wishbone offense. This decision led to a rebirth in Army Football during the 1984 season.

Response was initially mixed. Offensive coordinator Charlie Taaffee said, "We were at rock-bottom offensively. It was a gutsy decision and one that certainly needed to be made. But to be frank with you, we all knew that whatever we were going to go to would be better than what we were playing."

Army athletic director Carl Ullrich said, "Had not Air Force been so successful, I would have thought - boy, we're really desperate." Linebacker Jim Gentile said, "Talk about West Point building military leaders, it took real guts for Coach Young to make that decision."

Meanwhile, the coaching staff had to learn everything there was about their new offense prior to spring practice. Taaffe had a little experience with it a decade ago at Georgia Tech. He said, "We had to do our homework a little more, that's for sure. Only about a half-dozen teams [in Division 1-A] run the wishbone, so it wasn't hard to figure where to go to look for help."

The staff watched reels and reels of film of the Air Force wishbone and made trips to Wyoming and Mississippi State. The Bulldogs head coach Emory Ballard developed the wishbone offense for the Texas team in the 1969 season headed by Darrell Royal. The football coaching staff of Auburn, headed by head coach Pat Dye and offensive coordinator Jack Crowe spent four days at West Point helping implement the unorthodox offense.

The wishbone offense is a successful system for most of the major college teams that use it. It was no longer fashionable, as Young explained, "Most people got out of the wishbone not because it was stopped, but because the fans didn't like it. They wanted to see the football in the air. I just want to see the football in the end zone. In one week's time, it's very difficult for an opponent to get ready to defense the wishbone. And I believe it allows our offensive linemen to be aggressive and fire off the football."

In an interview with Mike Poorman of the Football Annual in the summer of 1985, Jim Young was asked about his decision to switch, "I think you go with what you think your personnel dictates. I felt that here at West Point we didn't have the ability to throw the football out of the pro offense, but we did have the ability to run an option attack. That's why we made the adjustment."

Asked about how important it was that the wishbone succeed, Young said, "Very important. Any time you make a decision you've got to be willing to stay with it. You have to go into it feeling it's the right decision right off the bat. In this case, it certainly was the right decision. It was a style of attack our players really believed in and related to."

1984 Army Football Coaching and Support Staff

The Army coaching staff remained mostly the same for their second season at West Point. Led by head coach Jim Young, it included defensive coordinator Bob Sutton, offensive coordinator Charlie Taaffee (his fourth season), defensive backs Johnny Burnett (sixth season), defensive perimeter Jay Robertson (first season), wide receivers John Simar, tight ends Greg Gregory, offensive backs Greg Seamon, defensive ends Jack Hecker (second tour, first under Tom Cahill from 1967-73), and offensive line Jim Shuck.

Other coaching staff included Tim Kish (defensive interior line), Pete Mahoney (offensive line & junior varsity), Doug Lowrey (linebackers & junior varsity), Charlie Blake (junior varsity), Herb Allen (graduate assistant & junior varsity), Gary Bastin (graduate assistant & defensive ends), and Rich Laughlin (graduate assistant & junior varsity).

Other support staff included Gene Benner (head trainer), Scott Lustig (admissions support & recruiting), Dick Hall (equipment manager), Bob Rogucki (strength training), Jim Wallace (assistant trainer), Jack Trainor (assistant trainer), Colonel Bob Berry (officer representative), Colonel Gerald Galloway (officer representative for academics), Lieutenant Colonel Jack Ryan (team physician), Major Bill Hopkinson (team physician), Captain Bob Johnson (assistant officer representative), Captain Greg Dyson (officer representative junior varsity), and Captain Jerry Araneo (officer representative junior varsity).

1984 Football Schedule

The 1984 football schedule would start at home against Colgate on Saturday, September 15th. The Cadets would then travel to Knoxville TN to face the University of Tennessee on the 22nd. Army would then return home for games with Duke (September 29th) and Harvard (October 6th).

They would then go on the road to Giants Stadium in East Rutherford NJ to play the Scarlett Knights of Rutgers University on Saturday, October 13th. The Cadets would then host the Quakers from the University of Pennsylvania on the 20th. Army would play indoors in the Carrier Dome at Syracuse the next Saturday. Air Force would then travel to West Point for their annual Commander-in-Chief's Trophy game on November 3rd.

The Cadets would travel to Chestnut Hill MA to face the Eagles of Boston College on Saturday, November 10th. Army would then play its first ever football game outside the United States, completing against Montana in the Mirage Bowl in Tokyo Japan on Friday, November 16th.

Originally, Army was to play Pitt at Michie on November 17th, but that game was cancelled. After playing ten straight weeks of football, the Cadets would have two weeks off, before playing Navy on December 1st at Veterans Stadium in Philadelphia.

Three games would be televised, the Air Force game by Lorimar Productions, Boston College by *CBS Television* and *Katz Sports*, and the Army-Navy game by *CBS Television*. The first five home games would kick off at 2 pm EDT. The game with the Falcons was originally scheduled to kick off at 12:20 EST, but was rescheduled for a night game. The Tennessee, Syracuse, and Boston College games were afternoon ones, while Navy would kick off at 12:20. The game in Japan would be played during Friday evening.

Spring Practice

Spring practice lasted five weeks, and the main effort was to introduce the wishbone offense and determine who might play in it. But before spring practice even began, Army faced some unexpected setbacks. Upcoming senior running back Elton Atkins, who led the team with 713 yards rushing and was a national leader in all-purpose running, informed the coaching staff he would not play in 1984. Freshman running back Travis Jackson, fourth in rushing last season, decided to resign from USMA. And mid-way through spring drills, rising junior quarterback Bill Turner, who started one game in 1983 and played in eight games the next season, turned in his gear.

The big question was how the offensive backfield would perform, with the fact that none of the four men on the first-string depth chart had played those positions last season. At quarterback, senior Nate Sassaman, who played back-up free safety, but was an option quarterback in high school, was ahead of junior Bob Healy, who started seven games in 1983 and passed for 913 yards (71-142-10).

Dee Bryant had come over from cornerback and Jarvis Hollingsworth from flanker, and were the preseason two-deep at halfback. Behind them was junior Kevin McKelvy (204 yards rushing in 1983), followed by hopefuls Benny Wright, Keith Basik, Clarence Jones, and William Lampley.

Doug Black was cut in preseason camp as a plebe, but had a successful intramural career for two seasons in eight man football, before his tactical officer (and future USMA Superintendent) Bob Caslen persuaded the coaching staff to give Black a second look. He started out 8th on the depth chart, and quickly rose to the starting line-up, ahead of lettermen Dave Pratt and Tom Perry.

Army lost 22 lettermen to graduation from the 1983 team, including seven who started against Navy. As many as 46 lettermen were on hand when the Cadets started pre-season work in August, with 26 of the men having starting experience. The starters on the preseason depth chart on July 1st all were lettermen, except one, fullback Doug Black.

Other positions were sorted out in spring drills. The offensive starters, besides the backfield, were split end Scott Spellmon, left tackle Karl Heineman, left guard Vince McDermott, center Ron Rice, right guard Don Smith, right tackle Dave Woolfolk, and tight end Rob Dickerson. Nine of the group would start in the Cherry Bowl.

On defense, the starters going into preseason were left end Brad Allen, left tackle Jim Jennings, nose guard Rob Ulses, right tackle Mike Sears, right end Kurt Guitierrez, linebackers Jim Gentile and John Roney, cornerbacks Eric Griffin and Kermit McKelvy, and safeties Bob Silver and Mike Tease. Nine would start in the Cherry Bowl.

Summer

New Cadets arrived at West Point on July 2nd with their classmates of the USMA Class of 1988, and 53 plebes were listed at top prospects in the Army Football Media Guide. Fullback Andy Peterson, offensive tackle Bill Schleiden, and center Ed Scultz would letter during the 1984 season. Others would see some playing time during the season included offensive guards Jim Saganowich and Brian Ash, split ends Mark Charette and Eric Keltner, quarterback Tory Crawford, defensive tackle Gary Duncan, linebackers Ray Griffiths and Dave Leek, and halfback Ron Herring.

Captains

A decision was made before the season that the entire senior class would be the Captains of the football team, instead of one or two individuals normally. For each game, someone out of this group went to the officials huddle for the coin toss. "We don't have a team captain," said Jim Young. "All the seniors are responsible for leadership. They're learning to be great leaders and we are giving them the responsibility."

USMA Graduate Support

In a request published in the September 1984 issue of *Assembly*, the publication of the Association of Graduates USMA, head coach Jim Young requested individuals to write letters to the football team. He said later to my old friend Morris Herbert, Class of 1950, in an interview in the March 1985 *Assembly*, "I was amazed by the response. All year long, every week, every game, we received letters of encouragement. I don't believe the graduates of any other college would have come through and given us the support our grads did. You know, we also wrote a special letter to Army football lettermen just before the Navy game asking them to write the team. Over 80% of the lettermen we wrote to responded."

"To me, it was a very moving experience. It had a very positive effect. The football team realized that our graduates, young and old, have a great pride in West Point and they really care about the team. I think it brought home to our team the close ties that exist between grads and the Corps; ties that carry on through your entire life. It made a difference, no doubt about it. I hope you will mention how grateful I am to our alumni for the letters written to our team."

Season Predictions

Most predicted that Army would finish 1984 similar to the 1983 season, or worse, as the Cadets had not won more than four games since 1977 and had a 18-44-4 record during the last six seasons. One national publication went so far as to rank Army among "the worst 20 teams in the country." Looking at the team's schedule, many saw five solid losses to Tennessee, Syracuse, Air Force, Boston College, and Navy, with six toss ups with Colgate, Duke, Harvard, Rutgers, Penn, and Montana.

Colgate

Colgate (1-0) traveled to West Point to meet Army on Saturday, September 15th, before 32,032 fans at Michie Stadium, with the Red Raiders favored by 3.5 points. Colgate beat Connecticut, 9-3, the previous Saturday.

On the Cadets first offensive play, Nate Sassaman handed off to his fullback, Doug Black, for a six yard gain. That possession ended with a 27 yard field goal by Craig Stopa. On the next possession, Black scored on a 37 yard rush to finish a 98 yard drive, and Army led 10-0 at the end of the first quarter.

The Red Raiders responded with two field goal before William Lampley ran 33 yards for a touchdown. Colgate completed a passing touchdown and Sassaman scored on a 21 yard run, making the score 24-12 at halftime in favor of the Cadets. Army scored on four of their first five possessions.

The teams traded field goals in the third quarter. Sassaman and plebe fullback Andy Peterson both scored on one yard plunges in the final stanza. Army buried Colgate 41-15 by showcasing the wishbone attack with 441 yards on the ground. Three Cadets rushed for more than 100 yards - Black (124 yards), Sassaman (123), and Lampley (102). The Cadets only passed three times, completing two for 44 yards.

The Army defense limited the Red Raiders to 19 yards rushing and 299 passing, made two interceptions and recovered one fumble. Sassaman was named ECAC Division 1-A Offensive Player of the Week. Colgate finished the season with a 5-5 overall record unranked, while it was ranked as high as #10 in the Division 1-AA Poll in early October.

"This is a big step in the right direction for us," said head coach Jim Young. "But we haven't arrived yet. We still have a long way to go. But this team is really happy to get a win in this game since we didn't win our opener a year ago. Considering we only had two wins all of last year and we have one right now makes for a pretty good feeling. This is a completely different team than it was a year ago. We played with more poise and we are physically tougher. The players want to prove they can win here."

Tennessee

"Tennessee is an excellent football team," said Jim Young. "They are extremely well coached and have a great tailback in Johnnie Jones. They are a quick team defensively and probably have the best kicking game we'll face this year. It will be a great challenge to play on the road in front of more than 90,000 against one of the better teams in the nation."

Facing #19 Tennessee (2-0) on the road in Neyland Stadium in Knoxville TN before 89,639 fans on September 22nd, the Cadets (1-0) were outweighed 42 pounds per man. The game was televised locally, with John Ward and Bill Anderson announcing. The Volunteers were favored by 19.5 points.

Craig Stopa converted a 32 yard field goal on the first possession. The Volunteers scored on a rushing touchdown to make it 7-3 at the end of the first quarter. Army responded on its second possession to go ahead thanks to a Sassaman touchdown pass to Rob Dickerson for a yard. The Cadets were headed for another scoring late in the second quarter, but lost the football on the Volunteers 13 yard line, and Tennessee kicked a 46 yard field goal on the final play to tie it, 10-10, at halftime.

William Lampley ran in from the two for a touchdown to make it 17-10. Tennessee responded by scoring on two long drives in each quarter for a 24-17 lead late in the fourth quarter. Army's response was to put together an 80 yard, eleven play drive that ended with Sassaman scoring from the one with 1:17 left in the game. Jim Young then made a decision to go for one instead of two. Craig Stopa converted his 37th straight extra point, and Army tied Tennessee, 24-24.

"They say a coach should always win, that's the American way," said Young. "Well, if I had to make the same decision again, I'd do the same thing. When you're a 20-point underdog against a team like Tennessee and you've been losing to teams like that for the past ten years, the players deserve not to lose. I didn't want us to lose another coming back like we did."

"If we lost by one, it would have just another Army loss," said wide receiver Benny White. "And we've had plenty of them. But they'll be talking about this tie for weeks." The tie raised the profile of the previously maligned Cadets into the national limelight almost overnight. Army's gutty performance was noted by Tennessee head coach Johnny Majors. His team would drop out of the Top Twenty on Sunday.

Army rushed for 292 yards, had 82 yards passing (6-10-1), with 23 first downs and two turnovers. Black rushed for 120 yards, while Sassaman had 85. The ECAA named Doug Black their Rookie of the Week. Defensively, the Cadets allowed 182 yards rushing and 167 passing, forced four punts, and recovered one fumble.

Tennessee would finish the regular season tied for fifth in the Southeastern Conference (3-3) with a 7-3-1 overall record. The Volunteers lost to #11 Maryland in the Sun Bowl, 28-27, to finish 7-4-1.

<u>Duke</u>

Army (1-0-1) returned to Michie Stadium to host Duke (1-1) before 37,026 fans on Saturday, September 29th, with the Cadets favored by 3.5 points. "We were flat, but I think that's a tendency after our game with Tennessee last week," said Jim Young. "But it's also a reaction to what's gone on around us. Since the start of the season, we've gone from bums to heroes in a very short period. It's hard to keep your perspective in that situation."

The Cadets defense stopped the Blue Devils twice in the first quarter inside the five yard line, forcing Duke to convert two field goals and take a 6-0 lead. In the second quarter, the Cadets scored first on a Stopa 36 yard field goal and then Black went over from the one with 2:21 left in the half for a 10-6 halftime lead.

Duke's field goal was the only scoring in the third quarter to close to 10-9. A Blue Devils drive to the Army twelve ended with a lost fumble. Stopa kicked a 22 yard field goal in the fourth to lead Army to a 13-9 win.

Duke held Army to ONLY 300 yards rushing and 25 passing (1-3-0). Black went over 100 yards for the third straight week, rushing for 126. The Cadets lost two fumbles and made 16 first downs. Duke rushed for 151 and passed for 154 and lost two fumbles.

"A game like this would have been a loss for us in the past," said Nate Sassaman. "Everything remains a challenge for us," added Jim Young. Black for the second week in a row was named ECAC Rookie of the Week. Duke would finish the regular season tied for sixth in the Atlantic Coast Conference (1-5) with an overall 2-9 record.

Harvard

Before 40,504 fans at Michie, the Cadets (2-0-1) hosted Harvard (1-1) on the first Saturday of October, favored over the visitors by 16 points. The Crimson seemed to have figured out how to stop the wishbone. Army's deepest penetration was the Harvard 47. Then Doug Pavek intercepted a long pass at midfield. Army then marched down the field and halfback Dee Bryan scored on a six yard run. Stopa made a 32 yard field goal on the final play before the half ended, making the score 10-0.

The offense woke up from there in the second half, scoring four times. Sassaman hit Dickerson on a 20 yard touchdown reception after Harvard fumbled on their opening possession. The Crimson then added a field goal. Lampley scored on a seven yard rush to end an 80 yard drive in eight plays and up the score to 23-3 at the end of the third. Stopa converted a 48 yard field goal. The Crimson responded with a touchdown pass. Fullback Tom Perry scored from the one to make the final score, 33-11.

Army had 381 yards on the ground and 20 yards in the air (1-5-0), with 24 first downs and no turnovers. Sassaman had 127 yards rushing and 20 passing. Bob Healy came in near the end of the third quarter. Doug Black rushed for 97 yards while Bryant had 77. Defensively, the Cadets gave up 220 passing and 102 yards rushing, with 19 first downs, two interceptions and one fumble recovered.

The Army 3-0-1 record was the best since the 1958 season. Craig Stopa missed his first extra point kick in 41 attempts as a Cadet, though Sassaman, his holder, said "I think Craig got robbed. It looked like it went through and then went wide. The snap was all right, the hold was all right. The ref just botched it." Harvard finished tied for second in the Ivy League (5-2) with an overall record of 5-4, losing to Yale by three points.

Rutgers

Army traveled to East Rutherford NJ to play against the favored (7.5 points) Rutgers (3-2) before 34,752 in Giants Stadium. The Scarlett Knights were the home team.

Again, the Army offense could not get going, but the Army defense did not allow for any touchdowns in the first half. It took the Cadets 19 minutes to gain a first down, and then they lost the football on their own 31 yard line. The Scarlet Knights then converted a 44 yard field goal. Five plays later, Army lost another fumble and Rutgers booted another field goal. The Cadets were able to drive late in the first half, but Sassaman bobbled the snap on a Stopa field goal attempt with 20 seconds left. The halftime score was 6-0 in Rutgers favor.

With 3:07 to play in the third quarter, safety Mike Tease recovered a Scarlet Knights fumble. Army then marched 73 yards down the field, with Doug Black plunging over the goal line on fourth and one for a Cadets 7-6 lead going into the final quarter. The Cadets failed to score on its final four possessions. Midway in the fourth quarter, Rutgers scored on a twelve yard rush and a two-pointer to take the victory, 14-7.

Army rushed for a low 200 yards and passed for 35 (4-11-0), with 12 first downs and two turnovers. Rutgers rushed for 109 and passed for 167, with 18 first downs, one lost fumble, and one interception. Rutgers finished the season with a 7-3 record as an Independent and did not receive a bowl bid.

"A loss is tough to take any time," said Young. "We were in it all the way. But Rutgers played a physical game. They controlled the line of scrimmage. The way we came back from this loss will determine what kind of team we are." "There was a lot of sloppy execution on our part, especially in the first half," said Sassaman.

Pennsylvania

On October 20th, Army (3-1-1) played Pennsylvania (4-0) at Michie Stadium before a sellout crowd of 40,496 fans on Homecoming Weekend. The Cadets were favored by 11 points.

Army scored on its first five offensive possessions, rolling up 292 yards of total offense in the first half. Dee Bryant scored first on a five yard run as the Cadets marched 80 yards in ten plays. Doug Black plunged over the one yard to end a 15 play, 70 yard possession. Penn made a 46 yard field goal for a 14-3 Cadets lead in the first quarter.

Black rushed for a touchdown from the four. After Penn scored a rushing touchdown, Jarvis Hollingsworth rushed six yards for a score, making it 28-10 at halftime.

Black scored on another one yard plunge in the third quarter while the Quakers made a short field goal to close it to 34-13 going into the fourth quarter. With the reserves playing, Dickerson caught a nine yard pass from Bob Healy with senior John Lopes making the extra point kick. Tom Perry ended the scoring with a one yard touchdown run. It was a 48-13 victory, the highest Army score over 75 games since 1977.

The Cadets dominated time of possession with 36:59 and had 470 yards of total offensive, 379 rushing, and 91 passing (7-8-0), with 31 first downs and losing one fumble. Sassaman rushed for 107 yards and Black for 74. Defensively, Army held the Quarters to 89 yards rushing and 163 passing, recovered one fumble, and intercepted two passes, allowing 12 first downs. Penn won the Ivy League with a 7-0 record and overall 8-1 record. The Quakers were never ranked in the weekly Division 1-AA Polls.

Syracuse

Syracuse had won three of their first four games of the 1984 season, including a 17-9 victory over #1 Nebraska on September 29th. The Orangemen then lost three games in a row, including 21-3 to #19 Penn State. Syracuse (3-4) hosted Army (4-1-1) at the Carrier Dome on Saturday, October 27th, before 41,438 spectators. The Orangemen were favored by 7 points.

After Doug Pavek blocked a punt, the Cadets opened the game with two touchdowns by Black and Bryant in the first quarter and a 13-0 lead. Army allowed an Orangemen touchdown and field goal in the second quarter while losing starting safety Mike Tease to a season ending injury to his spinal cord. Syracuse lost their starting running quarterback and his passing back-up during the first half to injuries, but closed to 13-10 at halftime.

In came third stringer junior quarterback Mike Kmetz in the second half, who had never taken a snap in two seasons; and he led the Orangemen to a touchdown run and a field goal in the third quarter. Stopa made a 50 yard field goal to close the Syracuse lead to 20-16. Kmetz scored on an eight yard touchdown run for the only scoring in the final stanza, and the victory, 27-16.

Syracuse's defense limited Army to a season low 151 yards rushing and just 280 yards total offense (6-12-2-129 in passing), 14 first downs, and three turnovers. Sassaman gained just 37 yards and left the game in the third quarter due to cracked ribs. Black was held to a season low 29 yards.

The Syracuse offense had 22 first downs, 210 rushing yards, 110 passing, and had no turnovers. The Orangemen beat Pitt and Navy, then lost to #13 Boston College to finish the season with a 6-5 record. The Orangemen did not receive a bowl bid.

"It's a particularly disappointing loss for us," said Jim Young. "We had opportunities to win and we didn't." Young was disappointed in giving up 27 points to a team who was near the bottom in scoring, having only scored 66 in the previous seven games.

Air Force

In Army's first ever night game in Michie Stadium, the Cadets (4-2-1) battled visiting Air Force (5-3) on Saturday, November 3rd, with 39,000 fans present. The game was televised before a national audience on *ESPN*, with Jim Simpson and Paul McGuire announcing. The Falcons were favored by 7.5 points. A win against Army would earn the Falcons the Commander-in-Chief's Trophy. Bob Healy would start for the injured Nate Sassaman at quarterback.

The Falcons had lost to Western Athletic Conference rivals Wyoming and Utah on the road, beaten Navy 29-22 in Colorado Springs, and upset Notre Dame in South Bend, 21-7. Two weeks before the Army game, they lost to #7 and eventual 1984 national champion Brigham Young (BYU), 30-25, at home and had two weeks to prepare for the Cadets.

Kurt Gutierrez tackled a Falcons pass receiver in the end zone for a safety on the game's opening play. On their next possession, Craig Stopa converted a 48 yard field goal. Air Force responded with a field goal and a 39 yard touchdown reception over the middle to lead after the first quarter, 9-5. The Falcons gained 263 total yards in the first half, but only made a short field goal in the second quarter to lead 12-5 at halftime. "We weren't playing with much emotion in the first half," Stopa said. "Coach Young gave us a big halftime talk and that fired us up."

The Cadets defense played a major role in the second half, allowing the Falcons only 188 yards total offense while forcing five turnovers and holding them scoreless. Stopa converted a 50 yard field goal in the third quarter. Defensive back John Thomson recovered a Falcons fumble on the Cadets 47 yard line and then Scott Spellmon ran 41 yards on a reverse for a touchdown. After a

34 yard punt return by Bob Silver, Stopa made another field goal from 34 yards in the third quarter to allow Army to take an 18-12 going into the final period.

Stopa made two field goals of 26 and 27 yards in the fourth quarter to cement the 24-12 victory in the first leg of the Commander-in-Chief's Trophy for Army. In the process, Craig Stopa entered Army's record book for most career field goals (37) and most in a game (5). It was the fifth straight home win and Coach Jim Young called it his biggest win in his two years at USMA.

Army had 15 first downs, 245 yards rushing, 23 passing (3-5-0), and only one fumble lost. The Cadets defense limited the Falcons to 25 first downs, 150 yards rushing, 218 passing (16-28-2), and three lost fumbles. Black rushed for 77 yards, while Lampley had 49 yards, and Scott Spellmon made 41 yards on the ground. Benny White, Dee Bryant, and Doug Black each caught a pass from Rob Healy.

It was Army's first win of the season against a Division 1-A team with a winning record. Bob Healy started the game at quarterback and rushed for 73 yards and passed for 23. Sassaman handed off on an end around on Spellmon's long touchdown run. The win moved Army to a 5-2-1 record and moved it into consideration for a bowl bid.

Air Force finished third in the WAC with a 4-3 record with an overall regular season record of 7-4. The Falcons beat Virginia Tech in the Independence Bowl on December 31st to finish 8-4. They received votes in both the final *Associated Press* Top Twenty Poll and *United Press International* Coaches Top Twenty Poll, finishing 29th and 24th, respectively.

Boston College

Army traveled to Chestnut Hill on November 10th to battle eventual Heisman Trophy winner Doug Flutie and #16 Boston College (5-2) before 32,000 fans in Alumni Stadium in a night game televised by *CBS Television* and Katz Sports. Curt Gowdy (play-by-play) and Len Dawson (analyst) were the announcers.

BC had beaten then #9 Alabama 38-31 at Legion Field in their second game of the season. In their last three games, they had lost at #20 West Virginia 20-21, beat Rutgers 35-23, and lost at Penn State, 30-37. The Eagles were favored by 16.5 points.

Doug Black scored on a one yard plunge in the first quarter, but after an Eagles rushing touchdown, Flutie threw his first touchdown pass to make it 13-7 at the end of one quarter. The Eagles scored on another Flutie touchdown pass and on a 45 yard punt return to take a 28-7 lead. Jarvis Hollingsworth completed a halfback option pass to Rob Dickerson for five yards and a touchdown to close scoring to 28-14 at halftime.

BC made a field goal, and Nate Sassaman, playing with three cracked ribs and wearing a flak jacket, rushed for an eight yard touchdown. Stopa converted a 40 yard field goal to make it 31-24 going into the fourth quarter. The Eagles rushed for a touchdown, and Hollingsworth ran across the goal line from the nine. Flutie then spoiled the comeback with his third touchdown pass for the Boston College victory, 45-31.

The Cadets had 25 first downs, 349 yards rushing, and 60 passing (6-12-1), with one lost fumble. Boston College had 24 first downs, 156 rushing and 311 passing, with one lost fumble. Doug Flutie became the NCAA's all-time passing yardage leader, completing 19 of 29 passes for 311 yards. Sassaman completed four passes for 38 yards while Hollingsworth completed two passes. Sassaman had 136 yards rushing, while Black had 93 and Jones had 87.

The Eagles finished their regular season with four straight wins and a 9-2 record, highlighted by the Hail Mary touchdown pass by Flutie at the end of the Miami game televised nationally on *CBS Television* on November 23rd. While many fans assumed that play clinched Flutie's Heisman Trophy win, the voting was already complete before that game. Boston College finished the season with a 45-28 victory over Houston in the Cotton Bowl

Classic and a #4 ranking in the *United Press International* Coaches Poll and #5 ranking in the *Associated Press* Poll.

"We didn't win, but I'm proud of our kids," said Jim Young. "They have nothing to be ashamed of. They played well. He's [Flutie] certainly a great quarterback who makes BC a great team. I'm most impressed with his quick release and his competitive instincts."

Montana

The Mirage Bowl was a regular season NCAA college football game played in Tokyo, Japan, from 1977 to 1993. In 1986, it was sponsored by and renamed the Coca-Cola Classic. It was never considered a post-season game. It was named for the Japanese version of the Dodge Colt subcompact car. During the 1984 game, fans introduced "The Wave" to Japan; thanks partly to the Tennessee State marching band being present at the game. Montana was selected to play because the American Ambassador to Japan was native son former U.S. Senator Mike Mansfield.

Army and the University of Montana (2-7-1) met on Friday evening, November 16th, at Tokyo, Japan, in the eighth annual Mirage Bowl, in Olympic Memorial Stadium, where the 1964 Olympics took place. Montana was the designated home team and the Cadets were favored. There were over 60,000 Japanese fans with some Americans attending.

The first quarter started off with a Jarvis Hollingsworth nine yard touchdown run and a Grizzlies 42 yard field goal, to make it 7-3 at the end of the period. Montana went briefly ahead on a rushing touchdown. Doug Black and Nate Sassaman scored on one yard plunges while Craig Stopa made 24 yard field goal to make it 24-10 at halftime.

In the third quarter, Hollingsworth rushed in from the four yard line. Grizzlies quarterback Marty Mornhinweg threw a short touchdown pass. Clarence Jones went 68 yards for a touchdown and a 38-17 lead going into the fourth quarter.

Montana came back with two quick scores, a one yard plunge and a 62 yard touchdown pass reception to close the scoring to 38-31 with 6:29 remaining in the game. The Cadets responded with a time consuming 82 yard drive that Black finished with a 14 yard touchdown rush. "Both teams moved the ball readily," said Jim Young. "We moved it more."

Army rushed for 628 yards and passed for 51 (2-4-0), with 36 first downs and three lost fumbles. Montana rushed for 24 yards and passed for 417 yards (32-50-2). The Cadets punted only once, while the Grizzlies punted twice.

Army tied a NCAA record in having four players each rushing for 100 or more yards, a feat that had only happened three other times in college football history, the last time by the 1973 Alabama wishbone offense. The Cadets who accomplished this were Black (183), Sassaman (155), Jones (130), and Hollingsworth (124). The record still stands after the 2019 season.

The Grizzlies Mornhinweg set a school record for single-season passing yardage while Bob McCauley set a school receiving record. Army established five school records - most yards rushing (628), total offense (679), first downs rushing (34), total first downs (36), and most field goals in a season (15). All but the most rushing yards and field goals records still stand as Army records after the 2021 season.

Sassaman was named the game's most valuable player, while Jim Gentile was named outstanding defensive player. Mornhinweg received the game's Fighting Spirit Award. Montana finished their season in Japan with a 2-8-1 overall record. The Grizzlies finished eighth and last in the Big Sky Conference with a 0-7 record. Returning back from Japan, Army had two weeks to prepare for Navy.

Bowl Game Bids

Scouts from the Hall of Fame, Independence, Liberty, and Bluebonnet Bowls scouted Army and Air Force in their CIC game on November 3rd. Bowl representatives at the game said they were looking for teams that have a good following, and service academies will always bring people out.

On November 17th, representatives of the Cherry Bowl watched the Wisconsin at Michigan State football game, saying the Badgers were at the top of their list to attend the game on December 22nd. On November 20th, the *Associated Press* reported that Army and Virginia, who both had never gone to any bowl games, seemed on their way this year. Bowl bids would not be officially extended until 6 pm EST, Saturday, November 24th. The *Associated Press* reported that the Cherry Bowl has said it wanted Army and Michigan State.

On November 20th, the *New York Times* reported that Army was expected to play against Michigan State in the Cherry Bowl. Army athletic director Carl Ullrich said, "Yesterday, we've been contacted by the Cherry Bowl people and we're interested. Barring unforeseen circumstances, I believe we will receive a bid Saturday at 6 pm, and if so, we will accept." On November 21st, the *Associated Press* reported interest from the Hall of Fame Bowl for Army to play Wisconsin. The Cherry Bowl was reported as considering Army, Penn State, and Rutgers to play Michigan State.

On November 22nd, the *Associated Press* reported that the Freedom Bowl had dropped Rutgers from consideration and that Army had edged out Rutgers for the Cherry Bowl, even though the Cadets lost to Rutgers. On November 24th, Army accepted a bid to play in the Cherry Bowl against Michigan State, with the game being played at 1 pm EST on Saturday, December 22nd at the Pontiac Silverdome near Detroit.

Navy

Navy came into the Army game with a 4-5-1 record. The Midshipmen began the season at North Carolina with a 33-30 win. Navy then lost three straight times, versus Virginia (9-21), at Arkansas (10-33), and at Air Force (22-29); before beating Lehigh (31-14) and Princeton (41-3) in Annapolis and tying the Pitt Panthers, 28-28, on the road. On *ESPN*, Navy narrowly lost to

Notre Dame at Giants Stadium, 17-18. At the Carrier Dome, the Midshipmen were blanked, 0-29, by the Orangemen.

The highlight of their season was a 38-21 upset win over then #2 South Carolina in Annapolis. Injuries played a role in Navy's fortunes, as they lost star tailback and Heisman Trophy candidate Napoleon McCallum in a season-ending injury in the second game of the season. Quarterback Bill Byrne was injured during the Notre Dame game, so sophomore Bob Misch started in his place.

The Midshipmen had faced two wishbone offensives, the Razorbacks and the Falcons, losing to both. Six opponents were going to bowl games. Navy had won nine and tied one of the last eleven games against Army, with the only Cadets victory coming in 1977 by 17-14.

The 85th Army-Navy game was played on December 1st, at Philadelphia's Veterans Stadium before a sellout crowd of 73,180 fans (the first sellout since 1971). *CBS Television* broadcasted the game nationally, with Lindsay Nelson and Pat Haden announcing the game. Army was favored by 1 points. Navy was the designated home team.

The Cadets marched 80 yards in 16 plays on their initial drive when Clarence Jones went six yards around left end for the touchdown, making it 7-0 at the end of the first quarter. On the next Army possession, Doug Black plunged over the goal line from the one to finish that drive. The Midshipmen made a 40 yard field goal and Army led 14-3 at halftime.

Nate Sassaman finished two more Army drives with touchdown runs of nine yards in the third quarter and six yards in the fourth to up the score to 28-3. Navy tried to stage a comeback, first by a touchdown pass and two-point conversion to close it to 28-11. The Midshipmen mounted another scoring threat in the final minutes, but were stopped on fourth down at the Army one yard line.

"It was a great way to end the season," said head football coach Jim Young after the Navy game. "Especially since Army doesn't have that many victories over Navy recently. The players will remember this game forever."

"I'll live with this [defeat] until I die," said Navy tight end Mark Stevens, who lost a key fumble in the second quarter.

"The big thing we were worried about going into the game was early turnovers like in past games," said Army quarterback Nate Sassaman. "But the big thing was to keep everything in perspective and play with poise and confidence."

"We couldn't stop them," said Navy head football coach Gary Tranquill. "They didn't do anything out of the ordinary; they just out-'physicalled' us. They just kicked our butts. That big fullback [Black] punished us. Every second down was second and five or less. We could not do anything offensively."

"This was a great win for us a great finish to our regular season," said head coach Jim Young. "All of our other accomplishments this year wouldn't have meant as much if we hadn't won today. But we did win, and we can be proud of this team."

Army had 29 first downs, 432 yards rushing, 32 passing (4-5-1), only one turnover, and went on fourth and short twice and converted each time. The Cadets gained ground on their first 59 snaps, and only lost yardage on two plays.

Black rushed for 155 yards and set the Army single-season rushing record of 1,148 yards. Sassaman gained his last nine rushing yards out of his 154 yards in the game on his final carry for a total of 1,002 yards in the season. Black and Sassaman became the fourth and fifth Army players ever to rush for over 1,000 yards.

Navy had 22 first downs, rushed for 62, passed for 280 (22-39-0), and lost the football twice. Bob Misch set an Army-Navy record by completing 22 out of 34 passes for 280 yards.

<u>Awards and Recognitions</u>

Linebacker Jim Gentile and safety Eric Griffin were invited to and played in the Hula Bowl All-Star game in January 1985 in Honolulu. Doug Pavek was invited to and played in the East-West Shrine Game at Stanford Stadium.

The two wins over Air Force and Navy, the first since the 1977 season, earned Army its third outright Commander-in Chief's Trophy (the other being in 1972, the first year of CIC competition). With the Cadets running all over Navy, Army finished first among all Division 1-A schools in rushing, with an average of 345.3 yards per game. The team also finished #11 nationally in rushing defense, #20 in scoring, and #23 in total offense.

Jim Young was voted Coach of the Year by the Football Writers Association in New York. *The Associated Press, United Press International*, and ECAC recognized Doug Black, Craig Stopa, Nate Sassaman, Jim Gentile, Eric Griffin, Rob Dickerson, Doug Pavek, and Jim Jennings in their season ending all-star teams.

During the 1984-85 fall, winter, and spring seasons, the following Army varsity sports also beat Navy - 150-Pound Football (1-1 against the Midshipmen), Men's Soccer, Women's Volleyball (2-0), Women's Basketball, Rifle, Men's Swimming, Women's Swimming, Men's Indoor Track, Wrestling (a tie), and Men's Golf.

1984 Season Statistics

For the 1984 season, only the regular season statistics counted for team and NCAA records, except for the win-loss record. Army scored 310 points and gave up 212, for an average 28.2 - 19.3 per game. The Cadets had 249 first downs (22.6) and gave up 221 (20.1). 214 first downs were gained by rushing. The team had 857 snaps and gained 4,390 yards in total offense (399.1 ypg), while defensively allowing 744 snaps and 3,762 yards (342.0).

There were 779 rushes for 3,798 yards (345.3 ypg) versus opponents 420 attempts that gained 1,254 (114.0 ypg). The Cadets scored 34 rushing touchdowns and gained 4.9 yards per attempt. The defense allowed 12 touchdowns on the ground and 3.0 yards per rush.

Army completed 42 passes out of 78 attempts (53.8%), with five interceptions for 592 yards (53.8 ypg). They gained 14.1 yards per completion and 4 touchdown receptions. The Cadets gave up 188 completions out of 324 attempts (58.0%), with 11 interceptions for 2,508 passing yards. They allowed 13.3 yards per completion and 9 touchdowns passing.

Army lost 15 out of 32 fumbles during the regular season, while opponents lost 13 of 26 fumbles. The Cadets returned the 11 interceptions a total of 88 yards, while they gave up 26 yards on 5 Army passes intercepted. There were 49 penalties called on Army for 409 yards; while opponents had 49 calls for 421 yards. The Cadets averaged 36.8 yards per punt on 41 punts and opponents had 43 punts for an average of 36.3.

The Cadets were first nationally in rushing yards. Army averaged 37,826 attendance in five home games, 54,692 in three away games, and 55,967 in three neutral site games. Scoring by quarters was 66-47 (1st), 86-60 (2nd), 83-39 (3rd), and 75-66 (4th).

Leading rushers were Doug Black (264 attempts for 1,148 yards, 11 touchdowns, an average 4.3 yards per rush, and a long of 39), Nate Sassaman (1,002 yards on 189 runs, averaging 5.3, 7 touchdowns, and a long of 38), William Lampley (410 yards on 81 carries, 5.1 yard average, 3 touchdowns, and a long of 33), and Clarence Jones (292 yards on 36 attempts, 8.1 average, 2 touchdowns, and a long of 68). Sassaman's rushing yardage was the most by a Division 1 quarterback since 1971.

Sassaman passed for 28-56-3 and 364 yards with 2 touchdowns for a long of 37 yards. Rob Healy passed for 12-19-2 and 206 yards with 1 touchdown with a long of 61. Benny White caught 17 passes for 241 yards, 14.2 average, and a long of 61. Rob Dickerson had 11 receptions for 138 yards, a 12.5 average, 4 touchdowns, and a long of 34. Scott Spellmon caught 7 passes for 88 yards (12.6), and a long of 20.

Craig Stopa scored 77 points (#19 in nation) on 15 field goals (out of 17 attempts, including two made 50 yarders) and 32 points after touchdown (out of 35 attempts). Other leading scorers were Black (66), Sassaman (42), Hollingsworth (24), Dickerson (24), Lampley (18), and Dee Bryant (18).

Defensively (few statistics available), Jim Gentile had 103 tackles, 66 of them solo. Kurt Gutierrez had 40 stops, while Tom Malloy had 31 and Jim Brock had 21 tackles. Jim Jennings had 13 tackles for loss (TFLs), while Doug Pavek had 12 TFLs. Pavek had nine pass breakups, while Kermit McKelvy had seven. Mike Tease recovered three fumbles.

The 1985 squad set Army team records for most rushing yards in a game (628), total yards gained in a game (679), most rushing first downs in a game (34), total first downs in a game (36), most field goals made in a game (5), most rushing attempts in a season (779), most rushing yards in a season (3,798), most total yards in a season (4,390), most rushing first downs in a season (214), most total first downs in a season (249), and most field goals made in a season (15).

Greg Stopa set the Army record for most field goals made during the Air Force game (5) and season (15); while tying for fifth in longest field goal made (50 yards). Doug Black set the record for most rushes (264) and rushing yards (1,148) in a season. Nate Sassaman was fifth in rushing yards in a season (1,002) and fifth in total offensive yards in a season (1,366).

At the end of the 2020 season, the 1984 Army team still held the following season records: tied with first for most players having a 100 yard rushing game (5), sixth in rushing attempts, seventh in completion percentage (53.8%), eighth in rushing yards per game, eight in first downs, tenth in rushing yards, ninth in total offensive yards per game, and tenth in total offense. It was one of only two teams having two players who each rushed for 1,000 yards in a season (the other being the 2012 team).

Individuals from the 1984 season still holding season records include Nate Sassaman is tied for most 100 yard rushing games by a quarterback (7), tied for second for number of 100 yard rushing games; Doug Black is third in rushing attempts, seventh for number of 100 yard rushing games (5), and ninth for rushing yards; and Sassaman and Black are tied for fourth in combined rushing yards (2,150).

Clarence Jones is tied for fourth in fewest carries in a 100 yard effort (6) and fourth in highest yards per carry in a 100 yard game (21.7); and Craig Stopa has the highest field goal completion percentage (88.2%), third in field goals made, and tenth in field goals attempted.

Lettermen

The following individuals received letters for the 2018 season: Brad Allen, Marty Baptiste, Rich Baxter, Larry Biggins, Doug Black, Jay Bridge, Jay Brock, Dee Bryant, Matt Buckner, Dean Chamberlain, Lou Dainty, John Devlin, Rob Dickerson, Pete Edmonds, Jim Gentile, Dave Grasch, Eric Griffin, Kurt Gutierrez, Rob Healy, Karl Heineman, Jarvis Hollingsworth, Bill Horton, Jim Jennings, and Clarence Jones.

Also, Jeff Karsonovich, Bill Kime, Bob Kleinhample, Scott Krawczyk, William Lampley, Darold Londo, John Lopes, Tom Molloy, Joe Manausa, Church Matthews, Vince McDermott, Tim McGuire, Kermit McKelvy, Kevin McKelvy, Marlin Murphy, Mike Newsome, Billy Noble, Doug Pavek, Tom Perry, Andy Peterson, Dave Pratt, Ron Rice, John Roney, Bill Sanders, Nate Sassaman, Dan Sauter, and Dave Scheyer.

Also, Bill Schleiden , Gordon Scott, Mike Sears, Ed Shultz, Bob Silver, Don Smith, Scott Spellmon, Mike Staver, Craig Stopa, Dan Stredler, Steve Strifler, Mike Tease, John Thomson, Jeff Thor, Rob Ulses, Lloyd Walker, Benny White, and Dave Woolfolk.

Army Branch Selections

The seniors on the team graduated are members of the USMA Class of 1985 and were commissioned in the following branches (Air Defense Artillery) Jim Gentile and Mike Newsome; (Aviation) Jim Jennings, John Lopes, John Roney, Mike Sears, and Rob Ulses; (Field Artillery) Brad Allen, Marty Baptiste, Dean Chamberlain, Pete Edmonds, Jarvis Hollingsworth, Jeff Karsonovich, Tom Perry, Bob Silver, Mike Staver, and Dave Woolfolk; (Infantry) Dee Bryant, John Devlin, Kermit McKelvy, Marlin Murphy, and Nate Sassaman; (Military Intelligence) Bill Kime ('84) and Scott Krawczyk; (Ordnance) Church Matthews; (Quartermaster) Eric Griffin and Vince McDermott; and (Signal Corps) Karl Heineman.

Conclusion

It was now the end of the regular season. Jim Young said in an interview prior to the 1985 season, "The team had beaten Navy. The Army Football Team had accomplished all of its goals they had set for themselves at the beginning of the season. So in a way, it was like our season was over with. Our goal all along was to go to a bowl game. Not to win it. So after the Navy game, we had to come back down and reset our goal and almost get into a new season."

Army would finally go to a college football bowl game.

Chapter 5

1984 Cherry Bowl Game

On November 24, 1984, the Michigan Cherry Committee officially invited Michigan State University (6-5) and the United States Military Academy at West Point (7-3-1) to attend the inaugural Cherry Bowl on Saturday, December 22nd at the Pontiac Silverdome in Pontiac, Michigan. The Spartans were playing in their first bowl appearance in 18 years while the Cadets were attending their first bowl game ever. Army had played Michigan State once, at home in the 1931 season, winning 20-7.

Cherry Bowl History

Muddy Waters was head of the Cherry Bowl selection committee. The committee had decided on November 19th to select Michigan State and Army, and quietly informed the two institutions, who could not say anything officially, but were both excited about the proposed matchup.

Tom Martin, Cherry Bowl President, remarked that "Army and MSU are both fine teams that earned the opportunity to play in a post-season game. We, from the start, felt a personal kinship to a Big Ten team. The closer to home you make that Big Ten selection, the better chances of success. I had always felt that, given the choice, we would want one of the Michigan teams participating. Down the road, that may not be as important, but for the first game, it seemed to be obviously vital."

"Army was chosen, in part, again because of geographic, a northern team from the East. And it's a team with a strong national following. That institution reflects history, tradition, protocol, procedures, and scholarship. This match-up gives our fans a perfect blend of two skilled teams, one which they recognize and appreciate and the other, they know of but never get a chance to see. It's an excellent blend."

Three years before, Martin proposed the idea of holding a bowl game in the Pontiac Silverdome. He was a Grand Rapids native who returned to western Michigan after a 15 year absence in 1980 to work for the state's cherry industry. "Bowl games are only supposed to be held in places where the sun is hot and the water is warm. Some wanted us to get involved in the January 1982 Super Bowl, but time was too short to become involved. Other commodities, like cotton and oranges have bowl games, why not cherries?"

Michigan grew 75% of the nation's cherry crop and was a $125 million industry in 1984. Martin found support from multiple organizations, especially the Century Club that guaranteed the purchase of 50,000 tickets, against the seating capacity of 80,638 (second only to the Rose Bowl that year).

In April 11, 1984, after two years of planning, the Cherry Bowl received the unanimous endorsement of the NCAA Bowl Committee. Seven days later, the NCAA Council delayed a decision on the bowl game. There was a question of a post-season tournament to determine a national champion that was under consideration, and the Council wanted input before approving any more bowl games.

Michigan's three members of the Council come out supporting the Cherry Bowl ten days later in an interview with the *Grand Rapids Press*. The NCAA Council approved the Cherry Bowl on August 17th, the only one to be played in 1984 in the northern United States. The bowl committee was back in business for a 1984 game.

However, a Supreme Court ruling earlier in the year freeing conferences and institutions to make their own television deals was causing confusion over televising bowl games. It took until November 14th before the *Mizlou Television Network*, an independent sports network, signed a television agreement to show the game nationally on the *USA Network*.

The Cherry Bowl would be the fifth game of the 1984 bowl season starting at 1 pm EST, with the Florida Citrus Bowl starting thirty minutes earlier on *NBC Television* and the Sun Bowl on *CBS Television* starting at 3 pm EST. It was also the third bowl that would be played indoors, with the Bluebonnet Bowl in the Houston Astrodome and the Sugar Bowl in the Louisiana Superdome. A total of 18 games would be played in 1984-1985 bowl season.

The Cherry Bowl sold 70,336 tickets for the game. The other rookie bowl game for the 1984 season was the Freedom Bowl in Anaheim CA, between Iowa and Texas, which was reported as selling 25,000 tickets with an attendance of 24,093. The expected payout to each team was $1 million, but turned out to be closer to $800,000.

Michigan State Football History

Intercollegiate football arrived at East Lansing in 1896. The 1903-1915 seasons produced 13 winning seasons, two undefeated, and the first victories over Notre Dame and Michigan. Irish Four Horseman and Hall of Famer Jim Crowley took over as head coach in 1929 and produced four more winning seasons. Hall of Famer head coach Charley Backman had twelve winning seasons from 1933-1946 and played in the 1936 Orange Bowl.

The Spartans joined the Big Ten in 1949. Led by Hall of Famer head coaches Biggie Munn and Duffy Daugherty, came one national championship each, and participation in three Rose Bowls (1954, 1956, and 1966). It would have been more, but Big Ten policy restricted its members to just the Rose Bowl, and champions could not repeat. There had been 66 first-team All-American citations earned by Spartans players.

Michigan State had not appeared in a bowl game since its 1966 Rose Bowl 12-14 loss to UCLA. The undefeated 10-0 Spartans shared the national championship that season. They were Big Ten co-champions in 1978. The Spartans finished the 1983 season with a 4-6-1 record. This would be their fifth bowl game ever, with a record of 2-2 coming into the Cherry Bowl.

1984 Michigan State Spartans Football Season

For the 1984 season, the Michigan State Spartans were led by second year head coach George Perles. He succeeded Frank (Muddy) Waters in December 1982. Perles played a major role by molding a strong defense that won four Super Bowls for the Pittsburgh Steelers.

Members of his coaching staff included defensive coordinator/backs Nick Saban, defensive line Steve Furness, defensive line Greg Croxton, defensive backs Rick Kaczmarek, outside linebackers Dave Kaple, outside linebackers Norm Parker, inside linebackers Ted Guthard, receivers Charlie Baggett, tight ends/special teams Steve Beckholt, running backs Larry Bielat, offensive line Buck Nystrom, quarterbacks Bill Rademacher, offensive line Randy Zimmerman, and administrative assistant Ed Rutherford.

Michigan State opened the 1984 season at Boulder on September 8th against the University of Colorado. The Spartans led 24-0 after three quarters, but then withstood three touchdowns scored by the Buffaloes and a 32 yard missed field goal attempt with 22 seconds left in the game to win their opener, 24-21.

At home on September 15th, the Spartans led Notre Dame 17-0 at halftime. Michigan State led 20-10 going into the final quarter. But two Irish touchdown drives produced a 20-24 loss. Traveling to Champaign on September 22nd in a game played during a driving rainstorm, the Spartans stayed close in the first half before the Fighting Illini dominated, losing 7-40 in the only game during the season where Michigan State was not really competitive.

On September 29th back home, Michigan State suffered their third straight loss, 10-13, to Purdue. Despite giving up 335 yards passing to the Boilermakers, the Spartans defense only yielded one touchdown. Purdue converted a 30 yard field mid-way through the fourth quarter for the victory.

The Spartans traveled to Ann Arbor on October 6th to play the Wolverines. Michigan State went up 13-0 on a one yard plunge and an 87 yard punt return. The defense gave up one touchdown late in the second quarter, but two field goals salted away a 19-7 victory over Michigan, the first since 1978 and the season's highlight game.

The Spartans continued to win, beating Indiana 13-6 at home on October 13th by scoring all of its points in the fourth quarter on homecoming day and having two players rush 96 yards each. Hosting Ohio State on October 20th, the Spartans tried to repeat their 1974 upset of the Buckeyes. The Spartans scored on a kickoff return and a long pass play, but a 43 yard field goal attempt was missed in the final seconds, leading to a 20-23 loss.

At the Humphrey Metrodome in Minneapolis the next Saturday, the Spartans defense held Minnesota to little yardage in the second half while the offense used a field goal and home run passing to beat the Gophers, 20-13. Back home on November 3rd, the Spartans sacked Northwestern's quarterbacks and pounded the football for a 27-10 win.

The Spartans built up a 14-3 halftime lead in Iowa City and extended it 17-3 going into the fourth quarter. The Hawkeyes scored two touchdowns, but missed the two-point conversion with less than a minute left, as Michigan State upset Iowa's Rose Bowl plans, 17-16. At home on November 17th, it was a clash of the Big Ten's hottest teams. The Badgers led 14-10 after three quarters, and Wisconsin made two field goals to win the final game of the regular season for both teams, 20-10.

Six of eleven Spartans regular season opponents went to bowl games in the 1984 season. Michigan lost to national champion Brigham Young 24-17 in the Holiday Bowl played the day before the Cherry Bowl. Iowa soundly trounced Texas, 55-17, in the Freedom Bowl. Wisconsin lost to Kentucky 20-19 in the Hall of Fame Classic, Notre Dame lost to Southern Methodist, 27-20, in the Aloha Bowl, Purdue lost to Virginia, 27-24, in the Peach Bowl, and Ohio State lost to Southern California, 20-17, in the Rose Bowl.

Michigan State ended the regular season with a 6-5 overall record, with a tie for sixth place finish with Michigan in the Big

Ten with a 5-4 conference record. Dave Yarema had completed 54% of his passes for eight touchdowns and ten interceptions. Mark Ingram was the top receiver averaging 23 yards per catch. Veno Belk and Bobby Morse were Yarema's short-range targets.

Lorenzo White emerged as one of the Big Ten's top freshman rushers during the late part of the season. The team's rushing leader, Carl Butler, had minor injuries and made fumbles to give White his chance. Fullback Keith Gates cuts back better than most backs and was used on quick traps.

Opponents ran just 2.6 yards per carry against the Spartans. Michigan State had never faced a wishbone attack, but might benefit from facing Minnesota's option. It had a bend but not break secondary more than capable of big interceptions. Ralf Mojsiejenko was a great punter, but his place kicking had suffered from five missed extra points this season.

Six Spartans were recognized by either or both the *Associated Press* or *United Press International* on the first or second string 1984 All Big-Ten Conference Football Teams - linebacker Jim Morrissey, defensive back Phil Parker, running back Carl Butler, center Mark Napolitan, defensive lineman Kelly Quinn, and place kicker & punter Ralf Mojsiejenko. Bobby Morse finished fifth in the nation in punt returns with a 12.0 average and one touchdown, while Larry Jackson finished fifth in kickoff returns with 26.2 average and one touchdown.

Statistical Comparisons

Defensively, the Spartans were averaging 17.5 points allowed, 19.1 first downs, 328.6 total defense, 115.6 yards rushing, and 212.9 yards passing. The Cadets were averaging 19.3 points allowed, 20.1 first downs, 342.0 total defense, 114 yards rushing, and 228 yards passing.

Coming into the bowl game, Army was averaging 28.2 points, 22.6 first downs, 399.1 total yards offense, 345.3 yards rushing, and 53.8 yards passing. Michigan State was averaging 17 points,

12.6 first downs, 264.6 total yards offense, 140.6 yards rushing, and 123.9 yards passing.

The Cadets had lost 15 fumbles and 5 interceptions for a total of 20 turnovers. Army had recovered 13 fumbles and made 11 interceptions. The Spartans had lost 16 fumbles and 13 interceptions for a total of 29 turnovers. Michigan State had recovered 14 fumbles and made 13 interceptions.

Army Team in Michigan

After not attending an Army football game since I graduated in 1978 due to two overseas assignments, my family and I traveled up to Detroit for the game. It would be the first football game ever for my two young children. Everyone was happy that the game was indoors, given it was three days until Christmas, and I recall the weather was colder. We sat in the second deck surrounded by mostly friendly Michigan State fans. Army fans were outnumbered in the stadium by at least a 20-1 range.

The Army football team spent most of the week in Michigan before the game. The team stayed at the Troy Hilton Hotel. There were press conferences, ceremonies, and a team trip to a mall to do Christmas shopping. The team spent Tuesday night at Jason's for dinner and entertainment. Practices also occurred, and on Wednesday, Nate Sassaman said, "We're getting serious, knowing we're not just out here for a good time."

Army's right tackle Bill Kime is a member of the Class of 1984, while almost all of his classmates graduated in May 1984. But he had missed a semester due to football injuries and subsequent knee surgeries, so he was able to play on the 1984 squad. "I had a one-man graduation in the Hilton Hotel in Pontiac the night before the game. [Army assistant equipment manager] Dicky Hall painted a gold bar on the black stripe [of my helmet]. I was a second lieutenant."

Hall made sure that Kime understood that he played in the Cherry Bowl as a United States Army Officer. While his teammates returned to West Point after the bowl game, he reported to his basic officer course at Fort Huachuca AZ. He missed the White House reception in the Rose Garden when President Reagan presented the Commander-in-Chief's Trophy to the team in early 1985.

Bowl Entertainment

Fans were entertained pre-game with by two jazz groups and the MSU Spartans Marching Band playing both team's fight songs and the national anthem, sung by John McCollum, Bethany Wright, and Russelle Hunter.

The Spartans Marching Band returned at halftime by performing three sets of the James Bond's Goldfinger, Diana Ross' I'm Comin' Out, and Frank Sinatra's New York, New York. The Durland High School Band joined the Spartans band in forming Christmas trees that dissolved into cherry trees, and finally Michigan's band director emeritus, George Cavender, led the fans in the World's Largest Sing-a-Long.

Post-game, the Durand and Clio School Bands provided entertainment. Presiding over the activities was the 1984 National Cherry Queen, Miss Kimberlee Broome, a nineteen year-old student at Central Michigan University and a native of Gaylord, MI.

There were 832 Cadets in Dress Gray uniform for the game sitting in Section 117. After the football game was over, the academic officer, Lieutenant Colonel Gerald Galloway, handed out grades to the Army football players.

Pre-Game

The Army starting lineup was tight end Rob Dickerson, right tackle Dave Woolfolk, right guard Don Smith, center Ron Rice, left guard Vince McDermott, left tackle Jeff Karsonovich, split end Scott Spellmon, halfbacks Clarence Jones and Jarvis Hollingsworth, fullback Doug Black, and quarterback Nate Sassaman.

On defense for the Cadets, the starters were defensive ends Brad Allen and Kurt Gutierrez, defensive tackles Mike Sears and Jim Jennings, nose guard Rob Ulses, linebackers John Roney and Jim Gentile, cornerbacks Eric Griffin and Kermit McKelvy, and safeties Bob Silver and Doug Pavek. Tom Malloy actually started the game for the injured Brad Allen.

For Michigan State on offense the starters were flanker Mark Ingram, tight end Butch Rolle, right tackle Steve Bogdalek, right guard John Wojciechowski, center Mark Napolitan, left guard Jeff Stump, left tackle Doug Rogers, split end Larry Jackson, tailback Lorenzo White, fullback Keith Gates, and quarterback Dave Yarema. Rob Wasczenski actually started for Larry Jackson.

The Spartans starting lineup on defense were ends Kelly Quinn and Tom Allan, defensive tackles Jim Rinella and Dave Wolff, linebackers Anthony Bell, Jim Morrissey, and Thomas Tyree, cornerbacks Lonnie Young and Terry Lewis, and safeties Paul Bobbitt and Phil Parker. Joseph Curran actually started for Rinella, while Tim Moore started for Thomas Tyree.

Officials for the game were referee Don Bauer, umpire David Hicks, lineman Paul Weidner, line judge Bruce Maurer, back judge Roger Parramore, and field judge Andrew Pfaff; all coming from the Mid-America Conference (MAC). The game would be played indoors in 72 degree temperatures. Michigan State was a three or four point favorite to win the game.

Michigan State was the designated home team and wore green helmets, green jerseys, and white pants. Army work white jerseys, gold pants, and gold helmets. The Spartans game captain was Jim Morrissey, while the Army game captains were the entire team represented by Brad Allen.

The Spartans called and won the toss, and elected to defer to the second half. Army elected to receive. MSU would defend the goal to the left of the press box. The announcers were Ray Lane (play-by-play) and Jim Branstetter (analyst). The game started at 1:12 pm EST with 70,336 in attendance (87% capacity).

First Quarter

Ralf Mojsiejenko kicked off from the MSU-30 into the end zone for a touchback. Starting on their own 20 yard line, Black went up the middle for three yards, tackled by Joseph Curran and Dave Wolff. Sassaman went around the right side on an option keeper and was tackled by Parker after gaining four yards.

Parker tackled Sassaman for one yard off left tackle. Scott Krawczyk punted 36 yards to the MSU-36 (his first college punt ever), and Morse returned it eight yards before being stopped by Tom Malloy. The Cadets drive lasted 1:48 over eight yards over three plays.

On first down on the MSU-44, Yarema was sacked by Jennings for a loss of twelve. White went off right tackle for three, downed by Marty Baptiste. Yarema pass attempt to Ingram was out of bounds.

Mojsiejenko punted 60 yards to Darold Londo, who was tackled by John Jones after an eight yard return. Army was called for clipping, and penalized half the distance to the goal line to the WP-6. The Spartans drive lasted 1:45 with three plays losing nine yards.

Sassaman went around the right side on an option keeper for a gain of nine before he was stopped by Bell and Quinn. Black ran off the right guard for three yards and a first down, tackled by Morrissey. Bell tackled Hollingsworth after a pitch that gained of five yards around the right end out of bounds.

Sassaman went left on an option and was tackled by Lewis and Morrissey after a rush of four yards. A measurement showed the Cadets were short of the sticks. Black went up the middle, fumbled and lost the football. Sassaman recovered the football and was tackled by Timothy Moore and Quinn for no gain. On fourth and one, Krawczyk punted 51 yards where Bobby Morse fair caught the football. Army's drive took 2:06 time of possession to go 21 yards in five plays.

From the MSU-22, White went off left tackle for a gain of five, stopped by Ulses. Gentile tackled White who gained one yard up the middle. A Yarema pass to Morse in the right flat was incomplete. Mojsiejenko punted 46 yards to Londo, who was tackled by Robert Stradley and John McDowell after a return of ten. Michigan State's drive took 1:24 to go six yards in three plays.

From the WP-36, Sassaman went around the right side on an option keeper for twelve yards and a first down, stopped by Bobbitt. Phil Parker intercepted a Sassaman pass and returned it 18 yards before being downed by Jeff Karsonovich for the first turnover of the game. An illegal procedure call against Army was declined. The Cadets drive of two plays went twelve yards in 35 seconds.

From the WP-43, Yarema overthrew a deep pass to Ingram. Yarema dropped back for a pass, then rolled left for a gain of eight before he slid to the ground. On third and two, White went up the middle before being stopped by Sears and Gentile for a gain of one. Mojsiejenko then attempted a 52 yard field goal attempt that went wide left.

From the WP-35, Black went off right guard for three yards before being tackled by Tyree and Wolff. Hollingsworth went around the right end before being tackled by Parker after rushing for no gain. On third and seven, on a reverse, Bell tackled Spellmon on a reverse around the right for a loss of six. Krawczyk punted 36 yards to Parker, who returned it five yards before being stopped by Griffin. The Cadets drive took 2:05 time of possession to lose three yards in three plays.

From the MSU-37, White went around the right side before being tackled by Baptiste and Malloy after a rush of seven yards. Yarema pitched to White, who went around the left side for nine yards and a first down, stopped by Gentile. White went around right tackle for twenty yards and a first down, stopped by Silver and Dave Scheyer.

From the WP-27, White went left, then reversed his direction, and was tackled by McKelvy after a gain of four. Ulses tackled

White going off right tackle for a rush of three. On third and three, White went off right guard, cut left, then ran for a gain of eleven and a first down at the WP-9, before being stopped by Bill Sanders.

White went off right tackle and lost a fumble. Mark Ingram recovered the football and was tackled by Sears and Gentile at the WP-7 as the first quarter ended with the game scoreless.

Second Quarter

On second and goal at the start of the second quarter, White again went off right tackle after a pitch and Baptiste and Gentile stopped him after a gain of two yards. Yarema's pass attempt to Morse on the left side was intercepted by Kermit McKelvy in the end zone, then returned seven yards, tackled by Morse. The Michigan State drive took 4:09 time of possession to go 48 yards in nine plays.

Sassaman was tackled by Parker after a three yard rush around the right side. Sassaman gained one yard around the left before being downed by Tyree and Lewis. Clarence Jones went on a counter off left tackle for four yards before being tackled by Morrissey and Lewis. Krawczyk punt was partly blocked and went for 49 yards before Army's Dan Stredler downed the football at the MSU-38. The Army drive of three plays for eight yards took 2:12 time of possession.

Yarema pitched to White, who went outside left tackle before being stopped by Ulses and Jennings after a gain of six. Gentile and Jennings tackled White after a rush off right guard of three yards. Another pitch to White as he ran four yards and a first down around right tackle before being stopped by Baptiste and Jennings.

White caught a swing pass from Yarema to the left flat, but Gentile tackled him for a loss of three yards. Yarema then overthrew a pass on the left side to Robert Wasczenski. On third and 13, Yarema went back for a pass, scrambled, and then lost the football while being tackled by Bob Kleinhample for a loss of two yards. Jim Gentile recovered the football at the MSU-46. Michigan

State's drive of six plays went seven yards in 2:30 time of possession.

Black ran off left tackle and was tackled by Bobbitt and Morrissey after a gain of four. Clarence Jones went around the left side for seven yards on an option play and was tackled by Lewis after making a first down.

Bell tackled Jones after he rushed for four yards off the left tackle. Sassaman went around the right end on an option and gained eleven yards and a first down while being tackled by Young and Bobbitt. The Spartans were called for an inadvertent facemask and a five yard penalty.

From the MSU-15, Black went off left tackle for two yards before being stopped by Allan Jones. Sassaman pitched left to Jones, who gained seven and was tackled by Lewis. A measurement found the Cadets to be short of the marker. On third and one, Sassaman kept and ran to the left side for a gain of two yards, tackled by Shane Bullough and Lewis for a first down and goal on the MSU-4.

Clarence Jones went off right tackle four yards for the touchdown at 6:41 left in the first half for a 7-0 lead over the Spartans. Craig Stopa converted the extra point kick. The Cadets drive took 2:51 to go 46 yards in eight plays.

Stopa kicked off to the MSU-8, where Dempsey Norman returned it 14 yards before being tackled by Bill Horton and Gutierrez. Marty Baptiste was injured on the play. From the MSU-22, Gutierrez tackled White who ran around the left side for a three yard gain. Jay Brock then sacked Yarema for a loss of one. Rolle caught a pass and gained twelve yards and a first down before being stopped by Gutierrez.

Sears tackled White off left tackle after a gain of five. Yarema overthrew Gates on the right side. On third and five, Yarema's pass attempt to Norman on the left side was broken up and incomplete. Mojsiejenko punted 59 yards into the end zone for a touchback. The Spartans drive of six plays gained 19 yards over 2:49 time of possession.

With 3:46 left in the half, Black ran off right guard for one yard before being tackled by Rinella. Black then rushed off the left guard for another one yard gain before being stopped by Wolff. Bell stopped Clarence Jones on a counter off left tackle for a gain of three. Krawczyk punted 30 yards to Bobbitt, who returned it four yards. The Cadets drive of three plays went five yards in 1:49.

From the MSU-49, Yarema long pass along the right sideline to Wasczenski was intercepted by Doug Pavek at the WP-1 with 1:49 left in the second quarter. The Spartans drive of one play took eight seconds.

Hollingsworth was tackled by Young on a rush off right tackle for two yards. Black ran off the left guard for two yards, stopped by multiple Spartans. Michigan State called a time out. Sassaman dropped back to pass and rolled left out of the pocket before running out of bounds for a gain of 20 yards and a first down.

From the WP-25, Tyree and Bell tackled Sassaman on a keeper around the left side for six yards. Tyree stopped Black on a three yard rush off the right guard as the half ended. The Army drive of five plays went 33 yards in 1:49 time of possession. Halftime Score: Army 7, Michigan State 0.

Halftime

At halftime, Army had six first downs, 144 yards rushing, and zero passing yards (0-1-1), in 34 plays with time of possession of 15:25. Michigan State had five first downs, 82 yards rushing, and nine yards passing (2-10-2), in 31 snaps. The Cadets had one pass intercepted; while the Spartans had been intercepted twice and lost one fumble.

Spartans Lorenzo White was the leading rusher, with 89 yards in 17 attempts, while Cadet Nate Sassaman led Army with 73 yards rushing in eleven attempts. Rolle had one reception for twelve yards. Army's Scott Krawczyk had punted five times with an average of 40 yards and a long of 51. Ralf Mojsiejenko had punted three times for the Spartans, averaging 55 yards with a long of 60.

Third Quarter

With Army defending the goal to the right of the press box, Stopa kicked into the end zone for a touchback. From the MSU-20 on a pitch play, White rushed outside the right tackle for two yards before being stopped by Griffin and Roney. Jennings and Gutierrez tackled White of a loss of two yards. Down the left side, Rolle caught a Yarema pass for a gain of 19 yards and a first down, stopped by Silver.

From the MSU-39, Yarema's deep pass attempt for Rolle down the middle was intercepted by Doug Pavek at the WP-36. The Michigan State drive went four plays in 19 yards taking 1:51.

On a pitch, Hollingsworth went around the right side for three yards before being stopped by Young. Sassaman gained four on an option run off right tackle, tackled by Parker. Sassaman ran off left tackle for a twelve yard run and a first down, stopped by Morrissey.

Going off left tackle, Sassaman was tackled by Wolff after a two yard gain. Morrissey tackled Hollingsworth for no gain. On third and eight, Sassaman gained seven yards outside of right tackle before Allan stopped him. Young and Morrissey stopped Sassaman after he gained two yards and a first down to the MSU-32.

Black gained five off of right tackle, stopped by Bell and Morrissey. Black rushed off the left guard for four yards, tackled by Tyree and Curran. Sassaman gained one yard off right tackle, stopped by Bell. An official measurement gave the Cadets a first down.

Outside the left end, Sassaman ran for three before being stopped by Morrissey. Clarence Jones was stopped by Morrissey for no gain off left tackle. On third and seven, Sassaman went around the right end and was stopped by Tyree after a gain of four yards. Stopa missed a 32 yard field goal wide right with 6:13 left in the third quarter. The Army drive of 14 plays went 47 yards in 6:56 time of possession.

From the MSU-20, Yarema overthrew a long pass attempt to Norman down the left side, defended and broken up by Pavek, who almost intercepted the pass. On a draw play off right guard, White gained twelve yards and a first down before being stopped by Gentile.

The Spartans were then called for offside and lost five yards. McKelvy defended a lateral pass to the left side to White for a loss of a yard. Pavek and Gutierrez defended a pass reception to Rolle that gained twelve yards. Yarema pitched to Gates who ran two yards off left tackle before being stopped by Gentile. On fourth and two at the MSU 40, Mojsiejenko punted 58 yards to the WP-2 where it was downed by the Spartans. Michigan State went 20 yards in five plays with 2:22 time of possession.

Black ran up the middle and was tackled by Morrissey, Parker, and Bell for a two yard gain. Black rushed four yards off right tackle before being stopped by Parker. Tyree tackled Sassaman for no gain outside the left end. Krawczyk punt was partly blocked and went 18 yards to the WP-28. Malloy tackled the Gregory Smith for no gain by Malloy. A Spartans player pushed an Army player into Krawczyk during the punt. The Cadets drive went six yards in three plays with 2:03 time of possession.

Yarema pitched to White who gained six yards around the right end before being stopped by Silver and pushed out of bounds. Roney, Gentile, and Gutierrez tackled Gates after a two yard gain up the middle. Jim Gentile tackled Lorenzo White around the right end for a loss of three yards. On the play, Tom Malloy forced a fumble by White that was recovered by Kurt Gutierrez at the WP-21. The Spartans possession took 54 seconds to go five yards in three plays.

Sassaman gained nine yards around the left side, stopped by Tyree. Black gained six yards off right tackle and a first down, tackled by Parker and Morrissey. On a counter, Clarence Jones gained three off right guard, stopped by Tyree as the third quarter ended.

Fourth Quarter

Sassaman pitched to the right to Hollingsworth, who gained five yards before being tackled by Bobbitt and Curran. Tyree stopped Black's one yard plunge up the middle. On fourth and one, Sassaman went outside the right tackle and gained two yards and a first down before being stopped by Young, Rinella, and Allan.

From the WP-47, Sassaman pitched right to Hollingsworth, who dropped back for a halfback pass, and then tried to run. Wolff and Allan tackled Hollingsworth for no gain. Parker stopped Black off left guard for a four yard gain. Hollingsworth caught a Sassaman pass and gained ten yards and a first down before being stopped by Tyree and Bell. Thomas Tyree was injured on the play and left the game.

Sassaman gained eight yards outside the left tackle before stopped by Wolfe. Sassaman bootlegged to the right and gained seven yards and a first down before being tackled by Timothy Moore, Bobbitt, and Quinn.

At the MSU-24, Rinella stopped Black up the middle for two yards. On a pitch, Hollingsworth ran right, but Young dropped him for a loss of two yards. On third and ten, Hollingsworth ran a counter off right guard for three yards, stopped by Morrissey and Allan. Craig Stopa converted a 38 yard field goal for a 10-0 lead with 8:40 left in the game. The Army scoring drive of 59 yards took 7:14 in 16 plays.

Stopa kicked off to the MSU-8 to Norman, who returned it 15 yards before being tackled by Scheyer and Rich Baxter on the MSU-23. Yarema threw a pass to Ingram across the middle for a gain of 20 yards and a first down before being stopped by Pavek.

Morse caught a pass reception on the left side and gained eleven yards, tackled by Griffin. Rolle caught a pass and was tackled by McKelvy for another eleven yard gain and a first down on the WP-46 yard line. Yarema completed his fourth straight pass, this time to Rolle, who stepped out of bounds after a gain of eleven yards and a first down.

Malloy tackled Gates for a loss of a yard. Yarema lost a yard on a quarterback draw, but the Spartans were called for a hold and penalized twelve yards. Jennings then sacked Yarema for a loss of six. On a third and 19, Yarema's pass to Wasczenski was broken up by McKelvy. On fourth down, Mojsiejenko made the 60 yard field goal attempt, but the Spartans were then called for a delay of game and penalized five yards back to the WP-48.

After the penalty, Mojsiejenko 65 yard field goal attempt was short at 5:18 left in the game. "I felt confident that I was going to make it," said Mojsiejenko after the game. "I tried to hit it hard, but I got underneath it just a hair." The Spartans drive of eight plays gained 31 yards in 3:22 time of possession.

Doug Black gained a yard off left tackle and was stopped by Dave Wolff who caused an Army fumble recovered by Tom Allan at the MSU-49. The Cadets drive took one play for a gain of one yard took six seconds.

Kleinhample then sacked Yarema for a loss of three yards. The Spartans were called for illegal motion, but Army declined. Kermit McKelvy was injured on the play and left the game, and was replaced by Matt Buckner. Yarema immediately targeted the new defensive back by completing an 18 yard pass to Wasczenski across the middle for a first down, tackled by Matt Buckner.

Dave Yarema then threw a deep pass to Robert Wasczenski, who stopped and let Buckner and Pavek run by him, before making the catch for a 36 yard touchdown reception in the end zone corner for a touchdown, with 4:19 left in the fourth quarter. Michigan State decided to go for two-points.

Yarema rolled right for a pass and was pressured, and his two-point pass to Gates was incomplete short of the goal line, making the score 10-6 in favor of Army. Michigan State's drive took 53 seconds to go 51 yards in three plays. Talking about the two-pointer, Perles said, "We were interested in winning the game. It would have made it 10-8 and we'd just need a field goal to win. That's why you come to a bowl game."

Mojsiejenko kicked off into the end zone for a touchback. Timothy Moore tackled Hollingsworth outside the right end for a gain of twelve and a first down. Black gained two off right guard and was stopped by Morrissey and Rinella. Sassaman was tackled by Carter Kamana and Morrissey after making two yards around the left end. Jim Morrissey was injured on the play and left the field.

Bell and Bullough stopped Clarence Jones for no gain outside the left end. Krawczyk punted 38 yards to Morse on the MSU-26, who returned it six yards before being stopped by Kleinhample out of bounds with 1:58 left in the game. The Cadets drive of four plays gained 16 yards in 2:14 time of possession.

Yarema's pass on the right sideline to Rolle was incomplete. A swing pass reception by Gates to the left gained eight yards before being stopped by Ulses. The Spartans took a time out. Silver broke up a pass to Rolle on the left side. On fourth and two, Silver again broke up a pass from Yarema to Rolle on the left side. Michigan State turned the football over on downs with 1:17 left in the second half. The Spartans final drive of four plays gained eight yards in 41 seconds.

Sassaman gained three yards outside the right end, tackled by Morrissey and Curran. Sassaman was injured on the play and left the field. The Spartans took a time out with 1:10 on the clock. Sassaman came back into the game after the time out. Black gained a yard up the middle, stopped by several Spartans. Michigan State took their final time out with 1:05 on the clock. On a pitch, Clarence Jones gained nine yards around the left end and a first down, forced out of bounds by Parker.

Black went up the middle for a yard, tackled by several Spartans. Sassaman took a knee and lost three yards. Michigan State took their final time out with 0:50 on the clock. Sassaman took another knee for the win. The final Cadets drive of six plays gained nine yards in 1:17 time of possession.

The game ended at 4:03 pm EST and took 2:51 to play. Final Score: Army 10, Michigan State 6.

Post-Game

"This team has come as far as any team I've ever coached," Army Head Football Coach Jim Young said. "We had great senior leadership and came about as close to our potential as any team could. This makes our season. We had a big win over Navy, but if we didn't win today, we'd be a little sad. We're capable of playing big time college football. We have the ability to play with emotion, and to play all out. Size isn't always the main thing."

Talking to the *Assembly* after the season ended, Young was asked about his thoughts preparing to play a Big Ten team. He said, "Well, as I looked at their films, I thought we could stay with them. We knew they had a great defense, very quick and strong. But we didn't believe their offense would be able to move the ball that well. And that's the way it worked out."

Army had 15 first downs, 266 total yards, 256 yards rushing (71 attempts), 10 yards passing (1-2-1), and time of possession of 35:05. The cadets averaged 3.6 yards per snap. Army had two turnovers, one interception and one fumble lost; had one penalty for seven yards; were 6 for 18 in third down conversions; and were 2 for 2 in fourth down conversions.

Defensively, the Cadets intercepted three passes and recovered two fumbles; had a total of 70 tackles; ten tackles for loss; four sacks, and four pass break ups. The Cadets punted seven times for an average of 36.7 yards; and had no kickoff return yards. Army had the football for 14 possessions, scoring on two of them.

Nate Sassaman rushed for 136 yards in 28 attempts and a long of 20 yards. Doug Black rushed 57 yards on 22 runs with a long of six. Clarence Jones had 41 yards and one touchdown in ten attempts, while Jarvis Hollingsworth rushed ten times for 28 yards and a long of 12. Scott Spellmon lost six yards in his one rushing attempt. Sassaman completed one pass for ten yards and was intercepted once in two passing attempts. Hollingsworth completed his one pass reception.

Craig Stopa attempted two field goals, making one for 38 yards. Scott Krawczyk punted six times for a 39.8 average, with a long of 51. A blocked punt went 18 yards. Darold Londo returned two punts for 18 yards. Kermit McKelvy returned one interception for seven yards; while Doug Pavek had two interceptions with no returns.

Jim Gentile led the Cadets with eleven tackles (6 solo); followed by Jim Jennings and Kurt Gutierrez each with seven; and Mike Sears with five. Others with tackles were Kermit McKelvy (4), Marty Baptiste (4), Tom Malloy (4), Rob Ulses (4), Bob Silver (3), Doug Pavek (3), Bob Kleinhample (3), Dave Scheyer (3), Eric Griffin (2), John Roney (2), and one tackle each for Bill Sanders, Matt Buckner, Jay Brock, Clarence Jones, Jeff Karsonovich, Bill Horton, Mike Newsome, and Rich Baxter.

Jennings had three tackles for loss, Kleinhample had two, and Gentile, McKelvy, Sears, Malloy, and Brock had a TFL each. Jim Gentile and Kurt Gutierrez each recovered a fumble. Bob Silver broke up two passes, while Pavek and McKelvy each broke up one pass attempt. Jennings and Kleinhample each had two sacks while Sears and Brock had one sack each.

"After the Navy game, there were quotes in a Philadelphia paper about [Army] having a [Philadelphia] cream cheese defense," said defensive tackle Jim Jennings. The quote became bulletin board material, and it became a rallying cry for the Cadets, who have brought Army's football program back to national prominence after several years on the downside. Jennings continued, "We talked about that and made a vow last night to play solid defense. This was my last game and I wanted to go out with a bang."

"We had been playing a little soft in the secondary this year," defensive back Doug Pavek said. "We were letting the receivers catch the ball before we would come up. But we've worked hard on our technique of playing the ball when it's thrown. We felt for us to win, we had to get some turnovers. We knew that would be a critical factor. Our defensive line did a helluva job. They can take credit for the interceptions. They made the Michigan State quarterback throw on the move, and that created some things."

"Army was supposed to be wide open to the pass," said Spartans quarterback Dave Yarema after the game. "I kept trying to get somebody down the middle, but we couldn't. It made it real easy for the safeties to cover the wide receivers. I don't know why we didn't go to those crossing patterns a little earlier. I guess it took us a while to get it going."

Michigan State had 13 first downs, 244 total yards, 89 yards rushing (33 attempts), 155 yards passing (11-25-3), and time of possession of 24:55. The Spartans averaged 4.2 yards in 58 snaps. MSU had five turnovers, three interceptions and two fumbles lost; had four penalties for 26 yards; were 4 for 13 in third down conversions; and were 0 for 1 in fourth down conversions.

Defensively, the Spartans intercepted one pass and recovered one fumble; had a total of total of 105 tackles, four tackles for loss, and no sacks. MSU had 13 possessions and scored on one of them. The Spartans closed out the 1984 season with a 6-6 record.

"I thought we played the wishbone well at times," Michigan State Head Football Coach George Perles said after the game, "In fact, I thought we played it pretty decent all game. The turnovers were the difference. We told the team there was no reason to be down. We didn't want to spoil their Christmas. Maybe we emphasized defense too much for the game and not enough offense. We stopped their wishbone, but didn't move the ball well enough. We will learn and grow from this game."

Lorenzo White rushed for 103 yards in 23 attempts with a long of 20, while Keith Gates ran three times for three yards, and Dave Yarema had seven rushing attempts for a loss of 17 yards. Yarema passed for 11 completions out of 25 attempts and three interceptions for 155 yards passing and one touchdown and a long of 36.

Butch Rolle caught five passes for 65 yards and a long of 19; and Robert Wasczenski had two receptions for 54 yards and one touchdown of 36 yards. Catching one pass each were Mark Ingram (20 yards), Bobby Morse (11), Gates (8), and White (loss of three yards).

Ralf Mojsiejenko punted four times for an average of 55.8 yards and a long of 60. Bobby Morse returned three punts for 14 yards, while three players had one punt return - Paul Bobbitt (4 yards), Phil Parker (5), and Gregory Smith (0). Dempsey Norman returned two kickoff returns for 29 yards. Parker returned one interception for 18 yards. Ralf Mojsiejenko attempted two field goals, missing both.

Jim Morrissey had 16 tackles (7 solo), Anthony Bell had 14 (6 solo), and Thomas Tyree had 12 tackles (5 solo). Others with tackles were Phil Parker (9), Terry Lewis (8), Lonnie Young (7), Tom Allan (7), Dave Wolfe (6), Paul Bobbitt (5), Joseph Curran (5), Kelly Quinn (4), Jim Rinella (4), Timothy Moore (3), John Jones (2), Shane Bullough (2), Robert Stradley (1), John McDowell (1), Bobby Morse (1), and Carter Kamana (1). The team was credited with two tackles for loss, and Bell and Young each had one TFL. Allan recovered a fumble, and Parker intercepted a pass.

Army's Nate Sassaman, the 5 foot, 11 inch, 185-pound senior quarterback from Portland OR, was named most valuable offensive player of the 1984 Cherry Bowl. "I was looking for a good game to end my career on," said Sassaman, who played the entire game despite pulling a hamstring in the third quarter and cracked ribs that required a flak jacket the entire contest. "I was really sucking it down for a while, but I have the rest of my life to heal," Sassaman continued. "Doc says six weeks for the ribs to heal. I don't know if I could take shots (tackles) for one more year." "He's a tough leader, a winner," said head coach Jim Young.

Michigan State's junior free safety Phil Parker, 5-11, 178 pounds, was named the most valuable defensive player in the bowl game. Parker intercepted one of the two passes thrown by Sassaman, and returned it 18 yards in the first quarter. Parker also had nine tackles for the game, seven of them solo. "Pound-for-pound," said Perles about his two-time All-Big Ten safety, "Phil is one of the toughest players I have ever seen."

The 1985 Cherry Bowl between #20 Maryland and Syracuse (a 35-18 victory by the Terrapins) had 20,000 less fans and also faced decreased television revenues. The bowl committee was unable to meet the reported $1.2 million payout to each team and despite obtaining General Motors as a title sponsor. With the committee over $2 million over budget, the Cherry Bowl folded after two games. This ended post-season college football in Detroit until the advent of the Motor City Bowl in 1987.

1984 Season Statistics

During the 1984 season, the NCAA did not allow teams to include bowl game results to count for season statistics, except for the win-loss records of a team. For example, the 2021 Army Football Media Guide shows Doug Black rushing for 1,148 yards and Nate Sassaman rushing for 1,002 in the 1984 season. Had bowl records been included, Black would have had 1,205 yards and Sassaman would have had 1,138 yards for the season.

Conclusion

Army's storybook season had a dramatic ending. A smaller Army team, playing more on raw emotion than muscle; ran its devastating wishbone attack to near perfection; and its opportunistic defense took advantage of Michigan State turnovers to leave the first Cherry Bowl with the sweet taste of success and a win in the Cadets first bowl appearance ever by thumping Michigan State, 10-6.

Watching the bowl game from his Colorado Springs home, former Army head coach Earl "Red" Blaik commented, "This just proves they had the ability. They had a boy like Doug Black playing intermural ball and a boy like Nate Sassaman playing defense. Their coach was very bold to go to a Wishbone without any experience in it. It's amazing, but it just shows that coaching can get more out of them."

In the final *Associated Press* Poll, Army received 44 votes for 23rd place. The Cadets also received points in the *United Press International* Coaches Poll, finishing at 22nd place. Both polls that season were only for the top twenty teams. Army was the most improved team in the nation, having won six more games than the prior season. *Sports Illustrated* ranked Army #18 and *Sporting News* had the Black Knights at #19 at season end.

Sometime after the bowl win, head football coach Jim Young summed up the season by saying, "It is the most enjoyable year of coaching I've had in twenty years. This team came the farthest of any I have ever coached. We played as close to our potential as any team possibly could."

Inside the Hotel Thayer, there is a plaque that recognizes the 1984 Army Football Team. It reads:

(Hotel Thayer Logo)

1984 CHERRY BOWL FOOTBALL TEAM

(Front cover of the Cherry Bowl Program)

ARMY 10 - MICHIGAN STATE 6

COACH JIM YOUNG

WINNING SEASON 8 WINS, 3 LOSSES, 1 TIE

MOST VALUABLE PLAYER NATE SASSAMAN, QUARTERBACK

BEAT NAVY 28-11

DUTY HONOR COUNTRY

Chapter 6

The 1985 Football Season

It was a question that had not been asked at West Point since the beginning of the 1978 spring drills. With the success of the 1984 season, beating Navy and Air Force, bringing home the Commander-in-Chief's Trophy; plus the Cadets making their first appearance ever in a post-season bowl game - and winning the Cherry Bowl over Michigan State; as the Army 1985 Football Annual pondered, it took a while to sink in while the winter snow covered The Plain. But as spring practice soon began, the Question came at one of the press events, "Just what, Coach Young, are you going to do for an encore?"

"You know, it's a greater challenge coming up this fall than what we faced last year. To be successful for more than one single season is the biggest challenge. We won last season, and the expectations will certainly be higher on the part of the players, the people who support the program, and our opponents. Especially the opponents. They're going to be looking at us in a different light now."

In an interview with Morris Herbert, USMA Class of 1950, in the March 1985 *Assembly*, head football coach Young said, "A winning team must have a good offense, and a good defense against the run. A year ago [1983 season] we were ranked very high nationally in pass defense, and we lost nine games."

"Winning is difficult enough, but continuing to win is even harder! Every game [in the 1985 season] will be a challenge. We can't assume we're going to win. We can't say that our ability is going to beat anyone. We must rely on our mental qualities like toughness, our altitude, our hitting, and our intensity."

<u>1985 Army Football Coaching and Support Staff</u>

The Army coaching staff under head football coach Jim Young remained mostly the same for his third season at West Point. It included defensive coordinator Bob Sutton (3rd season), offensive coordinator Charlie Taaffee (5th), Johnny Burnett (7th, defensive backs), Jay Robertson (2nd, defensive perimeter & special teams), John Simar (7th, wide receivers), Greg Gregory (4th, running backs), Jack Hecker (9th, defensive ends), Tim Kish (2nd, interior defensive line), and Jim Shuck (3rd, offensive line).

"I'm not going anywhere. I like coaching at West Point," said Young to Herbert.

Other coaching staff were Bob Rogucki (strength & conditioning), Mike Stephens (assistant strength & conditioning), Gene Benner (head trainer), Jack Trainor (assistant trainer), Jim Wallace (assistant trainer), Charlie Blake (running backs), Alan Seamonson (linebackers & special teams), Scott Lustig (head JV coach & offensive line), Pete Mahoney (tight ends), Craig Johnson (quarterbacks), Dee Bryant (graduate assistant & offensive backs/receivers), Kermit McKelvy (graduate assistant & defensive backs), Brad Allen (graduate assistant defensive line), Jim Jennings (graduate assistant defensive line), Bob Silver (graduate assistant strength & conditioning), and Scott Krawczyk (graduate assistant strength & conditioning).

Other support staff were Colonel Bob Berry (officer representative), Colonel Jim Armstrong (officer representative academics), Lieutenant Colonel Jack Ryan (team physician), Major Bill Hopkinson (team physician), Captain Bob Gay (assistant officer representative), Captain Greg Dyson (assistant officer representative), Captain Bee Carlton (assistant officer representative), and Richard Hall (equipment manager),

<u>1985 Army Football Schedule</u>

The bulk of the schedule was announced around 1980 and consisted of eleven games with five home games, five away, and one at a neutral site, with each game on a Saturday afternoon. The schedule began on September 14th at North Carolina, September 21st versus Rutgers, and September 28th at Pennsylvania.

Army would play Yale at home on October 5th and Boston College at home on October 12th. The Cadets would play at Notre Dame on October 19th, then return home to play Colgate on October 26th and Holy Cross on November 2nd.

Army would travel to Colorado Springs to play Air Force on November 9th. The Cadets would end their regular season on November 16th at Pittsburgh. Army would have two weeks off before playing Navy at Veterans Stadium in Philadelphia on November 30th.

Prior to 1984, the games at North Carolina and Pittsburgh were cancelled. Home games with Western Michigan (September 14th) and Memphis State (November 16th) were scheduled to replace them. This produced a favorable schedule with seven home dates, three away games, and Army-Navy at a neutral site.

The four home games would kick off at 2 pm EDT in September and October, except for Boston College, which would kickoff at 8 pm ET. Kickoff would be at 1:30 pm ET for the two home games in November, as well as the away game at Penn. The away games at Notre Dame and Air Force would kick off at 1 pm locally. The Army-Navy game would kick off at 2:30 pm EST.

Originally, the only televised game would be Army-Navy on *CBS Television*. The Boston College game would be played in the evening due to it being broadcast on *ESPN*. The *USA Network* would televise the Notre Dame at South Bend. It is possible that a New Jersey television station televised locally the Rutgers game. Probably due to television, the Army-Navy game was moved to December 7th prior to the beginning of the season.

Bowl Games

For the 1985-1986 bowl season, there were 18 games scheduled to be played, beginning December 18th and ending on January 1st. Army had no contracts to attend any bowl for this season, and would be subject to an at-large bid if it won six or more games. The fact that Army would play Division 1-AA opponents Penn, Yale, Colgate, and Holy Cross had no bearing on bowl eligibility.

Spring Practice

Head coach Jim Young said in a summer interview, "We'll lack the experience we had a year ago. However, in spring practice, we did a lot of scrimmaging and I think accomplished quite a bit in that respect. One of our biggest question marks heading into the season will be at linebacker. We're losing a lot of experience there. I feel good about quarterback. We'll have to wait until the actual games to see how that position develops. Probably the biggest question mark we have right now is with the punting. We're not set at all as far as our punter."

Young had to replace eight starters on defense and five on offense, as well as his punter. A total of 41 lettermen returned for the 1985 season. "I think the legacy of our senior class is that we left with a different attitude than what had been there before," remarked Nate Sassaman, "The standards we set are the minimum standards. Now, it's up to the next class to continue the things we started."

"They can do it, but they have to realize that last year is over," said Young. "What I've really tried to emphasize with them is to be their own team. I don't think there's any set direction a team goes in establishing its own identity. That's not something you plan, step-by-step. I've tried to tell them to make it a new start, using the good things. You have to do that as a coach, because you can't keep harping on last year's team."

"Can we match the success of last season?" asked All-American candidate Don Smith. "It's possible. In fact, it's beyond possible, it's expected."

Summer

Over 1,000 men and women entered West Point on July 1st as members of the USMA Class of 1989. On the opening day roster against Western Michigan were 13 plebes (freshmen) - offensive tackle Dave D'Antonio, offensive guard Jack Frey, halfback Mark

Phillips, fullback Darren Miller, quarterback Mark Mooney, defensive ends Greg Gadson and Pat Muschamp, and defensive tackle John Garcia.

Also, linebacker Chip England, defensive back Rusty Haire, punters Bob Kroning and Bit Rambusch, and kicker Keith Walker. Additionally, freshman listed in the 1985 Army-Navy and/or Peach Bowl programs included offensive guard Mike Cannizzaro, defensive end Charles Scheretzman, linebacker Bob Duffy, and defensive back Matt Seymour.

Captains

Right guard Don Smith and defensive end Kurt Gutierrez were name captains of the 1984 Army Football Team. Don Smith was a candidate for multiple All-American lists.

Season Predictions

Here are some highlights of Army's opponents pre-season, thanks to the Army 1985 Football Annual: (Western Michigan) The Broncos had a 5-6 overall record in 1984, with three of their losses by five points or less; the team has 15 of its 22 starters returning for the 1985 season under fourth year head coach Jack Harbaugh (father of football coaches John and Jim).

(Rutgers) The Cadets might be looking seeking revenge for their first loss of the 1984 season. The Scarlet Knights had a 7-3 record under rookie head coach Dick Anderson, winning all six games at home, including beating nationally ranked West Virginia. But Rutgers was not invited to a bowl.

(Pennsylvania) After sharing the Ivy League championship for two seasons, the Quakers won the title during the 1984 season where Penn went 8-1, its only loss was to Army. The Quakers lost nine offensive and six defensive starters from that team, but are playing at home against Army in head Coach Jerry Berndt's fourth season.

(Yale) The Ellis finished 1984 with a 6-3 record, rebounding from a 1-9 record in 1983. Yale should have an explosive offense under head coach Carmen Cozza.

(Boston College) BC is about to begin "Life After Flutie." The Eagles have plenty of talent returning under head coach Jack Bicknell.

(Notre Dame) Gerry Faust might be looking for employment if he cannot improve on his 7-5 record from the 1984 season. Army should have all it can handle when it meets the Irish in Notre Dame Stadium, with six starters on offense and eight on defense.

(Colgate) For the first time in three years, the Red Raiders failed to qualify for the Division 1-AA Playoffs. Head coach Fred Dunlap thinks his team can return to being a dominant force in 1985.

(Holy Cross) Gill Fenerty could be the top running back in Division 1-AA in 1985 as he is only 38 yards shy of the Crusaders career rushing record after back-to-back 1,000 yard rushing seasons since he transferred from LSU as a freshman. Five starters return from each side as head coach Rick Carter plans for a banner year.

(Air Force) The Falcons are one of only three teams who have played in and won bowl games their last three seasons. Air Force also beat Notre Dame each of the last three years. Air Force is building its wishbone football tradition under second year head coach Fisher DeBerry.

(Memphis State) During head coach Rey Dempsey's first season, the Tigers finished with a 5-5-1 record, including a 17-17 tie with sixth rank Florida State. Five starters return on offense, while six return on offense.

(Navy) Despite suffering a season-ending ankle injury in the second game of his senior year during the 1984 season, USNA Superintendent Rear Admiral Charles Larson announced on January 12th that Napoleon McCallum would return in 1985 for a fifth year. The Midshipmen returned five starters on the offensive line and seven starters on defense.

For the first time in over twenty years, Army Football made the cover of a national sports publication, the 1985 GamePlan College Football Annual Preview. On the publication's start of season Stat-Key Ratings, Army's power rating was 111, versus opponents Notre Dame (115), Boston College (112), Air Force (111), Memphis State (111), Navy (110), Rutgers (110), Western Michigan (107), Colgate (100), Penn (95), Yale (95), and Holy Cross (NR). Illinois was at 118.

GamePlan predicted Army's 1985 success on top of its 1984 results, "More of the same should be in store this season. Army should again be a potent ground force that could match its 1984 output. Despite heavy graduation losses, the Cadets have a legitimate shot at winning seven or eight games this fall."

GamePlan also made predictions for several of Army's opponents - Notre Dame (minimum of eight wins and contend for Top Twenty honors), Air Force (best the school has ever fielded, could win its first-ever WAC crown), Boston College (won't generate the offense without Flutie, will be hard pressed to win seven or eight games), and Rutgers (will be facing a simply brutal schedule, six or seven wins will constitute a very successful campaign).

Continuing their predictions, Navy (face another tough schedule, to flirt with a winning record), Holy Cross (could match last year's won-lost record), Colgate (it wouldn't be all surprising if failed to make it to .500), Penn (are perennial favorites in the Ivy League), Yale (solid second behind Penn), Western Michigan (counting on 40 returning lettermen and a better bounce of the pigskin to get them back on the plus side of .500), and Memphis State (schedule is rugged, a very tough outfit, can forge a winning record).

Western Michigan

Army (0-0) hosted Western Michigan (0-1) at Michie Stadium on September 14th in front of 28,620 fans. It was the first meeting ever between the two teams, and the first Army game with a Mid-American Conference opponent since a 1960 game with Miami.

The Broncos opened their season the prior Saturday with a 17-0 loss at Northern Illinois. Running back Otis Cheathem rushed for 91 yards on 21 carries, while quarterbacks Jon VanSlooten and Chris Conklin completed 17 of 43 passes for 132 yards. Senior linebacker John Offerdahl had twelve tackles in the Northern Illinois game. The Cadets were favored in the game.

Clarence Jones, took a lateral from quarterback Rob Healy and raced 50 yards for a touchdown, with Craig Stopa converting the extra point kick to make it 7-0 in the first quarter. In the second period, Stopa made two field goals of 26 and 36 yard to extend the score to 13-0. Bob Healy scored from the two and then William Lampley rushed eleven yards for a touchdown to make it 27-0 at halftime.

Doug Black ran for a 32 yard touchdown in the third quarter. Benny Wright scored on a seven yard rush while Andy Peterson plunged over the goal line from the one yard line in the fourth quarter. With 1:15 to go in the game, the Broncos reserve quarterback Jon VanSlooten completed a two yard pass to Kelly Spielmaker to make the final score, 48-6.

Army had 22 first downs, 408 yards rushing, 41 passing (3-7-0), lost no fumbles, and had 30:55 time of possession. Western Michigan had 16 first downs, 159 yards rushing, 160 passing (16-30-2), and lost four fumbles. The Cadets offense scored on five of those turnovers.

Clarence Jones had 110 yards rushing on nine carries. Stopa made all points after touchdown attempts. Darold Londo returned a punt 51 yards. Doug Pavek and John Thomas each made an interception. The Cadets used four quarterbacks in the game - Healy, Tory Crawford, Mike Ryan, and Alan Edwards.

Western Michigan finished the 2018 season with a 4-4-1 Mid-American Conference record with a tie with Northern Illinois for fourth place. Highlights of the Broncos season was tying at second place Miami (10-10) and ending the year winning four out of five games. John Offerdahl was selected as MAC defensive player of the year. The Broncos finished with an overall record of 4-6-1 in head football coach Jack Harbaugh's fourth season.

Rutgers

Army (1-0) hosted Rutgers (0-0-1) on Saturday afternoon, September 21st at West Point in front of 39,761 in sold out Michie Stadium. The Scarlet Knights had tied #5 Florida, 28-28, the prior Saturday. Leading Rutgers were quarterback Joe Gagliardi and the rushing and receiving of Albert Smith. The Cadets were favored by 1 point.

Rutgers scored on their first possession on a two yard pass reception. Army responded with a 68 yard drive when quarterback Rob Healy plunged over the goal line from the one yard line. A blocked punt by John Thomson moments later resulted in a safety when the ball rolled through the end zone, making it 9-7 at the end of the first period.

Midway through the second quarter Craig Stopa converted a 47 yard field goal to build the lead to 12-7. On the final play of the first half, Scarlet Knights quarterback Joe Gagliardi passed 36 yards to split end Greg Raffaelli for a touchdown. Darold Londo intercepted the two-point conversion attempt, leaving Rutgers with a 13-12 lead at the half.

William Lampley rushed for a ten yard touchdown with 1:28 remaining in the third quarter to cap a 66 yard drive. Clarence Jones ran in the two-point conversion as the Cadets took the lead, 20-13. Rutgers went to the air as the Cadets had stopped their running attack.

With five minutes left in the game, the Cadets defense forced a Rutgers 26 yard field goal to close to 20-16. On the next Scarlet Knights drive, Rutgers reached the WP-20. On fourth down, Tom

Malloy and Lloyd Walker sacked Gagliardi for a loss of four yards. The Cadets then ran out the clock over the next eight plays as they marched to the RU-19 to win the game.

"We didn't handle the pitch," said Dick Anderson, the Rutgers coach. "We let them get outside and in general we handled it poorly. We played it soft and got knocked off our feet."

Army had 22 first downs, 230 yards rushing, 85 passing (7-11-1), lost one fumble, and had 29:48 time of possession. Rutgers had 19 first downs, 82 yards rushing, 222 passing (21-33-0), and lost no fumbles.

Rutgers finished the 2018 season with an overall record of 2-8-1 as an Independent in head football coach Dick Anderson's second season. Besides the Florida tie, the Scarlet Knights lost the next weekend to #9 Penn State, 10-17. Rutgers did win two of their last five games of the season to Richmond and Colgate.

Pennsylvania

Army (2-0) traveled to Philadelphia to play Division 1-AA Pennsylvania (1-0) on Saturday afternoon, September 28th at Franklin Field before 23,765. The Quakers had beat Cornell, 10-6, in Ithaca NY the previous Saturday. The Cadets were favored by 18.5 points.

Clarence Jones rushed for a one yard touchdown in the first quarter, with Craig Stopa converting the extra point kick to make it 7-0. The Quakers cross the fifty and Roy Saunders made a 41 yard field goal to close it to 7-3 in the second period. Jones scored on a six yard run to make it 14-3 at halftime.

On the Cadets first possession of the second half, Stopa converted a 40 yard field goal. After Larry Biggins intercepted a pass, Rob Healy rushed two yards for a touchdown to extend the score to 24-3 at the end of the third quarter.

William Lampley scored on a two yard run and then Stopa made a 41 yard field goal. Back-up quarterback Tory Crawford ran 22 yards for a touchdown to close the scoring at 41-3. The

Quakers only crossed the fifty yard line three times, never getting inside the WP-10.

Army had 33 first downs, 449 yards rushing, and 76 passing (6-10-0), one lost fumble, two punts, 55 yards penalized, and 34:34 time of possession. Penn had 15 first downs, 84 yards rushing, 162 yards passing (15-31-2), no lost fumbles, and 40 yards penalized. Doug Black rushed for 120 yards, while Lampley ran for 95 and Crawford gained 83 yards. Larry Biggins and Doug Pavek each intercepted a pass.

Pennsylvania finished the 2018 season with a 6-1 Ivy League record and the conference championship. Penn's only Ivy loss (6-17) was to at second place Harvard (5-2) on November 16th. The Quakers were tied on November 9th at Colgate (27-27). Penn finished with an overall record of 7-2-1 in head football coach Jerry Berndt's 5th season. At the end of the season, Berndt would leave to coach at Rice.

Yale

Army (3-0) hosted Division 1-AA Yale University (1-0) on October 5th in Michie Stadium at West Point in front of a sellout crowd of 40,602. The Bulldogs hosted Brown on September 21st to win a close 10-9 game. The scheduled game on September 28th versus the University of Connecticut was first postponed and then cancelled as Hurricane Gloria approached the Connecticut shore. The Cadets were favored to win by 28 points.

William Lampley opened the scoring in the first quarter with a seven yard rushing touchdown, followed by Craig Stopa making the extra point kick for a 7-0 lead. Benny White caught a 33 yard pass reception from Bob Healy in the second quarter. Yale responded with an eleven yard touchdown pass to close to 14-6.

With 1:29 left in the half, Army stopped the Bulldogs on the WP-10. Doug Black plunged over the goal line from the two yard line in the last minute of the first half. After a turnover, Craig Stop made a record setting 53 yard field goal with one second left. The

Cadets scored on four of their five possessions in the first half for a 24-6 lead.

The Yale Band was barred from performing a halftime show during the football game at West Point, minutes before it was supposed to begin. Carl Ullrich, the athletic director at the Military Academy, later said that the band's show, which made fun of some West Point graduates, was "not worthy of the privilege of being presented to 40,000 people in Michie Stadium."

Yale's John Duryea made a 27 yard field goal in the third quarter. Tory Crawford rushed for a four yard touchdown. Crawford then threw a pass to Scott Spellmon that gained 42 yards and a touchdown to extend Army's lead 38-9 at the end of the third stanza.

Kevin McKelvy rushed for an 18 yard touchdown, Alan Edwards scored on a six yard run, and Ed Cole went in from the three yard line to up the score to 59-9. Stopa converted the first seven extra-point kicks, while Keith Walker made the last kick. Yale reserves scored on a nine yard pass to end the scoring at 59-16. It was the most points scored on a Yale team in their entire 1,005 game history. The Cadets scored on five of their six possessions in the second half. Rob Healy was injured during the game.

"It was a hard fought during the first half," said Jim Young. "When we put those points on the scoreboard before the half, it took the momentum away from Yale."

Carmen Cozza, Yale's head football coach since 1965, added, "It was the poorest defensive effort since I've been here."

Army made 27 first downs, 378 yards rushing, 93 yards passing (4-4-0), one loss fumble, one punt, and 27:19 time of possession. Yale had 20 first downs, 132 yards rushing, 201 passing (18-35-4), one lost fumble, and two punts. Doug Black rushed for 122 yards in the game. The Cadets defense had not given up a rushing touchdown in 24 straight quarters. Reggie

Fullwood intercepted two passes, while Dave Berdan and Lou Dainty each intercepted a pass.

Yale finished the 1984 season with a 3-3-1 Ivy League record in fifth place. The highlight of the season was a 17-6 victory over Harvard on November 23rd in the Yale Bowl. The Elis had a 4-4-1 overall record in head football coach Carmen Cozza's 21st season.

Boston College

Army (4-0) hosted Boston College (3-3) on Saturday evening, October 12th, in front of another sold out crowd of 40,819 at West Point. The Eagles were favored to win by 1 points. Lindsey Nelson and Paul Hornung were the announcers for the *ESPN* broadcast.

The Scarlet Knights opened the season on August 29th in Giants Stadium with a 14-28 loss to #10 Brigham Young, the national champion of the 1984 season. Rutgers then beat Temple (28-25), lost to #17 Maryland (13-31), won at Pitt (29-22), and lost to Miami, Florida (10-45). On October 5th, Boston College had beaten Rutgers, 20-10, to even their record.

Army dominated on both sides of the ball against the Eagles. Tory Crawford started at quarterback for the injured Rob Healy. Craig Stopa opened the scoring by making a 52 yard field goal in the first quarter. Crawford scored from the one yard line, Clarence Jones ran ten yards across the goal line, with Stopa converting each of the extra points, to make it 17-0 at halftime.

Boston College got on the scoreboard with a six yard touchdown run in the third quarter to make it 17-7, ending the defensive streak at 26 quarters. Jones then rushed for a twelve yard touchdown and Crawford scored from 14 yards out to extend the Cadets lead to 31-7 at the end of the third quarter.

The Crawford ran for a seven yard touchdown and Jones crossed the goal line from the 13 yard line, with Stopa making his fifth and sixth PATs of the game. The Eagles reserves completed a 13 yard pass reception for the final touchdown of the game, 45-14.

"We mixed our plays up well," said Jim Young. "Saying that a wishbone offense like Army's improves with experience. They played a similar defense to what they did last season."

Jack Bicknell was shocked by the depth of the shellacking, saying, "I don't think they could play any better than that. They had it going and we couldn't seem to stop them."

Playing in front of representatives of the Sun, Liberty, and Holiday Bowls, Army passed only three times as the sophomore quarterback Tory Crawford made his first start. "What's the use of passing the ball when you can move up and down the field by running?" asked Crawford.

Army had 32 first downs, 503 yards rushing, 19 passing (2-3-0), two lost fumbles, 47 yards penalized, and 32:42 time of possession. Boston College had 21 first downs, 48 yards rushing, 424 passing (24-40-3), and lost two fumbles.

Doug Black rushed for 158 yards, Tory Crawford ran for 131 yards and three touchdowns, Clarence Jones gained 103 yards and three touchdowns, and William Lampley made 95 yards rushing. The Cadets defense sacked the Eagles quarterbacks five times. Bill Sanders, Doug Pavek, and Craig Rollins each had the interceptions, while John Thomson and Tom Malloy each recovered a fumble.

Boston College would lose their next four games to West Virginia, at Cincinnati, at #3 Penn State, and at Syracuse, before winning their final game at home versus Holy Cross, 38-7. In Happy Valley, the Eagles would lose by only 12-16 to the Nittany Lions in front of 82,000. Boston College would finish with an overall record of 4-8 in head football coach Jack Bicknell's fifth season.

Notre Dame

Army was ranked 19th in the *Associated Press* Poll and 20th in the *United Press International* Coaches Poll on October 15th. *Sports Illustrated* ranked the Cadets 18th. It would be the first time since the 1958 season that the Cadets played a game against the

Irish while ranked, a series of nine games in-between being unranked. It would also be the second straight game that Notre Dame was unranked.

The Cadets (5-0) traveled to South Bend to play at sold out Notre Dame Stadium on Saturday afternoon, October 19th, in front of 59,075 Fighting Irish fans. Notre Dame (1-3) opened the season with a 12-20 loss at Michigan on September 14th. Returning home, the Irish beat Michigan State, 27-10.

Notre Dame lost on the road at Purdue (17-35) and at Air Force (15-21), the loss being the fourth straight to the Falcons. The Fighting Irish now had two weeks to prepare for another wishbone attack offense. Notre Dame was favored to win by 6.5 points. Eddie Doucette and Kyle Rote were the announcers for the *USA Network* broadcast.

Two plays and 39 seconds into the game, an errant pitch by quarterback Tory Crawford was recovered by Notre Dame's Steve Lawrence on the WP-16. Five plays later, the Cadets defense forced a fourth and one on the goal line, but Pernell Taylor plunged over for the Fighting Irish first touchdown.

Quarterback Steve Beuerlein completed a 19 yard pass to flanker Tim Brown for another touchdown to end the first quarter leading, 14-0. Midway through the second quarter, William Lampley scored on a four yard run, with Craig Stopa converting the extra point, to close the score to 14-7 at the half.

On their first possession of the second half, the Cadets drove to the ND-4 where it stalled, forcing Stopa to convert a 22 yard field goal to close it to 14-10. Notre Dame scored on a one yard run to end the third period leading, 21-10. The Cadets could not generate any drives past the ND-48 the remainder of the game. The Fighting Irish kicked a 21 yard field goal in the final period to win, 24-10.

"We beat a real good team," Faust said. "I thought our defense played very well. In the last two games we've given up only two touchdowns to the wishbone - one passing and one rushing."

Army had 20 first downs, 196 yards rushing, 98 passing (5-10-0), one lost fumble, and 29:30 time of possession. Notre Dame had 22 first downs, 207 yards rushing, 186 passing (12-20-0), no lost fumbles, and five punts. Doug Black rushed for 93 yards.

Notre Dame would continue its home stand with three straight victories against Southern California (37-3), Navy (41-17), and Mississippi (37-14) to raise its record to 5-3. The Fighting Irish would never win another game during the 1985 season, losing at #1 Penn State (6-36), versus #17 Louisiana State (7-10), and at #4 Miami, Florida (7-58). Notre Dame's overall record was 5-6 in Gerry Faust's fifth and last season as head football coach for the Fighting Irish.

Colgate

Army was unranked after the loss to Notre Dame. The Cadets (5-1) hosted Division 1-AA #16 Colgate University (5-1) on Saturday afternoon, October 26th at sold out Michie Stadium in front of 40,621 fans for Homecoming Weekend.

After losing at Holy Cross, 21-24, on opening day, the Red Raiders had gone on a five game winning streak at Lafayette (30-14), at Cornell (21-20), versus Lehigh (32-14), at Dartmouth (54-28), and at Princeton (49-44). The Cadets were favored to win by 23.5 points.

Senior quarterback Rob Healy started; back in the lineup after missing two games due to fractured ribs. The Cadets scored 17 points in the first quarter, first when Craig Stop converted a 40 yard field goal. Healy completed a 65 yard touchdown pass to Scott Spellmon. Clarence Jones then ran six yards for a touchdown in a four play, 59 yard drive.

Tory Crawford broke away for a 27 yard touchdown run, juking two Red Raiders at the twenty with a spin move, to make it a 24-0 lead less than five minutes into the second quarter. The Red Raiders responded with a 38 yard field goal. A minute later, Jones scored again from the four yard line to add to the Cadets lead, 31-3. Colgate scored a touchdown with 32 seconds left to make it 31-

10 at halftime. Hundreds left the stands, figuring an Army rout was underway. Almost, but not quite.

Colgate scored on a two yard touchdown reception in the third quarter, before Doug Black plunged across the goal line from the two yard line to finish a 76 yard drive. After a Red Raiders one yard rushing touchdown, the score was 38-24 going into the final period.

Healy scored from the three yard line with 12:12 left in the game to extend the Cadets lead to 45-24, completing a 75 yard drive. Colgate quarterback Tom Burgess completed three touchdown passes of twelve, one, and eight yards in less than five minutes after two costly fumbles by the Cadets. On the last two drives, the Army defense stopped two-point attempts to win the game, 45-43.

"So close," Colgate wide receiver Tom Stenglein said after the game. "We were so close."

"The 'almost' hurts," said head football coach Fred Dunlap. "It really hurts. The kids and all of us are looking at all the things that got us in the hole in the first half. I'm very proud of the way we fought back, but now we know we were good enough to win the football game. You can't concede that many points."

"We were lucky to win the game," said Jim Young. "We simply didn't stop them. The fumbles made it a ballgame. Without the turnovers the game wouldn't have been nearly as close as it was. That's where the game nearly slipped away."

Army had 20 first downs, 414 yards rushing, 65 passing (1-3-0), two lost fumbles, and 26:38 time of possession. Colgate had 28 first downs, 184 yards rushing, and 239 passing (22-37-1), and no lost fumbles. Tory Crawford rushed for 136 yards, while William Lampley had 108. Craig Stopa was good on all six point after touchdown kicks. Doug Pavek intercepted a pass and his blitz on the final two-point conversion attempt forced a wobbly, incomplete pass.

Colgate finished the 1985 season with a 7-3-1 record in its last year as an Independent. The Red Raiders beat Columbia, tied Penn, lost at Rutgers, and won at Boston University to finish the tenth season under head football coach Frederick Dunlap. In the 1986 season, it would join the Colonial League, before it was later was renamed the Patriot League.

Holy Cross

Army (6-1) hosted the College of the Holy Cross (3-3-1) on Saturday afternoon, November 2nd at sold out Michie Stadium in front of 40,356 fans at West Point. The Crusaders had beaten Colgate ((24-21), lost at Massachusetts (3-27), won versus Delaware (22-6), won at Dartmouth (17-14), lost at Yale (15-19), were beaten at Connecticut (2-22), and tied Brown (20-20). The Cadets were favored to win by 22 points.

Holy Cross made a 23 yard field goal in the first quarter and then a 33 yard field goal in the second period to take a 6-0 lead. Tory Crawford ran for a six yard touchdown, while Craig Stopa converted the extra point kick for the Cadets to take the lead, 7-6. Four minutes later, Doug Black went over the goal line from the one yard line as Army led, 14-6, at halftime.

The Crusaders completed a seven yard touchdown reception in the third quarter, but the two-point pass attempt failed, closing the score to 14-12. On the second play of the fourth quarter, Crawford rushed four yards for a touchdown to extend the lead to 21-12.

The Cadets defense forced Holy Cross to punt. Matt Buckner blocked the punt and Leighton Drisdale recovered the football on the HC-16. Six plays later, Doug Black rushed for a two yard touchdown to make the lead 28-12. A pass interception by Doug Pavek set up the final score of the game, when Andy Peterson rambled 27 yards down the right sideline for a touchdown as the clock expired for an Army victory, 34-12.

Army had 20 first downs, 286 yards rushing, 29 passing (2-5-0), one lost fumble, 30 yards penalized, and 30:46 time of possession. Holy Cross had 17 first downs, 177 yards rushing, 152 yards passing (13-30-2), no fumbles, and 95 yards penalized. Doug Pavek intercepted both passes. Tory Crawford rushed for 134 yards, while Doug Black had 82 yards. Holy Cross running back Gill Fenerty rushed for 128 yards.

Holy Cross finished the 1985 season with an overall record of 4-6-1 in Rick Carter's fifth and final season. It was the Crusaders final year as an Independent, as it would join Colgate and other teams in forming the Colonial League during the next season in 1986.

Air Force

Army (7-1) would travel to Colorado Springs to play #5/#4 Air Force (9-0) on Saturday afternoon, November 9th in sold out Falcon Stadium in front of 52,103 fans. A win against Army would give Air Force the Commander-in-Chief's Trophy. The Falcons were favored by 12 points. Snow fell before the game and during the second quarter.

Air Force had won nine straight against Texas El Paso (48-6), at Wyoming (49-7), versus Rice (59-17), at New Mexico (49-12), versus #15 Notre Dame (21-15), at Navy (24-7), at Colorado State (35-19), versus Utah (37-15), and versus San Diego State (31-10).

Air Force scored on a one yard touchdown run in the first quarter. In the second quarter, senior quarterback Bart Weiss surprised the Cadets secondary with a 64 yard touchdown reception to wide receiver Ken Carpenter to make it 14-0 at halftime. On the second play of the third quarter, Weiss broke off on a 56 yard touchdown run. Weiss scored on a one yard keeper to make it 28-0 at the end of the third period.

The Falcons made a 22 yard field goal. Army drove down the field on a 67 yard drive, capped with Clarence Jones rushing in for a seven yard touchdown, with Craig Stopa making the extra point kick to close the score to 31-7. The Falcons finished with a 57 yard and a one yard touchdown runs to win the game, 45-7.

"They dominated us," said Jim Young after the game. "They just beat us, outcoached us, outplayed us and made the big plays. Bart Weiss gave us a lesson in wishbone football."

"Never in my wildest imagination did I think we would have a blowout like this," Fisher DeBerry, said. "Army is a well-disciplined team, but things just didn't go their way. This was a complete effort from the people on the field to the coaches upstairs. But the players are the ones who executed it, and they are the real heroes."

DeBerry continued, "That might have been the best our team has played this year. Our quarterback did a super job. And I can't say enough about our defense. They took a team that in five of its eight games had scored over 40 points and almost shut them out. They shut down a dad-gummed good offensive machine, I guarantee you."

Army had 10 first downs, 168 yards rushing, 18 passing (4-11-1), one lost fumble, eight punts, and 26:56 time of possession. Air Force had 24 first downs, 396 yards rushing, 105 passing (4-10-0), no lost fumbles, and three punts. Weiss had 114 yards rushing and 105 yards passing. Clarence Jones rushed for 39 yards, while Tory Crawford had 37, Rob Healy 34, and Doug Black 34 yards.

With their victory over both Navy and Army, the Falcons won the 1985 Commander-in-Chief's Trophy. Air Force would lose to #16 Brigham Young, 21-28, on November 16th, ending their ten game winning streak. Air Force would finish the regular season at Hawai'i with a 27-20 victory. The Falcons finished with a 7-1 Western Athletic Conference record tied with BYU.

Air Force was invited to the Bluebonnet Bowl to play unranked Texas. The Falcons won, 24-16, on December 31st. Air Force finished the 1985 season with an overall 12-1 record in Fisher DeBerry's second season. Air Force was ranked #8 in the final *Associated Press* Poll and #5 in the final *United Press International* Coaches Poll.

Memphis State

Army (7-2) hosted Memphis State (2-6-2) on Saturday afternoon, November 16th, at West Point in front of 34,000 fans with three inches of snow covering Michie Stadium. Memphis State was an Independent this season and this game would conclude their season. The Cadets were favored to win by 6.5 points.

In their six opening games, the Tigers won at Southwestern Louisiana (37-6), tied Mississippi (17-17), tied Murray State (10-10), lost at #6 Florida State (24-41), lost at Mississippi State (28-31), and beat Tulane (38-21). Memphis State then lost four in a row to Southern Mississippi, Alabama, Virginia Tech, and Tennessee.

Army quarterback Rob Healy rushed for a two yard touchdown with less than four minutes in the game, with Craig Stopa making the extra point kick. In the second quarter, Healy completed a 30 yard touchdown pass to Rob Dickerson. Healy ran in for a ten yard touchdown to extend the halftime lead at 21-0. The Tigers scored on a 60 yard pass in the third quarter, while William Lampley ran nine yards for a touchdown to make it 28-7 going into the final period.

Healy hit Dickerson for a three yard touchdown reception. Tory Crawford carried the ball three times in the fourth quarter, with touchdown runs of seven and five yards. The Cadets had no problems in the snow, winning 49-7. Army finished undefeated at home for the second straight year, a string of twelve victories.

Army had 21 first downs, 476 yards rushing, 60 passing (3-7-0), one lost fumble, one punt, 10 yards penalized, and 31:26 time of possession. Rob Healy rushed for 143 yards, while Doug Black ran for 95 yards. Craig Stopa converted on all seven PATs.

Memphis State had 9 first downs, 55 yards rushing, 161 passing (14-28-2), three lost fumbles, six punts, and 25 yards penalized. The Tigers finished the 1985 season with an overall record of 2-7-2 in Rey Dempsey's second and last season as head football coach.

Bowl Game Bids

An article on November 5th focused on Syracuse's bowl game chances mentioned that the Cherry, All-American, and Liberty Bowls might be looking at Army (then 7-1) as well as the Orangemen. Syracuse did go to the 1985 Cherry Bowl where they lost to Maryland, 18-35.

An *Associated Press* article on November 18th reported that the match for the Peach Bowl would include Illinois and Army. On November 19th, there was an article that stated that if Illinois (then 5-4-1) beat Northwestern that Saturday, it would play in the Peach Bowl against Army.

Around 6 pm Saturday, November 23rd, the Peach Bowl extended official invitations to the Illinois and Army to play in the game on December 31st.

Navy

Navy started the 1985 season with three straight losses to North Carolina (19-21), at Delaware (13-16), and at Indiana (35-38). On September 28th, the Midshipmen upset #20 Virginia in Charlottesville, 17-13. Air Force beat Navy, 24-7 at Annapolis on October 12th.

The Mids then beat Lafayette (56-14) and Pittsburgh (21-7) at home for a record of 3-4. Navy then lost their next three games at Notre Dame (17-71), versus Syracuse (20-24), and at South Carolina (31-34); to come into the Army-Navy game with a 3-7 record.

The 86th Army-Navy game was played on December 7th, at Philadelphia's Veterans Stadium before a sellout crowd of 71,640 spectators. *CBS Television* broadcasted the game nationally, with Brent Musburger, Ara Parseghian, and Pat O'Brien announcing. The Cadets (8-2) were favored to win by 7 points and were ranked second nationally in rushing (350.8). Vice President and former World War II Navy pilot George Bush was in attendance.

Navy quarterback Bob Misch completed a 13 yard touchdown pass to Troy Saunders on its opening possession in the first quarter. Todd Solomon converted the extra point kick to make the score 7-0. The Cadets responded by a long drive down field ending with a Clarence Jones ten yard touchdown run and a Craig Stopa extra point kick to tie the game. Army reached the N-2 midway through the second quarter, but the Midshipmen defense stopped the Cadets on downs. Rob Healy dislocated his shoulder and left the game.

In the third quarter, Army came up empty when Stopa missed a 37 yard field goal attempt. It was tied 7-7 going into the final period. The Midshipmen broke the tie with 8:26 to go on a five yard burst up the middle by fullback Chuck Smith, then Solomon added a 26 yard field goal with only 1:15 remaining to close out the scoring and the Navy victory, 17-7.

"Navy's game plan was excellent," said Jim Young after the game. "Just keep running McCallum. Now we've got to worry about a team in the Peach Bowl that throws the ball all over the place."

"I'm not going to even think about Illinois until I go home and get well," Healy said, nursing his aching shoulder. "West Point is going to be a pretty depressing place."

"McCallum runs the same every day," said Gary Tranquill, who denied reports he planned to quit if Navy lost. "Napoleon is always good. I've never seen him be bad. This was very sweet today. It's been as frustrating a season as I've ever gone through."

"We played great," McCallum said. "That's what it comes down to. This is the game I'm going to remember forever. Our game plan was to play hard, run through the people and don't fumble the ball."

Army had 19 first downs, 192 yards rushing, 96 passing (4-8-0), lost no fumbles, were 29 yards penalized, had three punts, and

24:50 time of possession. Navy had 28 first downs, 313 yards rushing, 84 passing (8-16-0), lost one fumble, punted two times, and were penalized 51 yards. Doug Black rushed for 64 yards and Clarence Jones gained 63 yards. Napoleon McCallum rushed for 217 yards. Craig Stopa converted his 61st PAT in a row during the game.

Navy finished the 1985 regular season successfully with a victory over Army. The Midshipmen overall record was 4-7 in Gary Tranquill's fourth season. Eric Fudge and Napoleon McCallum were the Navy captains.

Awards and Recognitions

Cadets offensive guard Don Smith was named to the Eastern Kodak All-American team. Smith was also named to the second team *Associated Press* All-American team, the first team *Associated Press* All-East team, and the first team ECAC team. Kicker Craig Stopa, center Ron Rice, and safety Doug Pavek were named to the ECAC team. Doug Black was named to the National Football Foundation and Hall of Fame's National Scholar Athlete team.

Doug Pavek was invited to and played in the 1985 East-West Shrine Game. Doug Black and Don Smith played in the Hula Bowl. Pavek finished nationally tied for fifth with 0.64 interceptions per game.

1985 Season Statistics

The following are the Cadets team offensive statistics for the 1985 season, excluding the bowl game. On offense, the team had 365 points (33.2 average); 246 first downs (204 rushing, 33 passing, and 9 by penalty); rushed for 3,700 yards (336.4 ypg) on 699 attempts (5.3 ypa) and 43 touchdowns; passed for 680 yards on 41 completions on 79 passes and 2 interceptions for 61.8 ypg, 8.6 ypp, 16.6 ypr, and 5 touchdowns; had 4,380 yards total offense on 778 plays, 398.2 ypg, 5.6 ypp, and 48 touchdowns; had 43 penalties for 299 yards; had 27 fumbles and lost 11 of them; had an average time of possession per game of 29:35; and converted 82 out of 155 third downs (52.9%).

On defense, the team allowed 203 points (18.5 average); 219 first downs (107 rushing, 101 passing, and 11 by penalty); 1,837 yards rushing (167.0 ypg) on 456 attempts (4.0 ypa) and 11 touchdowns allowed; 2,096 passing yards on 167 completions on 310 passes and 16 interceptions for 190.5 ypg, 6.8 ypp, 12.6 ypr, and 15 touchdowns; allowed 3,933 total yards on 766 plays, 357.5 ypg, 5.1 ypp, and 26 touchdowns; opponents had 61 penalties for 404 yards; converted 71 out of 155 third downs (45.8%); forced 26 fumbles and recovered 11 of them; and returned 16 interceptions (10.2 average).

For Cadets special teams statistics, punted 36 times for a 34.7 average; returned 29 kickoffs (21.9 average); returned 24 punts (11.5 average); made 9 out of 15 field goal attempts; and made 44 out of 44 point after touchdown attempts. For opponents' special teams statistics, punted 46 times for a 38.6 average; returned 55 kickoffs (18.4 average); and returned 13 punts (4.8 average).

The Cadets were first nationally in total turnovers; second in rushing yards behind Nebraska; fifth in turnover margin; sixth in punt returns; ninth in scoring offense; 15th in kickoff returns; and 21st in total offense. Army averaged 37,826 attendance in seven home games, 44,981 in three away games, and 71,640 in one neutral site games. Scoring by quarters was 64-38 (1st), 110-35 (2nd), 70-58 (3rd), and 121-72 (4th).

Doug Black had 950 yards rushing in 197 attempts for an 86.4 ypg, while Troy Crawford ran for 657 yards in 128 attempts for 59.7 ypg. Other individual rushing statistics were Clarence Jones (89-604), William Lampley (102-578), Rob Healy (107-537), Andy Peterson (23-112), Alan Edwards (7-91), Kevin McKelvy (5-45), Ron Herring (7-45), Benny Wright (11-38), Scott Spellmon (3-18), Bill Kim (3-15), Ed Cole (4-12), Cleveland Bazemore (2-6), Mike Ryan (2-4), Rod Mullins (1-3), Paolo Smith (1-3), Erik Gunhus (1-2), and Mark Mooney (1-minus 5).

Crawford and Jones each had 10 rushing touchdowns, while Lampley and Healy each had six. Others scoring rushing touchdowns were Black (5), Peterson (2), with Edwards, McKelvy, Wright, and Cole making one touchdown each.

Healy completed 27 out of 47 passes for 421 yards with four touchdowns and one interception. Crawford had 13 completions out of 29 attempts for 254 yards with one touchdown and one interception. Lampley made one out of three passes for five yards.

Benny White caught 13 passes for 213 yards and one touchdown. Scott Spellmon had ten receptions for 203 yards and two touchdowns, while Rob Dickerson scored two touchdowns on ten catches for 159 yards. Others with receptions were Black (3-40), Jones (3-40), and Lampley (2-25).

Jones returned six kickoffs for a 29.7 average and a long of 61, while Lampley returned six for a 30.5 average with a long of 49 and Bazemore had six kickoff returns for 67 yards. Others with kickoff returns were Peterson (3-27), Ron Herring (2-39), Edwards (1-22), Chance Conner (1-20), and McKelvy (1-10). Darold Londo returned 19 punts for an 11.4 average, while Conner returned three punts for a 5.0 average. John Thomson returned one punt 32 yards and Matt Buckner returned one punt for 13 yards.

Matt Buckner and John Thomson each recovered two fumbles, while Kurt Gutierrez, Tom Malloy, Jim Brock, Darold Londo, Jay Bridge, Robert Duffy, and Chance Conner recovered one fumble each. Forcing fumbles were Doug Pavek (3), Dave Scheyer (2), Reggie Fullwood (2), with Gutierrez, Malloy, Jim Brock, Lloyd Walker, Thomson, Tom Sharp, Craig Rollins, Chip England, and Lou Dainty each forcing one fumble.

Doug Pavek intercepted seven passes for 83 yards, while Dave Berdan (26 yards) and Reggie Fullwood (8 yards) each intercepted two passes. Intercepting one pass were Larry Biggins (9 yards), Craig Rollins (5), Lou Dainty (3), John Thomson (0), and Bill Sanders (0). Darold Londo intercepted a fumble and returned it 29 yards. No touchdowns occurred on interception or fumble returns.

Kurt Gutierrez defended six passes, while Doug Pavek, John Thomson, Darold Londo, and Reggie Fullwood defended five passes. Other passes defended were Chance Conner (3), Peel Chronister (2), Scheyer (1), Biggins (1), Buckner (1), Malloy (1), and Lloyd Walker (1).

Craig Stopa made nine out of 15 field goal attempts, with a long of 53 yards. Stopa made 44 out of 44 point after touchdown kicks. Bit Rambusch punted 36 times for an average of 34.7 with a long of 61 yards. Matt Buckner and John Thomson each blocked a kick.

Craig Stopa led the team in scoring with 71 points, followed by Clarence Jones with 62 and Tory Crawford with 60. Others scoring were Lampley (36), Healy (36), Black (30), Peterson (12), Dickerson (12), Wright (6), White (6), McKelvy (6), Edwards (6), Cole (6), Keith Walker (2), and a Team Safety (2).

Dave Scheyer led the team with 117 total tackles (73 solo), followed by Larry Biggins with 96, Doug Pavek with 90, and Kurt Gutierrez had 84. Others with tackled included Matt Buckner (77), Tom Malloy (72), Jim Brock (58), Lloyd Walker (55), Bob Kleinhample (54), John Thomson (41), Darold Londo (33), Jay Bridge (25), Tom Sharp (25), Ray Griffiths (22), Peel Chronister (21), and Mike Lover (19).

Also, Reggie Fullwood (18), Robert Duffy (16), Craig Collins (16), Bill Sanders (15), Dave Berdan (15), Chip England (13), Bill Horton (13), Chris Tierney (11), Tim McGuire (9), Chance Conner (8), Lou Dainty (7), Greg Gadson (5), Joe Carter (3), Charles Williams (3), Rob Dickerson (2), Rob Roggerman (2), Jeff Schorr (1), Bill Schleiden (1), and Charles Schretzman (1).

Lloyd Walker led the team with 13 tackles for loss, Brock had 11, while Gutierrez, Malloy, Scheyer each made seven TFLs. Others with TFLs were Kleinhample (5), Sharp (4), Thomson (3), Lover (3), Bridge (2), Fullwood (2), McGuire (2), Carter (1), Londo (1), Buckner (1), and Biggins (1).

The following Cadets started every game on offense during the 1984 season, including the bowl game: Doug Black, Rob Dickerson, Clarence Jones, William Lampley, Clint Pollitt, Ron Rice, Ed Schultz, and Don Smith.

On defense, the following started every game during the 1984 season, including the bowl game: Jim Brock, Matt Buckner, Kurt Gutierrez, Bob Kleinhample, Doug Pavek, and John Thomson.

The 1985 team finished third in scoring points in a regular season, behind the 1944 NCAA record holder and the 1945 teams. Craig Stopa set the then Army record for longest field goal, a 53 yard conversion against Yale.

At the end of the 2020 season, the 1985 team season records included most players with 100 yard rushing games, sixth in rushing touchdowns, ninth in total first downs, tenth in total offense, eleventh in fewest punts, and twelfth in rushing yards.

Individually in a season, Rob Healy ranked fifth in passing efficiency. Craig Stopa has the most consecutive points after touchdown made (44), tied for first in extra point completion percentage (100%), fourth in extra point kicks made, and sixth in extra point kicks attempted.

Doug Pavek is tied for fourth in interceptions made, tenth in passes defended, and tied for tenth in fumbles forced. Darold Londo is 14th in punt returns, 15th in punt return yards, and 17th in punt return average yardage. Lloyd Walker is tied for 15th in tackles for loss.

Lettermen

The following lettered during the 1985 season: Brian Ash, Cleveland Bazemore, Art Beasley, Dave Berdan, Larry Biggins, Doug Black, Jay Bridge, Jim Brock, Matt Buckner, Peel Chronister, Chance Connor, Tory Crawford, Lou Dainty, Rob Dickerson, Leighton Drisdale, Bob Duffy, Alan Edwards, Chip England, Jack Frey, Reggie Fullwood, Greg Gadson, Ray Griffiths, Kurt Gutierrez, Bob Healy, and Todd Hecker.

Also, Ron Herring, Bill Horton, Roderick Jackson, Clarence Jones, Bob Kleinhample, Ted Kostich, William Lampley, Wayne Locklin, Darold Londo, Mike Lover, Tom Malloy, Joe Manausa, Tom Mathers, Tim McGuire, Kevin McKelvy, Tom Meyer, Charles Moses, John Oleinik, Doug Pavek, Andy Peterson, and Clint Pollitt.

Also, Bit Rambusch, Ron Rice, Rob Roggerman, Craig Rollins, Bill Sanders, Dan Sauter, David Scheyer, Bill Schleiden, Gordon Scott, Tom Sharp, Ed Shultz, Don Smith, Scott Spellmon, Craig Stopa, Dan Stredler, Steve Strifler, John Thomson, Chris Tierney, Roy Tomlinson, Lloyd Walker, Benny White, and Benny Wright.

Army Branch Selections

The following seniors are members of the USMA Class of 1986 were commissioned in the following branches: (Air Defense Artillery) Dan Suter and Roy Tomlinson; (Armor) Doug Pavek and Rob Roggerman; (Aviation) Rob Healy, Darold Londo, Craig Rollins, and Craig Stopa; (Engineers) Doug Black, Don Smith, and Scott Spellmon; (Field Artillery) Cleveland Bazemore, Jay Bridge, Leighton Drisdale, Kurt Gutierrez, Bob Kleinhample, Wayne Locklin, Kevin McKelvy, Charles Moses, Ron Rice, Gordon Scott, Tom Sharp, Dan Stredler, and John Thomson; and (Infantry) Matt Buckner, Ted Kostich, Tom Malloy, Steven Strifler, and Chris Tierney.

Conclusion

There was now three and a half weeks to now prepare for the upcoming bowl game against Illinois. With the conclusion and disappointment of the Army-Navy game, the Cadets began preparations for the Peach Bowl. But first, the players needed to pass their term end examinations (finals) for their fall semester courses. The team needed to push away those negative thoughts and get itself ready to compete.

Chapter 7

1985 Peach Bowl Game

The Peal Bowl Committee announced on November 23rd that it was officially announcing invitations to the University of Illinois (6-4-1) and the United States Military Academy at West Point (8-3) football teams to play in the 18th annual bowl game at Atlanta-Fulton County Stadium on December 31st and be televised by *CBS Television*. Both institutions immediately accepted the bowl bids.

It would be the eighth time that Illinois and Army had played, the last being during the 1959 season at Memorial Stadium and a Fighting Illini 20-14 victory. Each team has won three, lost three, and tied one game in a short series that began in 1929 with four games played on the campus at Illinois, two in Yankee Stadium, and one in Cleveland.

Peach Bowl History

The Peach Bowl was first played in December 1968, a creation of George Pierre Crumbley Jr., who shepherded the bowl application through the NCAA in order to be a fund-raiser for charitable work. The bowl is the ninth oldest. It started as a second-tier bowl game played between also-rans but winning teams from the Atlantic Coast and Southeastern Conferences that drew small crowds in usually drizzly, near freezing conditions, being broadcast on the Mizlou Network mainly to the Southeast region.

The first three bowl games were played at Grant Field on the campus of Georgia Tech University. In 1971, the game moved to Atlanta-Fulton County Stadium, where it was played until 1992, when the bowl game moved to the Georgia Bowl. It was the first charity bowl, used to fund $100,000 a year to the Lighthouse Foundation, which funded charitable work on behalf of the state's deaf and blind populations.

Illinois would be the fourth Big Ten team to play in the Peach Bowl, following Purdue (1978), Iowa (1983), and Purdue (1984). There had been ten other Independent teams that had played in the bowl game before Army.

The bowl guarantee for each team was reported to be $500,000. Under Big Ten rules, Illinois would not have to share this with other conference members. Army would keep their payment, being an Independent. Both teams incurred considerable expenses, bringing a full squad of players and coaches, plus members of the institution and athletic department staffs. Army received $740,000 for attending the 1984 Cherry Bowl. The Corps of Cadets was on Christmas Leave, but the athletic department provided free tickets for those Cadets who attended in uniform.

The bowl committee was hoping for about 40,000 spectators in the 60,606 stadium. For the first time ever, a team from the South was not invited. Having two Northern teams may have affected the attendance for the game, as the bowl game averaged 39,000 in 1982-1984 and 52,000 in 1986-1988, all with at least one Southern team.

The bowl committee was teetering on the brink of bankruptcy in the 1970s and early 1980s. The bowl was originally managed by the Georgia Lions Club. The Metro Atlanta Chamber of Commerce took over and improved managing the bowl and later secured a spot during the building of the Georgia Dome to move into a first-tier bowl game.

Illinois Football History

Illinois began playing football in the 1890 season. The Fighting Illini was an original member of the Big Ten Conference, joining in 1896. Illinois claims five national championships (1914, 1919, 1923, 1927, and 1951) and had in 1985 won 13 Big Ten Conference titles. This would be the Fighting Illini's sixth bowl game (3-2).

Illinois was having much success in the 1980s. In the 1983 season, it had beaten Michigan, won the Big Ten championship, and went to the 1984 Rose Bowl game (a 45-9 loss to UCLA). Two seasons later under sixth year head football coach Mike White and future NFL quarterback Jack Trudeau, gave the Fighting Illini a formidable offense.

1985 Illinois Fighting Illini Football Team

The 1985 Illinois coaching staff was led by head football coach Mike White and included Max McCartney (assistant head coach), Bob Gambold (offensive coordinator & quarterbacks), Rich Solomon (defensive coordinator & secondary), Larry Holton (running backs), Bob Karmelowicz (defensive line), Shawn Watson (tight ends), and Bill Callahan (offensive line).

Also on the coaching staff were Bill Kollar (volunteer assistant coach & special teams), Mike Gohn (graduate assistant & offensive line), Dean Kreps (graduate assistant offensive line), Frank Blateri (graduate assistant & outside linebackers), John Wrenn (graduate assistance & quarterbacks/receivers), and Don Barlow (graduate assistant & defensive backs).

For Illinois in the 1985 season, the team aimed high for another Big Ten championship, a trip to the Rose Bowl, and a high national ranking. The Fighting Illini were ranked 11th in the preseason *Associated Press* Top 20 Poll and 10th in the *United Press International* Coaches Top 20 Poll.

The #11/#10 Fighting Illini opened at home versus Southern California on September 7th, losing 10-20, due to six Illinois turnovers. After beating Southern Illinois 28-25 the next Saturday, thanks to scoring 22 points in the third quarter; #20/NR Illinois traveled to Lincoln to play #18/#17 Nebraska. The Huskers beat the Fighting Illini, 25-52, due to seven turnovers by the visitors. Illinois would not be ranked in the two polls after that loss the remainder of the 1985 season.

Illinois upset #5 Ohio State, 31-28, at home on October 5th. Senior placekicker made a 38 yard field goal on the last play of the game, giving the Fighting Illini a come-from-behind victory over the Buckeyes. At Purdue the next weekend, the Fighting Illinois suffered a 24-30 loss to the Boilermakers. Purdue's Jim Everett and Trudeau combined for 67 completions on 114 pass attempts for 889 yards without any interceptions. A late drive by the Fighting Illini was stopped on their opponents' 13 yard line.

Illinois responded with two wins at Michigan State (30-17) and versus Wisconsin (38-25). At home on November 2nd, Illinois tied #4 Michigan, 3-3. Both teams had kicked field goals in the third quarter. In the fourth quarter, the Wolverines drove down to the UI-12 where Michigan fullback Gerald White lost the football on a fumble. Illinois drove down the field, and with time running out, Fighting Illini kicker Chris White attempted a 37 yard field goal, which hit the crossbar and bounced out, leaving the game tied.

The Fighting Illini were shutout by #6 Iowa, 0-59, as Hawkeye quarterback Chuck Long led his team to a 35-0 first quarter lead. Illinois beat both Indiana at home (41-24) and at Northwestern (45-20) to finish their regular season with a 5-2-1 Big Ten Conference record in third place. After losing two of their first three games, and three of its first five, Illinois solidified into an outstanding team that won four of its last six games and tied Michigan.

Illinois finished eighth nationally in passing yards (272.0). The Fighting Illini averaged 121.5 yards rushing. On defense, Illinois allowed 172.8 yards rushing and 215.2 passing. The team averaged 25 points per game, while giving up 27.2 points per game.

During the regular season, quarterback Jack Trudeau had passed for 2,938 yards. Trudeau was ranked fifth nationally in total offense with 264.9 yards per game. Reserve quarterbacks Jim Bennett and Keith Jones had thrown 16 passes during the season for 54 yards.

Thomas Rooks was the leading rusher with 718 yards on 133 carries, followed by Ray Wilson with 448 and Keith Jones had 142 yards. David Williams had 1,047 yards receiving on 85 catches, while Stephen Pierce had 614 yards, Cap Boso 369, Thomas

Rooks with 347, Anthony Williams 169, Darryl Usher 139, and Ray Wilson with 133 yards.

Todd Avery had three interceptions, while African Grant and Craig Swoope each had two. Keith Jones had 16 kickoff returns for a 21.3 average, while Dwayne Pugh had twelve (20.0) and Darryl Usher with eight (19.5). Usher had returned 27 punts for a 9.9 average. Chris White had made all 31 of his points after touchdown kicks. White made 14 out of 20 field goal attempts, with a long of 51 yards. Chris Little had 49 punts for an average of 40.4, sixth best in Illinois' history.

Mark Tagart led the Fighting Illini with 80 total tackles (60 solo), while Craig Swoope had 63 and Jim Blondell made 60. Scott Davis had nine sacks, while Guy Teafatiller had six and Alec Gibson made four sacks. Chris White was the leading scorer with 73 points, followed by David Williams with 52 and Thomas Rooks with 42.

David Williams finished the season third nationally in receptions per game (7.7), third in receiving yards per game (95.2), fourth in touchdown receptions (8), and fifth in receiving yards. For his career, he finished second in receptions with 245 in 33 games, fourth in yards per catch (7.4), and fourth in receiving yards (3,195) in the NCAA Division 1-A. Williams would be selected a consensus All-American in both the 1984 and 1985 seasons; and is a member of the National Football Foundation College Football Hall of Fame, inducted in 2005.

Jack Trudeau finished tenth on the NCAA Division 1-A career passing yards (8,146), 11th in total offense (8,096), and seventh in total offense per game (238.1). Trudeau had also set virtually all of Illinois school passing records, including pass attempts (1,151), completions (736), completion percentage (63.9%), total offense, touchdown passes (51), and total plays (1,318).

Thomas Rooks was the Fighting Illini all-time leader in rushing with 2,753 yards, second in career carries (540), and second in career touchdowns (24). Rooks held the school's career mark for receptions (98) by a running back.

Bowl Entertainment

The bowl sponsored a Pep Rally, a Parade, a Ball, pregame parties, and a post-game Players Award Banquet. The Marching Illini (The Nation's Premier College Marching Band) provided halftime entertainment during the 1985 Peach Bowl and played during the game. There were other bands who provided pregame entertainment.

Pre-Game

Starting for the Illinois offense were split end David Williams; tight end Cap Boso; offensive tackles Mark Dennis and Brian Ward; offensive guards Jim Juriga and Scott Kehoe; center Mike Scully; flanker Stephen Pierce; fullback Thomas Rooks; running back Ray Wilson; and quarterback Jack Trudeau.

Starting for the Illinois defense were defensive ends Scott Davis and Alec Gibson; defensive tackles Jim Blondell and Guy Teafatiller; linebackers James Finch, Mark Tagart, and Rob Glielmi; cornerbacks Todd Avery and Lance Harkey; and safeties African Grant and Craig Swoope.

Starting for the Army offense were split end Scott Spellmon; offensive guards Don Smith and Clint Pollitt; offensive tackles Joe Manausa and Ed Schultz; center Ron Rice; tight end Rob Dickerson; halfbacks Clarence Jones and William Lampley; fullback Doug Black; and quarterback Rob Healy.

Starting for the Army defense were defensive ends Tom Malloy and Kurt Gutierrez; nose guard Jim Brock; defensive tackles Bob Kleinhample and Lloyd Walker; linebackers Larry Biggins and Dave Scheyer; and defensive backs Matt Buckner, Peel Chronister, Doug Pavek, and John Tomson.

The game officials were from the Southeastern Conference, and included Jimmy Harper (referee), Pete Williams (umpire), Bert Ackermann (lineman), Ed Dudley (line judge), Joe DeLany (field judge), Al Graning (side judge), and Dick Pace (back judge).

Army was the designated home team and wore their gold helmets, black jerseys, and gold pants (and names on the back of their jerseys). Illinois wore orange helmets, white jerseys, and blue pants. The Fighting Illini were favored by 9 points to win. Gary Bender (play-by-play), Steve Davis (analyst), and John Dockery (sideline reporter) were announcers for *CBS Television* which broadcasted the game.

The Illinois team captains were Jack Trudeau, Craig Swoope, and Chris White. The Army team captains were Kurt Gutierrez and Don Smith. 1985 Peach Bowl Queen Sharon Langley flipped the coin. Army won the toss and elected to receive. Illinois defended the north goal.

It was 45 degrees, 60% humidity, with winds from the south at 15 mph at the kickoff. The game was played in cooler temperatures, heavy rain, and gusting winds, with the grass field becoming slick, sloppy, and muddy, before 29,857 spectators, with a kickoff at 3 pm EST. Dockery asked Army quarterback Rob Healy what about the weather, and Healy said, "This is Army weather!"

First Quarter

Chris White kicked off to the WP-6, where William Lampley returned the ball eight yards but fumbled it out of bounds at the WP-14. Rob Healy went wide right for a 16 yard gain and a first down at the WP-30, tackled by Craig Swoope. Bob Sebring stopped Healy after a gain of seven yards going to his right. Doug Black rushed four yards up the middle for a first down at the WP-41, stopped by Ron Bohm.

Todd Avery tackled Clarence Jones on a pitch after a six yard gain wide left out of bounds. Lampley went up the middle for twelve yards and a first down at the UI-41, stopped by Swoope. Healy went wide left for four yards, tackled by James Finch.

Avery and Jay Lynch tackled Clarence Jones for a one yard gain. Swoope stopped Healy after a four yard run to the left. On a fourth and one from the UI-32, Rob Healy stumbled and ran to the right for a loss of two yards, stopped by Mark Tagart. The Cadets had a turnover on downs at 11:52 on the clock. The Cadets drive took 3:05 went 54 yards in nine plays.

Ray Wilson ran four yards to the right side before being tackled by Bob Kleinhample. Dave Scheyer tackled Thomas Rooks for a loss of one yard. Jack Trudeau completed an eleven yard pass to Cap Boso for a first down at the UI-48, who was stopped by Scheyer.

John Thomson tackled Boso out of bounds after a two yard pass reception. Wilson ran for three yards to the left side, tackled by Jim Brock. Peel Chronister intercepted a pass from Jack Trudeau to David Williams for no return at the WP-35 with 9:28 on the clock. The Fighting Illini drive took 2:14 off the clock, going 19 yards in six plays.

Swoope and Avery tackled Lampley after a nine yard pitch to the right. Black went up the middle for three yards and a first down at the WP-47, stopped by Scott Davis. Healy ran wide right for five yards, tackled by Swoope. Healy ran left off tackle for five yards at the UI-43, stopped by Ed White and Tucker Jenkins. The official measurement gave the Cadets a first down.

Army took a time out with 7:26 on the clock. Tagart and Sebring tackled Healy after a five yard run to the right. On a pitch, Lampley rushed wide right for ten yards and a first down at the UI-28, tackled by Rob Glielmi.

Black ran up the middle for three yards, stopped by Guy Teafatiller. Glielmi tackled Healy after a three yard rush to the right. Rob Healy ran down the right sideline for a 22 yard touchdown and a first down at 5:47 on the clock. Craig Stopa converted the extra point to make the score, 7-0. The Cadets drive took 3:35 and went 65 yards in nine plays.

Stopa kicked off to the UI-2, where Wilson returned it 18 yards before being stopped by Kurt Gutierrez. Trudeau completed an eight yard pass to Anthony Williams on the ground. Brock tackled Rooks for a loss of one yard. David Williams caught a 20 yards reception for a first down at the UI-47, stopped by Matt Buckner.

Trudeau completed a six yard pass to Boso, tackled by Lou Dainty and Gutierrez. Army was called for a dead ball personal foul after the play and penalized 15 yards and a first down to the WP-32. Trudeau's pass to David Williams was out of bounds and incomplete, but Illinois was penalized five yards on the play for illegal procedure back to the WP-37. On the next play, Illinois was penalized five yards for a false start back to the WP-42.

On first and twenty, Tom Malloy tackled Rooks on a run to the left after a gain of five yards. Trudeau was pressured by Larry Biggins and his attempted pass was incomplete. Illinois was called for another illegal procedure on the play, but Army declined it.

On third and 15, Stephen Pierce caught a nine yard reception and was tackled by Thomson. Chris White made a 45 yard field goal at 2:11 to close the score to 7-3. The Illinois drive took 3:34 and went for 52 yards in 8 plays. Chris White kicked off to the WP-1, where Lampley returned it forty yards before being stopped by Ed White.

Bohm tackled Black after a one yard gain up the middle. Ron Bohm then stopped Rob Dickerson for a loss of seven yards on a reverse. On third and 16, Healy completed a seven yard pass to Lampley, stopped by Curtis Clarke. On fourth and nine at the WP-42, Bit Rambusch punted 46 yards to the UI-12, where Darryl Usher returned it 13 yards to the UI-26 before being stopped by Doug Pavek with 0:03 on the clock. The Army drive took 2:02 to go one yard in three plays.

On the final play of the first quarter, Trudeau completed a 19 yard pass to Anthony Williams for a first down at the UI-46 as the clock ran out, with the score, 7-3 in Army's favor, with Chronister and Scheyer making the tackle.

Second Quarter

Lloyd Walker sacked Jack Trudeau for a two yard loss. On second and 12, Trudeau completed a 13 yard pass to Pierce at the

WP-44, tackled by Bill Sanders. An official measurement gave the Fighting Illini a first down. Brock and Larry Biggins tackled Rooks for a loss of one yard. Trudeau threw a high pass to David Williams for an incompletion. On third and eleven, Trudeau completed a 19 yard pass to Pierce for a first down at the WP-26, stopped by Chronister.

Trudeau threw a twelve yard pass to Anthony Williams for a first down at the WP-14, tackled by Thomson and Chronister. On the next play, Illinois was penalized five yards for illegal procedure. Scheyer tackled Wilson after a four yard reception. Jim Brock sacked Jack Trudeau for a loss of ten yards. Army took a time out with 10:51 on the clock.

On third and 21 at the WP-25, Trudeau threw a 23 yard pass to Wilson, tackled by Pavek. Doug Pavek was injured on the play and left the game. Wilson ran to the right for a gain of one yard, stopped by Brock. On second and one, Jack Trudeau rolled to his right and threw a one yard touchdown pass to Cap Boso and a first down at 9:48 on the clock. Chris White made the point after touchdown kick and the Fighting Illini took the lead, 10-7. The Illinois drive took 5:17 and was twelve plays over 74 yards.

Chris White kicked off to the WP-2, where Lampley returned it 18 yards before being stopped by Mike McBain and Sean Lawlor. Ed White tackled Healy after a six yard gain to the right. Swoope stopped Clarence Jones ran left for no gain out of bounds. Sebring stopped Lampley after a two yard run to the right. On the play, Army was called for holding, but Illinois declined the penalty.

On fourth and two at the WP-28, Rambusch punted 41 yards to the UI-31, where Usher returned it eleven yards. Bob Kleinhample tackled Darryl Usher and forced a fumble that was recovered by Doug Pavek at 8:37 on the clock at the UI-42. The Cadets drive took 1:09 went 8 yards in three plays.

Bohm and David Aina tackled Clarence Jones for a three yard run up the middle. Healy completed a 17 yard pass to Scott Spellmon for a first down at the UI-22, tackled by Lance Harkey out of bounds on the left sideline. On a pitch, Clarence Jones rushed wide left for a four yard gain, stopped by Mark Kelly. Swoope tackled Lampley on a counter play after a five yard rush up the middle. On third and one at the UI-13, Lampley rushed up the middle for a one yard gain and a first down, stopped by Jim Blondell.

Healy rushed to the right for three yards, stopped by Lynch. Kelly and Teafatiller tackled Lampley out of bounds on a pitch play going to the right side for no gain. On third and seven at the UI-9, Healy ran left for six yards, stopped by Tagart and Bohm. The official measurement found the Cadets to be short of the sticks as the rain began falling heavily. Army called a time out with 4:58 on the clock.

On fourth and one at the UI-3, Black rushed up the middle, but Illinois was called on the play for being off sides and penalized half the distance to the goal line to the UI-1 and a first down. Doug Black plunged over the goal line for a touchdown at 4:52 left in the first half. A dead ball foul was called on Illinois for 15 yards; the penalty was assessed on the kickoff. Craig Stopa converted the extra point kick as Army took the lead, 14-10. The Cadets drive of 3:41 took nine plays and went 42 yards.

Stopa kicked off from the fifty into the end zone for a touchback by Ray Wilson. On first and ten at the UI-20, Trudeau completed a nine yard pass to the flat to Rooks, but the Fighting Illini were called for clipping and penalized 15 yards to the UI-14. Malloy tackled Trudeau after a two yard run to the left. A pass to Wilson was overthrown and incomplete. Peel Chronister intercepted a pass from Jack Trudeau at the UI-35 with 3:29 on the clock. The Illinois drive of 1:23 took three plays to go minus six yards.

Glielmi tackled Healy after a gain of two yards. On a halfback option, Clarence Lampley completed a 33 yard pass to Benny White for a touchdown and a first down at 2:48 left in the half. After Craig Stopa's conversion kick, Army now led 21-10. The drive of 0:41 covered 35 yards in two plays. Stopa kicked off to the UI-5, where Wilson returned it 19 yards before being stopped by Buckner.

Trudeau threw an incomplete pass to Usher out of bounds. David Williams completed a six yard reception before being tackled by Biggins. A Trudeau pass to Pierce was incomplete, but Army was penalized 15 yards for pass interference and a first down to the UI-45. Biggins tackled Boso after an eight yard pass reception. Boso caught a seven yard pass for a first down at the WP-40 before being stopped by Biggins.

Trudeau threw a seven yard pass to Usher, stopped by Walker. Boso caught a six yard pass for a first down at the WP-27, tackled by Gutierrez. Illinois took a time out with 0:46 on the clock. Trudeau completed a twelve yard pass to Pierce for a first down at the WP-15, stopped by Biggins. Trudeau's pass to Usher was high into the back of the end zone and incomplete.

On second and ten, pressured on a blitz by Doug Pavek, Jack Trudeau completed a 15 yard pass to David Williams for a touchdown and a first down at 0:22 left on the clock. Illinois called a time out. A pass to Cap Boso for two-points was incomplete, closing the score 21-16. The drive took 2:18 and went 76 yards in nine plays.

Chris White kicked off to the WP-18, where Kevin McKelvy returned it 13 yards, stopped by Keith Jones. Aina tackled Black going up the middle for a yard as the clock expired. The Army drive of one play for one yard took 15 seconds. At the half, Army led 21-16.

Halftime

At halftime, Army had 11 first downs, 145 rushing yards, 57 yards passing (3-3-0), no fumbles, one penalty for 15 yards, two punts, made two out of third down attempts, made one out of two fourth down conversions, had seven possessions, and 14:28 time of possession.

Illinois had 13 first downs, 0 rushing yards, 217 yards passing (21-28-2), one lost fumble, five penalties for 32 yards, no punts, made five out eight of third down attempts, made one fourth down conversion, and had five possessions.

Third Quarter

Stopa kicked off to the UI-1, where Keith Jones returned the football 20 yards, tackled by Gutierrez. Trudeau completed a five yard pass to Wilson, stopped by Scheyer. A pass to David Williams was incomplete. Trudeau ran wide to the right for seven yards out of bounds and a first down at the UI-33. David Williams caught a six yard pass reception before being tackled by Buckner out of bounds. Pavek and Biggins stopped Rooks after a nine yard shovel pass reception and first down at the UI-48.

Trudeau completed a twelve yard pass to Eric Wycoff for a first down at the WP-40, tackled by Biggins and Scheyer. Pavek stopped Rooks after a seven yard rush. Wilson ran five yards to the right for a first down at the WP-28, tackled by Malloy. Reggie Fullwood stopped Wilson after a six yard pass reception. Chronister tackled Wilson after an eight yard rush to the left for a first down at the WP-14.

Brock stopped Usher after a five yard reverse run to the right. Kleinhample tackled Wilson after a gain of four yards. A Trudeau pass to David Williams was incomplete into the end zone. On fourth and one on the WP-5, Trudeau sneaked up the middle for a four yard gain and first down on the WP-1, stopped by Scheyer. Army was called for being offside on the play, but Illinois declined the penalty.

Ray Wilson went wide right and broke two tackles for a touchdown at 10:01 on the clock. Illinois lined up to go for two, but were called for a delay of game and penalized five yards. Chris White converted the extra point kick and the Fighting Illini took the lead, 23-21. The drive of 4:59 took 15 plays in 79 yards.

Chris White kicked off to the WP-8, where Lampley returned it 22 yards before being stopped by Wycoff. On a pitch, Lampley ran to the right for six yards, tackled by Avery. Sebring stopped Healy for a gain of two yards out of bounds on the right sideline.

Healy rushed to the right for six yards and a first down at the WP-44, stopped by Sebring. Blitzed by Illinois, a Rob Healy pass intended for Benny White was intercepted at the UI-22 by Craig Swoope who returned it two yards before being tackled by Benny White at 8:46 on the clock. The Cadets drive took 1:07 over 14 yards in four plays.

Trudeau completed a four yard pass to David Williams, stopped by Buckner. Scheyer tackled Rooks after a gain of two on a delayed handoff. Buckner stopped Rooks after a three yard pass completion. On fourth and one at the UI-33, Chad Little punted 48 yards to the WP-19, where Tim Bourke downed it at 6:43 left to go in the third quarter. The Illinois drive took 2:03 with 7 yards on three plays.

A pitch to Clarence Jones went wide left out of bounds for six yards. Black rushed to the right for nine yards and a first down at the WP-32, stopped by Tagart. Black rushed for 27 yards up the middle and a first down at the UI-41, tackled by Ed White. African Grant stopped Black after a gain of eight yards up the middle. Lampley went right for five yards and a first down at the UI-27, stopped by Sebring and Tim Bourke.

Healy went right for eight yards, tackled by Glielmi. Clarence Jones ran up the middle, but Army was called for holding and penalized ten yards to the UI-29. On a pitch play, Glielmi and Swoope tackled Lampley after a three yard gain. On third and nine on a halfback option to the right side, Clarence Jones passed 26 yards to Scott Spellmon for a touchdown and a first down at 3:33 on the clock. Craig Stopa converted the extra point kick and Army retook the lead, 28-23. The Cadets drive took 3:10 and went 81 yards in 8 plays.

Stopa kicked off to the UI-1, where Keith Jones returned the ball 33 yards out of bounds. A Trudeau pass to Rooks was overthrown and incomplete. A pass to Wilson was incomplete. On third and ten, a pass to Boso was incomplete and almost intercepted. Little punted 41 yards to the WP-25 where it was fair caught by Darold Londo at 2:59 left in the third quarter. The Fighting Illini drive took 0:27 and no yards over three plays.

Jenkins tackled Black after a three yard gain to the left side. On a pitch, Lampley went wide right for six yards, stopped by Ed White and Swoope. Healy completed an eleven yard pass to Dickerson for a first down at the WP-45, tackled by Swoope. On a pitch play, Grant and Tagart stopped Wright after a one yard gain. Healy's pass intended for Black was incomplete. On third down and nine at the WP-46, Rob Healy went back for a pass and was sacked by Scott Davis for a loss of seven yards.

Rambusch punted 31 yards to the UI-30 to Usher, but the Fighting Illini were penalized five yards for being off side. On fourth and eleven, Rambusch punted 31 yards to the UI-25 to Usher, who returned it eight yards to the UI-33 with seven seconds left on the clock, tackled by Pavek. The Cadets drive took 2:49 in six plays for ten yards.

On the punt return, the Illini were penalized 15 yards for clipping back to the UI-18. Thomson tackled Rooks after a gain of four yards as the clock expired, with Army leading, 28-23.

Fourth Quarter

After going back for a pass, Trudeau ran four yards and was stopped by Scheyer. Sanders tackled David Williams after a four yard pass reception for a first down at the UI-30. Rooks went wide left out of bounds for a two yard gain. A deep pass attempt to David Williams was incomplete with Thomson defending.

On third and eight, a Trudeau pass to Anthony Williams was incomplete and almost intercepted by Thomson. Little punted 45 yards out of bounds at the WP-23 with 12:46 left on the clock. The Fighting Illini drive took 2:21 off the clock and went 14 yards in five plays.

Healy ran wide right for a seven yard gain, stopped by Teafatiller. Blondell tackled Lampley after a four yard gain off right tackle for a first down at the WP-34. Swoope stopped Healy after a three yard run to the left. Black went right for three yards, tackled by Glielmi. On third and four at the WP-42, Finch tackled Black after a two yard rush to the right. Rambusch punted 31 yards to the UI-27, where it was fair caught by Usher with 9:48 left in the game. The Army drive took 2:58 to go 19 yards in five plays.

Trudeau completed an eleven yard pass to Anthony Williams for a first down at the UI-38, stopped by Scheyer and Biggins. Scheyer tackled Ray Wilson after a run of five yards, and forced a fumble that was recovered by Jim Brock at the UI-42 with 9:19 on the clock. The Illinois drive 0:28 of two plays went 15 yards.

Sebring stopped Healy for a gain of one yard to the right. On a pitch play, Clarence Jones ran wide left for 18 yards and a first down at the UI-23, tackled by Davis. Healy ran wide right for 10 yards, but Army was penalized for holding back to the WP-30. On first and 17, Kelly and Sebring stopped Clarence Jones on a pitch play to the left after a gain of five yards. Army called a time out with 7:27 on the clock.

Bohm tackled Black after a three yard run. On third and nine at the UI-22, Healy's pass attempt to Benny White was broken up by Lawlor and incomplete. Craig Stopa converted a 39 yard field goal with 6:40 on the clock, extending the Cadets lead to 31-23. The Cadets drive of 2:40 went 20 yards in seven plays. Stopa kicked off on a line drive to the UI-14, where Keith Jones picked the football up and returned it six yards, tackled by Chip England.

Trudeau completed a five yard pass to Boso who was stopped by Buckner and Biggins. Rooks went up the middle for an eleven yard gain for a first down at the UI-36, tackled by Pavek. Trudeau went back for a pass, and ran out of bounds after gaining a yard. Lloyd Walker was injured on the play and left the field. Pierce caught a 20 yard pass reception for a first down at the WP-43, stopped by Pavek.

Scheyer tackled Rooks after a gain of seven on a delayed handoff. Boso caught a six yard pass reception and a first down at the WP-30, before being stopped by Gutierrez. Trudeau completed a seven yard pass to Keith Jones, tackled by Gutierrez. A pass attempt to David Williams was off his fingertips and incomplete.

On third and three at the WP-23, a pass to Rooks was broken up by Buckner and incomplete. Chris White attempted a 40 yard field goal, but the football hit the crossbar and was no good. Army football on the WP-23. There was 3:20 on the clock. The Illinois drive took 3:14 to go 57 yards in ten plays.

Lampley ran three yards to the left, stopped by Tagart. Black went up the middle for a one yard gain, stopped by Bohm. On a pitch, Lampley went wide right for a six yard rush out of bounds at the WP-33, stopped by Harkey. Ed White was injured on the play and left the field. An official measurement was made and Army earned a first down.

Glielmi tackled Lampley after a three yard run. Illinois called a time out with 1:49 to play. Black went left for four yards, tackled by Sebring. Illinois called a time out. On a pitch play, Davis stopped Lampley for no gain on third and three. Illinois called a time out with 1:36 on the clock.

Initially, the Army offense stayed on the field, then Coach Young had the punt team run out. Rambusch punted 32 yards to the UI-28, where Rob Dickerson tackled Usher after a one yard gain. The Army drive took 1:40 off the clock and went 17 yards in six plays.

Trudeau completed a nine yard pass to Anthony Williams who went out of bounds. With the clock at 1:20, a pass to David Williams was thrown over his head and incomplete. On third and one, Rooks caught a four yard pass reception for a first down at the UI-42, tackled by Scheyer.

The Cadets defense pressured Trudeau who threw incomplete; and he was called for intentional grounding. On second and 25, Trudeau completed a 19 yards pass to Pierce out of bounds at the UI-46. On third and six with 0:45 to play, Jack Trudeau hit David Williams at the WP-22 for a completed pass, and Williams ran across the goal line to for a 54 yard touchdown reception and a first down with 0:34 on the clock to make the score, 31-29, in favor of Army.

Illinois decided to go for two-points in an attempt to tie the game. As Jack Trudeau rolled to his right, Peel Chronister batted away the two-point pass attempt to David Williams. The Fighting Illini scoring drive took 53 seconds and went 71 yards over five plays.

An onside kick by Chris White was recovered by Dickerson at the WP-45. Healy took a knee for a loss of two yards as the clock ran out. Army won, 31-29.

Post-Game

"Victories like this are few and far between," said head football coach Jim Young after the game to his players. "You fought hard and earned everything you got. I'm proud of you."

Referring to Illinois quarterback Jack Trudeau, Young said, "We couldn't get a rush, so we knew we couldn't stop his possession-type passing game. We just tried to lay back and slow him down. I knew we would have to play hard to the last down to beat them."

"We thought we could get a big play," Young said of the halfback pass play. "But not two. My coaches didn't want me to call the play the second time. I wanted to make sure the other halfback could throw the ball."

Mike White, called the two big plays "perfectly executed by four different players and not so badly defended.'"

Army had 20 first downs, 291 yards rushing on 64 carries, 94 yards passing (5-8-1), had no fumbles, scored 24 points off of turnovers, were penalized four times for 50 yards, punted five times, made seven out of 14 third down attempts, made one of two fourth down conversions, and had 30:14 time of possession.

Illinois had 26 first downs, 77 yards rushing, 401 yards passing (38-56-2), lost two fumbles, punted three times, were penalized eight times for 67 yards, made nine out of 17 third down conversions, and made their only fourth down attempt.

Rob Healy rushed for 107 yards in 23 carries and scored one touchdown. Other rushers were William Lampley (16-76), Doug Black (15-73), Clarence Jones (8-31), Benny Wright (1-1), and Rob Dickerson (1-minus 7). Healy had three completions on six attempts for 35 passing yards and one interception.

William Lampley completed one pass for 33 yards and a touchdown. Clarence Jones completed one pass for 26 yards and a touchdown. Scott Spellmon caught two passes for 43 yards and one touchdown while Benny White had one reception for 33 yards and a touchdown. Dickerson (11 yards) and Lampley (7) each caught one pass.

Peel Chronister intercepted two passes with no returns that led to Army touchdowns. Doug Pavek and Jim Brock recovered fumbles that led to Cadets scores. Bob Kleinhample and Dave Scheyer forced the fumbles. Lloyd Walker had one sack. Jim Brock had 2.5 tackles for loss, while Scheyer and Lloyd Walker each had 1.0 TFL and Larry Biggins had 0.5 TFL.

Craig Stopa made one field goal for 39 yards. Stopa kicked off six times for a 66.2 average, with one touchback. Stopa converted all four points after touchdown kicks. Bit Rambusch punted five times for a 36.2 average. William Lampley returned four kickoffs for a 22.0 average, while Kevin McKelvy returned one kickoff for 13 yards. Rob Dickerson recovered the onside kick.

Dave Scheyer led the Cadets with 15 total tackles (nine solo), while Larry Biggins had ten, Doug Pavek made eight, and Jim Brock, Kurt Gutierrez, and Matt Buckner each had six tackles. Others with tackles included Peel Chronister (4), Bob Kleinhample (4), Tom Malloy (4), John Thomson (4), Bill Sanders (3), Lloyd Walker (2), Lou Dainty (1), Reggie Fullwood (1), Benny White (1), Chip England (1), and Rob Dickerson (1).

For Illinois, Thomas Rooks rushed for 35 yards in 10 carries, while Ray Wilson had 31 yards on eight attempts with one touchdown. Other rushers were Jack Trudeau (7-6) and Darryl

Usher (1-5). Jack Trudeau completed 38 passes on 56 attempts for 401 passing yards with three touchdowns and two interceptions.

Cap Boso caught nine passes for 52 yards and one touchdown, David Williams had seven receptions for 109 yards and two touchdowns, with Stephen Pierce (6-92), Anthony Williams (5-59), Ray Wilson (4-38), Thomas Rooks (4-25), Eric Wycoff (1-12), Keith Jones (1-7), and Darryl Usher (1-7).

Chris White missed on 40 yard field goal attempt. White converted on both PAT kicks. White kicked off four times for a 63.0 average, with one onside kick. Chad Little punted three times for a 44.7 average. Darryl Usher returned four punts for an 11.0 average. Keith Jones returned three kickoffs for a 19.7 average. Ray Wilson returned two kickoffs for 18.5 average.

Craig Swoope intercepted one pass and returned it two yards. Ron Bohm and Scott Davis each had a sack; each for a loss of seven yards. Mark Tagart had one tackle for loss of two yards.

Craig Swoope had eleven total tackles (eight solo), while Bob Sebring had nine, and Ron Bohm and Rob Glielmi each had seven. Others with tackles included Mark Tagart (6), Ed White (5), Todd Avery (4), Scott Davis (4), Guy Teafatiller (3), Mark Kelly (3), David Aina (2), Lance Harkey (2), Jim Blondell (2), African Grant (2), James Finch (2), Jay Lynch (2), and Tucker Jenkins (2). Mike McBain, Sean Lawlor, Keith Jones, Eric Wycoff, Tim Bourke, Chris White, and Curtis Claire each had one tackle.

Rob Healy was named Offensive Most Valuable Player of the Game while Peel Chronister was named Defensive Most Valuable Player of the Game. The *CBS Television* announcers awarded duo players of the game, Brian Healy and Jack Trudeau. It was Illinois' third consecutive bowl defeat in the 1980s; while Army's second consecutive bowl win. The game was considered the 8th top moment in Army Football in 2015 by the USMA athletic website.

The game saw 18 Peach Bowl records broken or tied. Team records tied or broken were: most combined points scored (60), most combined total offensive yards (863); most combined first downs (46), most combined passing yards (495), most points by a losing team (29); most passing first downs (19); most pass attempts (56); most passes completed (36); most passing yards (401); and tied most touchdowns passes (3).

Individual records set or tied (by Jack Trudeau) most passes attempted (56); most passes completed (36); yards passing (401); tied most touchdown passes (3); total offensive yards (407); (Cap Boso) most passes caught (9); (David Williams) tied most touchdown passes caught (2); and (Peel Chronister) tied most passes intercepted (2).

Army received 37 votes in the *Associated Press* Top 20 Poll, which would have ranked in 23rd place, while Army received votes in the *United Press International* Coaches Top 20 Poll.

Conclusion

Matt Zemek reflected on the bowl victory thirty years later, saying "Jim Young was a coach who found solutions to Army's problems In terms of a single-game performance, the 1985 Peach Bowl might have been his finest hour. Young wasn't just clever in this game; he realized something essential about coaching: Bold decisions aren't just valuable for what they bring to the table in terms of tactics; being bold can, in itself, inspire players to do more, to find levels of determination that might have been lacking. Bold coaching can stimulate players, generating the kinds of responses less creative coaching often fails to bring about."

Zemek continued, "This is really how Army won, and left the 1985 season saying, 'You know what? We had our struggles in big games, but we were still pretty darn good after all!' Yet, that's what Young and Army did against the Illini. Army snookered Illinois on two separate halfback-option passes. Army held that line by breaking up Trudeau's two-point pass conversion. In one moment, the prospect of losing -- not a game, but certainly a victory that meant so much to a band of brothers -- was wiped away. In one moment, a team that lost the two games it wanted to win in 1985 sealed the triumph which gave the season an enduringly satisfying taste. Not broken, but certainly battered, after losing to Air Force and Navy, the 1985 Army team responded to a series of disappointments with the resilience every West Point man hopes to display in a time of testing and trial."

Army started something big in 1984 with the conversion to the wishbone offense and going to and winning of two bowl games. The combined 1984 and 1985 seasons resulted in 17 victories for Army. Only 13 Division 1-A teams won more games over these two years.

Inside the Hotel Thayer, there is a plaque that recognizes the 1985 Army Football Team. It reads:

(Hotel Thayer Logo)

1985 PEACH BOWL FOOTBALL TEAM

(Front cover of the Peach Bowl Program)

ARMY 31 - ILLINOIS 29

COACH JIM YOUNG

WINNING SEASON 9 WINS, 3 LOSSES

MOST VALUABLE PLAYER:

OFFENSE - ROB HEALY (QB)

DEFENSE - PEEL CHRONISTER

DUTY HONOR COUNTRY

Chapter 8

The 1988 Football Season

Folks say in 2022 that the public seems to have a very short attention span. I think it always had, just with continuous news feeds bombarding everyone we may be more aware of than in the past. So the nation had thrilled with Army's success during the 1984 and 1985 seasons. The Army won only eleven games over the next two seasons, not really like the few wins as the Cadets had prior to the Wishbone seasons, but much of the public soon forgot about the Black Knights as they fell from the nation's sporting spotlight.

1986-1987 Army Football Teams

It would be hard for this Army fan to call the 1986 Army Football season a disappointment. With a 6-5 record, it was the third straight winning season - that had not happened at West Point since the 1966-1967-1968 seasons. Even more important, the Army Football Team returned the Commander-in-Chief's Trophy back to its original home for the second time in three years. So while the Cadets did not go to a bowl game, it was a successful season, especially beating, no, sinking Navy, 27-7.

Syracuse (5-6) were 6.5 point favorites in the opening game, but quarterback Tory Crawford rushed for 173 yards, Clarence Jones 92, and Andy Peterson 91, and won the Cadets' 13th straight victory at home, 33-28. In Evanston IL, Northwestern Wildcats (4-7) held Crawford to eleven yards rushing and forced two turnovers and a team total of 147 yards, upsetting 12 point favorite Army (by 12 points), 25-18.

Underdog (by 4.5 points) Wake Forest (5-6) defense held Crawford to 26 and the Cadets to 175 rushing yards and three lost fumbles to win, 49-7, and ending the home win streak. Crawford ran for 120 yards, Jones for 126, and Benny Wright for 103 to lead 19.5 point favorite Army over Yale (3-7), 41-24, in the Yale Bowl.

Crawford ran for 112 yards and Army 272 to help upset 16.0 favorite Tennessee (7-5), 25-21 in Knoxville. At home, head coach Jim Young went for a win rather than kick a field goal, and Crawford got sacked with time running out, as 9 point underdog Holy Cross (10-1) beat the Cadets, 17-14. Crawford had only 69 yards against the Crusaders.

Rutgers were 7 point favorites; dominated the first half, 21-0; had 21:33 time of possession, held Crawford to 53 yards, and won, 35-7, at Giants Stadium. Boston College was favored by 14.5 points, the Cadets lost five fumbles, Crawford had 47 rushing yards, and the Eagles won at West Point, 27-20.

Things got much better over the final three games. Crawford rushed for 165 yards over 8.5 point favorite Air Force, beating the Falcons, 21-11. Crawford rushed for 208 yards, all of it needed to beat underdog Lafayette, 56-48. Tory Crawford only rushed 94 yards, but for the first and only time this season, the Cadets beat someone while their quarterback did not get a 100 yard game. And that someone were the Midshipmen, for the second time in three seasons.

The 1987 season (5-6) opened with Holy Cross (11-0), and the Crusaders took advantage of two lost fumbles to score 20 points in the second quarter; extending their lead to 34-10 midway in the fourth, and upset 4.5 point favorite Army in its home opener. In a Saturday night road game, 6 point favorite Army beat Kansas State (0-10), 41-14. The Cadets then trumped The Citadel (4-7), 48-6. Tory Crawford rushed 120, 126, and 97 yards in those three games, 35.3% of Army's rushing yards.

In the second quarter at home against Wake Forest (7-4), Crawford was gang-tackled by the Demon Deacons defense and injured his knee. Mark Mooney came in and ran for 60 yards and a touchdown, passing for 45 yards on four out of five completions. But in the fourth quarter, he dislocated his big toe on his right foot, and Bryan Babb replaced him, as Army lost, 17-13. "I have never lost two quarterbacks," said Jim Young later. "You always figure you might lose one, but not two.

On the road against 19.5 point favored Boston College (5-6), Babb missed two touchdown receptions by inches in the final minutes, losing, 29-24, in his first varsity start. Back at home, Babb started against 19 point underdog Colgate (7-4) with a swollen groin, but left the game in the second quarter with a concussion. One week later, Bryan Babb underwent surgery to remove a cancerous tumor, missing the remainder of the season. The Red Raiders took at 12-3 lead into halftime, and held on as Mooney returned to the game, edging Army, 22-20.

For the next game at home against 6 point favorite Rutgers (6-5), there were seven starters injured and missing. Mooney had not practiced all week, but he started and rushed for 61 yards until he went down with a dislocated shoulder in the third quarter and a broken toe on his left foot.

Next man up Morrell Savoy rushed for 60 yards but was sacked twice for 22 yards, but led the Cadets to two touchdowns. On Army's final possession, Savoy went down with a sprained ankle. Fifth-string quarterback Bryan McWilliams finished the game, losing 27-14.

McWilliams started against 3.5 point favorite Temple (3-8), but he suffered a dislocated finger on his throwing hand in the first quarter. Otto Leone threw one time for a 64 yard touchdown that broke a 7-7 tie and won the game, 17-7, breaking the four game losing streak.

In Colorado Springs, Army did not lose a quarterback for the first time in six games, and Crawford started without practicing during the week. Air Force (9-4) had already beaten Navy, (23-13); and beat Army, 27-10, to take back the Commander-in-Chief's Trophy. Army then beat Lafayette (4-7), 49-37, and sunk 4 point underdog Navy (2-9) again, 17-3, to end the bizarre season of injuries. It was the Midshipmen's first season running the wishbone offense.

1988 Army Football Coaching and Support Staff

Head football coach Jim Young entered his sixth year at West Point assisted by offensive coordinator Jim Shuck (6th year) and defensive coordinator Bob Sutton (6th). Other assistant coaches included Johnny Burnett (10th, defensive secondary), Greg Gregory (7th, quarterbacks & offensive special teams), Jack Hecker (12th, wide receivers & punters), Tim Kish (5th, linebackers), Scott Lustig (7th, nose guards & special teams), Jay Robertson (5th, inside linebackers), John Simar (10th, halfbacks), and Bob Rogucki (6th, head strength & conditioning).

Other coaches included Gene McIntyre (assistant coach & fullbacks), Denny Doornbos (3rd, defensive tackles), Bob Forgrave (2nd, tight ends & offensive tackles), Lawrence Livingston (1st, centers & offensive guards), Andy Moeller (1st, defensive backs), Mark Charette (1st, graduate assistant & defensive line), Robert Duffy (1st, graduate assistant & linebackers), Dave Marks (1st, graduate assistant & running backs), and Craig Raymond (1st, graduate assistant & offensive line).

Other support staff included Ed Warinner (2nd, executive assistant to head coach & recruiting coordinator), Gene Benner (8th, head trainer), Dick Hall (14th, equipment manager), Robert Black (assistant trainer), Jim Wallace (assistant trainer), Mark Manley (assistant trainer), and Dave Lopez (assistant strength & conditioning).

Also, Colonel Barry Butzer (officer representative), Lieutenant Colonel Louis Csoka (officer representative academics), Lieutenant Colonel Jack Ryan (team physician), Lieutenant Colonel Jim Wheeler (team physician), Major Ken Beatty (officer representative academics), Captain Steve Heinecke (assistant officer representative), and Captain Jack Quinn (assistant officer representative).

1988 Football Schedule

The 1988 Army Football schedule originally published in the 1984 Army Media Guide consisted of Holly Cross (September 10th), Northwestern (September 17th), at Harvard (September 24th), Cornell (October 1st), at Yale (October 8th), open date (October 15th), Rutgers at Giants Stadium (October 22nd), Boston College (October 29th), Air Force (November 5th), at Vanderbilt (November 12th), and versus Navy at Philadelphia Veterans Stadium (November 26th).

By the beginning of the 1985 season, the game with Harvard had been cancelled with Northwestern moving to September 24th. A game at Washington in Seattle was scheduled for September 17th. Lafayette was now scheduled for October 15th.

By the December 1985, the Vanderbilt game had been moved to West Point from Nashville. The 1986 Army Media Guide replaced the October 1st game versus Cornell with one versus Bucknell University. Before the 1987 season began, the Army-Navy game was moved from November 26th to December 3rd; while the October 29th Boston College game was moved to November 19th to be played in Dublin Ireland.

All games were scheduled to be played on Saturday afternoons. At the beginning of the 1988 season, the following games were scheduled to be televised: Holy Cross *(Jefferson Pilot)*, Northwestern (tape delay, *Madison Square Market Network*), Rutgers (tape delay, *Madison Square Market Network*), Air Force (tape delay, *Madison Square Market Network*), Boston College (*ESPN*), and Army-Navy (*CBS Television*).

Bowl Games

There were 17 post-season bowl games for the 1988 season running from the California Bowl on December 10th to the Orange and Sugar Bowls on the night of January 2nd. Army had no commitments to any bowl game. To be bowl eligible, The Cadets would have to win six or more games. The games against Division 1-AA Holy Cross, Bucknell, Yale, and Lafayette teams would count towards this eligibility, but might count against Army when compared to other team's schedules.

Spring Practice

Army lost 27 lettermen and 14 starters from the 1987 team. Returning were 45 lettermen, 22 on offense, 19 on defense, and two kickers. There were two starters on offense and six on defense returning. "This time last year, we were looking for help on the defense," said Jim Young as spring practice ended."

"This year, it's just the opposite. We have more experienced players on defense than we do on offense. I think major concerns offensively are the quarterback and the offensive line in general, with center being a key element. On defense, the secondary is the major concern."

"We have a number of quarterback candidates with some game experience, but none who have distinguished themselves. It's difficult to say now where we'll be at quarterback come September. Hopefully, someone is going to step forward and prove he's capable of doing the job on a steady basis."

On the offensive line, Young expressed confidence that the Cadets will have a good one this season. He stated, "The offensive line is starting to come along. Few, if any, positions are set coming out of spring practice."

Reflecting on spring practice, Jim Young said "We've done a lot of experimenting and a lot of scrimmaging. I've been pleased with that aspect of it, although I don't think we're set a football team. This spring, as a coaching staff and a team, we've worked hard. We made a lot of progress. I think we had the finest spring here yet - finding out what we can do, finding out who can play."

Summer

On June 29th, 1,334 men and women arrived at West Point as members of the USMA Class of 1992 to start Cadet Basic Training or Beast Barracks. A total of 61 freshmen (or plebes) were listed in the 1988 Army Football Media Guide. Thirty of the freshman were products of the USMA Preparatory School at Fort Monmouth NJ. Ten would be listed on the roster for the Army-Navy game program. One, halfback Edrian Oliver, would letter for the 1988 season.

Captains and Preseason Recognitions

Seniors split end Chris Destito and linebacker Troy Lingley were named team captains for the 1988 season. Lingley made the preseason All-East first team by Street & Smith. Senior punter Bit Rambusch was named to the 1987 season All-East first team by the *Associated Press* and ECAC. Rambusch was a preseason All-East first team for a number of publications. Senior defensive tackle Josh Haines was an honorable mention to the *Associated Press* All-East team for the 1987 season.

The coaching staff also felt that senior kicker Keith Walker, senior linebacker Greg Gadson, senior linebacker Chuck Schretzman, junior fullback Ben Barnett, junior split end Sean Jordan, junior defensive back O'Neal Miller, and sophomore halfback Mike Mayweather would be likely all-star candidates during the 1988 season.

Season Predictions

The projected starting lineup on July 1st for the Army offense was split end Sean Jordan, left tackle Mike Braun, left guard Bill Gebhards, center Frank Brunner, right guard Jack Frey, right tackle Mike Karsonovich, tight end Rob Horn, left halfback Mike Mayweather, right halfback Calvin Cass, fullback Ben Barnett, and quarterbacks Mark Mooney, Otto Leone, or Bryan McWilliams.

The projected starters for the Army defense were tackles Josh Haines and Jon Brunner; nose tackle Dan Cooney; linebackers Greg Gadson, Chuck Schretzman, Troy Lingley, and John Robb; cornerbacks Mike Thorson and Earnest Boyd; and safeties Darryl Scherb and O'Neal Miller.

"In my opinion, it's [the 1988 season] a much tougher schedule than last year," head football coach Jim Young said during the summer. "I thought last year the schedule was a challenge each week, but they were fairly level opponents. This year, I think there is still a challenge each week. There's Washington, certainly a big team. The next week is Northwestern, and they're big. And the first one, Holy Cross, is a team that has beaten us two years in a row. That's a tough start."

"At the end of the season, there's Rutgers, which is tough for us. Then there's Air Force, Boston College, and Vanderbilt, which has a Heisman Trophy candidate [quarterback Eric Jones]. And of course, Navy. On the surface, in looking back over the last five years, it's one of the toughest schedules that we've been asked to play."

None of Army's regular season opponents were ranked in either the *Associated Press* Top 20 Poll or *United Press International* Coaches Top 20 Poll. Boston College was receiving votes in the *Associated Press* Poll that would rank them 29th. Washington entered the *Associated Press* Top 20 Poll on September 6 at 20th, and would climb on September 13th to 17th ranking (and #19 in the *United Press International* Coaches Top 20 Poll) prior to playing Army. No other Division 1-A opponent was in the polls except for bowl opponent Alabama (see next chapter).

For Division 1-AA opponents, Holy Cross was ranked first in the preseason NCAA Division 1-AA Football Committee Top 20 Poll. Lafayette would enter the poll after winning their second straight game on September 19th at #12.

Holy Cross

Army (0-0) hosted #1 Holy Cross (1-0) on Saturday afternoon, September 10th, before 33,136 fans at Michie Stadium. Corey McPherrin, Bob Casio, and Steve Martin were the announcers for Jefferson-Pilot Television. Holy Cross began its season the weekend before by beating Rhode Island, 49-7, its twelfth win in-a-row. Mark Mooney was the starting Army quarterback. Army was favored to win.

Army's Keith Walker made a 36 yard field goal early in the first quarter. Late in the first period, Holy Cross tied the game with a 34 yard field goal. Late in the second quarter, Walker converted a 36 yard field goal. With 41 seconds left in the first half, Walker made a 31 yard field goal to boost the Cadets lead to 9-3 at halftime. There were two Army fumbles inside the HC-5 during the first half that prevented more scoring.

Midway through the third quarter, Mike Mayweather rushed three yards for a touchdown to complete a 16 play, 86 yard drive, with Walker making the extra point to extend the score to 16-3. Otto Leone completed a 68 yard pass to Sean Jordan for the final scoring, 23-3, on the next-to-last play of the third quarter. Jim Young won his 100th game as a head football coach. The Crusaders crossed the fifty yard line only three times during the game.

Army had 22 first downs, 269 yards rushing on 74 carries, 102 passing (5-8-0), lost one fumble, punted five times, converted on five out of 19 third downs, and had 33:33 time of possession. Holy Cross had 9 first downs, 54 yards rushing, 165 passing (13-28-2), one lost fumble, six punts, had ten penalties for 109 yards, and made two out of 12 third down attempts. Mayweather rushed for 135 yards, while Ben Barnett had 85. Jordan caught two passes for 73 yards, while Calvin Cass two pass receptions for 20 yards.

Holy Cross would finish the 1988 season with a 3-1 Colonial League record for third place. The Crusaders would lose to Lafayette, 20-28, the weekend after the Army loss, and drop out of the NCAA Division 1-AA Top 20 Poll on September 20th. Holy Cross would then win eight straight games at Princeton, versus Harvard, versus Dartmouth, versus Lehigh, at Brown, at Colgate, versus Bucknell, and finishing at home against Northeastern, 52-30. The Crusaders finished the 1988 season with a 9-2 overall record in head football coach Mark Duffner's third season. In the final NCAA Division 1-AA Top 20 Poll, Holy Cross was ranked 19th.

Washington

#17/#19 Washington (1-0) welcomed Army (1-0) on September 17th to Husky Stadium in Seattle on Saturday afternoon with 66,128 spectators attending. The Huskies won their opening game at Purdue, 20-6, the weekend before. Otto Leone was the starting quarterback for Army. Washington was favored by 20.5 points.

The Huskies opened the scoring at 9:17 in the first quarter with a one yard rushing touchdown. Early in the second period, Washington made a 33 yard field goal. With 2:30 to go in the first half, Keith Walker converted on a 45 yard field goal attempt to make the score 10-3, after a 10 play, 48 yard drive. The Huskies drove down the field in a little more than two minutes to score on a ten yard touchdown pass with 18 seconds left to make the halftime score, 17-3.

On the third play of the Cadets opening possession in the second half, Otto Leone hit Sean Jordan for a 56 yard touchdown pass, with Walker making the point after touchdown kick to close the score to 17-10. The Huskies responded with a nine yard touchdown run mid-way through the third period.

The Cadets responded in the opening minutes of the fourth quarter when Calvin Cass rushed six yards for a touchdown to make the score, 24-17. Army drove down the field, but were stopped inches short of a first down on the UW-2. Late in the game, the Cadets drove again down the field and threatened to tie, when Chico Fraley intercepted a deflected Leone pass and returned it 72 yards for the final score, 31-17.

Army had 17 first downs, 275 yards rushing, 91 passing (4-13-2), one lost fumble, made nine out of 19 third downs, punted four times, and had 30:39 time of possession. Washington had 20 first downs, 130 yards rushing, 183 yards passing (17-25-1), no fumbles, punted five times, and converted on five out of 13 third downs. Leone had 73 yards rushing, while Mike Mayweather had 61, Ben Barnett 55, and Cass rushed for 40 yards. Jordan caught three passes for 81 yards. Mayweather and Barnett suffered injuries during the game.

Washington would finish the 2018 season with a 3-5 Pacific 10 Conference record, tied for sixth in the conference with

Oregon. After the wins to Army and San Jose State (35-31), Washington was ranked #16. Losses to #2 UCLA (17-24), #3 Southern California (27-28), and Oregon (14-17) dropped the Huskies from the polls on October 23rd. Washington would finish with an overall record of 6-5 in the 14th season under head football coach Don James. The Huskies did not play in a bowl game for the first time in ten seasons.

Northwestern

Army (1-1) hosted Northwestern (0-2) on September 24th in front of 36,978 fans on a Saturday afternoon. The Wildcats entered the game against the Cadets after losing to Duke (21-31) and Air Force (27-62). Army was favored by 13.5 points. Otto Leone was the starting quarterback for Army, with starters Mike Mayweather and Ben Barnett out with injuries.

There was no scoring in the first quarter, partly due to an Army fumble inside the NU-25. Keith Walker made a 33 yard field goal with 12:21 on the clock in the second quarter. Eight minutes later, Northwestern responded with a 59 yard drive by scoring on an eight yard touchdown run to take a 7-3 halftime lead.

Mike Thorson intercepted a Wildcats pass on the first play of the third quarter. Bryan McWilliams came into the game at quarterback for Army. The Cadets drove 64 yards down the field, fueled by 54 yards from fullback John Barth. Calvin Cass plunged over the goal line from the one yard line with 10:06 left in the third period. A two-point run failed, making the score, 9-7.

Pat Davie recovered a fumble on the NU-30. Paul Capriotti rushed two yards for a touchdown at 4:57 in the third quarter to extend the score to 16-7. Northwestern missed a 45 yard field goal attempt. In the final three minutes of the game, Cass rushed one yard for a touchdown for the final score and Army win, 23-7.

Army had 23 first downs, 446 rushing yards on 77 carries, no passing yards (0-4-0), one lost fumble, punted four times, made eight out of 17 third downs, and had 33:06 time of possession.

Northwestern had 15 first downs, 121 yards rushing, 183 passing (13-25-2), one lost fumble, converted on five out of 14 third downs, punted five times, and had 55 yards of penalties. Calvin Cass rushed for 142 yards, while John Barth had 90, Otto Leone 83, and Paul Capriotti rushed for 57.

Northwestern lost to Indiana (17-48) the next weekend. In their final seven games, they tied Minnesota and beat Wisconsin and Purdue. Northwestern finished with a 2-5-1 Big Ten Conference record, tied for seventh place with Ohio State. The Wildcats had an overall record of 2-8-1 in head coach Francis Peay's third season.

Morris Herbert interviewed head football coach Jim Young after the season ended. Young said, "The first three games were the key to whether or not we'd have a successful season. I felt we could easily be 0-3 or 1-2 after playing Holy Cross, Washington, and Northwestern. But, when we won two of those first three, I was convinced we'd have a pretty good year. Our defense carried us for the first three games until the offense started to jell."

Bucknell

Army (2-1) hosted Bucknell (0-3) on Saturday afternoon, October 1st, in front of 38,924 fans at sold out Michie Stadium. The Bison had lost their opening three games of the 1988 season to Villanova (17-30), Colgate (13-14), and at Penn (35-38). Army was favored to win. Bryan McWilliams was the starting quarterback for Army; and would start all the remaining games during the season.

Bryan McWilliams opened the scoring with a five yard touchdown run at 3:00 on the clock in the first quarter, with Keith Walker making the extra point kick. John Barth rushed for a one yard touchdown 16 seconds later to extend the score to 14-0.

Bucknell completed a 53 yard touchdown pass in the early part of the second quarter to close the lead to 14-7. Less than three minutes later, Sean Jordan rushed 16 yards on a reverse for a touchdown. Walker made a 31 yard field goal with 3:45 left in the first half, extending the score to 24-7. Barth rushed for a seven yard touchdown at 2:26 on the clock. Bucknell made a 33 yard field goal as time ran out to make the halftime score, 31-10.

Barth scored on his third touchdown early in the third quarter on a one yard plunge. McWilliams broke free for a 41 yard touchdown run to up the score to 45-10 midway through the third quarter. Early in the fourth quarter, plebe halfback Edrian Oliver scored on a two yard run, while junior halfback Pat Mangin scored on a one yarder to finish the scoring at 58-10. It was the most passing yards in a game this season.

Army had 25 first downs, 403 yards rushing on 74 attempts, 106 passing (4-5-0), no fumbles, punted twice, made nine out of 15 third downs, and had 33:56 time of possession. Bucknell had 21 first downs, 25 yards rushing, 336 passing (24-42-2), lost three fumbles, punted four times, and made half of their twelve third downs attempts.

McWilliams rushed for 116 yards, Calvin Cass 66, Anthony Thomas ran for 54, and Paul Capriotti 42 yards. The Cadets scored on nine of their eleven possessions, and four out of five Bison turnovers became Army touchdowns. Five Army quarterbacks, six halfbacks, and three fullbacks played in the game.

Bucknell finished the season with a 2-3 Colonial League record tied for third with Lehigh and Colgate. Bucknell finished strong, winning three of their last four games at Columbia (21-7), versus Davidson (21-13), and at Lehigh (35-32), before losing their final game at Holy Cross (7-38). The Bison finished with an overall record of 3-7 in head football coach George Landis third and last season.

Yale

Army (3-1) traveled to New Haven CT to play Yale (0-2-1) on Saturday afternoon, October 8th, on natural grass in the Yale Bowl in front of 17,898 spectators. Yale started their 1988 season with a tie at Brown (24-24); then had two losses to Connecticut (0-41) and at Navy (7-41). Army was favored to win by 29.5 points.

Midway through the first quarter, Keith Walker made a 42 yard field goal. Less than seven minutes later, the Bulldogs responded by making a 20 yard field goal to tie the game at 3-3. Early in the second quarter, Ben Barnett plunged over the goal line from the one yard line, with Walker making the point after touchdown kick, to make the score, 10-3, at halftime.

At 10:26 in the third quarter, Mike Mayweather rushed five yards for a touchdown. Four minutes later, Bryan McWilliams completed a 32 yard touchdown pass to Sean Jordan, extending the Army lead to 24-3. Walker converted a 28 yard field goal early in the fourth period.

Yale's Buddy Zachery broke a tackle at the line of scrimmage and ran 82 yards for a touchdown less than three minutes later. After a lost Cadets fumble, the Bulldogs quickly scored again on a six yard pass and a two-point reception at 6:35 left in the game to close the score to 27-18. Army responded with a 60 yard drive as McWilliams ran in an eleven yard touchdown to make the final score, 33-18.

"We are happy to get out of here with a victory," said head football coach Jim Young after the game. Army had 26 first downs, 426 yards rushing, 32 passing (1-3-1), one lost fumble, punted twice, were penalized eleven times for 100 yards, converted ten out of 16 third downs, and had 32:02 time of possession.

Yale had 14 first downs, 191 yards rushing, 97 yards passing (11-21-1), lost one fumble, punted five times, had 60 yards of penalties, and made five out of 15 third downs. Mike Mayweather had 155 yards rushing, while Ben Barnett 93, Bryan McWilliams 61 yards, and Calvin Cass ran for 39 yards. Buddy Zachery rushed for 105 yards, the first Army opponent to do so this season.

The Bulldogs finished with a 3-3-1 Ivy League record, good for fifth place. Yale beat Columbia, 24-10, on October 15th and finished a successful season by winning at Harvard, 26-17. The Bulldogs had an overall record of 3-6-1 in Carmen Cozza's 24th season.

Lafayette

Army (4-1) hosted #5 Lafayette (5-0) on Homecoming Weekend, Saturday afternoon, October 15th, in sold out Michie Stadium with 40,570 fans in attendance. The Leopards started the 1988 season with five straight victories over Kutztown (54-7), versus #1 Holy Cross (28-20), at Columbia (49-3), at Colgate (42-35), and at Bucknell (52-35). The win against the Crusaders vaulted them into the NCAA Division 1-AA Top 20 Poll at #12. Army was favored to win.

Mike Mayweather scored on an eight yard touchdown run with 9:29 on the clock in the first quarter, finishing an 80 yard drive in 13 plays. Keith Walker converted the PAT, making the score, 7-0. The Leopards responded early in the second period with a seven yard touchdown pass to tie the score. In the final minutes of the first half, Ben Barnett pushed two yards over the goal line for a touchdown, finishing a 92 yard drive, making it 14-7 at halftime.

Midway through the third quarter, Walker converted a 25 yard field goal to extend the lead to 17-7. With 14:14 left in the game, Barnett scored from the one yard line to finish a 68 yard drive and to up the score to 24-7.

Over three minutes later, the Cadets defense stopped the Leopards drive and forced a 48 yard field goal that made it 24-10. Lafayette drove down the field in the final minutes, scoring on a six yard touchdown run with 53 seconds left. Army recovered the onside kick to win, 24-17.

Army had 23 first downs, 450 yards rushing, 13 yards passing (1-4-1), no lost fumbles, punted three times, made eleven out of 18 third downs, and had 33:35 in time of possession. Lafayette had 24 first downs, 112 rushing yards, 286 yards passing (24-42-4), no fumbles, punted twice, and made seven of 14 third downs.

Barnett had 159 rushing yards, Mayweather 156, Bryan McWilliams had 95 yards, and Calvin Cass rushed for 34 yards. O'Neal Miller intercepted two passes. This was Army's 57th straight game it had scored in. The 450 yards were the most rushing yards in a game this season.

Lafayette dropped down to #7 in the Division 1-AA Poll. The Leopards beat Mercyhurst College (60-18) the next weekend, then were tied by Cornell, 21-21, and lost to Penn, 17-31, to drop out of the poll on November 8th. Lafayette finished with a 5-0 Colonial League record and the league championship. The Leopards had an 8-2-1 overall record in Bill Russo's eight season, but did not compete in the playoff.

Rutgers

Army (5-1) traveled down near the city to play Rutgers (4-2) on Saturday afternoon, October 22nd, at Giants Stadium before 31,318 spectators. Rutgers was the home team. Rutgers opened the 1988 season beating #15 Michigan State, 17-13. The Scarlet Knights then lost a close one to Vanderbilt. 30-31, at Giants Stadium.

Traveling to Happy Valley, Rutgers upset #15 Penn State, 21-16; then beat Cincinnati at home, 38-9. The Scarlet Knights split two road games, losing at Syracuse (20-24) while beating Boston College (17-6). Rutgers was favored by 10 points.

Army opened the scoring at 9:28 on the clock in the first quarter with a Keith Walker 45 yard field goal. Rutgers fumbled the football at the WP-12, where Greg Gadson recovered it.

The Cadets then dominated the second quarter with three straight touchdown runs. After a 48 yard pass from Bryan McWilliams to Mike Mayweather alone on the sideline, Mayweather scored two plays later on a four yard run with 9:37 left in the half. The Cadets started a drive on the RU-35, and ten plays later Mayweather ran for a one yard touchdown with 3:40 on the clock.

Sean Jordan burst for a 41 yard reverse run for a touchdown with 1:50 before halftime. Keith Walker made all three PATs to make it a 24-0 game at halftime. The Cadets had rushed for 237 yards in the first half, holding Rutgers to 63 yards rushing and nine passing. "The best half of football we have played all year," said Jim Young.

The Scarlet Knights woke up to score a three yard touchdown run at 9:31 in the third quarter. With 1:10 left in the period, Walker made a 21 yard field goal to make it 27-7 going into the final stanza. Reserve quarterback Scott Erney entered the game for the Scarlet Knights and engineered three scoring drives in the fourth quarter.

Rutgers kicked a 29 yard field goal and ran in a seven yard touchdown to make it 27-17 midway through the fourth period. In the final minutes, the teams traded touchdowns, first with Mayweather's third in the game from the eight yard line after a time consuming drive, and the Scarlet Knights one yard run to end the scoring, 34-24.

"Army came to play and they outplayed us in every phase of the game," said Rutgers head football coach Dick Anderson after the game. "They played aggressive, physical, hustling, disciplined football."

Army had 17 first downs, 372 yards rushing, 48 passing (1-2-0), lost one fumble, punted five times, made only five out of 15 third down attempts, were penalized 15 yards, and had 31:50 time of possession. Rutgers had 19 first downs, 166 yards rushing, 181 passing (19-36-1), one lost fumble, punted seven times, had seven penalties for 70 yards, and made eight out of 18 third downs. Mayweather rushed for 115 yards, Bryan McMillian had 93, Ben Barnett ran for 84, and Jordan rushed for 41 yards.

After losing to Army, the Scarlet Knights went into a tailspin, losing three more games to Temple (30-35), at Pitt (10-20), and #4 West Virginia (25-35 at Giants Stadium); before a season ending win against Colgate at home (41-22). Rutgers finished with an overall record of 5-6 as an Independent in Dick Anderson's fifth season.

Air Force

Army (6-1) hosted Air Force (5-3) on Saturday afternoon, November 5th, in sold out Michie Stadium, with 40,660 attending. It rained during the game. The Falcons went 2-2 in their opening games - winning at Colorado State (29-22), losing at San Diego State (36-39), beating Northwestern (62-27) at home, and losing at home to Wyoming (45-48). Air Force then won three in a row to New Mexico (63-14), Navy (33-24), and at Utah (56-49). At #2 Notre Dame, the Falcons lost, 13-41.

A win against Army would allow Air Force to win the Commander-in-Chief's Trophy. Air Force was favored by 1 points and was leading the nation in rushing yards per game. Army was receiving votes in the *Associated Press* Top 20 Poll for 29th place.

There was no scoring in the first quarter. Dee Dowis completed a 35 yard touchdown pass to halfback Albert Booker with 11:50 in the second quarter. Army responded as Bryan McWilliams ran a bootleg to the right for 46 yards. Two plays later, McWilliams rushed for a five yard touchdown with 7:48 to go in the half. Keith Walker converted the extra point kick to tie the score at 7-7.

On the next Cadets drive, Mike Mayweather rushed 52 yards into the red zone. With 2:48 on the clock, Ben Barnett went over from the one yard line for a touchdown and a Cadets lead that they would never give up. At halftime, it was 14-7 Army.

There was no scoring in the third quarter. A minute into the fourth quarter, McWilliams scored on a four yard touchdown run. Nine minutes and one second later, Mike Mayweather went in for a touchdown from the one yard line to make it 28-7 with 4:56 to play in the game. Dee Davis hit wide receiver Greg Cochran for a 21 yard touchdown pass, followed by a two-point run by halfback Greg Johnson, to end the game with an Army victory, 28-15.

Army had 18 first downs, rushed for 394 yards, no passing yards (0-3-0), no lost fumbles, punted five times, made six out of 17 first downs, and had 35:26 time of possession. Air Force had 13 first downs, had 176 yards rushing, 92 passing (4-10-0), one lost fumble, punted eight times, and made two out of eleven third down attempts.

Mayweather had 192 yards, outgaining the entire Air Force team, while McWilliams ran for 95, Calvin Cass gained 65 yards, and Barnett rushed for 45 yards. Greg Johnson led the Falcons with 46 yards rushing. Greg Cochran caught two passes for 35 yards, while Albert Booker had one reception for 35 yards.

Air Force lost their remaining three games to Brigham Young (31-49), at Texas El Paso (24-31), and at Hawai'i (14-19) to finish with a 3-5 Western Athletic Conference record tied for sixth place with San Diego State. The Falcons finished the 1988 season with a 5-7 overall record in Fisher DeBerry's fifth season.

Bowl Game Interest

The 7-1 record brought Army into the bowl picture for the first time since the 1985 season. A newspaper article on November 10th reported that Army was under consideration for the Sun Bowl to play Alabama (6-2). Also under consideration were Pittsburgh (5-3), Indiana (6-2-1), Colorado (7-2), and Syracuse (7-1).

Vanderbilt

Army (7-1) hosted Vanderbilt (3-5) on Saturday afternoon, November 12th, in sold out Michie Stadium in front of 40,339 fans. The Commodores opened the season with two wins against Mississippi State and at Rutgers, then lost three in-a-row at #13 Alabama, Duke, and at #15 Georgia. The highlight of the season was the 24-9 victory over #20 Florida on national television. However, close losses followed to Ole Miss (28-36) and at Kentucky (13-14) before Vanderbilt traveled to West Point. Army was favored by 3.5 points.

Bryan McWilliams opened the scoring at 10:38 in the first period with a 34 yard rush for a touchdown to finish a 71 yard drive. Keith Walker made the PAT. The Commodores completed a twelve yard touchdown pass with four minutes to go in the first quarter to tie the game. Vanderbilt took the lead with a 24 yard field goal with 10:00 left in the first half, 10-7. In the final minutes, Mike Mayweather scored on a one yard touchdown run for Army to retake the lead, 14-10, at halftime.

Walker made a 46 yard field goal on the opening drive in the third quarter. The Commodores scored on a 21 yard touchdown pass, but the two-point run attempt failed, making the score, 17-16, going into the fourth quarter. At 5:57 left in the game, the Commodores Johnny Clark made a 21 yard field goal to take the lead, 19-17.

With 3:08 left in the game, Army was on the WP-37. It took three plays to get into Vanderbilt territory. With a third and three on the VU-39. McWilliams ran around the right end for twelve yards. A pass to tight end Doug Baker gained 13 more. Mayweather rushed for twelve yards. McWilliams ran in from the two yard line for a touchdown with 1:28 to play. Walker's extra point kick made the final score, 24-19.

"We were thinking field goal," said Jim Young after the game. "You have to in that situation. Keith Walker was on the sideline, preparing himself for his first chance to be a last-minute hero.

"Everyone had it in their minds that we were going to score," remarked Bryan McWilliams. "At first, we were all thinking field goal, but when we moved downfield, I knew we were going to get it in."

"I've had several come-from-behind wins in my career," said Young. "However, back then then we drove the length of the field with the number one passing team in the nation [Purdue quarterback Mark Herrmann]. With the wishbone, this was the best come-from-behind win."

"Coming back and winning like that is the greatest feeling," said offensive guard Jack Frey, who was a starter in Army's stunning upset of Tennessee in the 1986 season. "We had shown that we had arrived in football."

Army had 20 first downs, 303 rushing yards, 27 passing (2-6-0), no lost fumbles, punted four times, made nine out of 17 third downs, and had 30:44 time of possession. Vanderbilt had 23 first downs, 94 yards rushing, 287 yards passing (23-37-2), no fumbles, punted twice, and made six out of 16 third downs.

McWilliams rushed for 145 yards, while Mayweather had 77, Ben Barnett ran for 57, and Calvin Cass rushed for 31 yards. The win solidified a berth opposite Alabama in the John Hancock Sun Bowl. With an 8-1 record, it was the best start for Army since the 1967 season.

The Commodores lost their final games at Memphis State (9-28) and to rival Tennessee (7-14) in Nashville. Vanderbilt finished with a 2-5 Southeastern Conference record tied for eighth place with Kentucky. The Commodores finished the 1988 season with an overall record of 3-8 in Watson Brown's third season.

Bowl Game Bids

On November 12th, unofficial bowl pairings were released and publicized. Official invitations would not go out until November 19th. Army received information that they would likely play Alabama in the John Hancock Sun Bowl.

Boston College

Both Boston College and Army traveled to Dublin on Tuesday, November 15th and held practices there for the next three days. Both returned home on flights the night of the November 19th. More than 250 Cadets, cheerleaders, and the West Point Glee Club attended with the official Army party. A substitute mule was provided by the Mule Society of Great Britain.

Events included a charity ball, a golf outing, a reception with US Ambassador Margaret Heckler, a concert with the Eagles band and our glee club, horse racing, and a black-tie benefit dinner to aid the Irish Arthritis Foundation (they received $375,000 from the game)..

The Eagles had beaten only Cincinnati (41-7) and Pitt (34-31) during the season. Boston College had lost to four ranked teams, #8 Southern California (7-34), at #16 Penn State (20-23), at #6

West Virginia (19-59), and #15 Syracuse (20-45). The Eagles had also lost at Texas Christian (17-31), Rutgers (6-17), and at Tennessee (7-10).

This was the first ever Emerald Isle Classic, part of the on-going millennium celebration, or 1,000th anniversary of the founding of the city of Dublin. The game was advertised as the first pairing of two Division 1 teams ever played in Europe (actually not, Richmond played Boston University in London on October 16th).

The game was played in a historic natural grass rugby stadium (wonderful according to the locals), and it was expected to draw 15,000 American tourists in a wide variety of tours of the city and country. The game and other activities generated about $30 million for Dublin businesses.

Army (8-1) and Boston College (2-7) played on Saturday afternoon, November 19th, before 42,525 spectators on the tall grass of Lansdowne Road Stadium (capacity 53,000). Roger Twibell and Lee Corso were the announcers on *ESPN* who televised the game back to the States on a half-hour delay (it was also re-shown later that night). Army was the designated home team and was favored by 2.5 points.

The Eagles tailback Mike Sanders scored on a 53 yard touchdown run mid-way through the first quarter. Two minutes later after a Cadets 69 yard drive was stopped, Keith Walker made a 26 yard field go to close the score to 7-3. Early in the second period, Boston College converted a 23 yard field goal.

Midway in the second quarter, the Eagles had a 49 yard pass completion that led to a four yard touchdown run to make it 17-3. An interception by O'Neal Miller put Army in scoring position late in the first half. With 42 seconds left in the first half, Calvin Cass rushed six yards for a touchdown and Walker made the point after touchdown kick for a 17-10 halftime score.

Mike Mayweather fumbled on the first play of the second half. Boston College recovered it, resulting in a one yard touchdown run, on a short 28 yard drive. The Cadets responded when Ben Barnett plunged over the goal line from the one yard line, making it 24-17.

Boston College scored on a one yard touchdown run early in the fourth quarter. Mayweather returned the kickoff 72 yards to set up his three yard touchdown run to close the score to 31-24. With four minutes left in the game, the Cadets drove down to the BC-5, but failed to convert a fourth down. Boston College responded with a final one yard touchdown, the third one on the day by fullback Ed Toner, to win the game, 38-24.

"They made the big plays and we didn't," said linebacker Greg Gadson after the game. "It was lack of intensity on our part. They had it more than we did."

Boston College quarterback Mark Kamphaus had not played since breaking his jaw two months earlier in a game against Texas Christian. "He won the game," said head football coach Jim Young. "He did everything a quarterback is supposed to do."

"The atmosphere charged people up," said Boston College head football coach Jack Bicknell. "I thought the atmosphere was electrifying. The environment was great. They didn't always know when to cheer, but they were cheering."

Army had 22 first downs, 233 yards rushing, 69 passing (5-10-0), two lost fumbles, punted three times, made ten out of 18 third down attempts, and had 32:58 time of possession. Boston College had 21 first downs, 215 yards rushing, 194 passing (15-20-2), no fumbles, punted twice, and made six out of ten third downs.

Mayweather rushed for 88 yards, Cass 78, Barnett ran for 46, and Bryan McWilliams had ten yards. The Cadets had their seven game winning streak snapped and it was the least rushing yards in a game this season.

Boston College lost at Temple, 28-45 to finish their 1988 season with a 3-8 overall record as an Independent in Jack Bicknell's eighth season. Army received the official invitation from the John Hancock Sun Bowl committee to play Alabama after the game and accepted it.

Navy

Navy won its first two games of the season to James Madison (27-14) and Delaware (30-3), The Midshipmen then lost two straight games to Temple (7-12) and at The Citadel (35-42). Navy beat Yale, 41-7. The Midshipmen then lost five straight, at Air Force (24-34), at Pitt (6-52), versus #1 Notre Dame (7-22) in Baltimore, at #13 Syracuse (21-49), and at South Carolina (8-19).

Army (8-2) would play Navy (3-7) on Saturday afternoon at 2 pm EST on December 3rd in Philadelphia at Veterans Stadium before 68,435 fans. It would be the 89th game between the two rivals. *CBS Television* broadcasted the game nationally, with Brent Musburger (play-by-play), Pat Haden (analyst), and John Dockery (sideline reporter) announcing. Army was favored by 10 points.

Navy came in the game in a spoiler role in their second season running the wishbone offense. If the Midshipmen won, then all three service academies had won and lost a game to the other two, the Commander-in-Chief's Trophy would be tied for the first time since 1976, and Air Force would retain the actual trophy it won during the 1987 season. An Army win would capture the trophy outright. Navy was the home team.

Young told Hebert in January, "We asked the football letterman from the classes of 1939, 1959, and 1969 to write to the team before the Navy game. The response was almost 100%. Every player receive a packet of those letters and telegrams on the Friday evening before Navy. I want everyone who wrote to know how very much all of us on the coaching staff and the Army team appreciate their thoughts and encouragement. That great support was an important part of our success in '88."

On the Midshipmen's second possession of the game, Navy drove down to the WP-28 before being stopped. Ted Fundoukos made a 44 yard field goal at 3:44 left in the first quarter. Army responded with a 16 play, 63 yard drive, finishing when Ben

Barnett plunged over the one yard line for a touchdown at 12:05 in the second period. Keith Walker made the point after touchdown kick as the Cadets took the lead, 7-3. Mike Mayweather went over 1,000 yards on the first play of the second quarter during the scoring drive.

Fundoukos converted a 34 yard field goal at 3:57 to close the score to 7-6. Long runs by Mayweather and Calvin Cass moved the Cadets into the red zone. With 2:03 left in the first half, Walker made a 22 yard field goal for an Army halftime lead of 10-6.

Midway through the third quarter, the Cadets defense forced Navy to punt from the N-18, giving the offense a short field. Walker converted on a 35 yard field goal to extend the score to 13-6 for his second of the game. Fundoukos scored his third field goal, this time from 34 yards, with 1:36 on the clock in the third period, to make it 13-9.

The Cadets had to punt on their first possession of the fourth quarter. On the second possession, they drove down the field. Faced with a fourth and two on the N-25, head football coach Jim Young decided to go for it rather than kick another field goal. Bryan McWilliams ran off to the right side for four yards. Two plays later, McWilliams kept on an option play and rushed for an eight yard touchdown with 6:01 left in the game for a 20-9 Cadets lead to finish off the 59 yard drive.

Navy drove in eight plays, gaining 64 yards to the WP-2. James Bradley scored on a two yard touchdown run at 1:35 on the clock. It was Navy's first touchdown since the third quarter of the 1986 game. The Midshipmen pass attempt for two-points failed. Mark Mooney fair caught the onside kick. The Cadets ran out the clock over the next three plays. Final score, Army 20, Navy 15.

"I'm proud of this team," said Young after the game. "Navy should be proud of the way it played, too. Both teams went at it with all they had." Later in January, Young said, "It's hard to single out any individual in this year's game. It was really the Team - and the leadership from top to bottom - that did the job for us. The key to winning was our mental preparation, and keeping that mental edge on every play throughout the game."

Army had 17 first downs, 244 yards rushing, 30 passing (2-3-0), no lost fumbles, punted three times, made eight out of 18 third down attempts, and had 29:59 time of conversion. Navy had 14 first downs, 164 yards rushing, 77 passing (7-15-0), no fumbles, punted three times, and made three out of 15 third downs. It was the fourth straight Navy game that the Cadets had not turned the ball over.

Bryan McWilliams rushed for 99 yards, while Ben Barnett had 55, Calvin Cass 50, and Mike Mayweather ran for 42 yards. McWilliams completed two out of three passes for 30 yards. Doug Baker (17 yards) and Sean Jordan (13) each caught one pass.

For Navy, Alton Grizzard rushed for 62 yards, Luther Archer ran for 54, Deric Sims 27, and James Bradley rushed for 21. Grizzard completed seven out of 15 passes for 70 yards. Archer caught four passes for 28 yards, while Jerry Dawson (14 yards), Kevin Voss (15), and Carl Jordan (10) each had one reception.

Navy finished the 1988 season with an overall record of 3-8 as an Independent during head football coach Elliot Uzelac's second season.

1988 Season Statistics

The following are the Cadets team offensive statistics for the 1988 season, excluding the bowl game. On offense, the team had 308 points (28.0 average); 229 first downs (203 rushing, 20 passing, and 6 by penalty); rushed for 3,815 yards (346.8 ypg) on 786 attempts (4.9 ypa) and 35 touchdowns; passed for 518 yards on 25 completions on 61 passes and 4 interceptions for 47.1 ypg, 8.5 ypp, 20.7 ypr, and 3 touchdowns; had 4,333 yards total offense on 847 plays, 393.9 ypg, 5.1 ypp, and 38 touchdowns; had 53 penalties for 409 yards; had 21 fumbles and lost 7 of them; had an average time of possession per game of 32:26; and converted 90 out of 190 third downs (47.4%).

On defense, the team allowed 197 points (17.9 average); 193 first downs (81 rushing, 103 passing, and 9 by penalty); 1,448 yards rushing (131.6 ypg) on 411 attempts (3.5 ypa) and 14 touchdowns allowed; 2,081 passing yards on 170 completions on 301 passes and 17 interceptions for 189.2 ypg, 6.9 ypp, 12.2 ypr, and 8 touchdowns; allowed 3,529 total yards on 712 plays, 320.8 ypg, 5.0 ypp, and 22 touchdowns; opponents had 59 penalties for 538 yards; converted 55 out of 150 third downs (36.7%); forced 12 fumbles and recovered 8 of them; and returned 3 interceptions (42.3 average).

For Cadets special team statistics, punted 40 times for a 39.8 average; returned 37 kickoffs (19.7 average); returned 20 punts (4.8 average); made 15 out of 18 field goal attempts; and made 35 out of 36 point after touchdown attempts. For opponents' special teams statistics, punted 49 times for a 37.5 average; returned 54 kickoffs (21.7 average); and returned 23 punts (10.0 average).

Mike Mayweather had 1,022 yards rushing in 191 carries for a 92.9 ypg, while Bran McWilliams ran for 749 in 140 attempts for 68.1 ypg, Ben Barnett rushed for 679 yards (61.7) and Calvin Cass gained 582 yards (52.9). Other individual rushing statistics were Otto Leone (55-223), Paul Capriotti (26-127), John Barth (25-117), Sean Jordan (11-86), Callian Thomas (15-77), Willie McMillian (2-28), Robert Westbrook (5-26), Dave Foye (9-22), Mark Phillips (1-15), Bit Rambusch (1-15), Bryan Babb (5-14), Pat Mangin (8-11), Tom Schermerhorn (2-9), Mark Mooney (5-8), Morrell Savoy (1-5), Myreon Williams (2-1), Edrian Oliver (2-0), and Anthony Noto (1-minus 1).

Mayweather rushed for 9 touchdowns, while McWilliams had 8, Barnett made 6, and Cass had 4 touchdowns. Others scoring rushing touchdowns were Barth (3), Jordan (2), Capriotti (1), Mangin (1), and Oliver (1).

McWilliams completed 13 out of 31 passes for 255 yards with one touchdown and two interceptions. Leone had ten completions out of 25 attempts for 249 yards with two touchdowns and two interceptions. Babb completed one pass for nine yards. Mooney completed one out of two pass attempts for five yards. Cass attempted two passes, both of them incomplete.

Jordan caught twelve passes for 289 yards with three touchdowns. Doug Baker caught seven receptions for 90 yards. Cass had two receptions for 20 yards. Others catching one pass were Mayweather (48 yards), Todd Mulville (46), Chris Destito (16), and Mark Phillips (9).

Mayweather returned 13 kickoffs for a 25.0 average and a long of 72 yards, while Oliver had eight returns for an 18.9 average and Capriotti returned six times for a 19.3 average. Others returning kickoffs were Cass (3 returns for 61 yards), Ed Givens (2-33), Schermerhorn (2-24), Taylor Gray (2-7), and Barth (1-12). Paul Wynn returned 14 punts for a 4.7 average, while Earnest Boyd had six returns for a 5.0 average. No touchdowns were scored on punt or kickoff returns.

Greg Gadson recovered four fumbles, while Troy Lingley, Pat Davis, Mike O'Toole, and Kevin Reed recovered one fumble each. O'Neal Miller, Will Huff, Jon Brunner, and George Godfrey each forced one fumble. Earnest Boyd intercepted five passes for 37 yards, while O'Neal Miller had four interceptions for 32 yards. Others making interceptions were Mike Thorson (3-26), John Robb (2-11), Greg Gadson (1-21), Pat Davie (1-0), and Troy Lingley (1-0). No touchdowns were scored on interceptions or fumble returns.

Earnest Boyd had ten pass deflections, while Mike Thorson and Darryl Scherb each had five. Others who had pass deflections were Chuck Schretzman (4), O'Neal Miller (3), Josh Haines (3), John Robb (2), Jon Brunner (2), Troy Lingley (1), Pat Davie (1), Greg Gadson (1), Bert DeForest (1), and Andy Olson (1). There were no kicks or punts blocked.

Keith Walker made 15 out of 18 field goal attempts, with a long of 46 yards. Walker made 35 out of 36 point after touchdown kicks. The team did not attempt any two-point conversion attempts. Bit Rambusch punted 40 times for an average of 39.8 and a long of 56 yards. Army had punts or kicks blocked.

Keith Walker led the team in scoring with 80 points, followed by Mike Mayweather with 54 and Bryan McWilliams with 48. Others scoring were Barnett (36), Jordan (30), Cass (24), Barth (18), Capriotti (6), Oliver (6), and Mangin (6).

Troy Lingley led the team with 161 total tackles (72 solo), followed by O'Neal Miller with 114, Pat Davie had 91, Greg Gadson 82, and Chuck Schretzman with 81 tackles. Others with tackles included Dan Cooney (79), Mike Thorson (77), Darryl Scherb (66), Josh Haines (61), Earnest Boyd (47), Will Huff (45), John Robb (44), Jon Brunner (24), Mike O'Toole (16), Bob Wagner (16), and Steve Stark (12).

Also, Bert DeForest (11), George Godfrey (10), Bit Rambusch (10), Andy Olson (7), Ed Givens (7), and Malcolm Perry (4). Kevin Reed, Craig Romanowski, Mike Sullivan, Rod Ofte, and John Nadolski each had three tackles. Having two tackles were Tim Ladouceur, Sterritt Armstrong, Greg Mogavero, Paul Wynn, and Chip England. Percy Coard and Scott Moore each had one tackle.

Greg Gadson led the team with six tackles for loss. Others with TFLs were Haines (5), Schretzman (4), Coney (4), Huff (3), Brunner (3), Robb (2), Lingley (2), Scherb (2), Davie (1), Boyd (1), DeForest (1), and Godfrey (1).

The following Cadets started every game on offense during the 1988 season, including the bowl game: tight end Doug Baker, split end Sean Jordan, tackle Mike Braun, center Frank Brunner, guard Bill Gebhards, and halfback Calvin Cass.

On defense, the following started every game during the 1988 season, including the bowl game: nose tackle Dan Coney, tackle Will Huff, linebackers Troy Lingley, Chuck Schretzman, and Greg Gadson, defensive backs Earnest Boyd, O'Neal Miller, Darryl Scherb, and Mike Thorson.

The Cadets were first nationally in total turnovers; and third in rushing yards behind Nebraska and Air Force. Nationally, Keith Walker finished ninth in field goal completion percentage. Mike

Mayweather was ranked tenth nationally in kickoff returns and 16th in all-purpose yardage.

Army averaged 38,435 attendance in six home games, 42,013 in two away games, and 47,426 in three neutral site games. Scoring by quarters was 47-33 (1st), 109-67 (2nd), 95-37 (3rd), and 85-89 (4th).

The 1988 team established a new Army record of 63 consecutive games without being shutout. The team tied the record for most games won, accomplished in ten other seasons, last by the 1985 team. Army also tied the series record against both Navy (41-41-7) and Air Force (11-11-1).

At the end of the 2020 season, the 1988 team still held the following Army season records: fourth in rushing attempts; fourth in rushing yards per game; fifth in passing yards per completion: seventh in rushing yards; eighth in passing yards per attempt; and tenth in rushing touchdowns.

Individuals holding Army season records included: (Mike Mayweather) sixth in kickoff return average and tied for seventh in number of 100 yard rushing games; (Otto Leone) fourth in passing yards per completion, eighth in passing yards per attempt, and ninth in passing efficiency; (Keith Walker) tied for third in field goals made, tied for fourth in field goal completion percentage, and tied for sixth in field goals attempted; (Troy Lingley) second in total tackles; (Earnest Boyd) tied for first in passes defended, tied for fourth in pass breakups, and tied for ninth for interceptions made; and (Greg Gadson) tied for second in fumbles recovered.

Awards and Recognitions

Punter Bit Rambusch was named to the *Associated Press* All-East first team. Sophomore halfback Mike Mayweather was named to the All-East second team by the *Associated Press*. Ben Barnett, Jack Frey, Sean Jordan, Mike Thorson, and O'Neal Miller were honorable All-East selections by the *Associated Press*.

Lettermen

The following players received letters for the 1988 season: (Seniors) Bryan Babb, John Barth, Earnest Boyd, Mike Braun, Frank Brunner, Jon Brunner, Chris Destito, Chip England, Jack Frey, Greg Gadson, Bill Gebhards, Rob Horn, Mike Karsonovich, Troy Lingley, Mark Mooney, Scott Moore, Pat Muschamp, Mark Phillips, Bit Rambusch, Darryl Scherb, Chuck Schretzman, Ed Schultz, Mike Sullivan, Steve Svoboda, and Keith Walker.

(Juniors) Pete Andrysiak, Sterritt Armstrong, Ben Barnett, Dan Cooney, Pat Davie, Bert DeForest, Dave Foye, George Godfrey, Taylor Gray, Josh Haines, Will Huff, Sean Jordan, Tim Ladouceur, Pat Mangin, O'Neal Miller, Todd Mulville, Rod Ofte, Andy Olson, Mike O'Toole, Yale Peebles, Mike Preisser, Carlton Rice, Tom Schermerhorn, Karl Schreiber, Steve Stark, Mike Thorson, Bob Wagner, and Paul Wynn.

(Sophomores) Doug Baker, Paul Capriotti, Calvin Cass, Greg Cleveland, Ed Givens, Joe Gudenburr, Otto Leone, Mike Mayweather, Bryan McWilliams, Larry Misa, Greg Mogavero, Chester Nadolski, Anthony Noto, Malcolm Perry, Bret Petkus, Kevin Reed, and John Robb; and (Freshman) Edrian Oliver.

Army Branch Selections

The following seniors are members of the USMA Class of 1989 who graduated and were commissioned in the following branches: (Field Artillery) Bryan Babb, Mike Braun, Jon Brunner, Chip England, Greg Gadson, Bill Gebhards, Rob Horn, Corwin Jackson, Troy Lingley, Scott Moore, Pat Muschamp, and Darryl Scherb; (Infantry) Frank Brunner, Chris Destito, Mike Karsonovich, Chuck Schretzman, and Mike Sullivan; (Air Defense Artillery) Earnest Boyd, Mark Mooney, and Bit Rambusch; (Engineers) Steve Svoboda; (Aviation) Jack Frey; and (Military Intelligence) John Barth. Also, Ed Schultz, a December 1988 graduate of the USMA Class of 1988, went into Field Artillery.

Conclusion

Sophomore Calvin Cass said after the 1988 season, "I don't think anybody visualized the type of season we had. After we beat

Rutgers, we knew we had a team that could beat anyone. Now we expect success."

"Perhaps the real key to our success this year was our leadership of the senior class," said Young after the season. "To be successful, you know Army must have strong leadership from our first classmen. The Class of '89 took charge before we played our first game. Their attitude and dedication molded a team spirit that made this team as good as any I've coached at West Point. This quality of oneness, togetherness, a feeling that the team can accomplish any task, overcome any setback, that's what set the 1988 Army team apart."

"It's the best team since 1958," said Earl Blaik in an article on November 20th. "I'm very happy. They're my team." On May 6, 1989, Blaik passed away in a nursing home in Colorado Springs at the age of 92.

Army had beat the Midshipmen three games in a row, won the Commander-in-Chief's Trophy, and tied the record of nine victories in a regular season for the first time since 1949 season. The Cadets returned to West Point to take term end examinations and had three and a half weeks to prepare for the Crimson Tide of the University of Alabama in the bowl game on Christmas Eve.

Chapter 9

1988 Sun Bowl Game

The Sun Bowl Selection Committee issued official invitations on November 19th to the University of Alabama (8-3) and the United States Military Academy at West Point (9-2) football teams to play in the John Hancock Sun Bowl at 12:30 pm EST on, December 24th in El Paso TX in the Sun Bowl Stadium.

Sun Bowl History

The game would be televised nationally on *CBS Television*. The network had broadcasted the bowl game continuously since 1968. This would be the 55th edition of the Sun Bowl football game. It was reported that each school received a million dollar payment for its bowl participation. Alabama would be the home team.

The Sun Bowl was first played on January 1, 1945, and with the Sugar and Orange Bowls, are the second-oldest bowl games behind the Rose Bowl. After three games at El Paso High School Stadium, it moved to Kidd Field, the stadium for the University of Texas at El Paso and initially played on January 1st or 2nd.

Since the 1958 edition, is has been played in late December. In 1963, the bowl game moved to Sun Bowl Stadium, on the campus of UTEP, where it remains to this day. John Hancock Financial became the bowl's first title sponsor in June 1986.

Alabama Football History

Alabama began playing college football in the 1892 season and this was in its 96th overall and 55th season as a member of the Southeastern Conference. The Crimson Tide had never played Army before this bowl game. Alabama has claimed eleven and four unclaimed national championships and 22 conference championships. Ten players had been inducted into the College Football Hall of Fame.

This would be Alabama's 41st bowl game with a 22-15-3 record, the last being on January 2, 1988 with a 24-28 loss to Michigan in the Hall of Fame Bowl last season. The Crimson Tide had played in the Sun Bowl in 1983 and 1986, winning each time versus Southern Methodist (28-7) and Washington (28-6). Alabama had played in ten different bowls, including the Rose, Cotton, Orange, Sugar Liberty, Bluebonnet, Gator, Aloha, Sun, and Hall of Fame Bowls.

1988 Alabama Crimson Tide Football Team

The 1988 season coaching staff was led by second year head football coach Bill Curry, first year offensive coordinator Homer Smith, and second year defensive coordinator Don Lindsey. Other members of the coaching staff were Phil Savage, Bob Ianello, Andy Christoff, John Guy, Tommy Bowden, Mac McWhorter, Jim Fuller, TJ Weist, Jeff Fitzgerald, Ted Roof, Gary Otten, Chip Wisdom, Larry New, Kelvin Croom, Jack Fligg, and Byron Braggs. Homer Smith was the Army head football coach during the 1974-1978 seasons.

Alabama finished the regular season with a 4-3 Southeastern Conference record that was tied for fourth place with Florida. Their overall record was 8-3. The Crimson Tide began the season ranked #14/#16 and won its first game at Temple, 37-0.

Another road game against Texas A&M on September 17th was postponed until December 1st when Coach Curry declined to make the trip, worried about oncoming Hurricane Gilbert. The hurricane made landfall in Mexico, and the weather was clear in College Station that Saturday, earning him the name from Aggie fans as "Chicken Curry."

The Crimson Tide won its next two games, versus Vanderbilt (44-10) and at Kentucky (31-27). Alabama lost defensive back Gene Jelks and running back and Heisman Trophy candidate Bob Humphrey to injuries during the game against the Commodores.

On Homecoming, October 8th, versus Mississippi, #12/#14 Alabama suffered a 12-22 loss, the first one ever to Ole Miss in the state of Alabama. This dropped Alabama out of the rankings in both polls.

Alabama went on to three straight victories at Tennessee (28-20), versus Penn State at Legion Field (8-3), and at Mississippi State (53-34). Quarterback David Smith had missed three games due to a knee injury but returned for the game against the Volunteers. Alabama was ranked #19/#16 on October 24th before the game with the Bulldogs.

The #18/#16 Crimson Tide then hosted #13/#16 Louisiana State on November 5th and lost in a close game, 18-19 before a national television audience on *CBS Television*. A victory against Division 1-A Southwestern Louisiana (17-0) followed before #17/#15 Alabama met #7 Auburn at Legion Field on November 25th. The Tigers won that game, 15-10.

#20/#15 Alabama then met Texas A&M at Kyle Field in College Station, beating the Aggies, 30-10, to end the regular season. Alabama came into the bowl game ranked #20 in both the *Associated Press* and *United Press International* Coaches Top 20 Polls.

Alabama averaged 175.1 yards passing and 154.6 yards rushing per game during the 1988 season. On defense, the Crimson Tide averaged 191.7 yards passing and 95.7 yards rushing per game.

Leading the Crimson Tide in rushing were Murray Hill with 778 yards and five touchdowns and David Casteal with 368 yards and six touchdowns. Left-handed quarterback David Smith had completed 135 out of 223 passes for 1,592 yards with seven touchdowns and seven interceptions.

Alabama had a quartet of quality receivers, including LaMonde Russell (29 receptions for 404 yards and one touchdown), Greg Payne (33-442-2), Marco Battle (28-367-0), and Howard Cross (19-226-3).

Derrick Thomas led the Crimson Tide defense with 88 tackles, followed by Keith McCants (78), Lee Ozmint (67), Tommy Cole (66), and John Mangum (66). Thomas has twelve TFLs while Cole has eleven. Willie Wyatt and Bethune had each recovered two fumbles during the season. Ozmint and Kermit Kendrick had each intercepted six passes, while Mangum had intercepted five. Thomas led the team in sacks.

Pierre Goode led the team in kickoff returns with 15 for a 22.3 average and one touchdown return. Chris Mohr had punted 58 times for a 42.7 average and a long of 63. Philip Doyle had made all 28 point after touchdown kicks this season. Doyle had made 19 out of 31 field goal attempts with a long of 52 yards. Freshmen Steve Webb, Darryl Pickett, and Stacy Harrison have led the team in kickoff coverage.

Guard Larry Rose and linebacker Derrick Thomas were selected to the All-SEC first team football team by the *Associated Press*. Derrick Thomas was a consensus All-American selection by eight different organizations; and would be elected to the College Football Hall of Fame in 2014, 14 years after his death.

Regarding his thoughts of Alabama being heavily favored in the bowl game, Army team captain Chris Destito said before the game, "We had heard all of that and maybe some of us believed it for a while. During our first practice in El Paso, we were hitting as hard as I've ever seen us hit. We were ready and we believed we could win."

"We must be able to stop them offensively, since it will be difficult for us to score many points, and not make many mistakes," said Jim Young before the game. "Defensively, they are big and quick. Offensively, they lost their star running back [Humphrey], but they have a big offensive line and an accurate passer."

Pre-Game

The starting offense for Alabama was split end Greg Payne, left tackle John Fruhmorgen, left guard Larry Rose, center Roger

Shultz, right guard Chris Robinette, right tackle Terrill Chatman, tight end Howard Cross, flanker Marco Battle, fullback Kevin Turner, tailback Murry Hill, and quarterback David Smith. Robert Stewart actually started at fullback for Turner.

The starting defense for Alabama was defensive tackle Tommy Cole, nose guard Willie Wyatt, defensive end George Bethune, linebackers Derrick Thomas, Greg Gilbert, Keith McCants and Willie Shephard, and defensive backs Spencer Hammond, Lee Ozmint, Charles Gardner, and Kermit Kendrick.

The starting offense for Army was split end Sean Jordan, tight end Doug Baker, tackles Mike Braun and Mike Karsonovich, guards Jack Frey and Bill Gebhards, center Frank Brunner, fullback Ben Barnett, halfbacks Calvin Cass and Mike Mayweather, and quarterback Bryan McWilliams.

The starting defense for Army was nose guard Dan Cooney, defensive tackles Josh Haines and Will Huff, linebackers Pat Davie, Greg Gadson, Troy Lingley, and Chuck Schretzman, and defensive backs Earnest Boyd, O'Neal Miller, Darryl Scherb, and Mike Thorson.

The officials for the 1988 Sun Bowl were from the Big Eight Conference and included JC Louderback (referee), Frank Gaines (umpire), Mark Hittner (linesman), George Hayward (line judge), Terry Porter (field judge), Duane Osborne (side judge), and Willie Weisbrook (back judge).

The Alabama team captains were Derrick Thomas and David Smith. Army team captains were Chris Destito and Troy Lingley. Verne Lundquist (play-by-play), Pat Haden (analyst), John Dockery (sideline reporter), and Jim Nantz (sideline reporter) were the announcers for *CBS Television*.

Alabama was favored by 14 points to win. Army dressed 129 players, while Alabama dressed 110. Though the Crimson Tide were the home team, they wore their white jerseys and pants with crimson helmets. Army wore their gold helmets, black jerseys, and gold pants. Two replacement mules were obtained by Army for the game, Solomon and Miss Elegant Ass.

Army won the toss and elected to receive. Alabama decided to defend the north goal. The weather was 50 degrees, with the wind blowing out of the southwest at 15-20 mph (official scoring sheet) or 5 mph (television broadcast). There were 48,719 spectators (94% capacity) at Sun Bowl Stadium on Christmas Eve, December 24th. The game kicked off at 10:12 am MST.

First Quarter

Philip Doyle kicked to the WP-4, where Mike Mayweather returned the football 26 yards, stopped by John Mangum. Bryan McWilliams on a keeper went around the left end and gained one yard, tackled by Derrick Thomas. Mayweather got the pitch and went around the right end for twelve yards and a first down to the WP-43, stopped by Lee Ozmint.

Mangum tackled Mayweather on a counter play after a two yard run. Mayweather was slightly hurt and limped off the field. Ben Barnett rushed up the middle for 51 yards and a first down to the UA-4, stopped by Charles Gardner. Keith McCants tackled Barnett after a three yard gain. Willie Shephard stopped Barnett for no gain.

On third and one, Mike Mayweather ran on a counter play over the right guard for a one yard touchdown at 12:04 on the clock. Keith Walker converted the extra point kick to make it 7-0 Army. The Cadets drive took seven plays to go 70 yards in 2:56. Bit Rambusch kicked off to the UA-2, where Pierre Goode returned it 20 yards, stopped by Mike O'Toole.

Troy Lingley tackled Murry Hill after a gain of two. David Smith's pass intended to Greg Payne on the sideline was overthrown. On third and eight, Smith completed a 19 yard pass to Hill for a first down, stopped by Mike Thorson.

A pitch to Hill around the right end gained two yards out of bounds, stopped by Pat Davie. Smith completed a ten yard pass to

Marco Battle down the left sideline out of bounds for a first down, tackled by Earnest Boyd.

Goode ran a counter over the left tackle for a gain of one yard, stopped by Davie. Smith overthrew Todd Richardson down the left sideline. On third and nine at the WP-44, Smith's pass went through the hands of LaMonde Russell. The Crimson Tide took a time out with the 10:05 on the clock. Chris Mohr punted 44 yards into the end zone for a touchback with the clock at 9:56. The Alabama drive went 34 yards in eight plays over 2:08.

A pitch to Mayweather went six yards, stopped by William Amelong. Mangum tackled Calvin Cass after a gain of five yards and a first down at the WP-31. McWilliams went around the right end for five yards, stopped by McCants. Mayweather went up the middle for a gain of four, stopped by McCants. On third and one at the WP-40, McWilliams went around the left end for five yards and a first down at the WP-45.

McWilliams fumbled but recovered the football for no gain. Shephard tackled Mayweather over left guard after a gain of four yards. On third and six on the WP-49, Derrick Thomas dropped Bryan McWilliams for a loss of two yards. Bit Rambusch punted 38 yards to the UA-15, where Murray Hill made a fair catch at 5:55 on the clock. The drive went 27 yards in eight plays that took 4:01.

On a pitch, Hill went around the left end for no gain, stopped by Josh Haines. Lingley tackled Hill after a three yard run. On third and seven, Smith faked a draw and then completed a 14 yard pass to Payne on his knees for a first down.

Chuck Schretzman tackled David Casteal who ran around the right end for two yards. Smith's pass to Robert Stewart across the middle was dropped. On third and eight at the UA-45, Smith completed a 13 yard pass to Payne along the right sideline for a first down at the UA-47, stopped by Thorson.

Stewart ran up the middle for a gain of three, stopped by Will Huff. Smith faked a draw and completed a 15 yard pass for a first down to Payne who went out of bounds on the right sideline at the WP-36. Smith overthrew Prince Wimbley on the left side. Hill ran over the right guard for a gain of 25 yards and a first down to the WP-11, stopped by O'Neal Miller.

Lingley tackled Hill after a one yard gain up the middle. On the next play, Alabama was called for holding and penalized ten yards. Smith's pass into the end zone was incomplete. On third and 19 at the WP-20, Smith overthrew Payne in the back of the end zone. Philip Doyle made a 37 yard field goal with 1:25 on the clock to make it 7-3 in favor of Army. The Alabama drive took 14 plays to go 65 yards in 4:30.

Philip Doyle kicked off to the WP-1, where Mike Mayweather returned it 30 yards, tackled by Jimbo Salem. Tommy Cole tackled Mayweather after a two yard run up the middle. Barnett went over the right guard for a gain of two yards, stopped by Thomas. Barnett rushed for 25 yards and a first down at the UA-40, tackled by Kermit Kendrick as the clock expired. At the end of the first quarter, the score was Army 7, Alabama 3.

Second Quarter

Barnett rushed six yards up the middle, stopped by McCants. McWilliams ran four yards and a first down at the UA-30, tackled by McCants. On first and ten, Bryan McWilliams ran around the left end for a 30 yard touchdown at 14:02. Keith Walker made the extra point kick to extend the score to 14-3. The drive went 69 yards in six plays over 2:23.

Bit Rambusch kicked off to the UA-1, where Pierre Goode returned it 26 yards, stopped by Greg Cleveland. Dan Cooney sacked Smith for a loss of ten yards. Smith completed an eleven yard pass over the middle to Kevin Turner, stopped by Jon Brunner and Lingley. On the next play, Army was called for off sides and penalized five yards. On third and four, Payne caught a pass for a six yard gain and a first down at the UA-40.

Haines tackled Turner after a gain of six yards up the middle. On a draw play, Hill rushed for 18 yards and a first down at the

WP-36, stopped by Miller. Smith completed a five yard pass to Payne, tackled by Miller. Greg Gadson tackled Hill after a three yard run over the left tackle. On third and two, Alabama was called for illegal procedure and penalized five yards. On an Army blitz, Smith completed a 25 yard pass for a first down to Russell who went out of bounds on the left sideline at the WP-8.

Haines tackled Casteal after a gain of one yard up the middle. Huff stopped Stewart up the middle after a gain of three yards. On third and goal at the WP-4, Greg Gadson tackled David Smith for a loss of one yard. Philip Doyle made a 22 yard field goal at 7:33 on the clock and closes the score to 14-6. The Alabama drive was twelve plays in 67 yards, taking 6:29.

Philip Doyle kicked off into the end zone, where Mike Mayweather returned the football 23 yards, stopped by Darryl Pickett. Willie Wyatt tackled Mayweather after a four yard run over left guard. McWilliams gained five yards around the right end, stopped by Amelong. On third and one at the WP-32, Mayweather ran on a counter play over the right guard for a two yard gain and a first down, stopped by Thomas Rayam.

On a pitch, Cass gained seven yards around the left end, stopped by Kendrick. Steve Webb tackled Barnett after a gain of two up the middle. On third and one from the WP-43, Cass ran on a counter play over the left guard for a gain of two yards and a first down, stopped by Amelong.

On a pitch play, Cass ran three yards around the left end, tackled by Kendrick. On a pitch going to the right side, Mayweather ran eight yards around the end and a first down at the UA-44, tackled by Webb.

On a counter play over the right guard, Mayweather ran six yards, stopped by Thomas. Mayweather was injured on the play and left the field. Calvin Cass overshot a halfback pass to a wide open Sean Jordan. On third and four from the UA-38, Barnett went over left tackle for nine yards and a first down, stopped by Lee Ozmint.

Charles Gardner stopped Cass after a gain of three yards over the left guard. Greg Gilbert tackled Mayweather after a two yard run over left guard. On third and five, a McWilliams pass to Doug Baker was incomplete. Keith Walker attempted a 41 field goal, which was blocked by Derrick Thomas at 1:47 on the clock. The Cadets drive took 15 plays over 53 yards in 5:46 time of possession.

On first and ten at the UA-24, Smith's pass to Russell went through his hands. Smith completed a 19 yard pass to Wimbley for a first down at the UA-43, stopped by Darryl Scherb.

O'Neal Miller nearly intercepted an attempted pass from David Smith. Miller broke up an attempted pass reception by Howard Cross. Alabama took a time out with 1:14 on the clock. On third and ten from the UA-43, Smith completed a 14 yard pass to Battle for a first down at the WP-43, stopped by Lingley.

Battle caught a 22 yard pass reception on his back for a first down at the WP-21. Alabama took a time out with 0:54 left in the first half. Smith completed a 14 yard pass to Payne for a first down at the WP-6, stopped by Thorson.

David Smith completed a six yard touchdown pass to Marco Battle at 0:35 on the clock. Philip Doyle made the point after touchdown kick to close the score to 14-13. The Alabama scoring play went 76 yards in eight plays over 1:12. Philip Doyle kicked off to the WP-33, where Pat Mangin returned it twelve yards along the left sideline to the WP-45, pushed out of bounds by Pickett.

Sean Jordan lost three yards on a reverse play when tackled by Spencer Hammond. Alabama was called for a dead ball personal foul and penalized 15 yards and an Army first down at the UA-43. On a pitch play, Cass ran eleven yards around the left end out of bounds for a first down at the UA-32.

A McWilliams pass over the middle for Baker was broken up by Ozmint and incomplete. On a pitch play around the left end, Cass gained five yards out of bounds on the sideline. On third and five at the UA-27 in the last seconds of the first half, Keith

Walker's 44 yard field goal attempt was blocked by Derrick Thomas. The Cadets drive went 28 yards in four plays for 0:35. The score at halftime was Army 14, Alabama 13.

Halftime

Army had 13 first downs, 232 yards rushing, zero passing (0-3-0), no fumbles, punted once, penalized five yards, and 15:41 time of possession. Alabama had 13 first downs, 59 rushing yards, 193 yards passing (14-24-0), no lost fumbles, punted once, and had 30 yards penalized.

Barnett had rushed 96 yards while Mayweather had 62 and one touchdown and McWilliams 48 and one touchdown. Murry Hill had rushed for 54 yards. Greg Payne had caught six passes for 66 yards, while Marco Battle had four receptions for 53 yards and one touchdown.

Third Quarter

Army will kick off and defend the south goal. Alabama will receive. Bit Rambusch kicked off into the end zone, where Pierre Goode returned the football to the UA-14, stopped by Schretzman.

Smith's pass to Payne down the left sideline was out of bounds and incomplete. Lingley tackled Wayne Shaw after a seven yard gain on a draw. On third down and three, Thorson pressured Smith whose pass to Battle was incomplete. Chris Mohr punted 47 yards to the WP-24, where Paul Wynn returned it 14 yards, stopped by Hammond, at 14:03. The Alabama drive was three plays over seven yards in 0:57.

McWilliams rushed for six yards around the right end, tackled by Shephard. McWilliams ran four yards around the left end at the WP-48, stopped by Gardner. An official measurement determined that it was an Army first down. On a pitch play, Mangum tackled Mayweather after a four yard run around the right end. McCants tackled Cass on a counter play that gained one yard.

On third and five at the UA-47, Derrick Thomas tackled Bryan McWilliams for a loss of five yards. Bit Rambusch punted

39 yards to the UA-13, where Murry Hill returned it 87 yards for a touchdown at 11:28 on the clock. Alabama was called on the punt return for clipping and penalized, with Murry Hill credited with a 16 yard return. The Cadets drive went 14 yards on five plays for 2:35.

On first and ten at the UA-15, Casteal rushed three yards over left tackle, stopped by Cooney. Smith passed eleven yards to Battle for a first down out of bounds on the right sideline at the UA-29. Russell caught a twelve yard pass reception for a first down at the UA-41, stopped by Lingley.

Smith threw a screen pass to the left side to Turner, who gained seven yards before being tackled by Boyd. Schretzman stopped Hill after a gain of one yard over left tackle. On third and two at the UA-49, Earnest Boyd broke up a pass attempt to Marco Battle. Chris Mohr punted 30 yards to the WP-22, where Wynn made a fair catch at 8:56 on the clock. The Alabama drive of six plays of 34 yards in 2:32.

George Thornton stopped Barnett after a gain of four yards up the middle. McCants stopped Barnett up the middle for no gain. On third and six at the WP-26, Thornton tackled McWilliams after a two yard run around left end. Bit Rambusch punted 43 yards to UA-31, where the ball went out of bounds at 7:13 on the clock. The Cadets drive took three plays for six yards in 1:43.

Smith completed a pass to Casteal, who broke a tackle and gained 13 yards and a first down to the UA-44, stopped by Scherb. John Fruhmorgen was injured on the play and left the field. Battle caught a nine yard pass reception along the left sideline, stopped by Boyd. On a pitch play, Will Huff ran through three blockers and tackled Murry Hill for a loss of four yards. On a third and five, Smith completed a six yard pass to the left side to Payne for a first down, tackled by Boyd.

Smith completed an 18 yard pass to Richardson along the left sideline for a first down at the WP-27, stopped by Scherb out of bounds. Jon Brunner tackled Russell after a four yard screen pass reception along the left sideline. Davie tackled Shaw after a gain of five yards up the middle. On the next play, a third and one, Alabama was called for illegal procedure and penalized five yards.

On third and six, David Smith completed a 23 yard touchdown pass to Greg Payne for a first down at 4:23 on the clock. Philip Doyle converted the PAT kick as Alabama took the lead, 20-14. The Crimson Tide scoring drive took eight plays in 69 yards over 2:50 time of possession.

Philip Doyle kicked off to the WP-3, where Mike Mayweather returned the football 28 yards, stopped by Steve Webb. Hammond tackled McWilliams after a gain of one yard around the right end. Barnett went up the middle, breaking several tackles, and rushed for 58 yards and a first down at the UA-10, stopped by Mangum.

Mayweather went three yards around the right end, stopped by Mangum. Gilbert tackled McWilliams after a one yard gain to the right side. On third and goal at the UA-6, Barnett went up the middle for three yards, tackled by Webb and McCants.

On fourth and goal, Bryan McWilliams pitched to Mike Mayweather, who rushed for three yards for a touchdown around the right end with 1:22 on the clock. Keith Walker made the point after touchdown kick as Army retook the lead, 21-20. The Cadets drive took six plays over 69 yards in 3:01 time of possession.

A dead ball foul on Alabama was called after the PAT play and the Crimson Tide was penalized 15 yards on the kickoff. Bit Rambusch kicked off from the fifty into the end zone for a touchback. On first and ten at the UA-20, Smith completed a pass to Payne for twelve yards along the left sideline for a first down at the UA-32.

A pass intended for Battle was overthrown. Davie tackled Hill after a gain of one yard over left tackle. On third and nine, Smith scrambled and completed an eleven yard pass to Cross to the right side for a first down at the UA-44, tackled by Boyd.

On first and ten, O'Neal Miller intercepted a David Smith pass and returned the football along the sideline for 57 yards and a touchdown at 0:07 on the clock. Keith Walker made the PAT to make it 28-20. The Alabama drive of five plays gained 24 yards in 1:15 time of possession.

A dead ball foul was called on Army for excessive celebrations after the interception return and the Cadets were penalized 15 yards to be assessed on the kickoff. Bit Rambusch kicked off from the WP-20 to the UA-12, where Pierre Goode returned it 15 yards to the UA-27. Smith completed an eleven yard pass to Shaw in the left flat for a first down at the UA-38 as the quarter ended. The score was Army 28, Alabama 20.

Fourth Quarter

On first and ten at the UA-38, Smith overthrew his pass to Battle. Smith dumped a pass to Shaw, who gained six yards before being stopped by Lingley. On third and four, there was a bad snap from center, and Smith fell on the ball, losing five yards. Chris Mohr punted 61 yards into the end zone for a touchback at 13:28. The Alabama drive was four plays for twelve yards that took 1:39 off the clock.

Thomas tackled McWilliams after a four yard gain around left tackle. On a pitch play to the right, Mayweather rushed for seven yards and a first down at the WP-31, stopped by Ozmint. A forward pitch from McWilliams that was dropped was ruled an incomplete pass. Hammond tackled Barnett after a gain of four yards over the left guard.

On third and six, McCants stopped Barnett for no gain. Army was called for holding on the play, but Alabama declined the penalty. Bit Rambusch punted 35 yards to the UA-30, where Murry Hill returned it seven yards, tackled by Mike O'Toole at 11:37 left in the game. The Cadets drive took five plays over 15 yards for 1:51 time of possession.

On first and ten at the UA-37, Smith completed a 20 yard pass to Wimbley to the left side for a first down at the WP-43. Smith threw a pass incomplete. Scherb tackled Shaw for a two yard gain. On third and eight, Smith completed a twelve yard pass across the middle to Battle for a first down at the WP-29, stopped by Scherb.

A pass to the left side intended for Payne was incomplete. Wimbley caught an eleven yard reception to the right side for a first down at the WP-18, tackled by Boyd. A pass intended for Wimbley to the left side was bobbled and incomplete. Battle caught a ten yard pass to the left side rolling on to his back to the ground at the WP-8. An official measurement determined that Alabama had made a first down.

Battle caught a four yard pass over the middle, tackled by Lingley. On a pitch play, Casteal gained two yards around the right end, stopped by Gadson. On third and goal at the WP-2, Greg Gadson sacked David Smith for a loss of 13 yards. Dan Cooney was injured on the play and left the field. Philip Doyle made a 32 yard field goal at 7:25 on the clock to close the score to 28-23 in favor of Army. The Alabama drive took twelve plays over 48 yards for 4:12 off the clock.

Philip Doyle kicked off into the end zone, where Mike Mayweather took a knee for a touchback. Amelong tackled McWilliams for no gain around the left end. On a pitch play, Mayweather gained one yard around right end, stopped by Mangum. Mayweather was injured on the play and left the field.

On third and nine, a McWilliams pass was batted down at the line of scrimmage and incomplete. Bit Rambusch punted 42 yards to the UA-37, where Murry Hill returned it nine yards before being tackled by Wyatt at 6:17. The Army drive of three plays for one yard took 1:08.

On first down and ten from the UA-46, Army was called for pass interference and penalized ten yards to the WP-44 to give Alabama a first down. Smith completed a 19 yard pass to the right side to Richardson for a first down at the WP-25, stopped by Thorson. Lingley stopped Hill on a draw play that gained five yards. Shaw went over left guard for 16 yards and a first down at the WP-4, with Miller making the tackle.

Huff tackled Shaw after a gain of two yards up the middle. David Casteal hurdled high in the air over the line of scrimmage for a two yard touchdown at 4:01 left in the game. Alabama went for a two-point pass, but Boyd knocked down David Smith's pass.

However, Army was called for holding on the play and penalized two yards. Haines tackled David Casteal short of the goal line and no good on his two-point run attempt. The score was now 29-28 in favor of Alabama. The Crimson Tide scoring drive went five plays in 54 yards over 2:16 time of possession.

Philip Doyle kicked off into the end zone, where Mike Mayweather took a knee for a touchback. Barnett went up the middle for twelve yards and a first down at the WP-32, stopped by Gardner. McWilliams ran around the left end for seven yards, tackled by Ozmint. On a pitch play, Cass went around left end for four yards out of bounds and a first down at the WP-43, stopped by Kendrick.

George Bethune sacked Bryan McWilliams for a loss of three yards. Willie Shephard tackled Bryan McWilliams running left for a three yard loss. On third and 16 from the WP-37, Charles Gardner intercepted a Bryan McWilliams pass tipped by Lee Ozmint, and returned it 16 yards to the WP-30 with 1:53 left in the game. The Cadets drive took six plays of 17 yards taking 2:08.

Rod Ofte tackled Casteal after a gain of six yards. Army took a time out. Turner went up the middle for three yards, tackled by Ofte. Army took a time out. Haines stopped Shaw after he ran up the middle for three yards and a first down at the WP-18. Haines tackled Casteal for a loss of two yards. Army took its final time out. Davie tackled Shaw after a gain of three over right guard.

On third and nine at the WP-17, Alabama was called for delay of game and penalized five yards. Quarterback David Smith took a knee for a loss of one yard as the clock ran out. The final Alabama drive was six plays going seven yards in 1:53 time of possession. The game ended at 1:40 pm MST, taking 3:28 to play. Final Score: Alabama 29, Army 28.

Post-Game

"I was very proud of our team," said Jim Young in January. "Alabama is certainly the best team we've played since I've been at West Point. They have great athletes, and they are well-coached. We went into the game believing we had a chance of winning, but we just we're able to contain their offense well enough to make it happen. Alabama was one of the better teams in the country. We played them and beat them in everything except the score."

Asked about whether Army could have played better today, Jim Young said, "Yes, we could have kicked two field goals. But Derrick Thomas is a great player." Speaking of Barnett's effort, Young said, "The thing about the wishbone is you never know who is going to get the yardage, so it's tough to defend. Alabama played it better late in the game.'"

"We thought they might have trouble with the wishbone," said Young, who ended his sixth season at West Point. "But they have a very fine quarterback who is an accurate thrower and though to defend."

"It was the first time we had faced the wishbone in several years, so it took us a whole first half to get used to it," said Alabama head football coach Bill Curry.

"They [Alabama's offense] just couldn't run the ball," said Army nose guard Dan Cooney after the game. "Smith would see those guys coming out of the backfield and hit them. That was damaging. We just had to stop the short pass."

"We didn't expect to have to pass this much, but had to when they stopped the run," said Alabama senior quarterback David Smith after the game. "I didn't mind, as I had a great time throwing all those passes. It was one of those days when I felt I couldn't miss anything. Everybody remembers their last game. It was a great feeling to win it."

Army had 19 first downs (17 rushing), 350 yards rushing on 61 carries, no passing yards (0-6-1), had one fumble but lost none, made six out of 14 third down attempts, converted it only fourth down attempt, punted five times, made two sacks, had three penalties for 32 yards, had two field goals blocked, returned one interception 57 yards for a touchdown, and had 28:07 time of possession.

Alabama had 30 first downs (23 passing), 95 yards rushing on 36 attempts, 412 passing yards (33-52-1), had one fumble but lost none, made eleven out of 19 third down attempts, attempted no fourth down conversions, punted four times, made one sack, had seven penalties for 70 yards, returned one interception 16 yards, had one kickoff return for a touchdown called back due to clipping, and had 31:53 time of possession.

For Alabama, Murry Hill rushed for 57 yards on 12 carries, while Wayne Shaw had 38 yards on seven carries. Others rushers included David Casteal (7-14), Kevin Turner (2-9), Robert Stewart (2-6), Pierre Goode 91-1), and David Smith (5-minus 30). Smith had 33 completions out of 52 passes for 412 passing yards with two touchdowns and one interception, with a longest pass of 25 yards.

Greg Payne caught nine passes for 107 yards and one touchdown, while Marco Battle had nine receptions for 99 yards and one touchdown. Other receptions were Prince Wimbley (3-50), LaMonde Russell (3-41), Todd Richardson (2-37), Kevin Turner (2-18), Wayne Shaw (2-17), Murry Hill (1-19), David Casteal (1-13), and Howard Cross (1-11).

Philip Doyle made all three field goals attempts, the longest from 37 yards. Chris Mohr punted four times for a 45.5 average and a long of 61. Murry Hill returned three punts for 32 yards. Pierre Goode returned four kickoffs for 76 yards. Charles Gardner returned one interception for 16 yards.

Keith McCants had 13 total tackles (7 solo), while John Mangum and Derrick Thomas each had six. Others making tackles included Kermit Kendrick (5), Willie Shephard (5), Charles Gardner (4), Lee Ozmint (4), William Amelong (4), Steve Webb (4), George Thornton (3), Greg Gilbert (3), Spencer Hammond (3), Darryl Pickett (2), George Bethune (2), Thomas Rayam (2), Willie

Wyatt (2), Brian Stutson (1), Jimbo Salem (1), and Tommy Cole (1).

Thomas had two tackles for loss, while Kendrick, Bethune, and Shephard each had one TFL. Bethune had one sack. Ozmint and Thomas had one pass breakup.

For Army, Ben Barnett had 177 yards rushing on 14 carries, while Mike Mayweather had 74 yards on 19 carries and Bryan McWilliams had 62 yards on 19 attempts. Other rushers included Calvin Cass (8-40) and Sean Jordan (1-minus 3). Mayweather scored two rushing touchdowns, while McWilliams scored one. McWilliams threw five pass attempts with one interception, while Cass threw one pass attempt.

Keith Walker attempted two field goals, having both of them blocked. Bit Rambusch punted five times for a 39.1 average, with a long of 42 yards. Paul Wynn returned one punt for 14 yards. Mike Mayweather returned five kickoffs for 119 yards. O'Neal Miller returned one interception for 57 yards and a touchdown.

Troy Lingley had nine total tackles (7 solo), while Earnest Boyd had eight and Darryl Scherb and Pat Davie each had seven tackles. Others making tackles were Josh Haines (6), Mike Thorson (5), Greg Gadson (4), O'Neal Miller (4), Chuck Schretzman (4), Will Huff (3), Rod Ofte (2), Mike O'Toole (2), Dan Cooney (2), Greg Cleveland (1), and Jon Brunner (1).

Gadson had two tackles for loss, while Cooney and Huff each had one. Gadson and Cooney each had a sack. Miller had one interception. Miller, Boyd, and Lingley each had one pass breakup.

The Sun Bowl's C.M. Hendricks Most Valuable Player Trophy was Alabama quarterback David Smith. The Jimmy Rogers Jr. Most Valuable Lineman Trophy went to Alabama linebacker Derrick Thomas.

The following Sun Bowl team records were broken in this game by Alabama: most first downs (30), most pass attempts (52), most pass completions (33), most total offense yards (507), and most net yards passing (412). For Army, the Cadets tied the record for fewest pass completions (0), last set by Utah State in 1960.

The following Sun Bowl individual records were broken during the game: (David Smith) most pass attempts, most pass completions, and most net yards passing; (Greg Payne) tied for most receptions (9); and (Marco Battle) tied for most receptions (9).

It was the first time since Jim Young switched to the wishbone offense at the beginning of the 1984 season that Army had lost a game when it threw six or fewer passes. The Cadets had won 25 games throwing that number of passes.

Army (9-3) received 4 votes in the final *Associated Press* Top 20 Poll after the January bowl games, ranking 28th. Alabama (9-3) was ranked 17th in both of the final Associated Press Top 20 Poll and *United Press International* Coaches Top 20 Poll.

Five Crimson Tide players were selected in the 1989 NFL Draft: linebacker Derrick Thomas, linebacker Greg Gilbert, punter Chris Mohr, tight end Howard Cross, and linebacker George Bethune.

Conclusion

In the 1989 Army Football Yearbook, it summarized the 1988 season and bowl game as "In 1988, despite early-season questions about his defense, his offensive line, and his quarterback, Young led the Cadets to a 9-2 record and an invitation to play Alabama in the John Hancock Sun Bowl. In the three weeks between the victory over Navy and the Sun Bowl, Young again was forced to answer the doubters. This time they questioned whether his players were out of their league. On Christmas Eve, the Army team gave its answer with a one-point loss that was two blocked field goals away from a win."

"As a team, we were down on what the media said about not supposing to be in this game," said Bryan McWilliams after the game. "I don't care about what kind of respect we're going to get or anything like that, we lost the game. We should have won it."

"There is no satisfaction," Jim Young said. "We came here to win, not to be satisfied. This wasn't a moral victory. This wasn't a respectable effort. That was a winning effort. We came here to win and we gave a winning effort."

Chapter 9

The 1996 Football Season

Prior Army Seasons

It had been seven seasons since Army had gone to a bowl game. The improvements during the 1995 season with its 5-5-1 record, especially since four of the losses were for less than a touchdown, made the prospects of the 1996 season promising.

Since the 1988 Sun Bowl, Army had three seasons with winning records and three losing seasons. The last two seasons under former head football coach Jim Young were moderately successful in both having 6-5 records. Young lost a close game to Navy in 1989 (17-19) and went on to win his final game at West Point against the Midshipmen, 30-20.

There were 18 bowl games after both the 1989 and the 1990 regular seasons ended, but there were nine Independent teams with better records each season who had the opportunity for post-season tilts.

Losses to Air Force each season allowed the Falcons to participate in the 1989 and 1990 Liberty Bowls; a bowl game that all three service academies had agreed to have the winner of the Commander-in-Chief's Trophy receive an automatic bid to attend.

A retiring Young recommended to the USMA leadership to promote his eight-year defensive coordinator, Bob Sutton, as the 31st Head Football Coach at Army. They did. In Sutton's first season in 1991, Army lost to The Citadel (14-20), but then upset favored Louisville (37-12) on the road, but then had a disappointing loss to Navy while the Cadets were favored by 10 points, 3-24, to finish the season with a 4-7 record.

During the 1992 season, Army beat who they were supposed to beat, lose to who was favored, except for losing to The Citadel (14-15) again and beating favored Northern Illinois (21-14). And Sutton would do something more important, Beat Navy (25-24), to make a 5-6 season record somewhat successful.

Things would repeat a little in 1993, with one upset win and one upset loss; another victory over the Midshipmen (16-14) that created the fourth tie in the history of the Commander-in-Chief's Trophy; and a winning season to boot (6-5). Army led the nation in rushing yards per game during the season. Only two Independents went to one of the 19 bowl games that season.

The 1994 season was a bit of a step backwards with a 4-7 record. The Cadets finally beat The Citadel (25-24), barely; lost to Boston University when favored (12-21); and ended the year with a victory over Navy, 22-20. Seven of Army's eleven games were decided by six or less points.

Things were much better during the 1995 season. The Cadets beat everyone who they were favored to (Lehigh, Colgate, and Bucknell), tied 1.5 point favorite Rice (21-21), and beat badly 13 point favorite Boston College at Chestnut Hill (49-7, nope, that is not a typo).

Six of Army's eleven games during the season were settled in the final minute, with four games coming down to the final play. Four of the five losses came to teams that played in 1995 bowl games (Air Force, Washington, Notre Dame, and East Carolina).

The Cadets came back from a 21-point second half deficit against the Fighting Irish to lose by one point, after attempting a two-point conversion tackled just short of the goal line. 14 of the last 20 Cadets contests had been decided by nine or less points.

Army finished its regular season, 4-5-1, and got set to play Navy (5-5) at Veterans Stadium in Philadelphia on December 2, 1995. In Charlie Weatherbie's first season as head football coach of the Midshipmen, and offensive coordinator Paul Johnson running the option offense, I'm sure the Mids had visions of their first winning season since 1982.

After a Cadets turnover in their first possession, Navy scored on a 22 yard touchdown pass. Army rebounded later in the first quarter when fullback John Conroy bulled over from the one yard line. Both teams missed scoring opportunities late in the first half and went into the locker room tied, 7-7.

Navy received the second half kickoff, and spent the third quarter driving 52 yards in 16 plays before Tom Vanderhorst made a 39 yard field goal. Vanderhorst added a 22 yard field goal with 12:33 left in the game for a 13-7 lead. With 8:23 remaining, Navy had a fourth and goal on the WP-1, Weatherbie choose to go for a touchdown instead of a field goal. The low pass from Chris McCoy to Cory Schemm fell incomplete. Army now had the football, 99 yards away to win the game.

What happened next became an immediate part of Army Football history. Conroy rushed for one yard. Conroy ran for twelve yards and a first down at the WP-14. Abel Young rushed for six yards. Steve Carpenter gained three yards. On fourth and one, Carpenter made a yard and a first down at the WP-24. Ronnie McAda hit John Graves for a 17 yard pass and a first down at the WP-41.

McAda ran for one yard. Demetrius Perry rushed for two yards. On third and seven, McAda completed a nine yard pass to Perry for a first down on the N-47. Carpenter ran for three yards. Jeff Brizic rushed for 18 yards and a first down at the N-26. Conroy rushed for six yards. Brizic gained five yards and a first down at the N-15.

McAda was tackled for a two yard loss. A pass was incomplete. On third down, McAda was sacked for a loss of twelve yards back at the N-29. On fourth and 24, Ronnie McAda rolled right, found Graves wide open running a corner route along the left sideline, and completed a pass to him. Graves gained 28 yards and was pushed out of bounds for a first down at the N-1, tackled by defensive back Kevin Lewis.

The Mids held Conroy for no gain on first and goal. On second and goal, John Conroy plunged over the one yard line for the touchdown with 1:03 remaining on the 19th play of a 99 yard drive. J. Parker made the point after touchdown kick to make it 14-13, Army. It was the fourth straight loss by Navy.

Army finished the 1985 season with a 5-5-1 record, and Bob Sutton won his fourth straight win over Navy, previously done only by Army Head Football Coaches Charles Daly (1913-1916) and Earl Blaik (1944-1947).

1996 Army Football Coaching and Support Staff

Bob Sutton was in his sixth year as head football coach at Army His leadership team consisted of Greg Gregory (associated head coach & offensive coordinator, 15th season at Army) and Denny Doornbos (defensive coordinator, 11th).

Other members of the coaching staff included Ted Daisher (defensive line, 2nd), Mike Dietzel (running backs, 4th), Mike Locksley (tight and split ends, 1st), John Loose (inside linebackers, 5th), Bill Sheridan (defensive backs, 5th), Ed Warinner (offensive line, 10th), and John Bonamego (special teams & recruiting coordinator, 4th).

Also, John Milligan (defensive backs, 1st), Kent Riddle (fullbacks & junior varsity, 2nd), Bill Mottola (offensive linemen, 2nd), Mike Sullivan (junior varsity head coach, 2nd), Steve Carpenter (graduate assistant), and Brian Tucker (graduate assistant).

Other staff included Jack Hecker (director of football operation, 21st), Dick Hall (equipment manager, 22nd), Tim Kelly (head athletic trainer, 10th), Tim Swanger (head strength & conditioning, 7th), Dave Allen (assistant trainer), Melissa Marks (assistant trainer), Steve Murray (assistant strength & conditioning), Scott Swanson (assistant strength & conditioning), Heath Bates (strength & conditioning), and Ed Stover (strength & conditioning).

Support staff included Colonel Kip Nygren (officer representative, 2nd), Lieutenant Colonel Owen Mullen (deputy officer representative), Lieutenant Colonel Bob Arciero (team physician), Major Bill Wilhelm (assistant officer representative), Captain Karl Heineman (assistant officer representative), Captain Dan Sauter (assistant officer representative), Captain Matt Oliver (assistant officer representative), and Captain Doug Pavek (special assistant, 3rd).

1996 Football Schedule

The 1996 season began on September 14th with a home game with Ohio University (first time ever), followed by another game at Michie Stadium with Duke University on September 21st. The Cadets would travel to the Dallas area for their first game ever with North Texas on September 28th. The game against the Mean Green was scheduled to replace a game at Rice that same weekend.

On October 5th, Army would host Yale. The Cadets would play Rutgers at Giants Stadium in East Rutherford NJ on October 12th. Tulane would visit West Point on October 19th. Army would travel to Oxford OH to play Miami University on October 26th. A home game with Lafayette College would follow on November 2nd.

The annual service academy clash with Air Force would be at Michie Stadium on November 9th. The Cadets would play indoors at the Carrier Dome at Syracuse on November 16th to finish up their regular season. The annual Army-Navy game would be in Philadelphia at Veterans Stadium on December 7th.

Home kickoffs would be at 1:30 pm, except the Duke game at Noon. For the away games, the kickoffs would be North Texas (3 pm EDT), Rutgers (1 pm EDT), Miami University (1 pm EDT), Syracuse (6 pm EST), and Army-Navy (Noon EST).

The overtime system adopted for the 1995 bowl games was expanded to all Division 1-A and 1-AA games. Army would not play an overtime game until the 1999 season. There were 111 teams in Division 1-A during the 1996 season, in nine divisions with eleven Independent schools.

CBS Television would broadcast the Army-Navy game on December 7th for the first time since the 1990 season. *ABC Television* had carried the game during the past five years. *Liberty-Fox* would televised the September 21st game with Duke University. *ABC Television* would broadcast the Air Force game on November 9th, while *ESPN2* cable showed the game at Syracuse on November 16th.

Bowl Games

There were 18 bowl games scheduled after the 1996 regular season, from December 19th with the Las Vegas Bowl; until the national championship game on January 2nd at the Sugar Bowl. Bowl eligibility was determined largely by each bowl selection committee, and was not restricted by teams playing multiple games with Division 1-AA opponents. Army had no bowl ties this season.

Almost all bowls had contracts with individual conferences and a few relied on at-large berths of winning teams. There were only two bowl games with at-large berths, the new Haka Bowl and the Independence Bowl. The Haka Bowl was supposed to be played on December 26th or 27th in New Zealand and received NCAA approval, but the bowl committee could not provide financial guarantees and the NCAA revoked its license.

Spring Practice

There were 43 lettermen returning, 18 from the offense, 22 from the defense, and 3 from special teams. There were five offensive starters returning, six from the defense, and three specialists.

"Our program has remained the same in structure over the years," said Bob Sutton. "I think the style that we play, with an emphasis on toughness and unity, contains the ingredients that you need to be successful in the long haul. All of us in the program realized we could be a winning football team against outstanding competition. I think we learned a lot about ourselves. We learned that we still have to take the next step, but that we'll be in a position to do that if we develop the right type of winning culture."

Sutton continued, "We're in position to take off now. That's really the challenge for all of us, take the last step. It takes unified effort by all involved. It takes the belief and toughness to pursue the objective. I think we have that as a program. We have to go out and prove it on eleven Saturdays."

"I was happy with the spring in most regards. We went in with three key areas to work on from a personnel standpoint, offensive line, defensive secondary, and punter. We still have some positions that won't be settled until preseason practice, but we made great progress. Our backfield is in pretty good shape. Defensively, we are most concerned with our two safety positions. We tried to address our concerns by sliding personnel around. Our primary concern [with the offensive line] will be to see who is going to step forward and provide us with the type of line play that we had last season."

Captains

Following spring practice, head coach Bob Sutton announced that he was naming seniors linebacker Ben Kotwica and tight end Ron Leshinski as team captains for the 1996 Army Football team for the season, voted by the team. Kotwica ranked second last season in tackles. Leshinski has started every game since plebe year at tight end (33 straight games). Both were expected to contend for All-East honors this season. Leshinski did suffer a broken leg during spring practice, but was expected back by the home opener.

The starting offensive line-up prior to preseason was split end Ron Thomas, left tackle Dave Beard, left guard Doug Chadwick, center Kyle Scott, right guard Jeff Enck, right tackle Tim Booth, tight end Ron Leshinski, fullback Joe Hewitt, left halfback Jeff Brizic, right halfback Rashad Hodge, and quarterback Ronnie McAda.

The starting defensive line-up was defensive ends Larry Angles and Scott Eichelberger, defensive tackle CW Estes, nose tackle Colin Kearns, linebackers Brian King, Stephen King, and Bet Kotwica, cornerback Garland Gray, safeties Bo French and Robert Brown, and halfback Tom Mullins. The placekicker was J. Parker, the punter was Scot Lord, and the long snapper was Rob Rodenmayer.

Summer

On July 1, 1996, less than 1,200 men and women arrived at West Point to join the USMA Class of 2000. The 1996 Army Football Media Guide listed 52 freshmen (plebes) as part of the football team. Of these, 13 had attended the USMA Prep School. One of the freshmen would letter during the 1996 season.

Preseason Recognitions

Potential all-stars included defensive back Robert Brown, defensive back Garland Gay, halfback Rashad Hodge, linebacker Stephen King, linebacker Ben Kotwica, tight end Ron Leshinski, quarterback Ronnie McAda, kicker J. Parker, center Kyle Scott, and split end Ron Thomas.

Season Predictions

The only Army opponent to be ranked in preseason polls was Syracuse, which was ranked 10th in the *Associated Press* Top 25 Poll and 13th in the *USA Today/CNN* Coaches Top 25 Poll. Syracuse actually rose in the ranks to #9/#11 before it played in its first game of the season.

Ohio

Army (0-0) opened its 1996 season and hosted Ohio University (2-0) on September 14th at Michie Stadium before 30,500 fans. Ohio had beaten Akron (44-14) and at Hawai'i (21-10) to open the season undefeated. Army was favored by 16 points to win.

Ohio quarterback Kareem Wilson completed three straight passes in the Bobcats opening drive to score on a twelve yard touchdown pass to take a 6-0 lead. Midway through the first quarter, the Bobcats Steve Hookfin went 63 yards for a touchdown, for a 14-0 lead over the Cadets. Army responded by driving 67 yards down the field when Joe Hewett scored on a two yard touchdown run at 2:43 in first quarter. J. Parker converted the extra point kick to close Ohio's lead to 14-7.

On their next possession, the Cadets drove 89 yards, finishing with Rashad Hodges four yard touchdown at 10:20 in the second quarter to tie the score at 14-14. With 2:59 left in the first half, Hewitt rushed for a two yard touchdown to complete a 78 yard drive to make the halftime score, 21-14, in favor of Army.

The Army defense tackled Wilson in the end zone for a safety with ten minutes left in the third quarter. Brandon Tilford recovered a fumble and returned it 19 yards for a touchdown to make it 30-14, with over five minutes left in the third period. Army drove 84 yards, where Jeff Brizic scored on a three yard touchdown run with 12:59 left in the game to up the score to 37-14. In the last minutes, Ohio scored on a two yard touchdown for the final score of the game, losing 37-20 to Army.

Army had 25 first downs, 324 yards rushing, 68 passing (6-13-0), no turnovers, had 90 yards of penalties, punted five times, and had 34:28 time of possession. Ohio had 20 first downs, 170 yards rushing, 140 passing (14-23-0), lost one fumble, punted five times, and had 41 yards in penalties.

Bobcats running back Steve Hookfin rushed for 103 yards. Joe Hewitt rushed for 90 yards, while Ronnie McAda ran for 64 and Ty Amey 45 yards rushing. Ron Leshinski caught three passes for 49 yards.

Ohio finished the 1996 season with a 5-3 Mid-American conference record, in fourth place. After losing to Army, the Bobcats lost the next weekend at Northwestern (20-37). Ohio then beat Eastern Michigan (7-0) before losing at Ball State (27-30). The Bobcats then won at Kent State (24-15), at home versus

Bowling Green (38-0), and at Western Michigan (38-0). Ohio finished the season with three straight losses at Miami University (8-24), at East Carolina (45-55), and versus Toledo (23-24). The Bobcats had a 6-6 overall record in Jim Grobe's second season as head football coach.

Duke

Army (1-0) hosted Duke University (0-2) on September 21st at Michie Stadium before 36,049 fans. Duke had opened the season with back-to-back losses, first at #3 Florida State (7-44) and at home versus Northwestern (13-38). Army was favored by 3.5 points to win. The *Liberty-Fox* network broadcasted the game, but the announcers were unknown.

Army opened the game in the first quarter with two touchdown drives. Ronnie McAda scored on an eight yard touchdown with 10:31 on the clock, with Parker making the extra point kick to take a 7-0 lead. McAda then threw an 82 yard touchdown pass to Ron Thomas for another touchdown. Duke responded with an eleven yard touchdown run to make it 14-7 at the end of the first period.

With nine minutes to go in the first half, Duke made a 27 yard field goal to close to 14-10. Army marched again, finishing with McAda's 13 yard touchdown run to make it 21-10 at halftime.

Bobby Williams scored on a 28 yard run to extend the score to 28-10 in the third period. Duke scored on a nine yard touchdown pass with 12:22 left in the game to close it to 28-17. With eight minutes left, Williams completed another drive by plunging over from the two yard line to finish the scoring at 35-17 for the Army victory.

The Blue Devils had beaten Army three straight times, including a last second loss in 1995. Army had not beaten Duke since the 1984 season. "It was extremely important to us to win this game," said Ronnie McAda after the game. "Especially when you can beat them up and down the field like we did today."

Army had 24 first downs, 304 yards rushing, 225 passing (7-8-0), two lost fumbles, punted three times, had three penalties for 41 yards, and had 33:24 time of possession. Duke had 20 first downs, 104 yards rushing, 220 passing (24-41-1), no lost fumbles, punted five times, and had two penalties for ten yards.

Ronnie McAda rushed for 88 yards, while Bobby Williams ran for 77, Jeff Brizic had 40, and Joe Hewitt had 41 rushing yards. Ron Thomas caught two passes for 101 yards.

Duke finished the 1996 season with a 0-8 Atlantic Coast Conference record for ninth and last place. After losing to Army, the Blue Devils lost their next eight games. The Blue Devils had three close losses versus Clemson (6-13), Maryland (19-22), and at Wake Forest (16-17). Duke finished with a 0-11 overall record in Fred Goldsmith's third season.

North Texas

Army (2-0) traveled to Irving TX to play North Texas (1-2) on September 28th at Texas Stadium in front of 20,413 spectators. The Mean Green opened the season with a victory over Illinois State (20-14), but then lost back-to-back games at #18/#23 Arizona State (7-52) and at Texas A&M (0-55). Army was favored by 17.5 points to win.

Midway through the first quarter, Jeff Brizic plunged over the goal line from the two yard line, with J. Parker making the extra point kick for the Cadets to take a 7-0 lead. North Texas responded with a 41 yard field goal with less than four minutes to go in the first period to make it a 7-3 halftime score. Early in the second quarter, quarterback Ronnie McAda was injured while scrambling 20 yards for a first down. McAda would miss the next two games.

Parker made a 39 yard field goal midway through the third quarter. Two minutes later, Parker converted a 34 yard field goal to make it 13-3. Demetrius Perry scored on a one yard run three seconds into the final period to up the score to 20-3. Perry would score from the one with less than four minutes left in the game to up the score to 27-3. The Mean Green completed a four yard touchdown pass in the final seconds for the final 27-10 score in an Army victory.

Army had 18 first downs, 331 yards rushing, 44 passing (4-6-1), one lost fumble, punted four times, and was penalized 38 yards, with 42:27 time of possession. North Texas had 8 first downs, 13 rushing yards, 162 passing (18-41-1), one lost fumble, punted seven times, and was penalized 38 yards.

Rashad Hodge rushed for 61 yards, Perry had 53, Joe Hewitt 51, and Jeff Brizic 36 rushing yards. Adam Thompson came into the game three plays into the second quarter for the injured Ronnie McAda at quarterback.

North Texas finished the 1996 season with a 3-2 Big West Conference record, tied for third place with Idaho. The Mean Green won at Northern Illinois (24-21) the weekend after the Army game, then lost versus Vanderbilt at home, 7-19. North Texas beat New Mexico State (13-0) before losing two games to Nevada (13-40) and at Utah State (13-21). North Texas finished with two wins at Boise State (30-27) and versus Idaho (24-17). It was their first season in the Big West Conference. North Texas finished with an overall record of 5-6 in head coach Matt Simon's third season.

Yale

Army (3-0) hosted Yale University (1-1) on October 5th at sold out Michie Stadium with 40,776 fans. The Bulldogs had won at Brown (30-0) to open the season and then lost to #10 Connecticut, 6-42. Army was favored by 36 points to win. Adam Thompson started at quarterback for Army for the injured Ronnie McAda.

Army's J. Parker converted a 23 yard field goal with three minutes left in the first quarter. Midway through the second quarter, Parker made a 39 yard field goal. Yale's Bob Masella picked off an Adam Thompson pass and returned it for 34 yard touchdown with three minutes left in the first half, as the Bulldogs took the lead, 7-6. With ten seconds left, Parker made his third field goal, this time from 34 yards, for Army to take a 9-7 halftime lead.

Jeff Brizic scored a touchdown from the one yard midway through the third quarter. Thompson completed a 37 yard touchdown pass to Ron Leshinski with 3:09 to go in the third period to make it 23-7. Yale's quarterback Blake Kendall was tackled in the end zone by Colin Kearns for a safety with three seconds left in the third stanza.

An interception by Mike Coerper set up another Army drive. Less than three minutes later in the beginning of the final period, Demetrius Perry scored a touchdown from the six yard line. Yale's defense recovered an Army fumble by reserve quarterback Johnny Goff in the end zone to make the score 32-13 with eleven minutes left. Reserve Army quarterback Charles Keen ran 16 yards for a touchdown with six minutes left for the final score, 39-13.

Army had 25 first downs, 333 rushing yards, 97 passing (6-9-1), lost two fumbles, punted three times, was penalized five times for 40 yards, and had 43:58 time of possession. Yale had 4 first downs, 44 yards rushing, 38 passing (4-17-2), lost no fumbles, was penalized three times for 17 yards, and punted eight times.

Demetrius Perry had 56 yards rushing, while Adam Thompson had 52, Jeff Brizic ran for 48, Lee Gibson 44, and Bobby Williams had 43 rushing yards. Ron Leshinski caught two passes for 49 yards.

Yale finished with a 1-6 Ivy League record, in eighth and last place. The Bulldogs beat Bucknell (23-21) the weekend after the Army game, but then lost their final six games, including 21-26 at Harvard. Yale had an overall 2-8 record in Carmen Cozza's 32nd and final season.

Rutgers

Army (4-0) traveled to Giants Stadium to play Rutgers University (1-4) on October 12th before 19,101 spectators. Army was favored by 5 points to win. Rutgers was the home team. Adam

Thompson started at quarterback for Army for Ronnie McAda who was injured.

The Scarlet Knights opened the season on August 31st with a victory over Villanova (38-28), then dropped four straight games versus Navy (6-10), versus #10/#11 Miami Florida (0-33), at #18/#16 Virginia Tech (14-30), and at Syracuse (0-42). Offensive leaders for the Scarlet Knights were quarterback Mike Stephans, running back Chad Bosch, and receiver Steven Harper.

Rutgers scored on a nine yard touchdown run with three minutes left in the first quarter to take a 7-0 lead. Army responded in the second quarter with three straight touchdowns. Adam Thompson completed a 23 yard touchdown pass to Ron Leshinski two minutes into the quarter. Three minutes later, Joe Hewitt broke for a 69 yard touchdown run up the middle. With one minute left in the first half, Bobby Williams rushed for a three yard touchdown, making it 21-7 at halftime.

Army continued its scoring blitz on its first two possessions in the second half. Midway through the third quarter, Williams scored on another three yard touchdown run. Three minutes later, Demetrius Perry ran for a 61 yard touchdown.

In the last minute of the third quarter, Rutgers scored on a 20 yard touchdown pass to make it 35-14. Charles Kean rushed for a twelve yard touchdown five minutes into the final period. Rutgers completed a 37 touchdown pass to make the final score, 42-21 for an Army victory.

Army had 31 first downs, 546 yards rushing, 36 passing (2-3-0), one lost fumble, one punt, had six penalties for 62 yards, and 36:01 time of possession. Rutgers had 18 first downs, 25 yards rushing, 246 yards passing (16-34-0), one lost fumble, punted five times, and two penalties for ten yards.

Demetrius Perry rushed for 127 yards, Adam Thompson 126, Joe Hewitt for 117, and Charles Kean had 59 rushing yards. J. Parker made all six extra-point kicks.

Rutgers ended the season with a 1-6 Big East Conference record, finishing in seventh place. After losing to Army, the Scarlet Knights lost at Boston College (13-37). Rutgers beat Temple (28-17), then lost their last three games to West Virginia, at #10/#13 Notre Dame, and at Pitt. Rutgers finished the 1996 season with a 2-9 overall record in Terry Shea's first season as head football coach.

Tulane

Army (5-0) hosted Tulane University (2-3) on October 19th at Michie Stadium in front of 35,971 tickets sold (about 12,000 chose to not attend) in heavy rain and gusting winds on Homecoming Weekend. Army was favored by 6.5 points to win and leading the nation in rushing (368 ypg).

The Green Wave opened their season on August 30th at Cincinnati with a 34-14 victory. Tulane then lost twice to Rice (14-21) and at Memphis (10-17) before beating Texas Christian (35-7). The Green Wave lost a close game to Louisville, 20-23, the previous weekend.

Less than five minutes into the game, J. Parker made a 27 yard field goal. The Green Wave responded five minutes later with a 24 yard field goal conversion to tie the score. In the final two minutes, Parker converted a 27 yard field go for a 6-3 lead.

"THIS IS PRIME-TIME ARMY TRAINING WEATHER," said an Army cheerleader when the crowd noise dropped temporarily in the first quarter over an amplified microphone to those devoted followers in the stands.

Ronnie McAda returned to as the starting quarterback from a deep bone bruise above his left ankle and completed a 33 yard pass on each of the first two Army possessions. McAda rushed five yards for a touchdown on the first play of the second quarter. Midway in the quarter, Joe Hewitt rushed for a 27 yard touchdown to make it 20-3 at halftime.

Bobby Williams scored on a three yard touchdown run in the final seconds of the third quarter to make it 27-3. Tulane completed a 17 yard touchdown reception early in the fourth quarter. With eight minutes to go in the game, Williams rushed for a 14 yard touchdown for the final score, 34-10.

Army had 25 first downs, 357 yards rushing, 103 passing (5-11-0), no lost fumbles, punted twice, no penalties, and 41:26 time of possession. Tulane had 10 first downs, 43 yards rushing, 134 passing (11-29-0), one lost fumble, punted seven times, and had six penalties for 49 yards.

Bobby Williams rushed for 111 yards, while Joe Hewitt had 91, Rashad Hodge 57, and Demetrius Perry had 50 rushing yards. Ron Leshinski caught three passes for 45 yards.

Tulane finished the 1996 season with a 1-4 Conference USA record, placing sixth in the conference standings. The Green Wave lost the remaining five games to #24 Southern Mississippi, Houston, #24/#23 Syracuse, at Navy, and at #18 Louisiana State. Tulane finished with an overall record of 2-9 in Buddy Teevens' fifth and last season.

Miami

Army (6-0) traveled to Oxford OH to play Miami University (4-4) on October 26th at Yager Stadium in front of 16,543 Redskins fans in wet, rainy conditions. Miami was led by quarterback Sam Ricketts, running back Ty King, and receiver Tremayne Banks. Army was favored by 1.5 points to win.

Miami opened the season with victories over Kent State (64-6) and at Ball State (16-6). The Redskins then dropped the next three games at Indiana (14-21), versus Bowling Green (10-14), and at Cincinnati (23-30). Miami then beat Central Michigan (46-14) and at Eastern Michigan (35-25) before losing at Akron (7-10) the weekend before playing Army.

On Army's first possession, Ronnie McAda completed a 39 yard touchdown pass to Rod Richardson, with J. Parker making the extra point kick. Parker converted a 33 yard field goal with five minutes left to go in the first half, to make it 10-0 at intermission.

Early in the third quarter, Parker made a 21 yard field goal. In the opening minute of the fourth quarter, Bobby Williams rushed for a five yard touchdown. Jeff Brizic followed minutes later with a two yard touchdown run. Miami scored on a four yard touchdown pass in the final 39 seconds for the final score, 27-7, for an Army victory.

Army had 29 first downs, 408 yards rushing, 60 passing (4-7-0), no turnovers, had five penalties for 41 yards, punted three times, and had 43:18 time of possession. Miami had 12 first downs, 53 rushing yards, and 176 passing (16-35-0), no turnovers, punted five times, and had four penalties for 20 yards.

Joe Hewitt had 148 yards rushing, while Bobby Williams had 99, and Jeff Brizic 78 rushing yards. Rod Richardson had two catches for 45 yards.

Miami finished with a 6-2 Mid-American Conference record, in a tie for second place with Toledo. The Redskins won their final two games at Toledo (27-7) and versus Ohio (24-8) to finish with an overall record of 6-5 in Randy Walker's seventh season.

Lafayette

Army (7-0) hosted Division 1-AA Lafayette College (3-3) on November 2nd at sold out Michie Stadium in front of 39,269 fans. Army was favored to win.

The Leopards had opened their season with a win over Millersville (29-17), then dropped a game with Northeastern (6-36). Lafayette won two games back-to-back versus Cornell (30-19) and at Harvard (17-7). The game at Fordham on October 12th was cancelled after a Rams player collapsed and died during the pre-game warmups. The Leopards came to Army have lost two games in a row, at Columbia (0-3) and at Colgate (9-40).

Jeff Brizic scored on a one yard touchdown run in the opening three minutes. J. Parker made a 23 yard field goal 14 seconds left in the first quarter. Brizic rushed for a two yard touchdown run in the opening minutes of the second quarter. The Leopards completed a six yard touchdown reception with nine minutes left in the half. Army responded with a Ronnie McAda 40 yard touchdown pass to Brad Miller two minutes later for a halftime lead of 24-7.

McAda completed a 27 yard touchdown pass to Brizic in the opening minutes of the third quarter. Adam Thompson completed a 31 yard touchdown pass to Chris Dunning with 3:34 left on the clock in the third period.

The Leopards defense recovered an Army fumble and returned the football 66 yards for a touchdown in the opening minute of the fourth quarter. Three minutes later, Parker made his second field goal, this one from 23 yards. In the last minute, Lafayette scored on a 15 yard touchdown run, to make the final score, 41-21, for an Army victory.

Army had 22 first downs, 321 yards rushing, 180 passing (10-10-0), had three lost fumbles, punted two times, and 36:04 time of possession. Lafayette had 11 first downs, 83 rushing yards, 147 passing (11-17-1), one lost fumble, and punted eight times.

Lafayette finished the 1996 season with a 2-2 Patriot League record, placing in fourth in the standings. The Leopards won their next two games versus Bucknell (23-7) and Holy Cross (38-21) before losing to their rival Lehigh, 19-23, in their final game of the season. Lafayette finished with an overall record of 5-5 in head coach Bill Russo's 16th season.

Air Force

Army (8-0) hosted the United States Air Force Academy (5-3) on November 9th at West Point at sold out Michie Stadium with 41,251 fans attending. It was the largest crowd in 20 years. Air Force was favored by 3 points to win. Army was leading the nation in rushing, followed at second by the Falcons. Brent Musburger and Dick Vermeil were the announcers for *ABC Television*.

Air Force opened their season with big wins versus San Jose State (45-0) and at Nevada Las Vegas (65-17). On September 21st, the Falcons lost a close game at Wyoming, 19-22. Air Force rebounded with a home win versus Rice (45-17) on September 28th.

Air Force hosted Navy on October 12th, and lost a close game, 17-20. The Falcons rebounded by beating #8/#9 Notre Dame, 20-17, in South Bend in their first overtime game the next Saturday. Air Force then spanked Hawai'i at home, 34-7. The Falcons lost a heartbreaker to Colorado State (41-42) the weekend before the Army game.

Late in the first quarter, J. Parker converted a 31 yard field goal. Nakia Addison scored on a 25 yard touchdown run, with Dallas Thompson making the extra point kick for the Falcons to take a 7-3 lead midway through the second quarter. With four minutes left in the first half, Joe Hewitt rushed for a four yard touchdown, with Parker making the PAT kick, to give the Cadets a 10-7 lead going into intermission.

There was no scoring in the third quarter. Parker converted a 45 yard field goal with 13:39 left in the game to extend the Army lead to 13-7. Safety Jerrold Tyquiengco intercepted Beau Morgan's pass at the AF-35. Six plays later, Hewitt rushed for a four yard touchdown to make it 20-7, with eleven minutes to play. Parker made a 28 yard field goal with 5:26 to go for the final score and an Army victory, 23-7.

"When our defense plays like that, I don't know how many teams can beat us," said sophomore fullback Joe Hewitt after the game. "We earned a lot of respect with this. I don't think anyone in the country is going to say we're in league with Nebraska, but I think we can line up against anybody."

"It's tough to put into words," center Kyle Scott said of the rare victory over the Falcons. "There is a vast cultural difference between the two service academies. Army prides itself on a foxhole mentality and sees Air Force as the military's leisure class. The Cadets also thought Air Force to be haughty with its long winning streak. They were confident, but if we had won seven in a row, I'd be confident, too. To take that confidence away feels great."

Army had 18 first downs, 260 yards rushing, 125 passing (7-9-0), no turnovers, punted four times, had one penalty for 15 yards, and had 38:20 time of possession. Air Force had 11 first downs, 69 yards rushing, 148 passing (12-24-1), no fumbles, punted seven times, and had two penalties for ten yards.

Nakia Addison led the Falcons rushers with 38 yards. Joe Hewitt had 161 rushing yards, while Bobby Williams had 47 yards. Ron Leshinski had three catches for 29 yards, while Jeff Brizic caught one pass for 67 yards. Heisman Trophy candidate Beau Morgan had six yards rushing and 148 passing. It was the lowest rushing yards in a game in head coach DeBerry's tenure at Air Force.

The Falcons finished the 1996 season with a 5-3 Western Athletic Conference record for fourth place in the Pacific Division. Air Force won at Fresno State (44-38) in overtime, then lost another close game at San Diego State (23-28) to end the season. Air Force finished with an overall record of 6-5 in Fisher DeBerry's 13th season.

It was the first victory by Army over Air Force in eight years. It was also the first time since 1978 that the Falcons had lost to both Army and Navy in the same season. Army received 281 points from voters to be ranked 22nd in the *Associated Press* Top 25 Poll. In the *USA Today/CNN* Coaches Poll, the Cadets were ranked 23rd.

Syracuse

#22/#23 Army (9-0) traveled to play #19 Syracuse University (6-2) in the sold out Carrier Dome on November 16th in front of 49,257 indoor Orangemen fans. Syracuse was favored by 18.5 points to win. Army was fourth ranked in total defense (224 ypg) entering the game. Ron Franklin and Lou Holtz were the announcers for *ESPN2*.

#9/#11 Syracuse opened the season to two losses versus #24/#22 North Carolina (10-27) and at Minnesota (33-35). Syracuse dropped out of the rankings after the two losses. The

Orangemen then won six straight games before playing Army, versus #18/#16 Virginia Tech (52-21), versus Rutgers (42-0), versus Pitt (55-7), at Boston College (45-17), at #18/#17 West Virginia (30-17), and at Tulane (31-7). The Orangemen returned to the Top 25 rankings after beating the Mountaineers. The team was led by quarterback Donovan McNabb.

Ten minutes into the game, the Orangemen scored on a three yard touchdown run. Donovan McNabb completed a one yard touchdown pass at 9:38 mark in the second quarter to make it 14-0. Ronnie McAda completed a seven yard touchdown pass to Ron Leshinski two minutes later. With one minute left in the first half, Syracuse scored on a nine yard run to make it 21-7 at halftime.

Midway through the third quarter, J. Parker made a 24 yard field goal to close the score to 21-10. McNabb threw a nine yard touchdown pass three minutes later. The Orangemen rushed three yards for a touchdown late in the third period to make it 35-10. Demetrius Perry scored on a one yard run midway in the fourth quarter. With 1:26 left in the game, Syracuse scored on a ten yard run for the final score, 42-17, for Army's first loss of the season.

"They executed on offense," said Jim Young after the game. "You've got to give them some credit in there somewhere. We didn't probably play as well as we could like, but you've got to recognize they're very good and they did a heck of a job executing out there. They didn't make many mistakes."

"I'm disappointed with the loss," said quarterback Ronnie McAda. "We've come this far and we still have another game. We've got Navy. We're 9-1, we can't be disappointed with the season. We should have played them closer than we did."

"It was very important we kept the [Army] defense on their toes," said Donovan McNabb. "They were looking for the outside option and we hit them with the play-action pass. Our receivers got open and it was my job to hit them."

Army had 18 first downs, 288 yards rushing, 88 passing (11-18-0), no turnovers, punted four times, had five penalties for 38 yards, and had 32:24 time of possession. Syracuse had 12 first downs, 222 rushing yards, 285 yards passing (18-19-0), one lost fumble, punted once, and had eight penalties for 45 yards.

Syracuse's Malcolm Thomas rushed for 111 yards and two touchdowns, only the second opponent running back to do so this season. Joe Hewitt rushed for 120 yards, while Ronnie McAda had 58, Demetrius Perry 42, and Bobby Williams had 38 rushing yards. Orangemen Jim Turner caught four passes for 90 yards, while Quinton Spotwood had three catches for 73 yards. Donovan McNabb threw for 285 yards, the highest by an opponent quarterback this season.

Syracuse finished the 1996 regular season with a 6-1 Big East Conference record and was the league's co-champion, tied for first with #13 Virginia Tech and #14 Miami Florida. After playing Army, the Orangemen won at Temple (35-15) but then lost to #23 Miami Florida (31-38).

#23/#22 Syracuse was invited to play in the Liberty Bowl, where they defeated Houston, 30-17. Syracuse finished with an overall record of 9-3 ranked #21/#19 in the two polls during Paul Pasqualoni's sixth season as head football coach.

After the loss to Syracuse, Army dropped out of the polls on November 18th, still receiving votes but falling to #27/#26. On November 25th, Army was ranked 24th in both polls. On December 2nd, Army rose one spot in both polls to 23rd.

Navy

Navy began the 1996 season with two wins, first on September 7th at Rutgers (10-6) and then versus Southern Methodist (19-17) on September 21st. A close loss followed at Boston College (38-43). The Midshipmen then won three in a row, versus Duke (64-27), at Air Force (20-17), and at Wake Forest (47-18).

Navy was beaten by #19/#21 Notre Dame, 27-54, in the Emerald Isle Classic in Dublin Ireland on November 2nd. The Midshipmen then won three in a row, versus Delaware (30-14), versus Tulane (35-21), and at Georgia Tech (36-26) to finish their regular season prior to the Army-Navy game.

Because both Army and Navy had beaten Air Force, the winner of this game would take home the Commander-in-Chief's Trophy. Navy (8-2) ran the option offense this season under offensive coordinator Paul Johnson. Army (9-1) was ranked #23 in both polls and led the nation in rushing. Navy (8-2) was favored by 2 points to win.

The Independence Bowl had announced that the winner of the Army-Navy game would receive the at-large berth to play against a Southeastern Conference opponent, speculated to be Auburn or Louisiana State.

The Army-Navy game was played on December 7th in Philadelphia at sold out Veterans Stadium in rainy conditions before 69,238 spectators. Sean McDonough (play-by-play), Terry Donahue (analyst), Michele Tafoya (sideline reporter), and Mike Mayock (sideline reporter) broadcasted the game for *CBS Television*. Navy was the home team. Army wore gold helmets, white jerseys, and gold pants.

The Cadets lost their leading rusher, Joe Hewitt, to a knee injury early in the first quarter. At the end of the first quarter, J. Parker converted a 22 yard field goal. Navy's Patrick McGrew rushed for a seven yard touchdown with 9:33 on the second quarter clock, with Tom Vanderhorst making the PAT kick, to make it 7-3 in favor of the Midshipmen. Three minutes later, Chris McCoy completed a 15 yard touchdown pass to LeBron Butts to make it 14-3.

After an Army fumble on the kickoff gave Navy the ball at the WP-20, Omar Nelson ran 18 yards, then McCoy rushed for a two yard touchdown with five minutes left in the half to make the score, 21-3. Ronnie McAda broke loose and rushed for a 44 yard touchdown at 2:39 on the clock, with Parker making the extra point kick. An interception of a McCoy pass gave the Cadets the ball back. With 39 seconds left, Parker converted a 35 yard field goal. The halftime score was 21-13 in favor of the Midshipmen.

On the second play of the third quarter, Bobby Williams broke free down the left sideline on an 81 yard touchdown run. McAda stretched the football over the goal line on the two-point conversion effort, but the officials ruled that he had fumbled it into the end zone, making the score 21-19, Navy. A fumble by Army gave the ball to the Midshipmen on the WP-22, but Vanderhorst missed a 42 yard field goal attempt.

After a 45 yard run by McAda, Demetrius Perry rushed for a three yard touchdown with 4:43 left in the third quarter to complete the 77 yard drive. Navy stopped the two-point conversion run, but Army took the lead, 25-21. Navy returned the kickoff to the WP-39 and were aided by a personal foul penalty by the Cadets for a hit out of bounds. Vanderhorst made a 31 yard field goal with two seconds left in the third quarter to close the score, 25-24.

With 6:35 to play, Parker converted his third field goal of the day, from 20 yards, to make the score 28-24. Navy had two chances to regain the lead in the final minutes. On the first, the Midshipmen failed on four tries from inside the WP-4.

Navy got the ball back 56 seconds later on the N-43, with the stronger passer Ben Fay coming in at quarterback for McCoy. Fay completed a 24 yarder to Astor Heaven, 13 yard to Neal Plaskonos, and then receiver Pat McGrew drew an Army holding call that gave the Midshipmen a first and ten on the WP-10.

Two passes went out the back of the end zone over the hands of LeBron Butts. On third down, the pass slipped out of Fay's hands for an incompletion. Garland Gay intercepted a fourth down pass in the end zone with ten seconds left in the game to win the game. ARMY 28, Navy 24.

"We've been a great second half time all year and there was no reason to think we wouldn't be one this afternoon, too," said Navy head football coach Charlie Weatherbie. "But we didn't execute very well when we came out."

"I don't want to take anything away from Army because it is a very good team. But if I had done my job they wouldn't have had the 44 yard touchdown and that's what turned the game around," said Navy linebacker Clint Bruce. "We didn't do our jobs the way we should have done them and that made a big difference in this game."

"Losing this game will still hurt even if we get a bowl bid, but I tried to make our players understand that they've come a long way, though a few things slipped through our fingers today," continued Weatherbie.

"Army played tough," confessed Omar Nelson. "Army was fighting and scratching and not giving up. They made the most of their opportunities. That's what they did today. And we didn't."

Army had 17 first downs, 340 yards rushing, 116 passing (5-10-0), lost two fumbles, punted three times, had six penalties for 55 yards, and 32:29 time of possession. Navy had 18 first downs, 153 rushing yards, 144 yards passing (8-20-2), no fumbles, punted four times, and had four penalties for 25 yards.

Navy's Omar Nelson had 74 rushing yards, while Chris McCoy had 47 yards, Patrick McGrew 19, and Corey Schemm had 13 rushing yards. Chris McCoy's touchdown was his 16th of the season, breaking the Navy record held by Heisman Trophy recipient Joe Bellino. McCoy completed six out of 14 passes for 107 yards with one touchdown and one interception. Ben Fay completed two out six passes for 37 yards and one interception.

Astor Heaven caught two passes for 67 yards, while Corey Schemm had two receptions for 37, and LeBron Butts (15 yards), Neal Plaskonos (13), Omar Nelson (8), and Patrick McGrew (4) each had one catch. Safety Gervy Alota led the Midshipmen with 16 tackles (8 solo). Linebackers Clint Bruce and Jason Coffey each had ten tackles.

Ronnie McAda had 134 rushing yards, while Bobby Williams had 104, Demetrius Perry with 54, Jeff Brizic 25, Joe Hewitt had 18, Rashad Hodge with six, and Scot Lord had minus one rushing yard. Ronnie McAda completed five out of ten passes for 116 yards. Bobby Williams (43 yards), Brad Miller (30), Jeff Brizic (16), Ron Leshinski (15), and Ron Thomas (10) each had one reception. Ronnie McAda was selected as the most valuable player of the game for the second time in three years.

On December 8th, Navy received an invitation to play in Hawai'i on Christmas Day. Navy played in the Aloha Bowl on December 25th against California (6-5) and won, 42-38. The Midshipmen finished the 1996 season with a 9-3 overall record in Charlie Weatherbie's second season as head football coach. Navy received votes in the *Associated Press* Top 25 Poll good for 27th place.

Army was down 18 points to Navy in the second quarter. This game was the largest comeback ever by Army in the series. Army won its fifth Commander-in-Chief's Trophy and was the fifth straight win over the Midshipmen. The ten wins in a season were the first ever by an Army team. On December 9th, both polls dropped Army from a 23rd ranking to 24th.

The win against Navy brought Bob Sutton the honor of being the first head football coach to beat Navy in five straight games. Army also tied the mark of winning five straight games over Navy during the 1927 and 1930-1933 seasons with three head coaches during that period (there were no games with Navy in 1928 or 1929).

Bowl Game Bids

On Sunday, December 8th, the Bowl Alliance announced their line-ups, and then the remainder of the bowl's issued their invitations; with teams selected accepting (or rejecting) the invitation. Auburn officials were expecting an invitation to the Peach Bowl to play Clemson, but with the Alliance's selections, the Tigers (7-4) received an invitation from the Independence Bowl. Army had received their invitation on Saturday in their locker room after Beating Navy from Bowl Chairman Rick Holland. Both would meet on December 31st for the game.

In the 1996 season, there were eleven teams that played as Independents. Five of these teams had winning records in the regular season - #24 Army (10-1), Navy (8-2), East Carolina (8-3), #18 Notre Dame (8-3), and Louisiana Tech (6-5). Army and Navy went to bowl games. East Carolina and Louisiana Tech did not receive any bowl bids.

It was reported that Notre Dame was offered to play Auburn in the Independence Bowl after they lost to Southern California on November 30th and were no long being considered by the Bowl Alliance for their bowl games. The Fighting Irish turned down the invitation, believing the Tigers were an unworthy opponent and the bowl was an unworthy destination. Funny, the Fighting Irish went to the 1997 Independence Bowl and played Louisiana State. Through the 2022 season, Notre Dame has never played Auburn.

1996 Season Statistics

The following are the Cadets team offensive statistics for the 1996 season, excluding the bowl game. On offense, the team had 350 points (31.8 average); 252 first downs (198 rushing, 45 passing, and 9 by penalty); rushed for 3,812 yards (346.5 ypg) on 740 attempts (5.2 ypa) and 33 touchdowns; passed for 1,142 yards on 67 completions on 104 passes and 2 interceptions for 103.8 ypg, 11.0 ypp, 17.0 ypr, and 8 touchdowns; had 4,954 yards total offense on 844 plays, 450.4 ypg, 5.9 ypp, and 42 touchdowns; had 47 penalties for 449 yards; had 27 fumbles and lost 11 of them; had an average time of possession per game of 37:40; converted 84 out of 168 third downs (50.0%), and converted 15 out of 25 fourth downs (60.0%).

On defense, the team allowed 192 points (17.5 average); 158 first downs (56 rushing, 87 passing, and 15 by penalty); 979 yards rushing (89.0 ypg) on 325 attempts (3.0 ypa) and 12 touchdowns allowed; 1,840 passing yards on 150 completions on 301 passes and 8 interceptions for 167.3 ypg, 6.1 ypp, 12.3 ypr, and 11 touchdowns; allowed 2,819 total yards on 626 plays, 256.3 ypg, 4.5 ypp, and 26 touchdowns; opponents had 39 penalties for 275 yards; converted 45 out of 138 third downs (32.6%); converted 8 out of 20 fourth downs (40.0%); forced 13 fumbles and recovered 6 of them; and returned 2 interceptions (28.0 average).

For Cadets special team statistics, punted 34 times for a 40.9 average; returned 32 kickoffs (21.7 average); returned 25 punts (6.2 average); made 18 out of 21 field goal attempts; and made 40 out of 40 point after touchdown attempts. For opponents' special teams statistics, punted 63 times for a 40.3 average; returned 61 kickoffs (20.5 average); and returned 23 punts (6.7 average).

Joe Hewitt had 839 yards rushing in 141 carries for an 83.9 ypg, while Bobby Williams ran for 611 in 94 attempts for 55.5 ypg, Demetrius Perry rushed for 473 yards (52.6), and Ronnie McAda gained 459 yards (51.0).

Other individual rushing statistics were Jeff Brizic (71-321), Adam Thompson (51-223), Rashad Hodge (32-2210, Lee Gibson (21-147), Ron Thomas (20-104), Charles Kean (18-98), Coby Short (17-89), Ty Amey (18-75), John Johnson (21-66), Johnny Goff (8-27), Vaughn Carpenter (7-26), Brad Miller (2-16), Reno Ferri (3-9), Robert Lalumondier (2-5), Craig Stucker (2-4), and Scot Lord (1-minus 1).

Williams rushed for 8 touchdowns, while Hewitt, Perry, and Brizic each had 6. Others scoring rushing touchdowns were McAda (4), Kean (2), and Hodge (1).

McAda completed 55 out of 87 passes for 954 yards with five touchdowns and no interceptions. Thompson completed 12 out of 17 passes with three touchdowns and two interceptions. Hewitt led the team in all-purpose yardage with 85.0 ypg. McAda led the team in total offense with 157.0 ypg.

Ron Leshinski caught 17 passes for 259 yards and three touchdowns. Ron Thomas had eleven receptions for 163 yards and one touchdown, while Jeff Brizic caught nine passes for 188 yards and one touchdown.

Others catching passes were Rod Richardson (6-81 with one touchdown), Brad Miller (5-169 with one touchdown), Chris Dunning (5-61 with one touchdown), Rashad Hodge (4-45),

Bobby Williams (3-84), Demetrius Perry (3-40), Joe Hewitt (2-11), Coby Short (1-28), and John Johnson (1-13).

Thomas returned 21 kickoffs for a 23.2 average and a long of 52, while Richardson had six returns for a 20.7 average and Miller returned two for 37 yards. Kurt Ruch (10 yards), Brizic (17), and Johnson (17) each returned one kickoff. Miller returned 22 punts for a 6.5 average, while Richardson had two returns for 0.5 average, Matt Rodgers returned one punt for ten yards. Ken Rowland returned one blocked punt for three yards. No touchdowns were scored on any punt or kickoff returns.

Robert Brown, Ben Kotwica, Garland Gay, Colin Keans, Brandon Tilford, and Kurt Ruch each recovered one fumble. Tilford returned a fumble for 17 yards for a touchdown. Ruch, Chad Suitonu, and Joe Stanyer each forced a fumble. Jerrold Tyquiengco intercepted three passes for 17 yards, while Matt Rogers had two interceptions for 52 yards. Others making interceptions were Mike Coerper (0), Garland Gay (17), and Joe Sachitano (3). No touchdowns were scored on interceptions or fumble returns.

Stephen King and Garland Gay each had six pass breakups, while Tom Mullins had five and Jerrold Tyquiengco had four. Others with pass breakups were Robert Brown (3), Ben Kotwica (3), Joe Sachitano (2), CW Estes (2), Colin Kearns (2), Brandon Tilford (2), Donald Augustus (2), Scott Eichelberger (1), Scott Sprawls (1), Jeff Forgach (1), Jamar Mullin (1), and Justin Brandon (1). Matt Rogers blocked a punt.

J. Parker made 18 out 21 field goal attempts, with a long of 45 yards. Parker made 40 out of 40 point after touchdown kicks. The team attempted two-point conversion rushes twice without scoring. Opponents scored on one of two attempted two-point passes. Army scored twice on an opponent's safety, one time by CW Este. Scot Lord punted 34 times for an average of 40.9 and a long of 60 with no blocked punts.

J. Parker led the team in scoring with 94 points, while Bobby Williams had 48 and Jeff Brizic had 42. Others scoring were Perry

(36), Hewitt (36), McAda (24) Leshinski (18), Kean (12), Thomas (6), Hodge (6), Tilford (6), Miller (6), Dunning (6), Richardson (6), and Estes (2).

Stephen King led the team with 70 total tackles (43 solo), followed by Joe Sachitano with 68, Robert Brown with 52, Ben Kotwica had 49, and CW Estes with 47 tackles. Others with tackles included Scott Eichelberger (46), Larry Angles (45), Garland Gay (44), Jerrold Tyquiengco (44), Colin Kearns (37), Brandon Tilford (28), Tom Mullins (27), Scott Sprawls (26), Donald Augustus (25), Kurt Ruch (16), Len Kennedy (15), Bo French (15), Chad Suitonu (13), Matt Rogers (12), Brian King (12), Joe Stanyer (8), Mike Coerper (8), Tony Bianchi (8), Scott Fagan (7), Jeff Forgach (7), and Hise Gibson (6).

Having three tackles were Jason Walker, Kevin Koger, and Mike McCoy. Having two tackles were Jamar Mullen, Ken Rowland, Rob Rodenmayer, Ryan Miedema, Justin Brandon, and Scott Williams.

Estes and Angles led the team with eleven tackles for loss. Others with TFLs were Eichelberger (9), Sachitano (7), Stephen King (6), Kearns (6), Kotwica (4), Suitonu (3), Gay (2), Stanyer (2), Tyquiengco (1), Tilford (1), Sprawls (1), Brian King (1), Coerper (1), Forgach (1), and Brandon (1).

CW Estes led the team in sacks with 6.0, while Scott Eichelberger had 5.0 and Colin Kearns had 4.0 sacks. Others with sacks were Larry Angles (2.0), Stephen King (1.0), Chad Suitonu (1.0), Mike Coerper (1.0), Tony Bianchi (1.0), Scott Fagan (1.0), and Hise Gibson (1.0).

The Cadets were first nationally in rushing yards per game; sixth in rushing defense; ninth in total defense, 18th in scoring defense, and 37th in pass efficiency defense. J. Parker was ranked sixth nationally in field goals made per game and 24th in scoring. Army averaged 37,273 attendance in six home games, 32,400 in two away games, and 36,271 in three neutral site games. Scoring by quarters was 60-51 (1st), 110-69 (2nd), 91-36 (3rd), and 118-68 (4th).

The 1996 team established a new Army record for ten games won in a season; highest total offense yardage, fewest interceptions thrown; highest completion percentage; most field goals made in a season; most consecutive games holding an opponent to less than 55 yards rushing; most consecutive games holding an opponent to less than 105 yards rushing; most first downs; and tied for first for most players achieving a 100 yard rushing game.

At the end of the 2020 season, the 1988 team still held the following Army season records: first for fewest interceptions thrown (2); first in completion percentage; first for most field goals made in a season; first for most consecutive games holding an opponent to less than 55 yards rushing (5); first for most consecutive games holding an opponent to less than 105 yards rushing (8); and tied for first for most players achieving a 100 yard rushing game (5).

Also, second in total offense yards per game; second in passing yards per completion; fifth in total offense yards; tied for sixth in rushing yards per game; seventh in first downs made; seventh in total offensive yards per play; seventh in fewest punts; ninth in rushing yards; tenth in rushing attempts; tenth in punting average; and tied for 16th in rushing touchdowns.

Individuals holding Army season records included (Bobby Williams) tied for eighth in longest rush against Navy (81 yards); and tied for 15th in fewest carries in a 100 yard game (8-127); (Joe Hewitt) twelfth in rushing yards per game (83.9); and (Ronnie McAda) first in completion percentage (0.632); third for passing efficiency; tied for fifth for passing yards per attempt (11.0); tied for eight in total offensive yards per play; and ninth for total offense in a game against Duke (313 yards).

Also, (Ron Thomas) tied for first for least receptions to achieve a 100 yard game against Duke (2); tied for 13th for most 100 yard reception yards (1); and 17th in kickoff return average; (Scot Lord) 14th in punting average; (Brad Miller) tied for ninth in number of punt returns (22); (Larry Angles) tied for ninth in tackles for loss (15); (CW Estes) tied for ninth for quarterback sacks (6); and (Scott Eichelberger) tied for 15th for quarterback sacks (5).

Also, (J. Parker) first for most field goals made (18); tied for first in extra point conversion rate (100%); tied for first in most field goals made in a row (11); tied for second in field goal completion percentage (85.7%); tied for fourth for most field goal attempts (21); seventh for most points scored (94); eight in extra points made (40); and eighth in extra points attempted (40).

Awards and Recognitions

Bob Sutton was the recipient of the Bobby Dodd Coach of the Year Award. Ron Leshinski was invited to and played in the 1997 Hula Bowl.

Lettermen

The following individuals earned letters from the 1996 season: Larry Angles, Donald Augustus, Dave Beard, Tony Bianchi, Tim Booth, Justin Brandon, Jeff Brizic, Robert Brown, Doug Chadwick, Jeremy Chapman, Mike Coerper, Dan Cox, Jeff Dietz, Chris Dunning, Scott Eichelberger, Jeff Enck, CW Estes, Scott Fagan, Jeff Forgach, Rich Fredricks, Bo French, Garland Gay, Hise Gibson, Lee Gibson, and Joe Hewitt.

Also, Rashad Hodge, Guy Huntsinger, Charles Kean, Colin Kearns, Len Kennedy, Brian King, Stephen King, Ben Kotwica, Ron Leshinski, Scot Lord, Ronnie McAda, Mike McCoy, Brad Miller, Mike Morrison, Jamar Mullen, Tom Mullins, Eric Olsen, J. Parker, Demetrius Perry, Jorn Pung, Neal Ravitz, and Rod Richardson.

Also, Rob Rodenmayer, Matt Rogers, Kurt Ruch, Joe Sachitano, Kyle Scott, Coby Short, Nate Smith, Scott Sprawls, Joe Stanyer, Chad Suitonu, Ron Thomas, Adam Thompson, Brandon Tilford, Jerrold Tyquiengco, Mike West, Bobby Williams, Theo Unbehagen, and Matt Yost.

Army Branch Selections

The following members of the USMA Class of 1997 graduated and were commissioned in the following branches: (Field Artillery) Tony Bianchi, Tim Booth, Jeff Brizic, Doug Chadwick, Mike Coerper, Dan Cox, Scott Eichelberger, CW Estes, Rich Fredricks, Lee Gibson, Charles Kean, Colin Kearns, Stephen King, Ron Leshinski, Ronnie McAda, Mike McCoy, Tom Mullins, Demetrius Perry, Rob Rodenmayer, Kyle Scott, and Nate Smith; (Air Defense Artillery) Guy Huntsinger; (Armor) Mike West (Engineers) Jorn Pung, and Coby Short; (Aviation) Hise Gibson, Ben Kotwica, J. Parker, and Jerrold Tyquiengco; (Signal Corps) Donald Augustus and Rashad Hodge; and (Ordnance) Garland Gay and Ron Thomas.

Conclusion

On the strength of one of the finest seasons in its proud football history, Army would return to postseason play for the first time in eight years, heading south to face Auburn University in the 21st annual Poulan Weed Eater Independence Bowl in Shreveport LA on December 31st. The Cadets had term-end examinations (finals) to successfully complete prior to attending and a few players healing from injuries hoping to return to the field.

Chapter 11

1996 Independence Bowl Game

On December 7th, Bowl Chairman Rick Holland visited the celebrating Army Football Team in their locker room after their victory over Navy, and officially extended an invitation for the Cadets to attend the Poulan Weed Eater Independence Bowl. The USMA leadership and team immediately accepted the bowl bid. The next day, the Bowl Committee invited Auburn University (7-4) to play the United States Military Academy at West Point (10-1) in the 21st edition of the bowl game on Tuesday, December 31st, at 2:30 pm CST in Shreveport LA. The Tigers immediately accepted. The payout was reported to be $800,000 for each team.

Auburn athletic director David Housel said after the bowl game was over, "I've been to a lot of bowls, but never one where the people have been so great. They go out of their way to make sure you have a good time. And it is genuine, not phony. Everywhere I've gone people have told me, 'Good to have you in Shreveport.' Some of these other bowls live on reputation. But this one should be called the People's Bowl."

Independence Bowl History

The Independence Bowl was started in 1976 and received its name from the United States Bicentennial that year. All twenty prior editions had been played on the natural grass of the Independence Stadium (capacity 50,459), known at the State Fair Stadium until 1981. The 1976 game also used the name Bicentennial Bowl.

During its first five years, the bowl game had the Southland Conference champion play against an at-large opponent. It then moved to inviting two at-large teams. In 1995, the bowl featured a team from the Southeastern Conference against an at-large opponent. Army had received a bowl bid in the 1977 season to play Louisiana Tech, but USMA leadership turned it down.

In 1990, the postseason event became one of the earliest college bowl games to use a title sponsor, becoming the Poulan Weed-Eater Independence Bowl. Poulan was a division of AB Electrolux Home Products.

Auburn Football History

Auburn University started playing football in 1892 with an overall record of 579-346-48. The Tigers joined the Southeastern Conference (SEC) in 1932 as one of the five original members. Auburn had previously been in the Southern Intercollegiate Athletic Association (SIAA) in 1895-1921, then joined the Southern Conference (SoCon).

Auburn was the 1957 national champion, and some would argue it was national champion in 1913 and 1983. The Tigers have won seven SIAA, one SoCon, and five SEC championships, the last in 1989.

Auburn has played in 24 bowl games with a 12-10-2 record. On January 1st, the Tigers lost 13-42 to Penn State in the 1995 Outback Bowl. Auburn had played in eleven different bowls, with six appearance in the Gator and four in the Sugar, but never in the Independence Bowl.

Auburn has had 49 First Team All-Americans, two Heisman Trophy recipients (Pat Sullivan in 1971 and Bo Jackson in 1985), and two Outland Trophy recipients (Zeke Smith in 1958 and Tracy Rocker in 1988). Auburn had five members inducted in the College Hall of Fame.

1996 Auburn Tigers Football Team

Auburn was led by fourth year head football coach Terry Bowden with offensive coordinator and receivers Tommy Bowden and defensive coordinator and secondary Bill Oliver. Other members of the coaching staff were Rodney Allison (running backs), Jimbo Fisher (quarterbacks), Jack Hines (inside linebackers), Lionel James (tight ends), Pete Jenkins (defensive line), Rick Trickett (offensive line), Joe Whitt (outside linebackers), Will Muschamp (graduate assistant), and Bryan Fisher (graduate assistant). About 20 days before the game, Tommy Bowden accepted the head coaching job at Tulane, so Allison acted as offensive coordinator during the bowl game, while Terry Bowden called the plays.

Auburn began their 1996 season ranked #16 in the polls. The Tigers opened at home against Alabama Birmingham on August 31st, and blanked the Blazers, 29-0, with Jared Holmes kicking five field goals. Auburn dropped to #18, but still shutdown Fresno State at home, 62-0, the next weekend.

The #15 Tigers traveled to Oxford to face Ole Miss on September 14th, and won its first SEC game of the year, 45-28. The next Saturday, #13 Auburn hosted some other Tigers, this time from Baton Rouge. The #21 Louisiana State took advantage of three missed field goals and one missed PAT to eke out a win, 19-15.

#20 Auburn's quarterback Dameyune Craig ran for a pair of fourth quarter touchdowns to defeat South Carolina at home, 28-24. On October 12th, #18 Auburn traveled to Starkville and handily beat up their hosts Mississippi State, 49-15. The shoe was on the other foot when the #16 Tigers traveled to Gainesville to face #1 Florida, 51-10, as the Gators had 625 yards of total offense while Auburn only had 173 total yards.

Bobby Bowden, head football coach at Florida State, was down in New Orleans in late December getting his team ready to play for the national championship against Florida in the 1997 Sugar Bowl. He spoke on Sunday at the First Baptist Church and provided some stories about his son Terry asking for advice.

"A couple of years ago, I told him I'd give him advice by phone at halftime of an Auburn-Florida game. He did call, and I told him to just keep doing whatever you're doing because you're winning. This year, he called me at halftime [Florida was leading

21-10]. I told him to call 911. There is nothing I can do to help you."

Returning home, but letting the visiting Razorbacks a 7-0 first quarter lead, the #24 Tigers scored four straight touchdowns to beat Arkansas, 28-7. Division 1-A Northeast Louisiana (known now as Louisiana-Monroe) were supposed to be an easy game, but the Indians led from late in the second quarter to late into the final stanza. After making an 18 yard field goal, NLU led 24-21 with 2:51 left in the game. Craig led #22 Auburn on a 70 yard drive with a Kevin McLeod six yard touchdown to win, 28-24.

The unranked Georgia Bulldogs (3-5) visited Jordan-Hare Stadium to face #20 Auburn at home in their 100th meeting. The Tigers went up 28-14 at halftime, but then Georgia scored on a 67 yard touchdown pass in the fourth quarter, then took 67 seconds to march 82 yards for the tying score, 28-28, to force the game into the SEC's first ever overtime.

Each side scored a touchdown in the first three overtime periods. In the fourth one, Georgia ran one yard for a touchdown, but Dameyune Craig was tackled one yard short on a fourth and three to give the Bulldogs a big upset, 56-49.

#15 Alabama (9-2) and unranked Auburn (7-3) met at Legion Field on November 23rd. The Crimson Tide reeled off 17 points before the Tigers made a 34 yard field goal in the first quarter to make it 17-3 in favor of Alabama.

In the second quarter, it was Auburn's turn to score 17 points. Craig completed a 57 yards touchdown pass to Karsten Bailey streaking down the sidelines. Freshman Brad Ware intercepted a pass and returned it 34 yards for a touchdown to tie the game. Holmes connected on a 34 yard field goal to make it 20-17 Tigers at halftime.

Holmes made his third field goal in the third period to up the lead to 23-17. Alabama completed a six yard touchdown pass with 26 seconds left in the game to tie the game. Jon Brock made the PAT kick for Alabama to win the game, 24-23.

Auburn's offensive team statistics season averages were points per game (33.3), first downs (21.2), rushing yardage (153.3), passing yardage (234.0), total offense (387.3), and penalty yardage (58.5). The Tigers averaged 20.7 yards per kickoff return, 9.3 yards per punt return, 9.2 yards per interception, 3.9 yards per rush, 7.4 yards per pass, 13.4 yards per completion, 5.4 yards per play, 40.2 yards per punt, 42% third down completion percentage, 54% fourth down completion percentage, and 29:38 time of possession.

The Tigers had 17 fumbles and lost nine of them; completed 192 out of 348 passes with 19 touchdowns and 13 interceptions; made 24 rushing touchdowns; and had a total of 47 scores. On kicking, Auburn made 43 out of 45 extra-point kicks and 13 out of 20 field goal attempts. Auburn's 785 plays consisted of 348 passes and 437 rushes. Their quarterbacks were sacked 32 times for 223 lost yards.

Auburn's defensive team statistics season averages included points per game (22.5), first downs (19.7), rushing yardage (131.2), passing yardage (239.2), total offense (370.4), and penalty yardage (56.3). The Tigers allowed 19.3 yards per kickoff return, 8.0 yards per punt return, 8.8 yards per interception, 3.3 yards per rush, 7.3 yards per pass, 13.8 yards per completion, 5.1 yards per play, 40.2 yards per punt, 39% third down completion percentage, and 21% fourth down completion percentage.

The team forced 23 fumbles and recovered 14 of them and allowed 190 completions out of 361 passes with 15 touchdowns and 22 interceptions. The Tigers allowed 17 rushing touchdowns and a total of 33 scores. On kicking, Auburn allowed 31 out of 32 extra-point kicks and 5 out of 13 field goal attempts. Opponents had 795 plays consisted of 361 passes and 434 rushes. The defense made 28 sacks for 186 yards and returned three interceptions for touchdowns out of 22 returns. One punt return was returned for a touchdown out of 26 punt returns.

Auburn led the nation in interceptions per game (2.0); tied for most takeaways (36), and tied for second nationally for turnover margin (+14). Auburn stood fourth nationally in consecutive games without being shut out (45).

Leading rushers for the Tigers were Rusty Williams with 439 yards on 80 carries, while Fred Beasley had 428 yards on 94 attempts and Markeith Cooper ran 351 yards on 64 carries. Dameyune Craig had gained 486 yards on 123 attempts, but lost 279 for a net rushing total of 207 yards. Craig had completed 169 out of 310 passes for 2,296 yards with 16 touchdowns and 10 interceptions. Jon Cooley was the back-up quarterback with 23-38-3-278 and three touchdowns.

Karsten Bailey was the leading receiver with 592 yards on 45 catches with three touchdowns. Tyrone Goodson caught 36 passes for 642 yards and six touchdown, while Robert Baker had 526 yards on 34 receptions for five touchdowns. Baker was the leading punt returner averaging 10.0 on 23 returns with one touchdown. Baker was also the leading kickoff returner with 21 returns averaging 21.6.

Jaret Holmes had made 13 of 20 field goals for a long of 50 yards, with one blocked kick. Holmes also was the leading punter, averaging 42.0 on 48 punts, with a long of 60 with two punts blocked. Holmes was 43 out of 45 on PAT kicks. Brad Ware and Jayson Bray led the team each with four interceptions, while Antwoine Nolan had three with Martavius Houston, Ricky Neal, and Marcellus Mostella each intercepting two passes.

Takeo Spikes led the team with 119 total tackles (75 solo), while Ricky Neal had 111, Martavius Houston 83, Jimmy Brumbaugh 80, and Marcellus Mostella 80 tackles. Houston had eight tackles for loss, while Neal had five. Mark Smith led the team with 5.0 sacks, while Leonardo Carson had 4.5 and Brumbaugh made 3.0 sacks. Brad Ware and Jayson Bray each had four passes defended. Bray had 9 pass breakups while Ware had 8. Mostella, Ware, Ryan and Taylor Carson each recovered two fumbles. Brumbaugh and Larry Melton had each blocked two kicks or punts.

Sophomore linebacker Takeo Spikes was a second-team All-American. Spikes and junior placekicker Jaret Holmes were both consensus first-team All-SEC selections for the 1996 season. Junior offensive lineman Victor Riley was a consensus second team selection, while junior wide receiver Tyrone Goodson, sophomore nose guard Jimmy Brumbaugh, and sophomore safety Martavius Houston were selected for the Coaches' All-SEC second team. Tackle Jeno James was All-SEC freshman team selection.

Auburn finished the regular season with 4-4 Southeastern Conference record, good for third place in the South Division. The Tigers overall record was 7-4. Neither team had played any common opponents, nor had Auburn played against an option offense during the season.

"The majority of my coaches have lived and coached during the option era and they know what it is all about," head coach Terry Bowden said. "The problem is, it can truly make you look silly the way a good, disciplined team like Army runs it. Air Force used it to beat Notre Dame. Army played Syracuse so good. Navy used it to beat Georgia Tech before they played Army. This is a great, great challenge for us."

Auburn had about eight morning practices from December 12th through 20th. The players then took a Christmas break until December 26th, reporting for an evening practice in Shreveport. The Tigers practiced each morning from Friday, December 27th through Sunday at Captain Shreve High School's Caddo Parish Stadium. On Monday, the team practiced in the evening.

"I think our players are going to practice hard," Bowden said. "They want to set the tempo for next season. It would be awful good for us to do that and have a good feeling going into next year."

Bowl Activities

On Thursday, December 26th, there was an Independence Bowl Press Conference welcoming Auburn to Shreveport. Friday began with a Fellowship of Christian Athletes Breakfast at the Bossier Civic Center. A hospital visit was planned for the players, followed by a team awards party. Saturday evening, the team had a dinner at the Cowboy's Club.

On Monday, there was the Joint Press Conference at the Expo Hall with both teams, followed by the Minuteman Luncheon. A Harrah's Mardi Gras Preview was held Monday evening for the team.

Comments that got the most laughs at the Minutemen Luncheon when players asked the opposing head coach questions - Army player asks Terry Bowden if his relationship with Bob Sutton was any better than his father's was with Florida head coach Steve Spurrier. The younger Bowden said, "[Sutton] probably has got a lot more class than the coach from Florida." An Auburn player asked Sutton what kinds of fish could one catch now in the once-polluted Hudson River. Sutton's answer was, "You could catch a lot of things in the Hudson, old tires, bathtubs, coaches who don't beat Navy."

Auburn and Army had met two times previously, with both games at West Point. In 1922, the Tigers (8-2) lost to the Cadets (8-0-2) 19-6. The next season, Army (6-2-1) beat Auburn (3-3-3), 28-6. The United States Military Academy is the only service academy that Auburn has played, never having played Navy or Air Force.

Army did have an all-time record of 12-13-1 against teams currently in the SEC. Its last SEC opponent was Vanderbilt in the 1991 season, a 41-10 loss at Michie Stadium. The Cadets last SEC win was on the road in 1990 against Vanderbilt, 42-38. There were 31 players on the Army roster from Texas, four from Louisiana, and none from Arkansas, Alabama, or Oklahoma.

"In a sense, if we can be 7-4 and be in the Independence Bowl in a very disappointing season, it's a credit to our program," said Terry Bowden prior to the game. "In a normal year, we win two out of the three of those losses [to Louisiana State, Georgia, and Alabama] and we're playing on January 1st."

"With two weeks off, we've learned what it takes to finish games," said Takeo Spikes. "You can make a lot of excuses, but it's time for someone to step up and make some plays. We had high expectations. We also had a lot of bad luck. It's frustrating. We didn't achieve our goals, but we found out that we didn't give up. We're young, and we didn't know how to finish games."

"I don't think any of us planned what our record would be," said Bob Sutton before the game. "Our goal was to be 1-0 every week. The players never talked in terms of winning nine straight games, and I credit them for that because they were getting increased exposure and still keeping their focus. We think we are a good running team. Our defense, without question, has allowed us to step up a notch. We've had outstanding line play. We've had a tremendous number of three-and-out plays."

A few days before the game, reflecting on how Syracuse struck first on a 38 yard pass on the first snap, Auburn tight end Jessie McCovery said, "I think we need to come out and make something happen on our first possession. We need to take the wind out of them and get them thinking this team Auburn is for real. If we let them hang in there, and you've got to stop their running game, it could be a long day for us."

The Freedom Shrine was rededicated before the game, officiated by the Secretary of the Army, Togo West, Jr. and NFL quarterback David Woodley. Other pregame entertainment included 200 dancers from Shreveport and Bossier City dance teams, then the Auburn University Marching Band took the field for a seven minute performance, including the national anthem.

Nearby Barksdale Air Force Based housed the official party from the Department of the Army and USMA, as well as the 50 Cadets of the Army Pep Band, plus 200 other Cadets taking a break from their Christmas Leave to support the Army Football Team. The base provided 200 volunteers to support the visiting Army team and bowl activities.

The two teams did not sell out their ticket allocations, leaving more than 10,000 tickets unsold. Army sold 9,200 out of its 10,000 allocation, while Auburn sold 3,000 out of its 12,000 allocation. Area ticket sales were near an all-time high, being about 23,500 tickets sold.

Pre-Game

Auburn came into the bowl game receiving votes in both polls, ranking 29th in the *Associated Press* Top 25 Poll and 28th in the *USA Today/CNN* Coaches Top 25 Poll. Army was ranked 24th in both polls.

The Auburn starting lineup on offense was wide receivers Tyron Goodson and Karsten Bailey, tight end Jessie McCovery, tackles Jim Roe and Jeno James, guards Leonard Thomas and Victor Riley, center James Kiger, fullback Kevin McLeod, tailback Rusty Williams, and quarterback Dameyune Craig.

The defensive starting lineup for the Tigers was ends Charles Dorsey and Leonardo Carson, nose guard Jimmy Brumbaugh, linebackers Quinton Reese, haven Fields, Takeo Spikes, and Marcellus Mostella, cornerbacks Antwoine Nolan and Rodney Crayton, and safeties Martavius Houston and Brad Ware. Jayson Bray started for Nolan while Ricky Neal started for Fields.

The Army defensive starters were end Scott Eichelberger and Larry Angles, defensive tackle CW Estes, nose guard Colin Kearns, linebackers Stephen King, Ben Kotwica, and Chad Suitonu, cornerbacks Tom Mullins and Garland Gay, and safeties Robert Brown and Jerrold Tyquiengco. Brian King started for Suitonu.

The Cadets starting offensive line up was tight end Ron Leshinski, left tackle Dave Beard, left guard Doug Chadwick, center Kyle Scott, right guard Jeff Enck, right tackle Rich Fredericks, split end Ron Thomas, right halfback Jeff Brizic, left halfback Bobby Williams, fullback Demetrius Perry, and quarterback Ronnie McAda.

The officials for the bowl game came from the Pacific 10 Conference. They were Jim Fogltance (referee), Walt Wolf (umpire), Jim Rinne (linesman), Cappy Anderson (line judge), Jim

Northcott (back judge), Bill Gaskins (field judge), and Brian O'Cain (side judge).

ESPN broadcasted the Poulan Weed Eater Independence Bowl game nationwide. Craig Bolerjack (play-by-play), Rod Gilmore (analyst), and Merril Hoge (sideline reporter) were the announcers for the game. There were 41,366 spectators, including my family and myself. The prices in the concession stands in the stadium were hot dogs ($2), nachos ($2), peanuts ($1), popcorn ($1), soft drinks ($2 and $1), and beer ($4 and $2).

Auburn was the home team. Army wore gold helmets, white jerseys, and gold pants. The Tigers wore white helmets, blue jerseys, and white pants. The Cadets in the stands wore Dress Gray ("If it rains, we'll all smell like sheep," said a Firstie (senior) in the stands). Auburn was favored by 7.5 points to win.

Seniors linebacker Ben Kotwica and tight end Ron Leshinski were the Army team captains. Auburn used game captains throughout the 1996 season, but it is not known who called the toss in this game. Auburn won the toss and elected to receive. Army would defend the south goal.

The game started at 2:41 pm CST. The weather was 74 degrees, winds coming from the east at 10 mph, overcast, 87% humidity, and muggy. There was a light drizzle during the first quarter. Players said the field was slippery and spongy, with the sidelines mostly a quagmire of mud.

First Quarter

Eric Olsen kicked off 65 yards to the end zone, where Robert Baker returned it 26 yards before being stopped by Reno Ferri and Matt Rogers. Dameyune Craig completed a 48 yard pass down the left sideline to Tyron Goodson for a first down at the WP-26, tackled out of bounds by Robert Brown. Craig rushed left for 14 yards and a first down at the WP-12, stopped by Ben Kotwica.

Scott Eichelberger tackled Willie Gosha out of bounds after a four yard pass reception to the left side. Garland Gay stopped Karsten Bailey after a five yard pass completion to the left side.

On third and one on a pitch play, Fred Beasley ran right two yards for a first down at the WP-1, tackled by Colin Kearns.

On a pitch play to the left side, Jerrold Tyquiengco tackled Beasley for a loss of six yards. Ben Kotwica and Stephen King sacked Craig after losing his footing for a loss of seven yards back to the WP-14. On third and goal, Craig's pass to Goodson was in the end zone and incomplete.

Jaret Holmes made a 31 field goal at 10:59 on the clock for Auburn to take a 3-0 lead. The Tigers scoring drive took nine plays to go 60 yards in 4:01 time of possession. Holmes kicked off 65 yards to the end zone, downed by Ron Thomas for a touchback.

Brad Ware and Antwoine Nolan stopped Demetrius Perry after a six yard gain to the right side. Army called a time out with the clock at 10:22. Perry rushed up the middle seven yards for a first down at the WP-33, tackled by Nolan. Haven Fields stopped Perry after a four yard run up the middle. Ronnie McAda ran left eight yards for a first down at the WP-45, stopped by Quinton Reese.

Rodney Crayton defended a pass attempt to Ron Leshinski up the middle that popped up his pads and fell incomplete. Perry rushed five yards up the middle, tackled by Jimmy Brumbaugh. On third and five at the fifty yard line, Charles Dorsey tackled McAda for a loss of one yard. Scot Lord punted 51 yards into the end zone for a touchback at 7:51 on the clock. The Cadets drive took 3:08 over seven plays that went for 29 yards.

On first and ten from the AU-20, Craig completed a twelve yard pass to the left sideline to Bailey for a first down at the AU-32, stopped by Kotwica and Gay. A pass attempt to Erick Lowe was overthrown and incomplete. Craig was in the shotgun to pass, but rushed to the left side for 27 yards and a first down at the WP-41, tackled by Stephen King and Eichelberger.

Markeith Cooper caught an eight yard pass over the middle, stopped by Chad Suitonu. A pass attempt to Goodson was defended by Tom Mullins. On third and two at the WP-33, Gay tackled Craig after a gain of one yard to the left. On fourth and one, Kevin McLeod ran up the middle for two yards and a first down at the WP-30, stopped by Brown.

Dameyune Craig completed a 30 yard touchdown pass to Tyrone Goodson for a first down with the clock at 5:20. Jaret Holmes converted the PAT kick to make the score 10-0. The Auburn scoring drive took eight plays to go 80 yards in 2:31 off the clock. Holmes kicked off 57 yards to the WP-8, where Ron Thomas returned the football 36 yards to the WP-44, tackled and pushed out of bounds by the kicker Holmes.

Ricky Neal stopped McAda after a five yard gain to the right. Perry rushed five yards up the middle and a first down to the AU-46, tackled by Dorsey. On first and ten reverse play, Ron Thomas fumbled the football for a loss of four yards, and the Tigers Brad Ware recovered it at the WP-34 with 4:19 on the first quarter clock. The Cadets drive took 1:01 in three plays with six yards gained.

Craig completed an eight yard pass to Gosha, tackled by Donald Augustus. A pass attempt to Bailey was incomplete. Craig completed a six yard pass to Baker for a first down to the WP-20, stopped by Mullins. A pass attempt to Hicks Poor was incomplete. A pass from Craig to Baker was incomplete. On third and ten, a pass attempt to Baker was incomplete, but Army's Tom Mullins was called for pass interference and penalized ten yards and an Auburn first down at the WP-10.

On first and goal, Dameyune Craig rushed up the middle for eight yards before being stopped by Ben Kotwica, who forced a fumble that was recovered by Robert Brown at the WP-2 with 2:56 on the clock. The Tigers drive went 32 yards in six plays over 1:23 time of possession.

Perry rushed up the middle for six yards before being tackled by Bobby Daffin. McAda rushed for no gain. On third and four, Perry ran three yards up the middle, stopped by Neal and Takeo Spikes. Scot Lord punted 58 yards to the AU-31, where it was downed with 0:58 left in the first quarter. The Army drive took 1:58 over nine yards in three plays.

Craig completed a 32 yard pass to Gosha for a first down at the WP-33, where Mullins pushed him out of bounds. Rusty Williams took a pitch and rushed left for 13 yards and a first down at the WP-24, tackled by Brown and Mullins. Craig was tackled for a loss of one yard at the WP-25 as the clock ran out. At the end of the first quarter, the score was Auburn 10, Army 0.

Dameyune Craig was walking to the sideline when the Cadets fired their artillery cannon to mark the end of the first quarter. The gun's noise rocked the stadium for the first time, causing Craig to duck in surprise.

Second Quarter

On second and eleven at the WP-25, Craig ran up the middle for three yards, stopped by Brown. Under pressure, Craig completed a twelve yard pass to the left side to Baker for a first down at the WP-10, tackled by Tyquiengco. Kotwica tackled Rusty Williams for no gain on a pitch play. Craig completed a three yard pass to the right side to Jessie McCovery, stopped by Gay.

On third and six, Dameyune Craig passed seven yards to Willi Gosha for a touchdown at 12:17 on the clock. Jaret Holmes made the extra point kick to make the score, 17-0. The Tigers scoring drive took 3:41 to go 69 yards over eight plays. Holmes kicked off 65 yards into the end zone, where Ron Thomas downed it for a touchback.

Marcellus Mostella tackled Bobby Williams after he rushed five yards up the middle. Neal stopped Jeff Brizic after a gain of three yards up the middle. On third and two, McAda ran right five yards for a first down at the WP-33, stopped by Ware. McAda's pass attempt to Chris Dunning was incomplete. On the next play, Army was called for illegal procedure and penalized five yards.

Spikes defended a pass attempt to Ron Thomas that was incomplete. On third and 15 at the WP-28, McAda's attempted pass to Ron Thomas was incomplete and broken up by Crayton. Scot Lord punted 39 yards to the AU-33, where Robert Baker returned it one yard at 10:11 on the clock. On that play, Auburn was called for an illegal block and penalized ten yards to the AU-24.

My family and I were sitting on the bench seats in the middle of the east stands directly behind the Auburn bench, in the middle of mostly Shreveport area fans. A group of six or eight gentlemen sat directly behind us, and they were all high school football officials.

At this point, they began to point out how poorly the officials on the field were working, being out of position and making fun of how they got the ball ready for play. I also heard criticism of things called and not called. It was interesting, very educational, but I felt they were a bit disrespectful of the game's officials.

On first and ten, Rusty Williams was dropped after a loss of three yards. Craig completed a twelve yard pass to Baker, stopped by Mullins. On third and one, Beasley ran right for two yards and a first down to the AU-35, tackled by Stephen King.

Tyquiengco stopped Beasley for no gain on the run. Joe Sachitano tackled Beasley after a run of two yards to the right. On third and eight, Craig completed an 18 yard pass to Gosha going out of bounds for a first down at the WP-45.

A pass to Goodson was incomplete, but Auburn was called for holding on the play and penalized 17 yards back to the AU-38. On first and 27, Craig's pass attempt to Goodson was incomplete. Auburn called a time out with the clock at 6:46. Craig completed a 25 yard pass over the middle to Gosha, stopped by Augustus.

On third and two, Kotwica tackled Craig after a gain of one yard up the middle. A measurement was taken, and it was short. On fourth and one, Beasley ran four yards off right tackle and a first down at the WP-32, stopped by Stephen King.

Rusty Williams ran nine yards up the middle, stopped by Mike Coerper. On the next play, Army was called for being off sides, and penalized five yards, which resulted in an Auburn first down at the WP-18. Mike Coerper tackled Rusty Williams for a loss of four yards on a pitch play. A pass attempt to the right side for Bailey was dropped and incomplete.

On third and 14 at the WP-22, Ben Kotwica and Stephen King sacked Dameyune Craig for a loss of ten yards. Craig was injured on the play and lay on the field for several minutes before he was able to get up and walk to the sidelines.

Jaret Holmes converted a 49 yard field goal at 3:15 left in the first half, making the score 20-0. The Auburn scoring possession of 15 plays went 44 yards in 6:56 off the clock. Jaret Holmes kicked off 65 yards on a line drive into the end zone, where Ron Thomas returned the football 28 yards, stopped by Reese.

On a counter play, Brizic rushed up the middle for eight yards, tackled by Spikes. On a pitch play, Brizic ran right for nine yards and a first down out of bounds to the WP-45, stopped by Spikes. Joe Hewitt rushed up the middle for one yard, tackled by Brumbaugh and Mostella. Ronnie McAda completed a 33 yard pass to the right side for Bobby Williams for a first down at the AU-21, tackled by Martavius Houston.

McAda rushed left for 18 yards and a first down to the AU-3, stopped by Houston. On first and goal on a counter play, Bobby Williams ran left for a three yard touchdown with 1:15 left in the second quarter. J. Parker made the extra point kick to make the score, 20-7. The Army scoring drive took 2:00 to go 72 yards in six plays.

Eric Olsen kicked off 52 yards to the AU-13, where Eric Hines-Tucker returned the football 21 yards, stopped by Sachitano. Craig completed a 15 yard pass to Gosha out of bounds for a first down at the AU-49, tackled by Gay.

Craig passed for seven yards to Cooper, stopped by Mullins. Baker dropped a pass from Craig. On third and three, Craig rushed eight yards out of bounds and a first down to the WP-36. Craig completed a 24 yard pass to Baker out of bounds for a first down at the WP-12, stopped by Gay.

On first and ten, Dameyune Craig passed to Karsten Bailey, who gained four yards before Garland Gay forced a fumble that was recovered by the Army team at the WP-4 with 19 seconds left in the half. The Tigers drive took 56 seconds over 62 yards in six plays.

On first and ten, Ronnie McAda took a knee for a loss of two yards as the clock expired. This Army possession of one play took 19 seconds. The halftime score was Auburn 20, Army 7.

Halftime

At halftime, Army had seven first downs, 78 yards rushing, 33 passing (1-5-0), lost one fumble, had three penalties for 20 yards, punted three times, made one of four third down attempts, and had 10:32 time of possession. Auburn had 20 first downs, 65 yards rushing, 284 passing (19-28-0), lost two fumbles, had two penalties for 27 yards, made seven of eleven third down attempts, made two of two fourth down conversions, and had not punted.

Halftime entertainment included performances by the 330 members of the Auburn band and the presentation of the Omar N. Bradley "Spirit of Independence Award" ceremony to the Veterans of Foreign Wars by Generals Colin Powell and Norman Schwartzkopf.

At the conclusion of the award ceremony, the bowl sponsor, Poulan Weed Eater gave away a vintage 1946 Ford truck. After the game, attendees could catch a range of celebrations at casinos, night clubs, and other holiday sights.

Third Quarter

Jaret Holmes kicked off 65 yards into the end zone for a touchback. Spikes tackled Bobby Williams after a rush of five yards. Leonardo Carson and Neal stopped Bobby Williams after a one yard gain up the middle. On third and four, Neal and Mostella tackled Perry after a three yard run up the middle. Scot Lord punted 31 yards to the AU-40, where Robert Baker returned the football five yards, stopped by Scott Eichelberger with 13:15 on the clock. The Army drive of 1:45 went nine yards in three plays.

Craig completed a 14 yard pass to Bailey for a first down at the WP-41, stopped by Augustus. A pass from Craig to Gosha was dropped incomplete. Brown tackled Gosha after a four yard reception. On third and six, Craig's pass to Goodson was incomplete. Jaret Holmes punted 37 yards into the end zone for a touchback at 12:09 in the third quarter. The Auburn drive went 18 yards in four plays taking 1:06 off the clock.

Brumbaugh tackled Hewitt after a gain of two yards up the middle. Spikes stopped Brizic for a loss of a yard. On third and eleven, Carson and Neal tackled McAda for a loss of two yards. Scot Lord punted 45 yards to the AU-36, where Robert Baker returned it 17 yards to the WP-47, tackled by Ben Kotwica at 10:19 on the clock. The Army drive was three plays in 1:50 losing three yards.

Craig completed a ten yard pass to the right side for Gosha to the WP-37, stopped by Gay. There was an official measurement that declared a first down for Auburn. Brown tackled Rusty Williams after a gain of four yards off right tackle. A Craig pass to Baker was to the left and incomplete. On third and six, a pass attempt to the right side Bailey was incomplete. Robert Brown was injured on the play and left the field.

On fourth and six, Ben Kotwica blitzed the quarterback, but Dameyune Craig sidestepped him and rushed around the right side and down the sideline for a 33 yard touchdown and a first down at 8:51 to go in the third quarter. Auburn took a time out and decided to go for two. Craig's pass attempt was incomplete and the conversion failed, making the score, 26-7. The Auburn scoring drive took 1:28 to go 47 yards in five plays.

At this point, some of the local fans in the stands (those not wearing team colors) started to leave the stadium. I mentioned to a few of the high school referees that Army was going to come back, and those fans leaving would be missing all of that. I'm pretty sure the referees did not believe me.

Holmes kicked off 65 yards into the end zone for a touchback. Neal tackled Hewitt after a three yard gain. Hewitt rushed twelve yards and a first down to the WP-35, stopped by Ware. Bobby Williams ran 14 yards up the middle and a first down to the WP-49, stopped by Ware.

Spikes and Neal tackled Hewitt after a three yard gain. Perry ran six yards up the middle, stopped by Brumbaugh. On third and one, Bobby Williams gained two yards up the middle and a first down at the AU-40, tackled by Brumbaugh.

Brumbaugh and Carson stopped Perry after a gain of three yards. Neal and Crayton tackled Bobby Williams after a three yard rush. On third and four, Perry ran two yards, stopped by Brumbaugh. On fourth and two, Brizic ran two yards and gained a first down at the AU-30, tackled by Crayton.

Carson stopped Perry for no gain. Spikes tackled Perry after a gain of three yards up the middle. On third and seven, Brizic ran for four yards, stopped by Carson. Army took a time out at 2:40 and decided to go for it. On fourth and three at the AU-23, McAda's pass to Dunning in the end zone was defended by Crayton and incomplete with 2:34 on the clock. The Cadets lost the football on downs. The Army drive took 6:17 to go 57 yards in 14 plays.

Craig completed a 49 yard pass down the middle to Baker for a first down at the WP-28, stopped by Augustus. Tyquiengco defended an attempted pass over the middle to Goodson. Tyron Goodson was injured on the play and left the game. Rusty Williams rushed 15 yards up the middle and a first down at the WP-13, stopped by Brown.

On the next play, Auburn was called for a false start and lost five yards. On first and 15, Rusty Williams rushed left 18 yards for a touchdown with 1:04 left in the third quarter for a 31-7 Auburn lead. Auburn called a time out and decided to go for two.

Dameyune Craig's pass attempt was overthrown in the back of the end zone and no good. The Auburn scoring drive took 1:40 to go 77 yards in four plays. Jaret Holmes kicked off 65 yards into the end zone where Thomas took a knee for a touchback. More of the local fans began to leave the stadium, and quite a number of Auburn fans, too.

Neal tackled McAda after a rush of four yards to the left side. McAda went back for a pass and then ran left six yards for a first down at the WP-30, stopped by Neal. On a pitch play, Brizic ran right three yards to the WP-33, tackled by Neal and Houston as the clock expired. At the end of the third quarter, the score was Auburn 32, Army 7.

Fourth Quarter

Defensive coordinator Bill Oliver noted that the Cadets have had a tendency to play some of their best football in the fourth quarter. Oliver said on December 21st after an Auburn practice, "That is when they start beating people physically. It is really going to be a challenge for us."

On second and seven at the WP-33, McAda completed a 13 yard pass to the right side to Ron Thomas for a first down at the WP-46, tackled by Fields. Nolan and Fields tackled McAda after a five yard gain to the right. On second and five on a counter play, Bobby Williams broke free around the left side and ran 34 yards for a first down at the AU-15, stopped by Crayton.

Brumbaugh tackled Brizic after a gain of one yard up the middle on a counter play. Brumbaugh and Carson stopped Perry after a rush of two yards. On third and seven, Demetrius Perry rushed twelve yards up the middle for a touchdown at 12:44 left in the game. J. Parker converted the PAT kick to close the score to 32-14. The Cadets scoring drive took 3:20 to go 80 yards in nine plays.

Eric Olsen kicked off 60 yards to the AU-5, where Robert Baker returned the football 19 yards before being stopped by Len Kennedy. Craig completed a nine yard pass to the right side to

Gosha who was forced out of bounds by Gay. McLeod rushed three yards off left guard for a first down at the AU-36, tackled by CW Estes.

Stephen King stopped Rusty Williams for a one yard gain to the left. Dameyune Craig fumbled the snap, CW Estes tried to recover it, but Craig fell on the football for no gain. After the play, the officials gave the Army pep band a sideline warning to quit playing after the snap of the ball.

The Army fans in the stands started yelling loudly prior to and after the next snap. On third and nine at the AU-37, a pass from Craig to Baker was thrown out of bounds to the right sideline for Baker and incomplete, defended by Mullins. Jaret Holmes punted 46 yards to the WP-17, where Brent Turner downed it at 10:25 on the clock. The Auburn drive of five plays, 13 yards, took 2:19 time of possession.

Dorsey tackled Perry after a two yard run up the middle. McAda completed a swing pass to Perry, who was dropped for a nine yard loss by Mostella. On third and 17, McAda completed a five yard pass down the middle to a falling Leshinski. Scot Lord punted 34 yards to the WP-49, Baker returned it 23 yards at 8:31 on the fourth quarter clock. On the play, Auburn was called for an illegal block and penalized ten yards back to the AU-43.

On first and ten, Craig attempted a pass for Poor to the left sideline which was incomplete. Cooper rushed for four yards up the middle, tackled by Stephen King. On third and six, Dameyune Craig's deep pass was intercepted by Tom Mullins, who first ran up the right sideline and then cut across the field, returning it 66 yards, stopped by Markeith Cooper and Dameyune Craig to the AU-17 with 7:18 left in the game. The Tigers drive of three plays for four yards took 1:13 time of possession.

Neal stopped Perry after a gain of two yards off left guard. Perry rushed for five yards off right tackle, tackled by Spikes and Neal. On third and three, Bobby Williams rushed nine yards on a counter to the left for a first down at the AU-1, tackled by Neal.

On first and goal, Bobby Williams ran around left end for one yard and a touchdown with 5:50 to go. J. Parker made the extra point kick to make it 32-21. The Army scoring drive took four plays to go 17 yards in 1:26. J. Parker tried an onside kick, going nine yards to the WP-44, where it was recovered by Hicks Poor for Auburn.

Kotwica tackled Rusty Williams after a run of nine yards up the middle. Beasley rushed two yards to the right side for a first down at the WP-33, stopped by Scott Sprawls. Beasley slipped and fell on the ground for a loss of one yard. Army called a time out with 4:34 on the clock. On the next play, Auburn was called for a false start and penalized back five yards. Kearns and Kotwica stopped Rusty Williams off right tackle after a gain of three yards. Army called another time out with 4:24 left.

On third and 13, Rusty Williams ran for seven yards up the middle, stopped by Brown. Auburn called a time out at 3:39. On fourth and six at the WP-29, Dameyune Craig's pass was behind Willie Gosha and incomplete. Auburn lost the football on downs with 3:37 to go at the WP-30. The Auburn drive took 2:15 off the clock over six plays that went 15 yards.

Army had no time outs. McAda completed a six yard pass to Brizic with a knee down when he caught it. Brumbaugh tackled Bobby Williams after running a delay draw up the middle and gained two yards. On third and two, McAda passed to Ron Thomas, who was hit by Mostella and dropped along the left sideline in bounds for a gain of one yard. On fourth and one, Brizic ran a counter off right tackle for four yards and a first down at the WP-42, tackled by Neal.

McAda completed a 29 yard pass to Rod Richardson down the middle for a first down at the AU-29, tackled by Nolan and Ware. Mark Smith stopped McAda for a loss of one yard. On second and eleven, Ronnie McAda completed a pass to Rod Richardson at the WP-17, and Richardson ran it across the goal line for a 30 yard touchdown reception with 1:27 left in the game.

Army decided to go for two. Bobby Williams ran a counter to the right across the goal line for the two-point conversion to close the score to 32-29. The Army scoring drive took 2:10 to go 71 yards in seven plays. J. Parker kicked ten yards on an onside kick, and Army's Matt Rogers recovered the football for Army at the WP-45.

A McAda threw a deep pass to near the goal line to Richardson that was broken up Ware and incomplete, stopping the clock with 1:15 to play. McAda completed a 14 yard pass to the right side to Bobby Williams for a first down on the AU-41, stopped by Neal.

McAda then completed a 27 yard pass down the right sideline to Bobby Williams, who was tackled hard out of bounds by Ware for a first down at the AU-14 with the clock stopped at 0:55. Bobby Williams was injured and down on the sideline out of bounds after the play and the officials held up play.

Spikes tackled Perry after a gain of four yards up the middle. McAda spiked the football to stop the clock with 33 seconds left in the game. Head football coach Bob Sutton decided to go for a tie and head into overtime, sending the kicking squad out on the field.

The south goal post was tilted, but J. Parker's 27 yard field goal attempt was wide right and would have missed had the goal post been standing straight. The final Army drive took six plays in 45 yards in 58 seconds of possession.

Auburn had the football, and Dameyune Craig took a knee and lost two yards as the clock ran out. Final Score, Auburn 32, Army 29. The game ended at 6:02 pm CST, taking 3:21 in real time to play.

Post-Game

"We were not thinking about taking a second shot at the end zone," said head football coach Bob Sutton after the game. "We would have been happy going into overtime. That is why we didn't throw one more time. It was the best chance we had to get set and kick the ball. I would do it again. The only thing we would have done differently is to try to center the ball a little more. If we had thrown and gotten a sack or we had thrown and got an interception; everybody is going to ask, why didn't you go send it into overtime?"

"It was a good snap, a good hold. You saw what happened, it went wide right," said J. Parker. "I kicked the ground a little bit. I walked off the field, and it was total emptiness. My teammates gave something back to me. They gave me back my energy. They just said, Great season, great career."

"We came out and pretty much controlled the game, but they are the military, and they never give up," said Dameyune Craig after the game. "You have to feel proud to have a group like this defending your country."

"We were playing extremely well in the first half and they were not in their game," said head football coach Terry Bowden after the game. "They took over and started doing their thing and we did not play as well then. They started making big plays and it made for a great finish. Army didn't deserve to lose. But we fought hard enough to win. We needed this win for the morale of our players. In a year where it seems like you have been snake bit, you just start to think that bad things may happen. A win like this does not make up for some of the close losses, but it makes for a lot more positive offseason."

"Army did not lose its enthusiasm," said bowl chairman Rick Holland. "The team hit hard and never quit, but hey were up against raw talent and speed."

Army had 18 first downs (12 rushing), 257 rushing yards on 56 carries, 148 passing (10-16-0), one lost fumble, punted six times for an average of 43.0, had three penalties for 20 yards, made two sacks of 17 yards, made four out of 13 third down attempts, made two out of three fourth down attempts, and had 30:12 time of possession.

Auburn had 27 first downs (13 rushing, 12 passing), 161 yards rushing on 36 attempts, 372 yards passing (24-40-1), lost two fumbles, punted two times for a 41.5 average, made seven out of 16 third down attempts, made three out of four fourth down conversions, and had five penalties for 47 yards.

For Auburn, Dameyune Craig rushed for 75 yards on 13 carries and one touchdown, while Rusty Williams ran 72 yards on 12 attempts and one touchdown, Fred Beasley rushed for five yards on eight carries, Kevin McLeod ran five yards on two attempts, and Markeith Cooper had one four yard run. Craig completed 24 out of 40 passes for 372 passing yards, with two touchdowns and one interception.

Willie Gosha caught ten passes for 132 yards with one touchdown, while Robert Baker had five receptions for 103 yards, Karsten Bailey gained 39 yards on four receptions, Tyrone Goodson caught two passes for 78 yards and one touchdown, Markeith Cooper had two receptions for 15 yards, and Jessie McCovery caught one pass for three yards. Dameyune Craig lost one of two fumbles, while Karsten Bailey lost one fumble.

Jaret Holmes made both of his field goal attempts. Holmes punted twice for a 41.5 yard average. Holmes kicked off seven times for a 63.9 average with no touchbacks. Robert Baker returned four punts for 6.3 average. Baker returned two kickoffs for a 22.5 average. Eric Hines-Tucker returned one kickoff for 21 yards.

Ricky Neal led the team with 15 total tackles (8 solo), followed by Jimmy Brumbaugh with nine (6 solo), Takeo Spikes had seven (5 solo), and Leonardo Carson with seven (3 solo). Also having tackles were Brad Ware (4), Marcellus Mostella (4), Antwoine Nolan (4), Charles Dorsey (3), Haven Fields (3), Martavius Houston (3), Rodney Crayton (3), Quinton Reese (1), Bobby Daffin (1), Jaret Holmes (1), Mark Smith (1), Markeith Cooper (1), and Dameyune Craig (1).

Ricky Neal, Takeo Spikes, Leonardo Carson, Marcellus Mostella, and Charles Dorsey each had a tackle for loss. Brad Ware recovered a fumble with no return. Rodney Crayton had three pass breakups while Takeo Spikes had one.

For Army, Demetrius Perry ran 80 yards on 19 attempts and one touchdown, Bobby Williams rushed for 79 yards on eleven carries and two touchdowns, while Ronnie McAda had 46 yards on 13 carries, Jeff Brizic gained 33 yards on nine attempts, Joe Hewitt ran five times for 21 yards, and Ron Thomas one rush that lost 20 yards.

Ronnie McAda completed 10 out of 16 passes for 148 yards and one touchdown. Bobby Williams caught three passes for 74 yards, Rod Richardson had two receptions for 59 yards and one touchdown, Ron Thomas caught two passes for 13 yards, while Jeff Brizic (6), Ron Leshinski (5), and Demetrius Perry (minus 9) each had one reception. It was Ron Leshinski's 22nd birthday on game day. Ron Thomas lost one fumble.

Scot Lord punted six times for a 43.0 yard average, with no touchbacks or inside the red zone. Eric Olson kicked off three times for 59.0 average with no touchbacks. J. Parker kicked off two times on onside kicks for an average of 9.5 yards. Parker missed his one field goal attempt. Mike West was the holder on place kicks. Ron Thomas returned two kickoffs for a 32.0 yard average. Tom Mullins intercepted one pass and returned it 66 yards.

Garland Gay led the team with eight total tackles (7 solo), with Robert Brown had six (5 solo), Stephen King with six (4 solo), and Ben Kotwica with six (4 solo). Also having tackles were Tom Mullins (5), Donald Augustus (3), Scott Eichelberger (3), Jerrod Tyquiengco (3), Mike Coerper (2), and Joe Sachitano (2). Having one tackle each were Chad Suitonu, Colin Kearns, Len Kennedy, Scott Sprawls, CW Estes, Reno Ferri, and Matt Rogers.

Ben Kotwica, Jerrod Tyquiengco, Mike Coerper, and Stephen King each had one tackle for loss. Ben Kotwica and Stephen King each had a sack. Garland Gay and Ben Kotwica forced a fumble. Robert Brown recovered a lost fumble with no return. Jerrod Tyquiengco, Robert Brown, and Tom Mullins each had one pass breakup.

The bowl game's Offensive Most Valuable Player was Auburn's quarterback Dameyune Craig. The Defensive Most Valuable Player was shared by linebackers Takeo Spikes and Rickey Neal, both of Auburn.

Both teams set the combined total offensive yards record for the Independence Bowl (898). Army set the record for most points scored in the fourth quarter (22). Auburn set a new Independence Bowl record for most first downs, most yards passing (372) and most total offensive yardage (533). Terry Bowden won his 100th career football game as a head coach with this bowl win.

Dameyune Craig set Independence Bowl records for his passing yardage (372) and total yardage (447). Jaret Holmes 49 yard field goal was the second longest in bowl history. Willie Gosha set the bowl record for receptions. It was the second time that two receivers had each had 100 yard reception days (Willie Gosha with 132 and Robert Baker with 104 yards).

Conclusion

Shreveport *The Times* sports reporter Scott Ferrell wrote this to end his January's 1st article about this bowl game, "This Independence Bowl was everything a football fan could ask for. And it not surprising. The I-Bowl is becoming one of the more traditionally entertaining games of the bowl season. If people want to laugh about Shreveport as a non-resort location, fine. But if you want to make fun of the I-Bowl game, you're mistaken. Two teams that won't be in the top 10 this year gave a Top 10 performance. And that's all any college football fan can ask."

Chapter 12

The 2010 Football Season

Prior Army Seasons

It had been 13 seasons and six head coaches since Army West Point had had a winning football season. After the successful 1996 season, head coach Bob Sutton had three seasons of 4-7, 3-8, and 3-8 before being fired on the streets of Philadelphia after losing to Navy, 9-19, in December 1999. Sutton ran the Flexbone offense, but it faced difficulty by USMA's decision to join Conference USA beginning in the 1998 season.

USMA hired Todd Berry as its 32nd head football coach, and he installed a heavy passing attack that sometimes gained lots of yards, but few victories. At Cincinnati opening the 2000 season on September 4th, I witnessed Berry have the offense come out in a wishbone formation on the first play of the game, and then quickly move into his passing formation. Fun to watch, sometimes, but not many wins.

Four seasons Army fans suffered as Berry's records of 1-10, 3-8, 1-11, and finally 0-6 in the 2003 season led to his firing after losing at Louisville, 10-14, in a game I also attended. In stepped in defensive coach John Mumford, who finished the season without a win. The 0-13 record still stands as an NCAA FBS record.

USMA then hired veteran head coach Bobby Ross, who won a national championship at Georgia Tech more than a decade before. Ross ran a more pro set offense and had some good runners, but still had three losing seasons of 2-9. 4-7, and 3-9. Army left Conference USA after the 2004 season and returned to being a FBS Independent. Many felt Ross, while brilliant, was maybe past his prime; he finally admitted that and resigned after the 2006 season.

From Ross' staff, USMA elected to hire Stan Ross, a successful NFL offensive lineman, as the 35th Army head football coach. Brock ran a similar pros-set offense in 2007 to Ross', and got a similar result, a 3-9 overall record. Under pressure from USMA leadership and the Army fan base, he introduced an option run-oriented offense for the 2008 season, some called it the Brockbone that finally returned Army Football to its wishbone roots. But again, Brock only led Army West Point to a 3-9 season.

This time USMA purposely recruited and hired a triple-option oriented head football coach named Rich Ellerson as the 36th head football coach in December 2008. Ellerson promptly opened the 2009 season with a win at Eastern Michigan, 27-14, something that none of his last four predecessors had done. The Black Knights lost their home opener to Duke (19-35), then beat Ball State, 24-17.

Two losses followed, at Iowa State (10-31) and versus Tulane (16-17) before Army West Point beat Vanderbilt in a thriller at home in overtime, 16-13. Three more losses followed at Temple (13-27), hosting Rutgers (10-27), and at Air Force (7-35). The Black Knights beat VMI at home (22-17) and at North Texas (17-13). Army needed just one game to be bowl qualified, and had they beat Navy, they had a primary agreement to play in the EagleBank Bowl against an Atlantic Coast Conference opponent.

Army West Point lost to Navy, 3-17, in Philadelphia's Lincoln Financial Field. Navy finished their season 10-4, and was receiving votes in final *Associated Press* Poll and *USA Today* Coaches Poll that week and in the final rankings. It was the closest the Black Knights had come to beating the Midshipmen since the 2006 game (14-26). In the 2009 season, Rich Ellerson won more games in a season (5-7) since Army went away from triple option offense in 2000.

"We made significant strides last season," Ellerson said. "But those were the first steps towards returning this program to the level at which we'd like it to be. There is still much work to be done."

2010 Army Football Coaching and Support Staff

There were no changes in the coaching staff for the 2010 season. The leadership of the Army West Point Football coaching staff consisted of head coach Rich Ellerson, associate head coach and offensive guards & centers Gene McKeehan (2nd season), offensive coordinator and quarterbacks Ian Shields (2nd), co-defensive coordinator and linebackers Payam Saadat (2nd), and co-defensive coordinator and safeties Chris Smeland (2nd).

The remainder of the coaches included linebackers and special teams John Brock (4th), cornerbacks Tony Coaxum (4th), wide receivers Andy Guyader (2nd), defensive tackles Captain Clarence Holmes (8th), whip linebackers Robert Lyles (4th), defensive ends John Mumford (11th), fullbacks and special teams Joe Ross (2nd), offensive tackles Bill Tripp (2nd), slot backs and recruiting coordinate Tucker Waugh (9th), strength and conditioning Bret Gerch (2nd), and director of football operations Major Chad Bagley (5th).

2010 Football Schedule

The 2010 football schedule was announced on October 29, 2009, and consisted of five home, four away, and three neutral site games. Army West Point would start on the road at Eastern Michigan on Saturday, September 4th, in a night game. The Black Knights would then host Hawai'i and North Texas on September 11th and 18th, before going back on the road to play Duke on September 25th.

Army West Point would then host Temple on October 2nd. The Black Knights would travel to New Orleans to play Tulane in a late afternoon game in the Louisiana Superdome on October 9th. Rutgers would then host the Black Knights on October 16th at the New Meadowlands Stadium at East Rutherford NJ. After two weeks off, Army West Point would host the Virginia Military Institute (VMI) and Air Force on back-to-back Saturdays (October 30th and November 6th).

The regular season would end on the road, first with an away game with Kent State on November 13th, followed by a tilt with Notre Dame in in the new Yankee Stadium in the South Bronx on November 20th. The Black Knights would then have three weeks off to prepare for their annual game with Navy, to be played on December 11th at 2:30 pm EST at Lincoln Financial Field in Philadelphia PA.

Originally, Army West Point was supposed to play Arkansas State on September 11th, but that game was cancelled. The Rutgers game was originally scheduled as an away game at Rutgers Stadium in Piscataway NJ. All home games would kick off at noon each Saturday.

On July 1st, the *CBS Sports Network* announced that Dave Ryan (play-by-play) and Jason Sehorn (analyst) would be announcing all Army West Point home games (Hawai'i, North Texas, Temple, VMI, and Air Force). There would be a different sideline reporter at each game. The *CBS Television* network would broadcast the Navy game. The *NBC Television* network would broadcast the Notre Dame game. During the season, *ESPN3* picked up the Duke and Rutgers games, while local area stations showed the Eastern Michigan, Tulane, and Kent State football games.

Spring Practice

Spring practice began on February 17th. The Black Knights had their first spirited intra-squad scrimmage on Saturday, February 27th. There had been far fewer position changes than a year ago. Malcolm Brown switched from slot back to wide receiver. Nate Combs moved from whip bandit to the mike linebacker position.

There would be seven more practices in pads left on the spring schedule, including a second scrimmage on March 6th, and the annual Black & Gold Game on Saturday, March 27th. The Gold squad beat the Black squad, 42-35.

"The spring was a success, both with recruiting and practice," Ellerson said. "We are a better football team today than we were before spring practice started. We made some great gains physically. We are more at home with our offense and defense. We explored some options from a personnel standpoint, and there have been some positives to come out of that experiment. We like where we are and we are hard back at it."

Bowl Games

On April 16th, USMA announced that it had entered into a partnership with the Bell Helicopter Armed Forces Bowl to play in that game if Army West Point was bowl qualified. The Armed Forces Bowl was slated to feature teams from Conference USA and the Mountain West Conference. If either conference failed to fill their slot, Army West Point would be able to claim the opening.

Summer

Nearly 1,400 New Cadets arrived on July 1, 2010 to begin Cadet Basic Training, commonly called Beast Barracks to join the USMA Class of 2014. USMA announced a list of 55 plebes for the upcoming football team, with 27 coming from the USMA Prep School and 28 direct admits.

The following plebes lettered during the 2010 season - slot backs Jon Crucitti (9 games) and Raymond Maples (1 start, 9 games); defensive back Justin Trimble (11 games); linebackers Reggie Nesbit (4 games) and Zach Williams (4 games); defensive end Quentin Kantaris (1 start, 8 games); quarterback Matt Luetjen (2 games); and wide receiver Anthony Stephens (9 games). Other freshman who played but did not letter were slot back Julian Crockett and safety Tyler Dickson.

Captains

Senior linebacker Stephen Anderson, who served as one of the three team captains during the 2009 season, will continue in that role in the 2010 season. Game captains were named for each of the first seven games. On October 26th, the Army West Point Football

Team named its permanent Captains - Anderson, senior defensive end and long snapper Carson Homme, senior defensive end Josh McNary, and senior slot back Patrick Mealy.

Pre-Season Camp

The starters on the pre-season defensive depth chart were defensive ends Josh McNary and Marcus Hilton; defensive tackle Mike Gann; linebackers Nate Combs, Mike Rodriguez, Stephen Anderson, and Steven Erzinger; cornerbacks Antuan Aaron and Richard King; and safeties Donovan Travis, and Donnie Dixon or Jordan Trimble.

The starters on the pre-season offensive depth chart were wide receivers Davyd Brooks and Austin Barr; tackles Anees Merzi and Jason Johnson; guards Frank Allen and Seth Reed; center Zach Peterson; slot backs Brian Cobbs and Patrick Mealy; fullback Jared Hassin; and quarterback Trent Steelman.

Starting specialists were placekicker Alex Carlton, kickoff Matt Campbell, punter Jonathan Bulls, holder Kolin Walk, kickoff returner Patrick Mealy or Malcolm Brown, punt returner Josh Jones, and long snapper Carson Homme.

Preseason camp opened on August 2nd. The team donned pads and had contact drills on August 6th. On August 14th, the team conducted a scrimmage. On August 27th or 30th, there was a mock game played. The leading tackler returning from the 2009 season, linebacker Andrew Rodriguez, suffered a back injury that would cause him to miss the entire season.

"The offense in general has made leaps and bounds since last year," senior offensive tackle Jason Johnson said. "The cohesion level is much better than it was last year. It feels like everyone is on the same page and knows what they're doing. There is a lot more trust in the huddle."

The team introduced a new uniform style on August 9th. In addition to a new look for both home and road games, Army will sport a special "Dress Gray" uniform style as a tribute to the U.S.

Corps of Cadets and the Long Gray Line when the Black Knights square off against Air Force.

Army would continue wearing black jerseys (with gold swatches) and gold pants (with a black stripe) for its home games, while donning white jerseys (with black swatches) and gold pants (with a black stripe) on the road.

The Black Knights will also feature a white-pants (with thin gold and black stripes) option, an "India Whites" style, for road games played in warm weather climates. The word "Army" will be printed in small lettering centered on the chest of both jerseys above the uniform number, with the words "West Point" emblazoned along the back name plate atop the jersey number.

Pre-Season Recognitions

Senior Josh McNary was named to watch lists for the Lott Trophy, the Bronko Nagurski Trophy, the Lombardi Award, the College Football Performance Awards, and the Burlsworth Trophy. McNary was named on April 30th to preseason second team All-American team by *NationChamp.net*. He was named preseason honorable mention All-American by Consensus Draft Services on June 4th. Senior defensive end and long snapper Carson Homme was on the watch list for the NFF Awards, and on September 30th, Homme was announced as a semifinalist.

Season Predictions

The Bleacher Report predicted that "A revitalized Army team, as second-year coach Rich Ellerson may finally have the pieces to make a marked improvement on the Black Knights offense and defensive scheme. Air Force transfer fullback Jared Hassin and any combination of Army quarterbacks might just hold the keys to whether the Knights can submit a winning record in 2010."

Phil Steele predicted the ranking of Army's opponents - #16 Notre Dame, #31 Temple, #47 Air Force, and #48 Navy. He said, "This is the Cadets most experienced team (16 returning starters) since 2004 and it is also the second year of Rich Ellerson's schemes. Army almost made it to a bowl game last year at 5-7 with a couple of near misses. This year my main set of power ratings calls for them to get bowl eligibility and that would put them in the Armed Forces Bowl. This is easily Army's best team since their 1996 bowl Squad." Army West Point was one of only six teams with 26 or more seniors on their roster, and twelve of them would start in the opening game.

Eastern Michigan

Army West Point began its 121st season playing college football at Eastern Michigan's Rynearson Stadium on Saturday evening, September 4th. The Black Knights were 1-8 all-time in season openers on the road, achieving their first victory in 2009 at Ypsilanti MI. Army West Point honored the 1st Infantry Division, The Big Red One, by wearing their patch on their right shoulder, with the USMA patch on their left shoulder.

The Black Knights were favored by 9 points to win. It was cloudy and windy for the game and 66 degrees at the 7 pm EDT kickoff before 11,318 fans. The game was televised on a campus station, with Matt Shepard and Rob Rubick announcing with Jeff Fulton on the sidelines.

Eastern Michigan scored a touchdown in the first quarter to take a 7-0 lead. Sophomore linebacker Nate Combs suffered a knee injury on the first series, and would be out for the season. Josh Jackson recovered an Eagles fumble on the EMU-15. Jared Hassin rushed for a three yard touchdown, and Alex Carlton kicked the extra point to tie the game, 7-7.

After the Eagles lost the football on a fourth and two, starting quarterback Trent Steelman led the Black Knights to the EMU-24 before Carlton missed a 41 yard field goal attempt. During this Black Knights drive, there was a ten minute power failure, and the teams agreed to play with no scoreboard and reduced field lighting.

Donovan Travis intercepted a deep pass at the WP-15 and returned it thirty yards with 6:30 left in the first half. Army West Point drove down the field in 13 plays where Hassin scored a three yard touchdown with 0:40 seconds left. Eastern Michigan quickly scored to tie it up, 14-14 at halftime.

Army West Point opened the third quarter with a nine play, 75 yard drive with Patrick Mealy running eleven yards for the touchdown, upping the score, 21-14. Bill Prosko forced and recovered a fumble on the kickoff at the EMU-32. Carlton made a 42 yard field goal to extend the lead to 24-14. The Eagles then drove 74 yards in eleven plays to score on a one yard plunge, but missed the extra point, with 2:29 left in the third quarter to make it 24-20.

Eastern Michigan scored on a ten yard touchdown pass, taking the lead for the first time, 27-24, with 2:59 to go. Jared Hassin ran seven yards across the goal line for the winning touchdown with 38 seconds on the clock. The Eagles drove across midfield, but Josh McNary hurried the quarterback into making an incompletion to end the game, 31-27, with a Black Knights victory.

Army West Point had 21 first downs, 309 yards rushing, 65 passing (5-11-0), lost one fumble, was penalized seven times for 70 yards, and had 31:29 time of possession. The Eagles had 20 first downs, 285 rushing yards, 31 passing (4-9-1), lost two fumbles, and had no penalties. Army West Point had won their last five games all by less than eight points.

Patrick Mealy rushed for 81 yards, while Malcolm Brown and Jared Hassin both had 68, Brian Cobbs gained 60 yards, and Steelman a net of 35 rushing yards. George Jordan caught three passes for 34 yards while Mealy and Austin Barr each had one reception. Stephen Anderson had ten total tackles, while Josh McNary had eight and Chad Littlejohn had seven. There was one sack, by Mike Gann and Chad Littlejohn.

Eastern Michigan would finish the 2010 season with a 2-6 conference record in the Mid-American Conference and an overall 2-10 record. The Eagles finished tied for fifth place with Central Michigan in the West Division. The highlight of the season was two conference victories, the first an overtime win at Ball State (41-38) and the second, a 21-17 victory at Buffalo.

Hawai'i

Army West Point (1-0) hosted Hawai'i (0-1) on Saturday, September 11th, for their first home game of the season before 30,042 fans in Michie Stadium. The Black Knights had lost their last two home openers since their 14-7 overtime win over Rhode Island in 2007. Army West Point would honor the 25th Infantry Division, nicknamed Tropic Lightning. It was 66 degrees at kickoff with the weather clear and crisp. The Black Knights were favored by 3 points to win. Andy Nicholas was the *CBS Sports Network* sideline reporter.

The Rainbow Warriors arrived on Thursday to New York to avoid jet lag. Hawai'i lost their opening game at home to #14 Southern California, 36-49. The Warriors run-and-shoot offense showed quick strike capability with three touchdowns taking less than seven plays and under three minutes, passing for 459 yards in their first game. Hawai'i was ranked first in the nation in passing coming into their game with the Black Knights.

The Rainbow Warriors scored on a 26 yard pass reception, going 81 yards in ten plays to take the lead, 7-0, in a lengthy five minute drive. After a Black Knights punt, Hawai'i took less than three minutes to drive 50 yards for an eleven yard touchdown pass to increase their lead to 14-0 at the end of the first period.

Hawai'i scored on a 48 yard pass to cap a five play drive of 88 yards, extending their lead to 21-0, with 11:31 left in the second quarter. Malcolm Brown rushed from the four for the touchdown to finish a 13 play, 75 yard possession taking seven minutes. The first half ended with the score, 7-21 in favor of the Rainbow Warriors.

Jared Hassin scored on a 16 yard run to cap the 68 yard opening drive in eight plays to close the score 14-21. Brian Cobbs recovered a muffed reception on the kickoff, and Malcolm Brown plunged over the goal line from the one to tie the game, 21-21, with 7:10 left in the third quarter.

Trent Steelman left the game with a shoulder injury, and Max Jenkins came in at quarterback. Jenkins scored on a one yard run, for a 28-21 lead with 5:35 left in the third quarter. It was Jenkins first snap at quarterback, first carry, and his first touchdown. Hawai'i responded with a touchdown run after four plays to tie it, 28-28 late in the third period.

"We kind of gathered ourselves as the second quarter wore on," remarked Rich Ellerson after the game. "We settled down and we stopped them once and then we got a drive. We came out to start the second half with a nice drive. Then we got some turnovers, and the takeaways, as always, will give you an opportunity. That's the best thing we could do with the Hawai'i offense, and that is keeping them over there (on the sideline) watching our offense. We were able to do that with a takeaway in the kicking game and a takeaway on defense. We got the ball in scoring position, and we got ourselves back in it. Frankly, that's what it was going to take against an outfit like that."

After a long 16 play drive, Carlton's 37 yard field goal attempt was blocked. The Black Knights defense forced a three an out with 5:39 left in the game. On the tenth straight rushing play, Jenkins was hit and lost the football at the UH-27 with 24 seconds left in the tied game. Two pass completions and a personal foul penalty moved the Rainbow Warriors to the WP-14 where Scott Enos converted the winning 31 yard field goal with seven seconds left, 31-28.

"It was a hard-fought contest," said Rich Ellerson. "I'm proud of how our team took some shots early and bounced back. We kept believing, and we just battled and battled and battled. That character will give us a chance every week we play. We need to build on that. We need to find another play; we need to find another play on offense, defense and in the kicking game. Every phase of the game had a chance to make a difference there. If we can get into an uphill fight like that physically, we can dig a hole for ourselves and battle back like that, then we can win some football games."

"We had chances all the way through. When the game comes down to a single play, you have to count all of them. You can't just count the one that catches your imagination at the end. There were 100 chances, and what we need to do, as empty as we feel right now, is to be excited about how we competed."

Ellerson continued, "We need to be together. We talk about this brotherhood. Well, that will pay off for us. We'll hold onto each other. Each and every one of us will be accountable and will take responsibility for that. We'll get better. Our most experienced guy has exactly one year and two games of experience in this offense and this defense. The beautiful thing is where we are as competitors, and where we are as a team. If we make sure that is not jeopardized and we find a way to dig our cleats in a little bit deeper and we find a way to make one more play, this team will win some football games."

Army West Point had 19 first downs, 250 yards rushing, and 58 passing (4-6-0), with two lost fumbles and almost 38 minutes of possession time. Hawai'i had 20 first downs, 10 yards rushing, and 343 passing (25-37-0), and lost two fumbles. The Black Knights were penalized ten times for 68 yards, while the Warriors had five for 45 yards.

Hawai'i quarterback Bryant Moniz had a great day passing to his five receivers and three passing touchdowns. Jared Hassin rushed for 83 yards, while Patrick Mealy had 41 yards and Trent Steelman had 40 rushing yards. Steelman passed 3-4-0 for 38 yards and Jenkins 1-2-0 for 20. Davyd Brooks caught three passes for 49 yards, while Mealy had one reception for nine.

L.B. Brown had six total tackles, followed by Stephen Anderson with five. Josh McNary had three tackles for loss (all sacks) and Christopher Swain had one. McNary forced a fumble and Marcus Hilton recovered it. Brian Cobbs recovered another fumble. Josh McNary was named honorable mention defensive linemen performer of the week by the CFPA.

The Rainbow Warriors had five tackles for loss. Hawai'i would finish the season with 7-1 record in the Western Athletic

Conference with a share of the conference championship with Nevada and Boise State; and an overall 10-4 record. The Warriors would lose to Tulsa in the Hawai'i Bowl on December 24th. Hawai'i would receive votes in the final *Associated Press* Top 25 Poll and *USA Today* Coaches Top 25 Poll at the end of the season.

North Texas

The Black Knights (1-1) hosted North Texas (0-2) at Michie Stadium on Saturday afternoon, September 18th in front of 24,689 fans. The temperature was 65 degrees and partly sunny with almost no wind. Katy Murphy was the *CBS Sports Network* sideline reporter for the game.

The Mean Green lost at Clemson, 10-35, and a close loss at home versus Rice, 31-32. Army West Point would face another high-flying attack, as North Texas ranked 23rd in the nation averaging 282.5 yards per game. It would be their fourth matchup against the Cadets, with Army West Point winning each game in 1996, 1997, and 2009.

The Black Knights would wear the patch of the 1st Cavalry Division, the "First Team," on their right shoulders. Army West Point ranked eighth in the nation in rushing yards per game (279.5) and Josh McNary was tied for 11th in sacks per game (1.5). The Black Knights were favored by 5.5 points to win.

Patrick Mealy scored on a nine yard and Alex Carlton made the extra point for a 7-0 lead in the opening drive. Jordan Trimble intercepted a Mean Green pass attempt in the end zone for a touchback with seven seconds left in the first quarter to dwarf a North Texas scoring drive.

Steve Anderson then recovered a fumble at the NTU-14. Malcolm Brown crossed the goal line from the two for a 14-0 lead. Alex Carlton missed a 50 yard field goal attempt in the final seconds of the first half.

Trent Steelman rushed for 20 yards across the goal line with 5:52 left in the third quarter and a 21-0 lead. Alex Carlton made a 23 yard field goal to extend the score to 24-0 with 12:24 left in the game. North Texas quarterback Riley Dodge attempted to pass down the field, but sacks by Mike Gann and Josh McNary had the Mean Green turn the ball over on downs. The Black Knights then rushed ten times to the NTU-20 before taking a knee two times in the victory formation.

"It's hard to win a football game, and it's especially hard to shut a football team out," said Rich Emerson. "That was a great day for our defense because our defense hasn't felt great coming off the field the last couple of games. They have such high standards and expectations for themselves. We respect North Texas. Keeping those guys out of the end zone and getting those takeaways when we needed them was really big in terms of the outcome."

"We didn't have a lot of magic out there. I think at halftime, coach [Ian] Shields and the guys put together a short list of things that would create opportunities for our guys and we were able to string some plays together and get some first downs and we drove the ball more like we're accustomed to. I think what we're going to need to do here is routinely find those 20 and 30 yard plays. When you're playing on a long field like that, you need to find a way to create a shorter field. We need to find some of those chunks. That was the part of the puzzle that was missing in the first half. In the second half, I think we made those adjustments and found those plays. "

Army West Point had 22 first downs, rushed for 292 yards and passed for 45 yards (5-10-0) with 34:35 time of possession, no turnovers, and only two penalties. The Black Knights defense gave up 11 first downs, 95 yards rushing, 106 passing (14-29-1), four sacks, and recovered a fumble. It was the first shutout since beating Akron 20-0 in 2005, the first shutout at Michie since beating Colgate 30-0 in 1993, and first home shutout of an FBS opponent since 1991.

Sophomore slot back Brian Cobbs rushed for 75 yards, with Trent Steelman had 68, and Patrick Mealy with 46 yards rushing. Barr caught two receptions for 18 yards, with Davyd Brooks (12 yards), George Jordan (9), and Crucitti (6) had one reception each. Jonathan Bulls punted six times for an average of 41.5 yards.

Jordan Trimble had 9 tackles, Stephen Anderson eight, and Josh McNary, Antuan Aaron, and Steven Erzinger each had five. McNary and Mike Gann had two tackles for loss, with Trimble, and Jarett Mackey having one each. McNary had two sacks with Mackey and Gann having one apiece. Anderson recovered a fumble and Trimble made an interception. There were seven pass breakups.

North Texas beat Florida Atlantic, 21-17, the week after losing to Army West Point. Their biggest victory came at Western Kentucky, 33-4. North Texas also won at Middle Tennessee, 23-17. The Mean Green lost their final game of the season at home against Kansas State, 41-49. North Texas finished the season with a 3-5 record in the Sun Belt Conference, finishing tied for fifth in the conference with Florida Atlantic and Louisiana-Lafayette. The Mean Green had an overall record of 3-9.

Duke

Army West Point (2-1) went on the road to Durham NC to face Duke University (1-2) at Wade Wallace Stadium on Saturday afternoon, September 25th. The game was televised on *ESPN3*, with Ryan Rose and Jay Taylor announcing. Duke was favored by 6.5 points.

The Blue Devils began their season with a win at home against Elon College, 41-27, but then lost at Wake Forest 48-54. Duke was blown out at home by #1 Alabama, 13-62. Army West Point again faced a top-25 passing attack. The Blue Devils were ranked #19 with 288.0 yards per game. Army West Point was ranked 29th in the nation in pass defense (160.0 yards per game).

The Black Knights honored the 82nd Airborne Division ("All-Americans") for the game. The Black Knights wore their India Whites uniforms. At kickoff, the temperature was 93 degrees, partly cloudy, with wind blowing from the southwest at nine mile per hour with kick off at 3:04 pm EDT in front of 27,289 fans.

On the third snap, Stephen Anderson picked off Sean Renfree's pass and returned it 36 yards to the DU-3. Brian Cobbs scored around the left end on the Black Knights first play of the game, and Alex Carlton made the extra point kick, 7-0 at 13:41 on the clock.

The Black Knights drove down the field on twelve plays in over six minutes before Cobb's 15 yard touchdown run was nullified by a holding penalty. Carlton's 33 yard field goal attempt was blocked. Donnie Dixon intercepted on the next play and returned it 20 yards to the DU-5. Trent Steelman plunged over the goal line for the touchdown and a 14-0 lead.

Duke responded, scoring a ten yard touchdown run by their running quarterback Brandon Connette to close the lead to 14-7 with 1:33 left in the first quarter. The Black Knights moved down the field in nine plays to the DU-4. Brian Cobbs rushed for a touchdown around the left side at 5:27 left in the second quarter, 21-7 for the halftime lead.

On Duke's second snap in their opening possession, Jarett Mackey ripped the ball out of the receiver's hands after catching a twelve yard pass and Donovan Travis recovered it at the DU-34. On the next play, Trent Steelman hit Raymond Maples for a touchdown reception and a 28-7 lead with 12:35 on the clock.

On the next drive, Josh McNary recovered an unforced fumble by the Duke quarterback at the WP-47. Steelman faked an option and lofted the ball down the left hash to Austin Barr for a 34 yard touchdown reception to extend the lead to 35-7 with 6:31 left in the third quarter.

Blue Devils Conner Vernon scored on a 58 yard touchdown to close to 35-14 on the first play of the fourth quarter. Richard King intercepted a pass in the end zone to end a Duke drive. The Blue Devils drove 67 yards for a touchdown with 1:41 left in the game to close the scoring at 35-21. Army West Point recovered the onside kick. After a one yard gain, Max Jenkins took a knee twice in the victory formation, winning for the third straight time at an opponent's home field.

"Well, there were a lot of great things in that football game and there were some things we don't like," said Ellerson. "We need to finish a game like that better. We are not used to being in a situation where you've got somebody by the throat. We need to make sure we can play people and they know what to do and what is expected. We don't play on our heels - we play on the edge, we play aggressively. That is their opportunity to develop and we don't expect the opponent to go down the field in 20 odd seconds, ever."

"Offensively we moved the ball well at times but we needed those turnovers to create points. That is offense, defense and special teams all playing together. That is how you win football games. You don't win it on one side of the ball. Cleary the defense getting those early takeaways and putting us in good scoring position and the offense being able to capitalize on it. That is why turnovers are such an important predictor of success. If you can win the turnover battle you've got a great chance every week."

Ellerson continued, "Our first goal is to win the next game. Regardless of what happened last week, we are going to refocus and go to work. That is what our guys are doing. They are getting more comfortable with this role; they are getting more comfortable with this expectation -- that is what the scoreboard is supposed to look like. That is a powerful thing - learning how to win. We are starting to do that. We have to enjoy this and then go to work on it. Clear and get ourselves refocused. We have a great challenge next week."

Army West Point had 17 first downs, 248 yards rushing, 85 passing (4-6-0), no turnovers, one flag for ten yards, and held the ball for 39:57. Duke had 16 first downs, 111 yards rushing, 261 yards passing (17-30-3), and five turnovers. The Black Knights converted 8 out of 17 third downs and one for one on fourth down attempts, while the Blue Devils made one out of eight third down attempts.

Trent Steelman had 62 yards rushing, Malcolm Brown 46 yards, and Jon Crucitti had 44 rushing yards. Austin Barr caught three passes for 51 yards, while Raymond Maples caught one 34 yard touchdown reception. Army West Point quarterback Trent Steelman was named Rivals.com Player of the Week.

Stephen Anderson had eight tackles and a pass breakup, Josh McNary and Marcus Hilton each had six, and Kingsley Ehie and Ty Schrader each had five. Hilton had one sack and tackle for loss, while McNary and Jordan Trimble each had half a tackle for loss. McNary and Donovan Travis both recovered fumbles, while Anderson, Donnie Dixon, and Richard King intercepted one pass.

For Duke, Conner Vernon had eight receptions for 129 yards and a score, while Brandon Braxton had the other touchdown reception. Desmond Scott rushed for 34 yards. Abraham Kromah has 13 total tackles.

Duke would end its season with a 1-7 record in the Atlantic Coast Conference and an overall record of 3-9. The Blue Devils finished tied in fifth place with Virginia. Highlights of their season were back-to-back victories at Navy (34-31) and at home to Virginia (55-48).

Temple

Army West Point hosted Temple University (3-1) at Michie Stadium on Saturday afternoon, October 2nd. The temperature was 64 degrees at kickoff with 8 mile per hour winds and sunny before 33,065 fans. Chris Frasse was the *CBS Sports Network* sideline reporter.

The Owls opened the season with wins against Villanova (31-24), Central Michigan (13-10), and Connecticut (30-16). Temple led at #20 Penn State until near the end of the third quarter, losing 13-22. The Owls were averaging 146.5 yards rushing and 159.5 passing. Temple was favored by 6 points.

Army West Point honored the 1st Armored Division, "Old Ironsides." The Black Knights were eighth in rushing yards per game (274.8) and third nationally in turnover margin (+2.25).

L.B. Brown forced a fumble on the opening kickoff that was recovered by Ty Schrader at the TU-27. On the fourth play,

Steelman went over the goal line from the two, with Alex Carlton converting the extra point for a 7-0 lead. The Owls ran in a three yard touchdown to complete an 81 yard drive in seven plays, but had a bad snap on the extra point attempt, making the score, 7-6 in favor of the Black Knights.

Carlton missed a 50 yard field goal attempt. Temple's Matt Brown ran 42 yards for a touchdown to allow the Owls to take the lead, 13-7, with 4:05 left in the first quarter. The Black Knights responded with a 79 yard drive in 18 plays when Steelman scored a touchdown from the seven, retaking the lead, 14-13, with 9:08 left in the second quarter.

Jonathan Bulls punted the ball 69 yards where it was downed on the TU-1. The Owls suffered a three and out, and their punt was returned by Josh Jackson to the TU-31. Steelman hit Austin Barr for a touchdown reception and a 21-13 halftime lead.

The Black Knights opened the second half with Trent Steelman going over the goal line from the three to extend the Army lead to 28-13 with 8:05 left in the third quarter. The Owls scored three plays later on a trick play, a 24 yard reception, and a two-point pass to close the score to 28-21.

The Owls drove down the field, and on the first play of the final quarter, scored on an eight yard reception to tie the game 28-28. Matt Brown ran eleven yards for a touchdown for the Owls to take the lead, 35-28. On the next Temple drive, Matt Brown rushed 23 yards, then seven, and a final 20 yards for a touchdown to extend the score 42-28. With 4:20 left, Army West Point went 80 yards in twelve plays with Steelman scoring from the five to close the score, 35-42, with 1:13 left. An onside kick was recovered by Temple, who ran out the clock.

"That's tough to take," said Rich Ellerson after the game. "We are going to look at that, and there are so many things we do well, but we don't play well in critical situations. We allow some huge plays. We don't match up very well in space, and I thought we got exposed in space, defensively. Offensively, we went out and went three and out in some critical situations. By-and-large, I thought we battled against a very gifted and talented football team. We battled, but in a day like that you need to take every opportunity. You couldn't squander an opportunity, and we did. I'm proud of the way we battled. We continued to compete. We believed we were going to find a way somehow, some way. It was every phase. We did some great things from a field position standpoint with the kicking game. If you're going to beat a team like Temple, you have to be hitting on all cylinders. You can't pass up an opportunity."

"I don't think we had a long way to go [for bowl qualification]. We needed a couple more plays. That's a bowl team we're playing out there. That's a team that went to bowl game last year and is playing great football this year. They have some really accomplished football players that have been playing for a long time. We had them on their heels and we had an opportunity. We have to find a couple of plays. That's going to be the case every week. That was not one of our best days. We know what great days feel like, and we're going to have some great days ahead, but it's not going to be magic. It's going to be a lot of hard work and some tough decisions and a lot of really focused practice time."

Both teams had 22 first downs. Army West Point rushed for 235 yards and passed for 124 (9-17-0), with no turnovers, 31:02 time of possession, and no sacks against the Owls. Temple rushed for 256 yards and 151 passing yards (8-17-0) with one fumble. The Owls Matt Brown rushed for 226 yards and four touchdowns and Michael Campbell caught five passes for 124 yards for two scores.

Malcolm Brown rushed for 71 yards, Steelman 65, and Jared Hassin had 58 yards. Steelman was 9-16-0 with one touchdown pass to Austin Barr. Hassin caught three passes for 29 yards, Barr two for 47, and Malcolm Brown two for 33 yards. Jonathon Bulls punted four times for a 45.8 yard average. Jonathan Bulls was named honorable mention punter performer of the week by the CFPA, as did Trent Steelman for honorable mention quarterback performer of the week.

Stephen Anderson had eight total tackles, while Steve Erzinger had seven, Jarrett Mackey and Donovan Travis had five each. Anderson had two tackles for loss, Josh McNary 1.5, and

Mike Gann had 0.5 TFL. L.B. Brown forced a fumble that Ty Schrader recovered. Erzinger, Antuan Aaron, and Richard King each had a pass breakup.

Temple would finish the season with a 5-3 record in the Mid-American Conference and an overall record of 8-4. The Owls finished in third place in the East Division behind Miami and Ohio, both teams they lost to. Temple was the only FBS team with more than six wins that was not invited to a bowl game.

Tulane

Army West Point (3-2) traveled down to New Orleans to play Tulane University (2-2) at the Louisiana Superdome on late Saturday afternoon, October 9th. The game was televised on a campus station with Todd Graffagnini and Steve Barrios announcing with Jimmy Ordeneaux on the sidelines. Tulane was favored by 1 point. The game was indoors in front of 28,756 spectators.

The Green Wave opened their season with a win over Southeastern Louisiana (27-21), then two losses to Mississippi (13-27) and at Houston (23-42), and a win last week at Rutgers (17-14). They were tied for 11th in Sacks and 14th in Tackles for Losses nationally.

Army West Point ranked first in time of possession (35:00), second in turnover margin (+2.00), third in turnovers lost (3), ninth in rushing (266.8), and with Oregon State, had not thrown an interception. The Black Knights had not turned the ball over for three straight games, the first time since the 1946 season. The Black Knights wore the 10th Mountain Division patch during the game.

After a Green Wave three and out, Jared Hassin ran up the middle for a nine yard touchdown, with Alex Carlton converting the extra point for a 7-0 lead with 8:10 left in the first quarter. Tulane recovered a Trent Steelman fumble on the WP-27 and then scored on a pass reception to tie the score, 7-7, with 1:23 left in the opening period.

Antuan Aaron recovered a fumble at the TU-36. Steelman hit Davyd Brooks on a fade route in the corner for an eight yard pass reception to finish an eight play drive and up the score to 14-7. On the kickoff, Zach Watts forced a fumble and recovered it on the TU-26. Alex Carlton converted a 35 yard field goal four plays later to extend the score, 17-7.

On the kickoff, L.B. Brown forced a fumble and Donovan Travis recovered it on the TU-30. Alex Carlton missed a 40 yard field goal attempt. The Black Knights drove 66 yards in five plays as Steelman went over from the one with 1:59 to go in the second period to make it 24-7 at halftime.

The Black Knights drove 76 yards on their opening possession in the second half, with Jared Hassin scoring from the seven to extend the lead, 31-7, with 7:11 to go in the period. Tulane responded with an 18 play drive for 87 yards in eight minutes, scoring on a five yard pass reception making it 31-15 with 14:16 left in the game. After a Josh Jackson kickoff return of 42 yards to the TU-49, Alex Carlton made a 33 yard field goal, 34-15.

Tulane took 96 seconds to go 64 yards in nine plays to score on a five yard pass reception to close it to 34-23 with 2:32 to go in the game. On an offside kick, Donovan Travis scooped the ball up and returned it 31 yards to the TU-8. Brian Cobbs rushed over the left end from the eight for the final touchdown, 41-23. Army West Point won their third road game of the year (first since 1967 season) and fourth in a row on their opponent's home field.

"I don't think that the road has a lot to do with it," remarked Rich Ellerson. "I think that our guys are playing a little bit better in different phases each week. We are doing a great job on the turnover battle. When you do that, you've got a great chance to win. When we won the turnover battle, it's hard to overcome something like four to one. That's hard to overcome. We are running the ball well and we are being opportunistic. Defensively, we can finish a lot cleaner than that. We need to. We need to continue to grow there. That was progress."

"It started off a little shaky," said Trent Steelman. "This just shows how this team can overcome adversity and the character. Just being able to fight through those things, and that's what you have to do to be a good team. Tulane, they are a great defense. We saw on film that they could run and that they were going to be able to run. They are big up front. We just came in and tried to take care of business. That's what we did."

Army West Point had 20 first downs, 312 rushing yards, 31 passing (3-5-0), one lost fumble, and 35:44 time of possession with three sacks. Tulane had 17 first downs, 63 yards rushing, 235 yards passing (23-41-0), and three lost fumbles.

Jared Hassin rushed for 144 yards, Trent Steelman had 85 yards, and Malcolm Brown 41 yards. Davyd Brooks had one pass reception for a touchdown, while Hassin (14 yards) and Austin Barr (9 yards) each had a reception. Hassin was named Player of the Week.

Antuan Aaron had seven total tackles, while Josh McNary, Chad Littlejohn, and Steve Erzinger each had six. Josh McNary had two tackles for loss (both sacks), while Aaron (sack), Stephen Anderson, and Mike Gann each had one TFL. McNary, Littlejohn, Zach watts, and L.B. Brown forced a fumble. Aaron, Watts, and Donovan Travis recovered fumbles. Josh Jackson had two pass breakups, while Erzinger, Brown, Richard King, and Parker Whitten each had one.

Tulane's quarterback Ryan Griffin completed 20 out of 34 pass for 211 yards and three touchdowns. Casey Robotom caught six passes for 63 yards and two scores. Joe Kemp caught six for 57 yards. Trent Mackey paced the Green Wave defense with 17 tackles, while Austin Jacks had two tackles for loss.

After losing to Army West Point, Tulane beat Texas El Paso (34-24) and Rice (54-49).Tulane would finish their season with a 2-6 record in Conference USA in sixth and last place in the West Division. The Green Wave had an overall record of 4-8.

Rutgers

Rutgers University (3-2) would host Army West Point (4-2) in the first college football game played at New Meadowlands Stadium (now called Giants Stadium) on Saturday afternoon, October 16th. Casey Keefe of *CBS Sports* said "Army is actually a pretty solid team this year. They'll give Rutgers a fight." The game was broadcast by *ESPN3*, with Bob Picozzi and Curt Warner announcing.

The Scarlet Knights opened the season with back-to-back wins against Norfolk State (31-0) and at Florida International (19-14). Rutgers then dropped close games to North Carolina (13-17) and Tulane (14-17), before beating Connecticut, 27-24. Their rushing defense ranks tenth in the nation (90.2), ninth in scoring defense (14.4), and eighth in kickoff returns (27.2). Rutgers was favored by 7 points.

The Black Knights were tied for the lead in turnover margin (+2.00) and had the ninth ranked rushing attack in the nation (274.3). Army West Point would wear India Whites uniforms, honoring the 2nd Infantry Division. The temperature at kickoff was 58 degrees, mostly cloudy, with winds of 19 mile per hour coming out of the northwest in front of 41,292 in attendance.

After a Scarlet Knights three and out, Alex Carlton missed a 40 yard field goal attempt. Trent Steelman was injured early in the game. Zach Watts blocked a Scarlet Knights punt and the football was recovered by Sean Westphal on the RU-12. Steelman returned to the field, and rushed for a three yard touchdown at 2:45 in the first quarter. Alex Carlton converted the extra point kick as the Black Knights took an early 7-0 lead.

Rutgers had a 19 yard field goal to close the score to 7-3 at 10:46 in the second quarter. Hassin ran for 50 yards to the RU-7 and two plays later scored from the two, making it 14-3 with 8:02 left in the half. With four minutes left in the second quarter, Steelman completed four passes while mixing rushing plays to move Army West Point 94 yards in 13 plays to the RU-4 with three seconds left. Alex Carlton converted a 21 yard field goal for a 17-3 halftime lead.

Army West Point opened with eleven straight rushing plays in a six minute drive, but Steelman threw incomplete on a fourth and three on the RU-23. Rutgers responded with a nine minute drive of 74 yards to the WP-3 as the third quarter ran out. On the next snap, the Scarlet Knights completed a touchdown pass to close the score to 17-10. Center Zach Peterson was injured on the next play and left the game.

A Donovan Travis interception was overturned by a personal foul call. Rutgers Chad Dodd completed an 18 yard pass for a touchdown to tie the game, 17-17 with 5:16 left. Rutgers Eric LeGrand was severely injured after tackling Malcolm Brown on the kickoff return, and he was transported to the hospital. The teams exchanged possessions throughout the fourth period. The game then went into overtime.

For the first time this season, Army West Point lost the toss and went on offense first. Alex Carlton converted a 26 yard field goal to make the score 20-17. Steve Anderson forced a fumble on the first Scarlet Knights snap, but Rutgers recovered it for a first down on the WP-13. Rutgers running back Joe Martinek scored on a one yard plunge to win the game, 23-20.

Army West Point had 21 first downs, 289 yards rushing, and 115 yards passing (8-14-0), with two fumbles lost, 29:09 time of possession, eight sacks made, and eight penalties for 94 yards. Rutgers had 17 first downs, a negative one yard on 35 attempts rushing, 251 yards passing (18-31-1), no lost fumbles, and twelve penalties for 63 yards. The Black Knights had eight sacks for 76 yards lost.

Jared Hassin rushed for 118 yards and Trent Steelman ran 102 yards. Brian Cobbs (47 yards), Hassin (30), and Davyd Brooks (24) each had two pass receptions, while George Jordan (8 yards) and Austin Barr (6) each caught one pass.

Steve Erzinger had 14 total tackles while Donovan Travis had twelve. Erzinger had 3.5 tackles for loss, while Josh McNary (2.5 TFL), Marcus Hilton (2.0), Jarrett Mackey (1.5), Chad Littlejohn (1.5), Stephen Anderson (1.0), Donnie Dixon (1.0), Travis (0.5), and Mike Gann (0.5). McNary had 2.5 sacks, while Erzinger (1.5), Mackey (1.5), Hilton (1.0), Dixon (1.0), and Gann (0.5).

Anderson forced one fumble. Travis made an interception. Erzinger and Dixon broke up one pass. Erzinger, Hilton, Dixon, and Gann each had one quarterback hurry. Steve Erzinger was named on October 18th as a CFPA honorable mention linebacker performer of the week.

Rutgers Mohamed Sanu rushed for 33 yards and Joe Martinek for 30 and one touchdown. Sanu caught six passes for 50 yards, while Jeremy Deering caught four for 76, Mark Harrison three for 51, and D.C. Jefferson had two receptions for 56 yards. Ted Dellaganna punted five times for a 45.0 average. Antonio Lowery had 19 total tackles, while Khaseem Greene had ten. Jonathan Freeny had two tackles for loss and recovered a fumble.

After beating Army West Point, Rutgers lost their remaining six games, including at South Florida (27-28) and versus Syracuse (10-13). Rutgers finished the season with a 1-6 record in the Big East Conference, finishing eighth and last in their conference. The Scarlet Knights had a 4-8 overall record.

Awards and Recognitions

McNary was named by Phil Steele on October 20th to the midseason fourth team midseason All-American team. On October 21st, McNary was named a quarter finalist for the Lott Trophy.

Named to the Phil Steele's midseason first team All Independent Team were linebacker Stephen Anderson, fullback Jared Hassin, defensive end Josh McNary, center Zach Peterson, offensive guard Seth Reed, and defensive back Donovan Travis.

Named to Phil Steele's second team All Independent Team were defensive backs Antuan Aaron and Donnie Dixon, offensive guard Frank Allen, offensive tackles Jason Johnson and Anees Merzi, wide receiver Austin Barr, punter Jonathan Bulls, running back Malcolm Brown, linebacker Steven Erzinger, defensive tackle Mike Gann, defensive end Marcus Hilton, punt returner Josh Jackson, and quarterback Trent Steelman.

Bowl Games

On October 26th, Army West Point signed a bowl agreement with the Military Bowl, sponsored by Northrop Grumman. Formerly called the EagleBank Bowl, the agreement will allow Army or Navy to play in this bowl in 2011 and 2012 if bowl eligible. Army West Point would also be an option for the 2010 Military Bowl if the Atlantic Coast Conference or Conference USA was unable to fill it.

Virginia Military Institute

Army West Point (4-3) hosted the Virginia Military Institute (3-4) to Michie Stadium on Saturday afternoon, October 30th.

VMI was playing in their 120th college football season. The Keydets had beaten Lock Haven (48-6), lost at William & Mary (0-45) and at Virginia (7-48), beat Presbyterian (24-13), lost at Stony Brook (9-27) and versus Liberty (7-41), and beaten Charleston Southern, 34-16, last weekend. VMI was in its first year running the traditional pro-style offense; almost even in rushing and passing plays, after running the spread option running attack for four seasons and leading the FCS in rushing twice.

Army West Point led the nation in turnover margin (+1.57), 3th in sacks (2.86), was ranked eighth in rushing (276.4), and the only FBS team not to have thrown an interception. Josh McNary was second in the nation in sacks (1.36) and #13 in tackles for loss (1.71).

The Black Knights wore Army Combat Uniform camouflaged pants, jerseys, and helmets, wearing the patch of the Army Special Forces, or Green Berets. Army West Point was favored by 33.5 points to win. Senior Thomas Hagan started for the injured Zach Peterson at center.

Nolan Melson would be the sideline reporter for *CBS Sports Network*. The temperature at kickoff was 53 degrees, mostly sunny, with 11 mile per hour winds from the northwest, before 32,410 fans at Michie Stadium. For the first time this season, Army West Point lost the toss.

Steelman plunged over from the one for a touchdown on the Black Knights second possession and Alex Carlton kicked the extra point at 4:08 in the first quarter. Jared Hassin ran 38 yards for a touchdown and a 14-0 score with 14:20 left in the first half. The Keydets were called for holding in the end zone for a safety at 2:35 left in the second quarter, extending the Black Knights lead to 16-0. Alex Carlton converted a 43 yard field goal with 21 seconds left for a 19-0 lead at halftime.

The Keydets drove down the field for 86 yards in 15 plays on their third possession for a touchdown from the one at 4:18 left in the third quarter, closing the score to 19-7. After Hassin rushed for 54 yards to the VM-27, Carlton made a 41 yard field goal to extend the score, 22-7, with 12:15 left in the game.

VMI drove down the field to the WP-32, but Eric Kordenbrock was intercepted by Donovan Travis who returned it for 37 yards, then lateralled to Jordan Trimble, who then went 42 yards for the touchdown, making it 29-7 with 8:56 to go in the game. The Black Knights then ran out the clock for the victory, 29-7.

"It was a hard-fought game," said head coach Rich Ellerson after the game. Don't let anybody tell you there's anything easy about this game. That was a very physical and hard-fought contest. Give a lot of credit to VMI, especially on the defensive side of the ball. They did some smart things, and they did them very well. Offensively, they were able to hand the ball off and do some things to us that should really be hard to do. If we do that against some other folks, now that that's on tape, we'll have some challenges. I'm excited that we found new ways to win in that we were much more poised late in the football game than maybe we have been."

"We love to win, it's good to win, it's hard to win and it's important to be able to win when you have a few guys nicked up and a few guys who weren't quite available. Hopefully we can be a healthier football team coming out of this week. We all hoped that coming out of the bye week we were going to wave a magic wand and be completely healthy, and the truth was that we weren't. So, there's a lot to be excited about. First and foremost, you won a game and it was hard-fought."

Army had 14 first downs, 316 yards rushing, and 65 passing (4-11-0), two lost fumbles, 30:27 time of possession, and one sack. VMI had 16 first downs, 123 yards rushing, 159 passing (20-36-1), and one sack.

Jared Hassin rushed for 158 yards, with Patrick Mealy (97 yards), Trent Steelman (42), and Brian Austin (21). Hassin caught three passes for 54 yards, while Austin Barr made one pass reception for eleven. Jared Hassin was named honorable mention running back performer of the week by the CFPA.

Donovan Travis had nine total tackles and Stephen Anderson had seven. Anderson, Kingsley Ehie, Richard King, Jarett Mackey, and Reggie Nesbit (sack) each had one tackle for loss. Ehie forced a fumble that VMI recovered. Travis got credit for an interception, and Jordan Trimble scored a touchdown. Travis, Ehie, and Josh McNary had one pass breakup.

For VMI, Chaz Jones rushed 72 yards with one touchdown and Gabe Itoka ran 55. Eric Kordenbrock was 5-27-1 for 139 yards. Itoka caught five passes for 35 yards, Mario Scott had four catches for 29, three receptions by T.J. Talley (45 yards) and Bryan Barnson (12), two catches by Chaz Jones (1), and one reception each by Tracy Hairston (30), Trent White (5), and Josh Favaro (2). Eric Church had 15 total tackles while Kris Ware had nine tackles and a sack. Alex Ray and Charlie Jones each recovered a fumble.

After losing to Army West Point, VMI lost their remaining three games to Coastal Carolina, at Old Dominion, and to Gardner-Webb. The Virginia Military Institute finished their season with a 2-4 record in the Big South Conference with an overall record of 3-8. The Keydets tied for fourth place with Gardner-Webb in the conference standings.

<u>Air Force</u>

"It's a challenge because to have a chance against Air Force we're going to have to play much better than we did," said Ellerson as he prepared his team to face the Falcons. "The good news is, we had a lot of guys step up and play well. We found a way to be successful against a determined and in many places a gifted opponent. The bad news is that if we don't play a lot better than we did just there, we don't have a chance. The good news is that we can play better than that, we can play a lot better than that, and we'll need to. We're going to need to be healthier, we're going to need to be smarter. What we can't do, we can't punt any better than that. We punted way too doggone much, but we're good at that."

Army West Point (5-3) would face the United States Air Force Academy (5-4) on Saturday afternoon, November 6th, before 38,128 fans at sold out Michie Stadium. The Commander-in-Chief's Trophy was on the line, thanks to the Falcons beating Navy on October 2nd in Colorado Springs. Air Force last won the CIC back in the 2002 season.

Air Force had started the season with two straight wins, against Northwestern State (65-21) and BYU (35-14), before losing at Oklahoma, 24-27. Three victories at Wyoming (20-14), Navy (14-6), and versus Colorado State (49-27) were followed by three straight losses, at San Diego State (25-27), at Texas Christian (7-38), and versus Utah (23-28).

The Falcons were second in the nation in rushing (313.6) and 26th in total offense (437.0). Their rushing defense was 109th in the country (205.4). Air Force would wear a special uniform design modeled after the flying suits and helmets worn by the USAF Thunderbirds air demonstration squadron with the back of each jersey saying either SERVICE or FREEDOM. The Falcons were favored by 6.5 points.

Army West Point was now fifth in turnover margin (+1.25), seventh in rushing (281.4), 17th in total defense (313.9), and 27th in rushing defense (117.8). The 1985 Army Peach Bowl championship team was there and met fans in Black Knights Alley. Army West Point was looking to win to become bowl qualified, and its first win against a service academy rival since

2005 at Colorado Springs. It was Senior Day, and 29 seniors were honored with their parents before the game.

Sam Roddy would be this week's sideline reporter for *CBS Sports Network*. Army West Point would wear their Dress Gray uniform with the patch of the 4th Infantry "Ivy" Division on their shoulders. The temperature at kickoff was 45 degrees, mostly sunny, with winds at 7 mile per hour from the east. Air Force won the toss and deferred, and would kick off to Army West Point.

On the Black Knights opening possession, Alex Carlton converted a 30 yard field goal for a 3-0 lead with 8:55 on the clock. Carlton converted on a 41 yarder to make it 6-0 with 4:50 left in the first quarter. Air Force drove down the field, and on the last play of the quarter, Donnie Dixon forced a fumble on the WP-6. The play was reviewed, and the Falcons had the ball on the WP-3. On the second snap of the second quarter, Tim Jefferson went over the goal line from the three to take the lead, 7-6.

Jefferson lofted a pass to Jon Warzeka for a 53 yard touchdown reception to extend the lead to 14-6 at 10:00 left in the first half. Army West Point responded, with Jacob Bohn rushing 18 yards for a touchdown, dragging a pair of defenders, with Alex Carlton kicking the extra point, closing the gap to 13-14 with 6:17 left. Steelman was intercepted by Anthony Wright, who returned the ball to the WP-23. Four plays later, Nathan Walker scored from the two for a Falcons halftime lead of 21-13.

Alex Carlton converted on a 46 yard field goal on the Black Knights second possession to close the score, 16-21, with 2:22 left in the third period. Jefferson hit Warzeka again for a 63 yard touchdown, 28-16, with 44 seconds on the clock in the third period.

Hassin fumbled the football, and Falcons Jordan Waiwaiole recovered the ball and returned it 52 yards for a touchdown at 12:39 left in the game, 35-16. Army West Point responded with a seven play drive, capped off with a Steelman to Austin Barr nine yard touchdown reception. Steelman's pass attempt for a two-point extra point failed, making the score 22-35 with 9:49 left.

A.J. Mackey looked like he forced a Jefferson fumble on the WP-1, but the booth review agreed that Air Force recovered it. Jefferson ran a quarterback sneak on the next snap to up the score to 42-22, with 6:27 left in the half. Quarterback Max Jenkins entered the game, but after two first downs and an illegal block penalty, the Black Knights punted. Air Force ran out the clock for the victory, 42-22.

"We're hurting a little bit," said Rich Ellerson. "We didn't do enough well. It's not a mystery. We didn't coach well enough and we didn't play well enough for it to be a good football game. It wasn't. That's devastating to our guys. There was no lack of effort. There was no lack of caring. There was no lack of investment. We didn't do the things that we have consistently done that have given us a chance in every football game. We know how to do this. We're better than that. That was going to be a hard game to win. If we go out there and play our best football game, it's going to be a hotly-contested game. That had a chance to be just a great football game, and we didn't put our best foot forward. Frankly, that's a shame. That's on me."

Army West Point had 19 first downs, 244 yards rushing, 81 yards passing (6-13-1), one lost fumble, with 30:46 time of possession. Air Force had 18 first downs, 277 yards rushing, and 124 yards passing (3-7-0), and no turnovers. The Falcons won the Commander-in-Chief's Trophy for the first time since 2002.

Jared Hassin rushed for 114 yards, Trent Steelman had 60, Patrick Mealy with 36, and Jon Crucitti ran for 18 rushing yards. Crucitti caught two passes for 32 yards, while Davyd Brooks (22 yards), Mealy (11), Austin Barr (9 yards), and George Jordan (7) each had one reception. Jonathan Bulls punted four times for a 42.2 yard average. Alex Carlton made three field goals of 30, 41, and 46 yards. On November 6th, Alex Carlton was named honorable mention place kicker performer of the week by the CFPA.

Donnie Dixon had twelve total tackles, with Stephen Anderson with nine. Anderson had 1.5 tackles for loss, while Dixon (1.0), Mike Gann (1.0), and A.J. Mackey (0.5). Dixon and

A.J. Mackey forced fumbles, but Army West Point was unable to recover any of them. Anderson had two pass breakups.

For the Falcons, Nathan Walker rushed 109 yards and a touchdown, while Asher Clark ran 89 and Tim Jefferson gained 57 and two touchdowns. Jon Warzeka caught two touchdown receptions for 116 yards and Mikel Hunter had an eight yard reception. Brady Amack had 13 total tackles, while Zach Payne had eight and Andre Morris had seven. Jordan Waiwaiole recovered a fumble and returned it 52 yards for a touchdown.

After the Army West Point victory, Air Force beat New Mexico (48-23) and at Nevada Las Vegas (35-20). Air Force finished their season with a 5-3 record in the Mountain West Conference and a 9-4 overall record. The Falcons finished tied for third in the conference standings with San Diego State and BYU. The Falcons beat Georgia Tech, 14-7, in the Independence Bowl on December 27th. Air Force would receive votes in the final *Associated Press* Top 25 Poll and *USA Today* Top 25 Coaches Poll at the end of the season.

Kent State

Army West Point (5-4) traveled to Dix Stadium to play Kent State (4-5) on Saturday afternoon, November 13th, before 17,222 spectators, including yours truly who attended this game. The game would be televised on a campus station, with Ty Linder and Rob Polinsky announcing. The temperature was 66 degrees at kickoff, mostly sunny, with seven mile per hour winds from the south southwest.

Kent State started the 2010 season with a 41-10 victory at home versus Murray State. The Golden Blazers then lost three in a row, at Boston College (13-26), at Penn State (0-24), and at Miami University (21-27). Kent State then beat Akron (28-17), lost at Toledo (21-34), before winning back-to-back games at Bowling Green (30-6) and versus Ball State (33-14). They lost last weekend to Temple at home, 10-28. The Golden Flashes were favored by 1 point to win.

The Golden Flashes came into the game with the #1 rushing defensive unit in the nation (69.33 yards per game), first in tackles for loss (9.33), and 11th in sacks (2.89). Offensively, they have been led by quarterback Spencer Keith with a 58% completion rate and 1,773 passing yards to receivers Sam Kirkland (43 catches for 493 yards) and Tyshon Goode (42 for 451).

Army West Point was now eighth in the nation in rushing (277.2), 11th in turnover margin (+0.89), #12 in penalties per game (4.7), and 24th in total defense (320.0). The Black Knights wore the patch of the 3rd Infantry Division, the "Rock of the Marne." Josh McNary returned to the field, after sitting out most of the Air Force game due to injury. The Black Knights seeking its sixth win of the season and bowl eligibility.

Sophomore fullback Jared Hassin finished the opening 57 yard drive in 11 plays by rushing twelve yards for a touchdown, with Alex Carlton converting the extra point for a 7-0 lead with 8:09 left in the first quarter. Dri Archer returned the kickoff 99 yards for a touchdown, but it was called back because of a Kent State holding call. Trent Steelman went over the goal line from the two to make it 14-0 with 2:03 left in the first period on a 63 yard drive.

Kent State ran and passed 80 yards down the field to score on a 19 yard run to close it 14-7 with 12:46 left in the second quarter. Steelman hit Davyd Brooks for a 41 yard pass reception, and the 74 yard drive in seven plays ended when Brian Cobbs went over from the two to make it, 21-7 with 4:25 left in the second period. Donovan Travis intercepted a deep pass by Spencer Keith, and returned it 50 yards to the KSU 22. Four plays later, Steelman ran over from the four for a touchdown with 2:00 left in the first half, 28-7.

After a Jonathon Bulls punt, Luke Wollet returned it 36 yards to the WP-29. Kent State completed a 24 yard pass on the first snap and scored two plays later from two to close the score to 28-14. Army West Point responded with a nine play, 82 yard possession with a 39 yard pass possession by Austin Barr and a five yard touchdown run by Raymond Maples to extend the Black

Knights lead to 35-18 with 7:32 left in the third period. Kent State made a field goal to close to 35-21 to end the third period.

Richard King intercepted a pass at the WP-46 and returned it 16 yards. Five plays later, Brian Cobb went over from the five yard line to make it, 42-21 with 13:07 left in the game. Tyshon Goode completed a 72 yard pass reception to close it to 42-28. The Black Knights responded with a nearly six minute possession with Carlton converting on a 49 yard field goal, 45-28. The Black Knights forced two turnovers and ran out the clock for the victory, 45-28.

"That was a hard-fought game," said Ellerson after the game. "I don't think anyone would have anticipated that score. It speaks to the resourcefulness of our opponent. I'm proud of our team; we kept finding another way to win. We've reached a landmark, and we've been working at it for a long time."

"It's an amazing feeling, knowing we accomplished a goal we set back in August as a team," remarked Stephen Anderson. "We talk about playing for the seniors and how it's our last go-around. You see on the field when things start to go bad, or something happens, we demand more from each other."

Army West Point had 20 first downs, 233 yards rushing, and 149 yards passing (9-10-0), no turnovers, one sack, and 38:02 time of possession. Kent State had 19 first downs, 185 yards rushing, 225 yards passing (13-25-3), and one lost fumble.

Jared Hassin had 75 yards rushing, while Brian Cobbs ran 64 yards, and Trent Steelman gained 37. George Jordan had four receptions for 46 yards, while Davyd Brooks two catches for 47, Hassin two receptions for 17, and Austin Barr one 39 yard reception.

Stephen Anderson had seven total tackles, while Chad Littlejohn had six. Jarett Mackey had one tackle for loss (a sack), while Anderson, Donnie Dixon, and Mike Gann each had one TFL. Anderson forced a fumble recovered by Gann. Richard King intercepted two passes while Donovan Travis had one. Dixon had two pass breakups, while Anderson, Travis, and King had one each. Josh McNary had two quarterback hurries.

Richard King was named honorable mention defensive back performer of the week by the CPFA. So was Matt Campbell, for honorable mention kickoff specialist who had two kickoffs for touchbacks.

For Kent State, Eugene Jarvis rushed 71 yards and a touchdown, while Giorgio Morgan ran 48 and Sal Battles gained 42. Morgan passed for 122 yards (5-9-2), while Spencer Keith passed for 95 (7-11-1). Tyshon Goode had seven receptions and one touchdown for 155 yards. Dorian Wood had 14 total tackles, while Brian Lainhart had twelve and Luke Batton had eleven. Future NFL star Roosevelt Nix had half a TFL.

After losing to Army West Point, Kent State lost at Western Michigan (3-38), and head football coach Doug Martin resigned on November 21st. The Golden Flashes ended their season with a victory over state rival Ohio University (28-6). Kent State finished their season with a 4-4 record in the Mid-American Conference and an overall record of 5-7. The Golden Flashes finished fourth in the East Division.

Bowl Games

Army West Point became bowl eligible for the first time since the 1996 season. It was the Black Knights fifth straight victory at a home opponent's stadium, including four in the 2010 season. It was the longest road winning streak since the 1966-1967 seasons.

Notre Dame

Army West Point (6-4) traveled to their second neutral site of the season to play against the University of Notre Dame (5-5) in the first college football game at the new Yankee Stadium on Saturday evening, November 20th. The two teams had met 22 prior times at the original Yankee Stadium, with the last meeting in 1966. This would be the 50th game, beginning with the first matchup in 1913. The game would be televised by *NBC*

Television, with Tom Hammond as play-by-play announcer, color analyst Mike Mayock, and sideline reporter Alex Flanagan.

The Irish were playing their first season under head football coach Brian Kelly using a spread attack. An opening versus Purdue (23-12) was followed by three straight losses to Michigan (24-28), at Michigan State (31-34 in overtime), and Stanford (14-37). Notre Dame then won three in a row, at Boston College (31-13), Pittsburgh (23-17), and Western Michigan (44-20).

Navy beat Notre Dame, 17-35, then Tulsa edged the Irish 27-28. The Irish then beat #15 Utah in its home finale, 28-3, the first over a ranked team since 2006. Freshman quarterback Tommy Rees had his first career start against Utah, throwing three touchdowns. The Irish were #21 in passing offense (272.6).

Army West Point would wear the patch of the 101st Airborne Division, the "Screaming Eagles." The temperature was 48 degrees at kickoff, mostly cloudy, with 11 mile per hour winds coming out of the north northwest, with 54,251 in attendance. Notre Dame was favored by 8 points to win the game. The Irish won the toss and elected to receive.

Notre Dame moved down the field to the WP-5 in eight plays, but Donavan Travis intercepted the pass in the end zone for a touchback. The Black Knights responded with a drive to the ND-2, where Alex Carlton converted a 20 yard field goal with 2:20 left in the first period, capping the 17 play drive going 78 yards that took almost nine minutes off the clock.

Notre Dame made a 47 yard field goal in the first minute of the second quarter. The Fighting Irish scored on a one yard touchdown plunge by Brian Hughes for a 3-10 Irish lead. An Irish 31 yard touchdown pass reception made the score 3-17 with 8:01 left in the first half.

Notre Dame's Darren Walls intercepted a pass for a 42 yard touchdown return down the left sideline, making it 3-24 at 14:00 in the third quarter. The Fighting Irish intercepted Trent Steelman again, converting on a 39 yard field goal to extend their lead to 27-

3 with 5:23 in the third period. The final score was an Army loss, 3-27.

Stephen Anderson said after the game, "It was a great atmosphere and something that really allowed us to be a part of something special. We talked about making history all week and winning the first game ever played in the new Yankee Stadium. It was something that was really something we wanted to do and let slip away."

"It was a disappointing loss," remarked Trent Steelman. "It's disappointing that we didn't come out and play the way we should have or the way we've been practicing all week. It's just the little things that got us today, not keying on our assignments. That's huge when you run this offense. At the same time, you have to take your hat off to Notre Dame and their defense today. They flew around and had a good game plan. At the same time, we have to really look at ourselves right now and see what we need to fix."

Army West Point had 8 first downs, 135 yards rushing, 39 passing (2-8-2), no fumbles lost, and 29:17 time of possession. Notre Dame had 15 first downs, 155 yards rushing, 214 passing (13-20-1), and two interceptions. Patrick Mealy rushed for 30 yards with Trent Steelman (24), Jared Hassin (23), and Brian Cobb (22) on a total of 43 attempts. Davyd Brooks (27 yards) and George Jordan (12) each had a reception.

Stephen Anderson had 10 total tackles, with Bill Prosko (8), Jarett Mackey (7), Steve Erzinger (6), Jordan Trimble (5), and Richard King (5). Anderson had 1.5 tackles for loss, while Mackey, Erzinger, and Mike Gann had one each, and Prosko had 0.5 TFL. Erzinger forced one fumble, but it was recovered by the Irish. Donovan Travis had his 5th interception of the season and one pass breakup. Anderson also had a pass breakup.

For the Irish, Cierre Wood rushed 88 yards, Tommy Rees passed for 214 yards, Tyler Eifert caught four passes for 78 yards and one touchdown, while Robby Tomy had four receptions (63 yards) and Michael Floyd had three receptions (63).

After beating Army West Point, the Fighting Irish narrowly defeated Southern California, 20-16, on November 27th. Notre Dame finished the season with an 8-5 record. The Fighting Irish were invited to the Sun Bowl, where they beat the Miami Hurricanes, 33-17. The Irish would receive votes in the final *Associated Press* Top 25 Poll and *USA Today* Coaches Top 25 Poll at the end of the season.

Awards and Recognitions

On November 4th Jordan Trimble (first team) and Carson Homme (second team) were named to the *ESPN* Academic All-American team. On December 3rd, Josh McNary became a finalist for the Burlsworth Trophy. Head coach Ellerson became a finalist for the Liberty Mutual Coach of the Year on December 13th (Gene Chizik of Auburn would be the winner).

Named by Phil Steele to the first team All Independent Team were linebacker Stephen Anderson, fullback Jared Hassin, defensive end Josh McNary, center Zach Peterson, offensive guard Seth Reed, and defensive back Donovan Travis.

Named to Phil Steele's second team All Independent Team were defensive back Donnie Dixon, offensive tackle Anees Merzi, wide receiver Austin Barr, punter Jonathan Bulls, linebacker Steven Erzinger, defensive tackle Mike Gann, kicker Alex Carlton, and quarterback Trent Steelman.

Bowl Game Bids

On November 30th, Army West Point accepted a bid to the Bell Helicopter Armed Forces Bowl at Noon EST on December 30th at Gerald J. Ford Stadium in Dallas. Southern Methodist University (SMU) would be the Black Knights' opponent, accepting their bid on December 5th.

Navy

On December 7th, USMA extended Rich Ellerson's contract for two years as head football coach at Army West Point. The terms of the agreement were not revealed. The new pact will extend the contract until the end of the 2015 season.

Army West Point (6-5) would face Navy (8-3) in the 111th edition of the rivalry in Philadelphia's Lincoln Financial Field on Saturday afternoon, December 11th. *CBS Television* would broadcast the game, with Verne Lundquist (play-by-play), Gary Danielson (color analyst), and Tracy Wolfson (sideline report). It was the first time since 1996 that both teams entered the showdown with winning records.

Navy started the 2010 season with a close loss against Maryland (14-17), then won a pair of games against Georgia Southern (13-7) and at Louisiana Tech (37-23). The Midshipmen lost at Air Force, 6-14, but then went on a three game winning streak at Wake Forest (28-27), Southern Methodist (28-21), and versus Notre Dame (35-17) before losing to Duke (31-34). Navy came into the Army game with three straight victories, at East Carolina (76-35), Central Michigan (38-37), and Arkansas State (35-19).

The Midshipmen were receiving votes in the national polls and were ranked fifth in rushing offense (302.6), 16th in turnover margin (+0.91), and 19th in pass efficiency (151.2). Senior quarterback Ricky Dobbs led the team in rushing at 80.6 yards per game and 13 touchdowns and had completed 54.8% of his passes for 10 touchdowns. Tyler Simmons led the team in tackles with 111 with Wyatt Middleton with 72 stops. Navy was favored by 7.5 points.

Army West Point entered the game eighth in rushing (260.3), 12th in turnover margin (+1.00), 25th in pass defense (190.9), and 27th in total defense (332.6). The Black Knights would wear a mixture of unit patches versus Navy. Malcolm Brown played in his first game since suffering a collarbone injury versus Rutgers. The temperature at kickoff was 45 degrees, with the weather partly sunny and the winds calm, with 69,223 fans in attendance. Navy won the toss, and elected to receive.

The two teams lost fumbles on each of their opening drives. Joe Buckley completed a 36 yard field goal to make it 3-0 with 11:57 in the first quarter. John Howell caught a pass from Dobbs for a 77 yard touchdown, extending the score to 10-0 with 8:44 on the clock.

With 3:56 left in the first period, Navy began an 85 yard drive in eight plays capped by a Brandon Turner 32 yard touchdown reception and a 17-0 lead, with 13:44 in the second quarter. Josh McNary recovered a Dobbs fumble at the N-23 that led to a Malcolm Brown five yard touchdown reception, with Alex Carlton making the extra point, to close the score to 17-7 with 8:19 left in the first half.

McNary forced another Dobbs fumble and Stephen Anderson recovered the ball at the WP-48. Army moved down the field to the N-3, where Tyler Simmons popped the ball out of Steelman's hands, and Wyatt Middleton grabbed it and ran 98 yards for a touchdown, making it 24-7 with 1:03 left in the first half.

The Black Knights opening drive took seven minutes before Alex Carton converted a 42 yard field goal to close the score to 24-10. Richard King intercepted Dobbs in the end zone for a touchback to end Navy's opening drive. After a Black Knights punt, Navy had a nine minute, 97 yard drive as Gee Greene rushed in for a 25 yard touchdown to make it 31-10 with 5:44 left in the game.

Trent Steelman completed a 45 yard touchdown pass to Malcolm Brown to close the score to 31-17 with 4:05 left. The Black Knights defense forced a three and out. Army West Point moved from its 39 to the N-8, but were unable to convert a fourth down. The Midshipmen took a knee in the victory formation, in a 17-31 Army loss.

"I've never wanted a game more than I wanted this one in my entire career," said Stephen Anderson. "Our team prepared and did as much as we could to feel like we were ready for this game. The way the season went, the ball just didn't bounce our way again. It comes down to going back to work. I didn't beat Air Force and I didn't beat Navy in my entire career here and that's something I'll never get over. I consider myself a competitor. As a team, we consider ourselves able to win any game we go into. Today just wasn't our day."

Anderson continued, "Of course, there's not a point that we felt we were going to be out of the game. We know four minutes is plenty of time. Our offense was getting it going. There was some let-down on the sideline, definitely felt that. That's just what we needed, a little spark. If we could have gotten the ball back a little quicker for our offense it could have been a little different ending."

"There's always more you can do," remarked Josh McNary. "You can't feel satisfied with your performance even as a unit, offense or defense, if your team doesn't win the game. Looking back on it, there's always some things we can improve upon. We're going to look back at it, scrutinize every single play. It's times like these where you really look back and reflect in detail, maybe I could have done that a little bit better, maybe I didn't perfect that, my technique on that particular assignment, on that particular play. We're just going to go back and critique ourselves pretty hard. I think all of us are our own worst critics, so we're all going to find something that we definitely could have done better."

"It's the Navy game, it was our last opportunity to beat Navy,". McNary answered in the post-game press conference. "This loss will probably be in the back of my mind forever, honestly. Knowing that we do have a bowl game in our near future definitely does bring some sense of relief. We do have a chance to avenge this loss with a win. I think it's a great opportunity at this bowl game to end on a good note and leave West Point on a positive note."

Army West Point had 20 first downs, 209 yards rushing, and 128 yards passing (11-20-0), with two fumbles lost, 34:27 time of possession, and one sack made. Navy had 16 first downs, 139 yards rushing, 186 yards passing (6-11-1), three fumbles lost, and three sacks made.

Trent Steelman rushed for 74 yards, Raymond Maples had 60, and Jared Hassin ran for 50 yards. Malcolm Brown had three pass receptions for 59 yards and two touchdowns. Catching two passes were George Jordan (21 yards) and Davyd Brooks (19), while Austin Barr (13 yards), Hassin (10), and Patrick Mealy (6) had one reception each. Jonathan Bulls punted five times for a 39.0 average, including three inside the twenty. Two of the leading rushing teams in the nation each had two passing touchdowns.

Stephen Anderson led the Black Knights with 12 total tackles, followed by Marcus Hilton, Donovan Travis, and Jarett Mackey with six each. Anderson and Mackey shared the one sack. Mackey had 1.0 tackles for loss, while Anderson and Mike Gann had 0.5 TFL. Josh McNary and Anderson each forced and recovered one fumble, while Donnie Dixon also recovered a fumble. Richard King intercepted a pass, while Travis had a pass breakup.

Ricky Dobbs rushed for 54 yards, while Alexander Teich ran for 47. Aaron Santiago had two receptions for 54 yards while Greg Jones had two for 23 yards, John Howell one touchdown reception for 77 yards, and Brandon Turner one touchdown reception for 32 yards. Tyler Simmons and Matt Warrick each had 13 total tackles, while Aaron McCauley had 11. Bill Yarborough, Jabaree Tuani, and McCauley each had a sack.

Wyatt Middleton recovered two fumbles, one returned for a 98 yard touchdown, and was named the game's Most Valuable Player. Navy won for the ninth straight time. Navy finished their season with a 9-4 record. They lost to San Diego State, 14-35, in the Poinsettia Bowl. The Midshipmen would receive votes in the final Top 25 *Associated Press* Poll at the end of the season.

Conclusion

For the first time since the 1996 season, this was not Army West Point's last game of the season. The Cadets has 18 days to prepare for their bowl game, prepare and pass their term end examinations (finals), and rest.

Chapter 13

2010 Armed Forces Bowl Game

On December 5th, the Bell Helicopter Armed Forces Bowl announced that Southern Methodist University (SMU) (7-6) and the United States Military Academy at West Point (6-6) football teams had been selected to play in the game on Thursday, December 30th at Gerald J. Ford Stadium in Dallas TX. It would be the fourth consecutive year that a service academy had played in the bowl, with Air Force playing in the 2007-2009 games.

"We couldn't be happier in having Army assist us in continuing our tradition of hosting a service academy," said bowl executive director Brant Ringler. "It only adds value to what we're trying to accomplish with our bowl game each year, and that is a full patriotic tribute to those who wear and have worn our nation's cloth."

"Knowing we have a bowl game in our near future definitely does bring some sense of relief," said Josh McNary. "We do have a chance to avenge this loss [to Navy] with a win. I think it is a great opportunity at this bowl to end on a good note and leave West Point on a positive."

The Armed Forces Bowl had an agreement with Conference USA and the Mountain West Conference to provide teams. Because of Texas Christian's selection to a BCS Bowl, the Mountain West only had four teams to fulfill its five bowl commitments. Army West Point had a contingency agreement if it was bowl eligible, so it was offered the bid on November 30th, with their opponent likely to be the loser of the Conference USA championship game between SMU and Central Florida.

Armed Forces Bowl History

On December 23, 2003, #18 Boise State beat #19 Texas Christian, 34-31, in front of 38,028 mostly TCU fans on their home field at Amon G. Carter Stadium for the first edition of the Fort Worth Bowl game, sponsored by the PlainsCapital Bank. The bank sponsored the bowl again in 2004. The 2005 edition did not have a corporate sponsorship. In 2006, Bell Helicopter Textron became the bowl's sponsor and the game changed its name to the Armed Forces Bowl.

Each of the previous seven games had been played at TCU's stadium, but when the TCU Board of Trustees approved in April 2010 a renovation project to begin immediately at the end of the TCU's regular season in November 2010, the bowl committee looked for a temporary home.

The committee reached out to SMU to consider hosting the bowl game, and the university agreed. On August 16th, it was announced that the bowl game would move to the Dallas enclave of University Park and Gerald J. Ford Stadium, home field for Southern Methodist University's football team.

"It was a pretty quick process," said SMU athletic director Steve Orsini. "Brant reached out to us that the TCU stadium may not be available for the bowl. It was a short conversation, because as soon as Brant asked us, we said we would be honored to help. I looked it as helping our great metropolitan area and our great athletic community. Anything we can do to help that community, like hosting the game while TCU improves their stadium, we're happy to do." SMU did not know at the time of this decision where it might go bowling.

Southern Methodist Football History

Southern Methodist played its first football game on October 10, 1915 against TCU, losing 43-0 at Fort Worth. The Mustangs overall win loss record was 452-480-54 at the conclusion of the 2010 regular season. SMU had won three national championships, in 1935, 1981, and 1982, as well as eleven Southwest Conference championships. Doak Walker won the Maxwell Award in 1947 and the Heisman Trophy in 1948. The football team had nine members of the College Football Hall of Fame and 16 consensus All-Americans in 2010.

SMU had a 5-6-1 bowl record coming into the 2010 season, with their first bowl game being played in the 1925 Dixie Classic against West Virginia Wesleyan, losing 7-9. They beat Nevada in the 2009 Hawai'i Bowl, 45-10.

2010 Southern Methodist Football Team

June Jones would begin his third season as head football coach for the Mustangs. His 2008 team went 1-11, but quickly rebounded to 8-5 and a bowl win during the 2009 season. Dan Morrison was the assistant head coach and offensive coordinator, while Tom Mason was the defensive coordinator.

Other members of the coaching staff were Jeff Reinebold (wide receivers), Wes Suan (running backs), Bert Hill (defensive line), Adrian Klemm (offensive line), Derrick Odum (secondary), Joe Haering (linebackers), Dennis McKnight (special teams), Randy Ross (director of football operations), Tom Hollinshead (director of high school recruiting), Steve Stigall (director of on-campus recruiting), and Mel deLaura (strength & conditioning).

"Once upon a time June Jones and I were on the same staff at Hawai'i, both young coaches, getting ready to play an option team, Air Force," said Rich Ellerson. "I remember in the locker room June saying, 'I hate this offense.' I remember saying, 'I hate to play against it.' Here we are umpteen years later getting ready to get after each other."

Jones continued, "Our kids got a taste of [winning] last year, and they will certainly want to finish that way again," said Jones. "It will be a challenge. All three years I've been here, we haven't beaten Navy, and Army runs a similar offense."

SMU was 7-6 during the 2010 football season running the run and shoot offense. They opened to a loss at Texas Tech (27-35), before beating Alabama Birmingham (28-7) and Washington State (35-21). Rival Texas Christian beat the Mustangs, 41-24. SMU then won back-to-back at Rice (42-31) and versus Tulsa (21-18) before losing in Annapolis to Navy, 21-28.

Houston then beat the Mustangs, 45-20. SMU won at Tulane (31-17), lost at Texas El Paso (14-28), before beating Marshall (31-17) and at East Carolina (45-38, in overtime). With a 6-2 Conference USA record and co-championship of the West Division (with Tulsa, who they had beaten), the Mustangs played at Central Florida for the conference championship, losing 7-17.

For the 2010 season, SMU averaged 26.6 points per game while giving up 26.4. The Mustangs were averaging 140.9 rushing yards and 273.8 passing (22nd in the nation). On defense, SMU was holding teams to 140.6 yards rushing and 221.8 passing.

A number of Mustangs were ranked in the top 50 nationally. These included Cole Beasley, 18th in receptions (6.5) and 29th in receiving yards (79.7); Darius Johnson, 27th in receptions (5.8); Aldrick Robinson, 12th in receiving yards (94.2); and Zack Line, 16th in rushing yards (107.0) and 49th in all-purpose yardage (119.2).

Also, Kyle Pardon, 42nd in pass efficiency (136.5) and 15th in total offense (290.8); Darryl Fields, 48th in kick returns (25.0); Taylor Reed, 12th in tackles per game (10.2); Pete Fleps, 43rd in tackles (89); and Ja'Gared Davis, 31st in sacks (0.7) and 47th in tackles for loss (1.2).

<u>2010 Army West Point Football Team</u>

Army West Point had previously met SMU twice in football. The first time was in 1928 at West Point, a close win by the Black Knights, 14-13. The second time was an Army victory during the 1967 season in Dallas, 24-6. Army West Point had been a member of Conference USA during the 1998 through 2004 seasons, and had posted a 3-5 record against their former conference foes since 2004. SMU joined Conference USA beginning with the 2005 season.

The Black Knights, had averaged 27.5 points per game against giving up 25.2; rushing for 256.0 versus 141.5 defensively, and passing for 82.1 yards while giving up 190.5 per game. The Black Knights were third nationally in time of possession (33:35), seventh in turnover margin (+1.08), eight in least number of penalties (4.6), and tenth in rushing offense.

Black Knights ranking in the top 50 nationally included Alex Carlton, 48th in field goals made (1.2); Josh Jackson, 48th in punt return yardage (7.3); Donovan Travis, 14th in interceptions (0.4); Richard King, 33rd in interceptions; and Josh McNary, 16th in sacks (0.8). 15 members of the Army West Point roster hailed from Texas.

Army West Point arrived in Fort Worth on Sunday, December 26th. They practiced that afternoon at Kennedale High School's field. The official Black Knights team headquarters was the Renaissance Worthington Hotel in downtown Fort Worth. There was a team welcome event at Billy Bob's Texas that evening.

Monday consisted of practice, a team dinner at Reata Restaurant, and a team comedy event that evening. Tuesday there was a Welcome Home a Hero event at the DFW Airport, morning practice, a visit to the Cook Children's Hospital, and Inside Army Football Radio Show that evening in the hotel.

Army West Point's demonstrated its strong fan base by selling out its allotment of tickets to the game. After the December 5th, there were only standing room only tickets available.

The two teams had a joint press conference Wednesday morning at the Omni Forth Worth Hotel, then enjoyed the Kickoff Luncheon. Later in the afternoon, there was a walk thru and team photos at the Gerald J. Ford Stadium in Dallas.

<u>Pre-Game</u>

For the Mustangs offense, the starters were left guard Kelvin Beachum, left guard Bryan Collins, center Blake McJunkin, right guard Kelly Turner, right tackle J.T. Brooks, wide receivers Aldrick Robinson, Darius Johnson, Cole Beasley, and Bradley Haynes, running back Zach Line, and quarterback Kyle Padron.

Starting for the SMU defense were defensive ends Taylor Thompson and Margus Hunt, nose tackle Marquis Frazier, linebackers Justin Smart, Taylor Reed, Ja'Gared Davis, and Pete Fleps, cornerbacks Ryan Smith and Richard Crawford, and safeties Chris Banjo and Justin Sorrell.

For the Army West Point offense, the starters were wide receivers Davyd Brooks and Austin Barr, left tackle Anees Merzi, left guard Frank Allen, center Zach Peterson, right guard Justin Reed, right tackle Jason Johnson, slot backs Patrick Mealy and Malcolm Brown, fullback Jared Hassin, and quarterback Trent Steelman.

Starting for the Black Knights defense were defensive ends Josh McNary and Todd Miller, bandit Jarett Mackey, nose guard Mike Gann, linebackers Stephen Anderson, Steve Erzinger, and Zach Watts, cornerbacks Josh Jackson and Richard King, and safeties Jordan Trimble and Donovan Travis.

The officials were from the Western Athletic Conference. The referee was Clair Gausman and the umpire was Rico Orsot. Other officials were Tim Schlenvogt (linesman), Lance Thompson (line judge), Steve Lindsay (back judge), Shane Standley (field judge), Matt Sumstine (side judge), and Charley Green (scorer).

For the game, SMU was the home team and wore their special home uniforms of white helmets, black jerseys (in honor of West Point), and white pants. Army West Point wore gold helmets, white jerseys, and gold pants. The Black Knights would wear the patch of the 1st Calvary Division on their right shoulder as well as the bowl patch. The Cadets attending the game wore Dress Gray uniforms.

ESPN televised the game nationally, with Beth Mowins doing play-by-play, with Ray Bentley as color analyst and Jon Berger as sideline reporter. SMU was a 7 points favorite. At kickoff, the temperature was 65 degrees, cloudy, with 16 mile per hour winds coming out of the south. Announced attendance was 36,742, which was 115 per cent of the stadium's capacity, and its largest football crowd ever in the stadium.

The SMU Captains were Chris Butler, Sterling Moore, Youri Yenga, Pete Fleps, and Kelvin Beachum. The Army West Point Captains were Stephen Anderson, Carson Homme, Josh McNary, and Patrick Mealy. The honorary team captain was General Craig R. McKinley, Chief of the National Guard Bureau and a 1974 graduate of SMU, who would perform the coin toss. He would also perform an induction ceremony for new recruits of all five branches at halftime. SMU won the toss, and elected to receive. Army West Point chose to defend the south end zone.

First Quarter

Matt Campbell kicked off at 11:02 am into the end zone for a touchback. At the SMU-20, starting quarterback Kyle Padron hit Aldrick Robinson deep for a 45 yard pass reception to the WP-35 and a first down. Cole Beasley caught a six yard pass to the right side. Zach Watts sacked Padron for a loss of eleven yards, and the quarterback lost the football. Josh McNary recovered it and returned it for a 55 yard touchdown. Alex Carlton converted the extra point for a 7-0 lead with 13:33 on the clock. The Southern Methodist drive went 35 yards in three plays, taking 1:27 off the clock.

Campbell kicked off to the SMU-2, where Kenneth Acker returned it 27 yards after being tackled by Steven Erzinger. Zach Watts and Stephen Anderson tackled Zach Line for no gain off left tackle. Line rushed off right guard for four yards before being stopped by Marcus Hilton. Padron threw an incompletion in the direction of wide receiver Keenan Holman towards the right sideline.

On fourth and six, Matt Szymanski went back to punt, then ran around the left end for an 18 yard gain out of bounds and a first down at the WP-49. On first down, SMU was penalized ten yards for an illegal downfield block to the SMU-41.

On first and twenty, under pressure from Black Knights defenders, Padron then completed a 23 yard pass to wide receiver Darius Johnson who caught it along the right sideline at the WP-36 out of bounds. Coach Ellerson called a timeout at 10:46 to challenge the call of a catch. The booth determined that the play stands.

Line then rushed left for twelve yards and a first down to the WP-24, stopped by Anderson. Padron ran right two yards out of bounds. Jarett Mackey tackled Line up the middle after a four yard gain. Wide receiver Cole Beasley dropped a pass up the middle on third down. Szymanski's 35 yard field goal attempt was wide right and no good, with 8:40 in the first quarter. The Mustangs drive of ten plays for 53 yards took 4:53 time of possession.

Austin Barr dropped a pass to the left side from Trent Steelman. On a counter play around the right end, defensive back Chris Banjo tackled Patrick Mealy after he gained 22 yards and a first down to the WP-42. Linebacker Taylor Reed tackled Jared Hassin up the middle after a five yard gain.

On second down, Davyd Brooks caught an eight yard Steelman pass to the right side for a first down at the SMU-45, stopped by defensive back Richard Crawford. Hassin ran six yards up the middle before being tackled by linebacker Pete Fleps. Steelman's pass to the right sideline for Mealy was incomplete, but Banjo was called for interference and penalized 15 yards and a first down to the SMU-24.

On a jet sweep, Brian Cobbs then rushed left for six yards, stopped by Fleps and linebacker Ja'Gared Davis. Davis stopped Mealy up the middle for a five yard gain and a first down at the SMU-13. On a pitch going left, Malcolm Brown ran 13 yards for a touchdown. Carlton's extra point attempt was blocked by Margus Hunt, making the score, 13-0, with 5:26 left in the first quarter. The Army West Point scoring drive went 80 yards in eight plays, taking 3:21 time off the clock.

Campbell kicked off to the SMU-3, and Acker returned it 17 yards, tackled by Erzinger. Anderson tackled Line after a gain of 14 yards up the middle and a first down at the SMU-34. Johnson caught a pass at the WP-47 and then went up the middle for 34 yards and a first down to the WP-34, stopped by Jordan Trimble.

Chris Swan tackled Robinson after a four yard reception to the left side and then fumbled the football; with Johnson recovering the football. The officials ruled that Robinson was down by contact to the ground before the fumble. On a high snap, Watts stopped Padron for no gain. Padron rushed for eight yards to the left side and a first down to the WP-22, tackled by Donovan Travis.

On first and ten, Stephen Anderson intercepted a Padron pass to the right side at the WP-15, and was stopped by wide receiver Bradley Haynes after an eight yard return to the WP-23 with 1:54 left in the first period. The Southern Methodist drive took 3:25 for 58 yards over six plays.

On a jet sweep to the right, Brown rushed for six yards, forced out of bounds by Banjo. Hassin ran for 13 yards up the middle and a first down to the WP-42, tackled by Banjo. Fleps stopped Hassin after a three yard gain off right tackle. On a pitch to the left, Banjo tackled Hassin for a six yard loss at the WP-39 as the clock ran out.

Second Quarter

On third and 13 at the WP-39, Steelman cut back to his left and ran for 14 yards and a first down to the SMU-47, tackled by Fleps. Hassin ran five yards up the middle, stopped by Reed. Fleps and Reed stopped Hassin after he gained five yards off right tackle and a first down to the SMU-37.

Linebacker Justin Smart stopped Mealy up the middle for a one yard gain. On a counter play up the middle, Mealy ran one yard, stopped by Reed. On third and eight, Mealy only gained one on a pitch to the left, stopped by Fleps. Jonathan Bulls then punted 32 yards, where Kingsley Ehie downed it at the SMU-2. The Black Knights went 43 yards in 5:48 over ten plays.

Pardon got out of his end zone with a 37 yard pass over the middle to Johnson and a first down to the SMU-39, stopped by Trimble. Mackey stopped Pardon for no gain. Josh Jackson intercepted a pass thrown over the middle by Pardon at the WP-32, and returned it for 38 yards up his left sideline out of bounds at the SMU-30 with 9:33 in the second quarter. The Mustangs drive of three plays that went 37 yards in 1:33 time of possession.

Reed stopped Mealy run off right guard after a gain of one yard. Brooks lost seven yards on a reverse going left, tackled by Banjo. There was an Army flag thrown on the play, but the officials picked it up without explanation. Steelman's pass to Barr to the left side was incomplete on third down. Bulls punted 25 yards to the SMU-11, where Crawford returned it ten yards, stopped by Anderson. The Army West Point drive lost six yards on three plays lasting 1:17 time of possession.

Watts stopped Line for a two yard gain off right tackle. Robinson caught an 18 yard pass over the middle, but SMU was called for holding and penalized back to the SMU-13. Anderson tackled Zach Line for a two yard loss on a shovel pass reception going to the left side. On third and twenty, Padron's pass to Holman was over the middle but was tipped by Black Knights defenders and incomplete. Szymanski punted 40 yards to the WP-49, where Josh Jackson fair caught the ball with 6:10 left in the half. The Southern Methodist drive of 2:06 lost ten yards in three plays.

On a pitch to the right, Hassin rushed eight yards before he was forced out of bounds by Crawford and Banjo. Reed stopped Steelman for a two yard gain off left tackle and a first down at the SMU-41. Fleps tackled Hassin after running up the middle for four. Taylor Reed forced Trent Steelman to fumble the football, which Brian Cobbs recovered with a two yard gain before being stopped by Reed. On third and four, Mealy rushed up the middle for seven yards and a first down, tackled by Davis at the SMU-28.

Defensive lineman Marquis Frazier tackled Hassin in the backfield for a loss of one. Under pressure, Steelman's pass to Brooks to the right side was incomplete. Steelman looked to pass on the next play, but ran towards the right sideline before being pushed out of bounds by Smart after a two yard gain. On fourth and nine, Alex Carlton converted on a 44 yard field goal to extend the Army West Point lead to 16-0, with 2:39 left in the half. The Black Knights scoring drive took 3:35 in nine plays for 24 yards.

Campbell squib kicked off 41 yards to the SMU-29. Aaron Davis returned it 14 yards before Josh Powell tackled him at the SMU-43. Erzinger and Anderson tackled Johnson after a two yard pass reception to the left side. Johnson caught a 13 yard pass to the right side from Padron for a first down out of bounds at the WP-42.

Back to pass, Padron scrambled before McNary stopped him after a rush of two yards. Jackson tackled Robinson for a six yard reception to the left side. With third and two on the WP-34, SMU called a time out with the clock at 1:19. Padron's pass attempt to Robinson into the left side of the end zone was off his finger tips and incomplete. SMU called another time out to discuss options. On fourth and two, Mike Gann stopped Padron for a loss of a yard on a quarterback sneak, with 1:09 left. The Mustangs had a turnover on downs. The Southern Methodist drive took 1:26 to go 22 yards in six plays.

Steelman rolled out left and gained a yard before going out of bounds. Banjo tackled Steelman after a two yard rush to the left side. SMU took their final time out at 0:52. Defensive back Justin Sorrell tackled Mealy after running a yard up the middle. Army West Point let the clock run down before taking a time out with 0:05 on the clock.

On fourth and six, Bulls then punted 36 yards to the SMU-24, where Crawford returned it six yards before being tackled by Carson Homme with no time left on the clock. The Black Knights drive of three plays lasted 1:09 and gained four yards. At the end of the first half, the score was Army West Point 16, Southern Methodist 0.

Halftime

At halftime, Army West Point had 10 first downs, 122 yards rushing on 28 carries, had completed one pass on four attempts for eight yards, and had 15:10 time of possession. SMU had 9 first downs, rushed for 49 yards on 14 attempts, made 10 passes out of 16 with two intercepted, and lost one fumble.

For the Black Knights, Jared Hassin had rushed for 48 yards while Patrick Mealy had 39. Stephen Anderson had six tackles with Zach Watts having four. For the Mustangs, Zach Line had rushed for 36 yards. Darius Johnson had caught five passes for 107 yards, while Aldrick Robinson caught three for 55 yards. Taylor Reed had eight tackles while Chris Banjo and Pete Fleps each had seven.

Third Quarter

Matt Syzmanski kicked off into the end zone for a touchback. Banjo tackled Mealy after he gained eight yards off right tackle. Hassin rushed four yards off left tackle and a first down to the WP-32, stopped by Smart.

Davis and Smart tackled Hassin after a three yard gain up the middle. Banjo and Frazier stopped Hassin after he ran three yards off left tackle. Steelman was stopped by Reed after running to the left side for three yards. On fourth and one at the WP-41, the Black Knights called a time out. Malcolm Brown went two yards for a first down at the WP-43 on a sweep around the right end, tackled by Crawford. Hassin then rushed up the middle 17 yards to the SMU-40, stopped by Sorrell.

Smart sacked Steelman for a five yard loss. Mealy gained nine yards up the middle before being stopped by Davis. On third and six from the SMU-36, Davis tackled Hassin on a pitch play to the right for a three yard loss. Bulls punted 31 yards to the SMU-8, where Chris Parks muffed the punt. SMU's Lincoln Schick recovered it at the SMU-8. The Army West Point drive took 6:04 off the clock going 41 yards in ten plays.

SMU opened their first possession of the second half with Zach Line running to the left side for 17 yards and a first down to the SMU-25, tackled by Travis. Beasley then completed a reception to the right side for 13 yards and a first down at the SMU-38, stopped by Travis and Erzinger.

Robinson caught a 13 yard pass reception over the middle for a first down at the WP-49. Hilton tackled Line after a 13 yard gain to the left side and first down to the WP-36. The Black Knights forced two back-to-back incompletions. On third and ten, Padron found Johnson on the right side for a twelve yard reception and first down, stopped by Bill Prosko at the WP-24.

Anderson and McNary sacked Padron for a loss of five. Padron's pass over the middle to Robinson was incomplete. On third and 15, Holman caught a 21 yard pass to the right side and was tackled by Travis and Trimble for a first down on the WP-8. Erzinger stopped Line for no gain off right tackle. Anderson tackled Line for no gain up the middle.

On third and ten, Kyle Padron hit Aldrick Robinson on a post route on the left side for an eight yard touchdown pass. Matt Syzmanski's extra point kick was good to close the score to 16-7, with 2:56 left in the third quarter. The scoring drive took six minutes in 13 plays to cover 92 yards.

Syzmanski kicked off into the end zone for a touchback. Reed stopped Raymond Maples for a run of four yards up the middle. Brown rushed seven yards around left end and a first down at the WP-31 before being stopped by defensive back Ryan Smith.

Frazier and Smart tackled Hassin after a three yard gain up the middle. Sorrell stopped Hassin for two on a pitch play to the right side. Army West Point called a time out with 0:26 left in the third period with a third and five from the WP-36. On a jet sweep going to the left, Smith stopped Cobbs for three yards as the clock expired.

Fourth Quarter

On the first snap of the fourth period, Bulls punted 35 yards where Ehie downed the ball on the SMU-26. The Black Knights drive of 3:06 time of possession went 19 yards in five plays.

Anderson tackled Johnson after a two yard reception over the middle. Line caught a pass to the right side from Padron for seven yards before being forced out of bounds by Jackson. Holman completed a five yard reception on the left side for a first down at the SMU-40, stopped by Anderson. SMU called a time out at 12:55.

Travis stopped Line after a two yard gain around the left end. Line rushed eight yards off right tackle and a first down at the fifty yard line after being tackled by Anderson and Travis. McNary stopped Line after a five yard gain on the left side to the WP-45. Padron pass to Johnson along the right sideline was incomplete.

On third and five, Holman made a ten yard reception over the middle for a first down at the WP-35, tackled by Travis and Jackson. Swain tackled Line after a seven yard gain up the middle. Kyle Padron completed a 28 yard pass at the goal line along the left sideline to Darius Johnson for a touchdown at 9:20. Matt Syzmanski made the extra point to close the score to 16-14. The Mustangs scoring drive for 74 yards lasted 5:35 in ten plays.

Syzmanski kicked off to the WP-11 where Raymond Maples fell on the ball. Hunt and Frazier tackled Hassin for no gain. Steelman's pass attempt near the right sideline to Brooks was incomplete. On third and ten, Steelman rolled to the left and then passed along the left sideline towards Barr that was incomplete. Austin Barr was injured on the play and left the field. Bulls punted 57 yards to the SMU-32, where Acker returned it six yards before being tackled by Homme. The Army West Point drive took 1:00 over three plays to gain no yards.

Richard King forced Line out of bounds after an eight yard rush to the right. Haynes caught a pass near the right sideline from Pardon for nine yards and a first down at the WP-45, forced out of bounds by Anderson. Line ran six yards to the right side, tackled by Anderson. Beasley caught a five yard pass along the left sideline for a first down at the WP-34.

Padron's pass attempt over the middle to Holman was incomplete. Anderson tackled Line after a one yard gain off left tackle. Jordan Trimble almost sacked Kyle Padron, but the quarterback escaped and rolled right, throwing a pass caught by Johnson near the right sideline that gained three yards before being stopped by Jackson. Southern Methodist lined up for a field goal attempt, then took a time out at 4:10.

Ray Bentley said that the wind was blowing "big time" right to left when head coach June Jones called the time out. When the Mustangs came out on the field, Bentley mentioned that the wind was now blowing a little into the kicker's face. On fourth and six on the WP-30, Syzmanski's 47 yard field goal attempt hooked wide left. The Mustangs final drive took 4:10 time of possession to go 32 yards in eight plays.

Army West Point took over on its thirty yard line. On a jet sweep to the left, Davis stopped Brown after a three yard rush. Reed tackled Steelman after he gained two yards off left tackle. SMU took their final timeout with 3:20 to play. On a third and five, Trent Steelman ran a bootleg around the left end for six yards and a first down at the WP-41, stopped by Frazier and Davis.

Reed tackled Mealy after a gain of one up the middle. Hassin ran for five yards to the left side, but was tackled by Smart. Facing a third and four on the WP-47, Coach Ellerson called a time out with 1:18 on the clock.

Steelman completed a pass to Davyd Brook along the right side for a 22 yard gain and a first down at the SMU-31, with Sorrell making the tackle. The Black Knights lined up in the victory formation and Steelman took a knee as the clock ran out. The final Army West Point drive went 39 yards in 4:05 in seven plays.

The game ended at 2:06 pm for an elapsed time of 3:04. The final score was Army West Point 16, Southern Methodist 14.

Post-Game

Following the end of the bowl game, Gary Sinise and The Lieutenant Dan Band provided a postgame concert at the Armed Forces Adventure Area.

"Well, first, what a hard-fought football game that is and how fortunate we were to win," said head football coach Rich Ellerson after the game. "That's an awfully good football team we played."

"We had eleven guys doing their job today," remarked linebacker Stephen Anderson. "That's the best part about playing the game, you get to play next to your brothers who trust you to do your job, and of course you trust them to do their job. It's a great feeling."

Ellerson continued, "You can't appreciate how much those guys have accomplished in their time here, because some of the big things they did, some of the things that will have the longest impact, longest legs, greatest impact over time, you can't see except for what happens out there between the white lines. I'm so happy for them that they had this day that they got this seventh win."

"We've been saying, Bring winning football back for two years, and they did. So they've earned a place. This senior class and this football team has earned a place with that pantheon of great Army football teams. They've brought something back to West Point that has been absent. It will flourish there because of the culture these guys have created for Army football."

"You can't turn over the ball - especially the way we did," said quarterback Kyle Padron. "I think we had three in the first half - my interceptions and the fumble. Army is a great team and anytime you do that, they're going to beat you. They [Army] did everything we expected them to. You just can't turn over the ball when you play a team like that."

Padron continued, "We came out and did the same game plan, we just executed better in the second half. I felt pretty comfortable from the first play on. The first throw was pretty tough on me. The wind got it a little bit and it floated a little bit. I've got great players surrounding me and I felt fine out there. The offensive line played a great game, all around, throughout the entire game and the receivers made some great catches, too."

SMU outgained the Black Knights 413-229 in total yards. Army West Point had 16 first downs (13 by rushing), 199 rushing yards in 50 carries for a 4.0 average, 30 yards passing (2-7-0), and 229 total yards, no fumbles lost, 4 tackles for loss, two sacks, and one forced fumble. Southern Methodist had 21 first downs (14 by passing), 118 yards rushing in 26 attempts, 302 yards passing (23-34-2) with one lost fumble, five tackles for loss, one sack, and one blocked kick.

The Black Knights had 29:19 time of possession, dominating in the second (9:51) and third (9:00) quarters while SMU dominated the first and fourth. Army West Point had no penalties, while SMU had three for 35 yards. The Black Knights were 4 for 12 in third down conversions, while the Mustangs were 6 of 11. Army West Point was 1 for 1 in fourth down conversions and SMU was 1 for 2.

For the Black Knights, Jared Hassin rushed for 82 yards in 18 carries, while Patrick Mealy had 11 for 57 yards, Malcolm Brown 5 for 31, Trent Steelman 10 for 27 yards, Brian Cobbs 2 for 11, Raymond Maples 2 for negative two yards, and Davyd Brooks had one carry for negative seven yards. Steelman passed for two completions on seven attempts for 30 yards, long of 22. Brooks caught both passes.

Jonathon Bulls punted six times for a 36.0 average with two into the red zone. Alex Carlton made one field goal and one of two extra-point kicks, the other being blocked. Matt Campbell kicked off four times for a 61.5 average and one touchback. Josh Jackson returned one interception 38 yards, while Stephen Anderson returned an interception eight yards.

Stephen Anderson had 14 total tackles (10 solo), while Donovan Travis had seven and Steve Erzinger had five. Other players with tackles were Josh Jackson (4), Zach Watts (4), Josh McNary (3), Jordan Trimble (3), Chris Swain (2), Jarett Mackey (2), Carson Homme (2), Marcus Hilton (2), while Mike Gann, Richard King, Bill Prosko, and Josh Powell each had one tackle.

Anderson had 1.5 tackles for loss, while Watts and Gann each had 1.0 and McNary had 0.5 TFL. Watts had 1.0 sack, while Anderson and McNary each had 0.5. Watts forced a fumble that was recovered by Josh McNary for a 55 yard touchdown return.

For the Mustangs, Zach Line rushed for 103 yards on 17 attempts, while Matt Szymanski gained 18 yards on one carry and Kyle Padron ran a negative ten yards on eight attempts. Padron completed 23 out of 34 passes for 202 yards, two touchdowns, and two interceptions, with a long of 45.

Darius Johnson caught nine passes for 152 yards and one touchdown, while Aldrick Robinson had five catches for 76 yards and a touchdown, Keenan Holman caught three passes for 36, Cole Beasley had three for 24, Line had two catches for 24 yards, and Bradley Haynes caught one pass for nine yards.

Szymanski punted one time for 40 yards. He kicked off three times for a 66.3 average and two touchbacks. Szymanski made both extra points, but missed two field goal attempts from 35 and 47 yards. Richard Crawford returned two punts for 16 yards, while Kenneth Acker returned one for six yards. Acker returned two kickoffs for 44 yards while Aaron Davis returned one for 14 yards.

Taylor Reed had 12 total tackles (11 solo), with Chris Banjo with nine and Ja'Gared Davis with eight. Others with tackles included Justin Smart (7), Pete Fleps (7), Marquis Frazier (5), Justin Sorrell (4), Richard Crawford (3), Ryan Smith (2), Bradley Haynes (1), and Margus Hunt (1). Banjo had 2.0 tackles for loss, while Davis, Smart, and Frazier each had 1.0 TFL. Justin Smart had the one sack. Taylor Reed forced a fumble that the Black Knights recovered. Margus Hunt blocked an extra point kick.

A total 57 Black Knights players participated in the game. Individuals not starting or appearing in individual statistics were Matt Luetjen, Antuan Aaron, Thomas Holloway, Sean Westphal, Ty Shrader, Josh Jones, Waverly Washington, Justin Trimble, Jacob Bohn, Jon Crucitti, Quentin Kantaris, Justin Schaaf, Joe Bailey, Brian Zalnerailtis, Parker Whitten, Matt Villanti, Mikel

Weich, Brad Kelly, Justin Allen, Kyler Martin, George Jordan, Mark Allen, and A.J. Mackey.

A total of 54 Mustangs participated in the game. Individuals not starting or appearing in individual statistics were: Chris Butler, Bryce Lunday, Ben Hughes, Darryl Fields, Chris Castro, Braden Smith, Brett Haness, Randall Joyner, Robert Parker, Victor Jones, Robert Mojica, Billy Dugal, Ryan Moczygemba, Stephen Nelson, Bryon Brown, Cameron Rogers, Mark Voosen, Lincoln Schick, Bryce Tennison, Jordan Favreau, Ben Gottschalk, Josh Emshoff, Jordan Free, Charles Clay, Marcus Holyfield, Patrick Fleming, and Mike O'Guin.

Senior linebacker Stephen Anderson was named Army's Most Valuable Player after registering a season-high 14 total tackles, 1.5 tackles for loss, and an interception return. Anderson finished his career with 298 tackles and 34 TFL. Sophomore wide receiver Darius Johnson was named SMU's Most Valuable Player and had the most receiving yards and receptions in Armed Forces Bowl history.

There were other Armed Forces Bowl records set in the game. Josh Jackson's 38 yard interception return was the longest, as was Josh McNary's 55 yard fumble return, and SMU's third quarter drive of 92 yards. Zach Line's 103 yards rushing was the eleventh best in Armed Forces Bowl history, while Kyle Padron's 302 passing yards were third best in this bowl. Alex Carlton's 44 yard field goal tied for third longest. Army West Point tied the bowl record for having no penalties.

2010 Season Statistics

The following are the Army West Point Football Team statistics for the 2010 season, including the bowl game. On offense, the team had 346 points (26.6 average); 239 first downs (179 rushing, 53 passing, and 7 by penalty); rushed for 3,271 yards (251.6 ypg) on 728 attempts (4.5 ypa) and 34 touchdowns; passed for 1,015 yards on 72 completions on 138 passes and 3 interceptions for 78.1 ypg, 7.4 ypp, 14.1 ypr, and 7 touchdowns; had 4,286 yards total offense on 866 plays, 329.7 ypg, 4.9 ypp, and

43 touchdowns; had 55 penalties for 532 yards; had 23 fumbles and lost 11 of them; had an average time of possession per game of 33:15; converted 89 out of 193 third downs (46%); converted 14 out of 19 fourth downs (74%); gave up 8 sacks for 62 yards; and scored 44 times out of 50 trips into the red zone (88%) with 36 of them touchdowns.

On defense, the team allowed 316 points (24.3 average); 228 first downs (103 rushing, 105 passing, and 20 by penalty); 1,809 yards rushing (139.2 ypg) on 426 attempts (4.2 ypa) and 18 touchdowns allowed; 2,588 passing yards on 187 completions on 327 passes and 14 interceptions for 199.1 ypg, 7.9 ypp, 13.8 ypr, and 22 touchdowns; allowed 4,397 total yards on 753 plays, 338.2 ypg, 5.8 ypp, and 43 touchdowns; opponents had 73 penalties for 563 yards; had 26 fumbles and lost 16 of them; converted 60 out of 144 third downs (42%); converted 10 out of 19 fourth downs (53%); made 25 sacks for 182 yards; scored 29 times out of 34 trips into the red zone (85%) with 25 of them touchdowns; and returned 14 interceptions (21.4 average).

For Black Knights special teams statistics, they kicked off 68 times for 59.3 average (normally from the thirty yard line), 4 touchbacks, and 0 for 1 on onside kicks; punted 56 times for a 38.9 average; returned 50 kickoffs (19.1 average); returned 20 punts (7.1 average); made 15 out of 22 field goal attempts; and made 41 out of 42 point after touchdown attempts.

For opponents' special teams statistics, they kicked off 60 times for 60.5 average, 7 touchbacks, and 0 for 1 on onside kicks; punted 52 times for a 36.9 average; returned 62 kickoffs (20.4 average); returned 22 punts (3.7 average); made 5 out of 7 field goal attempts; and made 37 out of 38 point after touchdown attempts.

Army West Point averaged 31,667 attendance in five home games, 27,103 in six away games, and 61,737 in two neutral site games. Scoring by quarters was 92-58 (1st), 112-76 (2nd), 79-66 (3rd), 60-110 (4th), and 3-6 (OT).

Jared Hassin had 1,013 yards rushing in 191 attempts for a 77.9 ypg, while Trent Steelman had 721 yards in 197 carries for a 55.5 ypg. Other individual rushing statistics were Patrick Mealy (101-470), Malcolm Brown (62-343), Brian Cobbs (50-302), Raymond Maples (47-208), Jon Crucitti (29-87), Jacob Bohn (15-75), Max Jenkins (14-55), Brian Austin (5-25), and Davyd Brooks (3-minus 4). Steelman had 11 rushing touchdowns, while Hassin (9), Cobbs (5), Brown (4), Mealy (2), and Maples, Bohn, and Jenkins had one touchdown each.

Steelman passed for 71 completions on 133 passes for 995 yards with 7 touchdowns and 3 interceptions. Jenkins passed for one completion on five passes for 20 yards. Brooks caught 15 receptions (238 yards and one touchdown), Jordan George had 15 passes (148 yards), Barr caught 14 passes (215 yards and 3 touchdowns), and Hassin had 12 receptions (154 yards). Others having pass receptions were Brown (5-92 and 2 touchdowns), Mealy (4-45), Crucitti (3-38), Maples (2-38 and one touchdown), and Cobbs (2 yards).

Josh Jackson returned 26 kickoffs for a 20.1 average and a long of 42 yards, while Brown returned 13 for a 21.0 average with a long of 34 yards. Other kick returners were Maples (3-15.3), Mealy (3-11.3), and Cobbs (2-18.0) with Donovan Travis (31.0), Julian Crockett (12.0, and Justin Schaaf (-1.0) returning one kickoff return. Jackson returned 18 punts for a 7.3 average while Zach Watts (7.0), Sean Westphal (3.0), and Josh Jones (0.0) each returned one punt.

Travis returned five interceptions for 68 yards, while Richard King had four for 16 yards and Stephen Anderson had two for 44 yards. Three Black Knights returned one interception during the season - Jackson (59 yards), Trimble (42 yards and a touchdown), and Donnie Dixon (20 yards). Josh McNary returned one fumble 55 yards for a touchdown, while Marcus Hilton returned one fumble for ten yards. McNary recovered two other fumbles for no return, while Anderson and Donovan Travis each recovered two without a return, and Dixon, Jackson, Watts, Antuan Aaron, Bill

Prosko, Ty Shrader, Josh Jones, and Todd Miller each recovered one fumble with no return.

Alex Carlton made 15 out of his 22 field goal attempts, with his longest being 49 yards against Kent State. Two attempts were blocked. He ended the season making 11 consecutive field goals. Carlton made 41 out of 42 extra point conversions, the other being blocked. The Black Knights did not attempt a two-point conversion. Matt Campbell kicked off 64 times for a 60.0 average and 4 touchbacks. Carlton kicked off four times for a 47.8 average. Jonathan Bulls punted 56 times for a 38.9 average.

Alex Carlton led the team in scoring with 86 points, with Trent Steelman with 66 and Jared Hassin having 54 points. Others scoring were Brown (36), Cobbs (30), Barr (18), Mealy (12), Maples (12), McNary (6), Trimble (6), Jenkins (6), Bohn (6), and Brooks (6), with one Team safety. Steelman led with 132.0 total offense yards per game followed by Hassin with 77.9. Jared Hassin led the team in all-purpose with 89.8 yards per game.

Stephen Anderson led the team with 108 total tackles (68 solo), followed by Steve Erzinger (76, 40 solo) and Donovan Travis (60, 34 solo). Others with tackles included Jarett Mackey (47), Josh McNary (46), Donnie Dixon (45), Jordan Trimble (38), Marcus Hilton (38), Josh Jackson (33), Chad Littlejohn (30), Mike Gann (28), Antuan Aaron (27), Kingsley Ehie (25), Richard King (23), and Zach Watts (20).

Also, L.B. Brown (16), Bill Prosko (16), Ty Shrader (14), Sean Westphal (11), Chris Swain (10), A.J. Mackey (9), Matt Campbell (6), Justin Trimble (5), Josh Jones (4), Brian Cobbs (3), Quentin Kantaris (3), Zach Williams (3), Carson Homme (3), Justin Schaaf (2), Josh Powell (2), and Reggie Nesbit (2). Having one tackle were Jacob Bohn, Malcolm Brown, Parker Whitten, Frank Allen, Kyler Martin, Trent Steelman, Todd Miller, Jon Crucitti, Jason Johnson, Justin Allen, and Waverly Washington.

McNary led the team with 12.5 tackles for loss. Others included Anderson (12.0 TFL), Gann (9.0), Jarett Mackey (6.5), Dixon (5.5), Erzinger (4.5), Hilton (3.0), Littlejohn (3.0), Jordan

Trimble (1.5), Aaron (1.0), Ehie (1.0), King (1.0), Watts (1.0), Swain (1.0), Nesbit (1.0), Travis (0.5), Prosko (0.5), and A.J. Mackey (0.5).

Josh McNary led the team in sacks with 10.0 for 86 yards lost. Others making sacks included Jarett Mackey (4.0), Hilton (2.0), Gann (2.0), Erzinger (1.5), Anderson (1.0), Dixon (1.0), Aaron (1.0), Watts (1.0), Nesbit (1.0), and Littlejohn (0.5). Zach Watts blocked a kick. Forcing fumbles were Anderson (4), McNary (3), Jarett Mackey (2), Watts (2), L.B Brown (2), while Erzinger, Dixon, Littlejohn, Ehie, Prosko, and A.J. Mackey forced one fumble each.

Donovan Travis had six pass breakups, while Anderson, Dixon, and Erzinger had five each. Others having pass breakups included King (3), McNary 92), Jordan Trimble (2), Jackson (2), Aaron (2), and L.B. Brown (2), with Ehie, Swain, and Whitten with one each. Marcus Hilton had four quarterback hurries, while McNary (3), Gann (2), Erzinger (1), and Dixon (1).

Jason Johnson, Seth Reed, Anees Merzi, Frank Allen, and Trent Steelman started every game for the offense this season. Josh McNary, Stephen Anderson, Mike Gann, Steve Erzinger, and Jarett Mackey started every game for the defense.

Jared Hassin finished the season being the 14th Black Knights ever to go over 1,000 yards in a season. Trent Steelman finished the season five passing yards shy of being the first Army player to pass for 1,000 yards and rush for 500 in the same season. Hassin and Steelman finished the season with a combined 1,734 rushing, 7th best for a rushing duo in Army's history. Alex Carlton's extra point miss ended his streak of 54 in a row, third longest in Academy history.

Army bowl records set in the 2010 Armed Forces Bowl still in effect as of 2019 season included most field goals made (1), fewest penalties called (0), fewest penalty yards (0), longest fumble return (55), longest field goal made (44), and most defensive reception yards allowed (152).

Army football records set during the 2010 season still in effect at the end of the 2020 season include most sacks in a season (25, tied with the 2016 season) and most sacks in a game (8, Rutgers).

Awards and Recognitions

Josh McNary was selected for and attended the 2011 East-West Shrine Game in Orlando FL on January 22, 2011. The Pat Tillman Award was presented to linebacker Josh McNary, who "best exemplifies character, intelligence, sportsmanship and service."

Lettermen

Those earning letters for the 2010 season were Antuan Aaron, Frank Allen, Justin Allen, Mark Allen, Stephen Anderson, Brian Austin, Joe Bailey, Austin Barr, Jacob Bohn, Chip Bowden, Davyd Brooks, LB Brown, Malcolm Brown, Jonathan Bulls, Matt Campbell, Alex Carlton, Brian Cobbs, Nate Combs, Jonathan Crucitti, Donnie Dixon, Kingsley Ehie, Steven Erzinger, Mike Gann, Tom Hagan, and Jared Hassin.

Also, Marcus Hilton, Carson Homme, Damion Hunter, Josh Jackson, Max Jenkins, Jason Johnson, Josh Jones, George Jordan, Quentin Kantaris, Brad Kelly, Richard King, Chad Littlejohn, Matthew Luetjen, AJ Mackey, Jarrett Mackey, Raymond Maples, Kyler Martin, Dan McGue, Josh McNary, Patrick Mealy, Anees Merzi, Todd Miller, Reggie Nesbit, Zach Peterson, Josh Powell, Bill Prosko, Seth Reed, and Justin Schaaf.

Also, Ty Shrader, Trent Steelman, Anthony Stephens, Christopher Swain, Donovan Travis, Jordan Trimble, Justin Trimble, Victor Ugenyi, Matthew Villanti, Kolin Walk, Waverly Washington, Zach Watts, Mike Weich, Sean Westphal, Parker Whitten, James Whittington, CeDarius Williams, and Zachary Williams.

Army Branch Selections

The Army West Point seniors in the USMA Class of 2011 went into the following branches (Field Artillery) Mark Allen,

Jacob Bohn, Chip Bowden, Jonathan Bulls, Matt Campbell, Donnie Dixon, Mike Gann, Marcus Hilton, Josh McNary, Anees Merzi, Zach Peterson, and Seth Reed; (Infantry) Stephen Anderson, Carson Homme, Jason Johnson, and Todd Miller; (Air Defense Artillery) L.B. Brown, Kingsley Ehie, Pat Mealy, Donovan Travis, and Mike Weich; (Armor) Emerson Follett; (Aviation) Tom Hagan; (Engineers) Sean Westphal; and (Signal Corps) Jordan Trimble.

Conclusion

The bowl win clinched Army West Point's first winning season since 1996 and snapped a two game losing record in bowl games. The Black Knights were now 3-2 in bowls, their last victory being against Illinois, 31-29, in the 1985 Peach Bowl. The win snapped Army West Point's 22 game losing streak to teams with winning records at the time of the game. It was the first time since the 1963 season that all three service academies had won seven games in a season. The win stretched Army West Point's winning streak to six games playing in an opponent's home stadium.

Inside the Hotel Thayer, there is a plaque that recognizes the 2010 Army West Point Football Team. It reads:

(Hotel Thayer Logo)

2010 ARMED FORCES BOWL FOOTBALL TEAM

(Picture of several team members with the bowl trophy)

COACH RICH ELLERSON

ARMY 16 - SOUTHERN METHODIST UNIVERSITY (SMU) 14

WINNING SEASON 7 WINS, 6 LOSSES

MOST VALUABLE PLAYER:

ARMY LINEBACKER STEPHEN ANDERSON

DUTY HONOR COUNTRY

Chapter 14

Post-Script

Now you have read the story of the first five Army West Point bowl teams, plus a little Army Football history of why it took USMA until 1984 to attend bowl games.

Volume 2 will continue with the next five Army West Point bowl teams. I believe very strongly Volume 3 will follow sometime in 2027-2028 with the story of the next five bowl teams.

A well-executed option running offense and a sound rushing defense produces a winning Army Football Team in these modern times. Sound running attacks and sound running defenses were also true in the Daly seasons, during most of the 1920s & 1930s, during the Blaik seasons, in the early Cahill seasons, and in 1977.

As I was finalizing Volume 1, and had not yet written this chapter, I was thinking which of the five first bowl teams was the best team? I will not do that, but I will present a strong reason for each team:

The 1984 Cherry Bowl Champions were the first to play and win a bowl game; and literally dominated their Big Ten opponent on defense.

The 1985 Peach Bowl Champions showed that 1984 was not a fluke, and showed off the wishbone offense was more than enough to take on a Top Five passing attack from a future NFL quarterback.

The 1988 Sun Bowl team showed off a wishbone attack that dominated one of college football's elite programs and truthfully, beat the Crimson Tide that day.

The 1996 Independence Bowl team's three touchdown comeback in the fourth quarter showed the fighting spirit of West Point athletes using the flexbone attack that really defeated their opponent.

The 2010 Armed Forces Bowl Champions dominated a run and shoot, high scoring, offensive attack in the opponent's home stadium packed with a record attendance; with the option running attack holding on to the football.

Bibliography

GENERAL SOURCES FOR ARMY AND COLLEGE FOOTBALL INFORMATION:

"Army West Point Football" Football. Last accessed on July 1, 2022. https://www.goarmywestpoint.com.

"Army Wishbone Trips Lafayette," *The Journal News*, September 15, 1974.

Association of Graduates of the United States Military Academy at West Point. *Classes of 1802 Bicentennial and 1902 Centennial Edition of Register of Graduates and Former Cadets*. West Point, NY: Association of Graduates, USMA, 2002.

Association of Graduates of the United States Military Academy at West Point. *Register of Graduates and Former Cadets*. West Point, NY: Association of Graduates, USMA, 2010.

Association of Graduates of the United States Military Academy at West Point. *Register of Graduates* Look-up for each Graduate. Last accessed on June 7, 2022. https://www.westpointaog.org.

Boyles, Bob, and Guido, Paul. *Fifty Years of College Football: A Modern History of America's Most Colorful Sport*. New York: Skyhorse Publishing, 2007.

Cohane, Tim. *Gridiron Grenadiers: The Story of West Point Football*. New York: C.P. Putnam's Sons, 1948.

Fienstein, John. *A Civil War: A Year inside College Football's Purest Rivalry*. Boston: Little, Brown, and Co., 1996.

Golden, Neal. *LSU Bowl Games: A Complete History*. Jefferson NC: McFarland & Company, 2021.

Hammond, T.W. *A Brief History of Intercollegiate Football at the United States Military Academy*. West Point, NY: Army Athletics Association, 1914.

MacCambridge, Michael, ed. *ESPN College Football Encyclopedia: The Complete History of the Game*. New York: ESPN Books, 2005.

National Collegiate Athletics Association. *Football Bowl Division Records*. Indianapolis, IN: NCAA, 2019.

Naval Academy Athletic Association. *2011 Navy Football Media Guide*. Sports Information Office: Annapolis, MD, 2011.

Palmer, John McA. "How Football Came to West Point." *Assembly*, January 1943, 2-4.

Phillips, Tommy A. *Penn State Bowl Games: A Complete History*. Jefferson NC: McFarland & Company, 2021.

Revsine, Dave. *The Opening Kickoff: The Tumultuous Birth of a Football Nation*. Guilford, CT: Lyons Press, 2014.

U.S. Department of Defense. United States Military Academy. Office of Athletic Communications. "Army's Storied Football History," excerpted with permission from Dineen, Joseph E. *The Illustrated History of Sports at the U.S. Military Academy*. Last accessed on October 6, 1999. https://www.usma.edu/athletics/varsitysports/football/history.htm.

U.S. Department of Defense. United States Military Academy. Office of Athletic Communications. *The 2005 Army Football Record Book*. West Point, NY: College Promotions Corporation, 2005.

CHAPTER 1 (1929-1931):

"Army-Navy Game Set for Here Dec. 13," *The New York Times*, November 15, 1930.

"Army-Navy Grid Truce in Offing," *Montana Standard*, May 29, 1931.

"Army-Navy Pick New York for Charity Game," *Altona Mirror*, October 8, 1931.

"Army, Navy Agree to Meet on Gridiron for Benefit of Unemployed," *Salt Lake Tribune*, October 7, 1931.

"Army's Football Schedule Ready," *United Press*, September 5, 1929.

"Army's Reception Worries Stanford," *The Bismarck Tribune*, December 19, 1929.

"Army Cadet's Neck Broken in Yale Game," *The Associated Press*, October 24, 1931.

"Army Coach Gives Stanford Praise; Strongest Foes of Year, Says Biff," *The Salt Lake Tribune*, December 30, 1929.

"Army Eleven to Meet 3 New Opponents in 1930," *The Associated Press*, December 7, 1930.

"Army Gridders Reach Heart of Rocky Mountains," *The Dubuque Telegraph Herald and Times Journal*, December 22, 1929.

"Army Squad Leaves for Game on Coast," *The New York Times*, December 19, 1929.

"Army Team Works Out in Desert," *The Port Arthur News*, December 22, 1929.

"Army to Take 110 Men West for Grid Battle," *The Tuscaloosa News*, December 16, 1929.

"Army Train Rolls Along," *The News Tribune*, December 20, 1929.

Bell, Bell. "Army Has Stiff Card and Unusual Problems," *The Associated Press*, September 9, 1929.

Braucher, William. "Farewell Game for Cagle and Biff Jones," *The Pittsburgh Press*, December 21, 1929.

"Cadet Gridders Reach Coast," *Beatrice Daily Sun*, December 23, 1929.

"Cadet Gridders to Wear Jerseys of Loud Colors," *The Associated Press*, September 9, 1929.

"Cadets Tackling Stiff Grid Slate," *United Press*, February 8, 1928.

"Cagle and Mates Defeated 34 to 13," *United Press*, December 28, 1929.

"Card-Army Agreement Favored," *United Press*, June 12, 1928.

"Coaches Favor Navy in Dispute," *United Press*, December 31, 1927.

"Contest Will Be Played Nov. 24 on West Point Field," *The Associated Press*, February 8, 1928.

Cromartie, Bill. *Army Navy Football: The Greatest Rivalry in All of Sports*. Atlanta, GA: Gridiron Publishers, 1996.

"Drop Celebrations to Make Trip Quick," *The Charleston Daily Mail*, December 21, 1929.

Edson, James Stewart. *The Black Knights of West Point*. New York: Bradbury, Sayles, O'Neill Co, 1954.

"500 Cheer Cadet Team to Victory," *The Associated Press*, December 19, 1929.

Kirshner, Alex. "What Army-Navy's disjointed history says about college football," *Banner Society*, December 12, 2019.

"Mother, Racing Death, Reaches Football Hero Kept Alive by Lung," *The Pittsburgh Press*, October 26, 1931.

Neil, Edward J. "Cadets Stage Comeback in Second Quarter to Win Over Midshipmen," *The Associated Press*, December 12, 1931.

Neil, Edward J. "Crowd of 70,000 Gives $600,000 for Charity," *The Associated Press*, December 14, 1930.

Neil, Edward J. "Ray Stecker Gallops 57 Yards to Give Cadets 6 to 0 Victory," *The Associated Press*, December 13, 1930.

"1926 Army Cadets football team," *Wikipedia*. Last accessed on June 10, 2022.
https://www.en.m.wikipedia.org.

"1926 Navy Midshipmen football team," *Wikipedia*. Last accessed on June 10, 2022.
https://www.en.m.wikipedia.org.

"1927 Army Cadets football team," *Wikipedia*. Last accessed on June 10, 2022.
https://www.en.m.wikipedia.org.

"1927 College Football Schedule and Results," *Sports Reference College Football*. Last accessed on June 17, 2022.
https://www.sports-reference.com/cfb/.

"1928 Army Cadets football team," *Wikipedia*. Last accessed on June 10, 2022.
https://www.en.m.wikipedia.org.

"1928 College Football Schedule and Results," *Sports Reference College Football*. Last accessed on June 17, 2022.
https://www.sports-reference.com/cfb/.

"1928 Notre Dame Fighting Irish football team," *Wikipedia*. Last accessed on June 10, 2022.

https://www.en.m.wikipedia.org.

"1928 Stanford football team," *Wikipedia*. Last accessed on June 10, 2022.
https://www.en.m.wikipedia.org.

"1929 Army Cadets football team," *Wikipedia*. Last accessed on June 10, 2022.
https://www.en.m.wikipedia.org.

"1929 College Football Schedule and Results," *Sports Reference College Football*. Last accessed on June 17, 2022.
https://www.sports-reference.com/cfb/.

"1929 Notre Dame Fighting Irish football team," *Wikipedia*. Last accessed on June 10, 2022.
https://www.en.m.wikipedia.org.

"1929 Stanford football team," *Wikipedia*. Last accessed on June 10, 2022.
https://www.en.m.wikipedia.org.

"1930 Army Cadets football team," *Wikipedia*. Last accessed on June 10, 2022.
https://www.en.m.wikipedia.org.

"1930 College Football Schedule and Results," *Sports Reference College Football*. Last accessed on June 17, 2022.
https://www.sports-reference.com/cfb/.

"1930 Navy Midshipmen football team," *Wikipedia*. Last accessed on June 10, 2022.
https://www.en.m.wikipedia.org.

"1930 Notre Dame Fighting Irish football team, *Wikipedia*. Last accessed on June 10, 2022.
https://www.en.m.wikipedia.org.

"1931 Army Cadets football team," *Wikipedia*. Last accessed on June 10, 2022.
https://www.en.m.wikipedia.org.

"1931 College Football Schedule and Results," *Sports Reference College Football*. Last accessed on June 17, 2022. https://www.sports-reference.com/cfb/.

"1931 Navy Midshipmen football team," *Wikipedia*. Last accessed on June 10, 2022. https://www.en.m.wikipedia.org.

"1931 Notre Dame Fighting Irish football team," *Wikipedia*. Last accessed on June 10, 2022. https://www.en.m.wikipedia.org.

"No Room for Navy on 1931 Army Chart," *United Press*, December 20, 1930.

"Red Cagle Guarded Close as Cardinals Overwhelm Cadets," *The Associated Press*, December 28, 1929.

Rooks, Commander A.H., *U.S. Navy. Entrance Requirements of U.S. Naval Academy*. Annapolis, MD: Naval Institute Proceedings, October 1935.

"Salvation Army to get Proceeds," *The Associated Press*, November 15, 1930.

Schoor, Gene. *100 Years of Army-Navy Football: A Pictorial History of America's Most Colorful and Competitive Sports Rivalry*. New York: Holt, 1989.

"Shift Army, Irish Game to Chicago," *Benton Harbor News Palladium*, February 11, 1930.

"Smalling, with Great Support, Outdoes Cagle," *United Press*, December 28, 1929.

"Soldier Field," *Wikipedia*. Last accessed on June 10, 2022. https://www.en.m.wikipedia.org.

"Special Train on Way to California," *Delphos Daily Herald*, December 21, 1929.

"Stanford Defeats Army Eleven, 34-13," *The New York Times*, December 29, 1929.

Stanford University, Athletic Communications Department. *2021 Stanford Football Media Guide*. N.p., 2021.

"Taps to be Sounded Today for Cadet Sheridan, Victim of Fatal Football Injury," *Prescott Evening Courier*, October 28, 1931.

"Trojans Preparing for Annual Tournament of Roses New Year's," *Frederick News Post*, December 21, 1929.

"Urge Charity Army-Navy Game," *Janesville Daily Gazette*, October 2, 1931.

U.S. Department of War. United States Corps of Cadets. *The Howitzer*, The Annual of The Corps of Cadets. N.p., 1929.

U.S. Department of War. United States Corps of Cadets. *The Howitzer*, The Annual of The Corps of Cadets. N.p., 1930.

U.S. Department of War. United States Corps of Cadets. *The Howitzer*, The Annual of The Corps of Cadets. N.p., 1931.

U.S. Department of War. United States Corps of Cadets. *The Howitzer*, The Annual of The Corps of Cadets. N.p., 1932.

U.S. Department of War. United States Military Academy. *Annual Report of the Superintendent*. Washington, DC: Government Printing Office, 1928.

U.S. Department of War. United States Military Academy. *Annual Report of the Superintendent*. Washington, DC: Government Printing Office, 1930.

"Westward Jaunt of Cadets Delayed by Blizzard at Chicago," *Abilene Morning News*, December 20, 1929.

"West Point Gridders Practice During Trip," *The Michigan Daily*, December 20, 1929.

Wilner, Barry, and Rappoport, Ken. *Gridiron Glory: The Story of the Army-Navy Football Rivalry*. New York: Taylor Trade Publishing, 2005.

CHAPTERS 2-3 (Bowls):

"Air Force Football" AF Football. Last accessed on May 2, 2022. https://www.goairforcefalcons.com.

"Army, Colgate in bowl picture," *The Associated Press*, November 18, 1977.

"Army after Independence," *The Monroe News Star*, November 18, 1977.

"Army Eyes Bowl," *The Associated Press*, November 5, 1962.

"Army Looking for Bowl Invite," *The Journal News*, November 18, 1977.

"Army May let Cadets Play in Bowl this Year," *The Associated Press*, November 11, 1968.

"Army Missing Sugar Bowls," *The Associated Press*, November 17. 1967.

"Army Not to Play in Any Bowl Game," *The Associated Press*, November 24, 1945.

"Army Possible Foe for Champion Tech," *The Town Talk*, November 18, 1977.

"Army Receptive to Rose Bowl Bid," *The New York Times*, November 28, 1933.

"Army Rejects All Bids for Bowl Games," *The Associated Press*, November 22, 1946.

"Army Rejects Bids to Play Bowl Game," *United Press International*, November 13, 1958.

"Army reportedly wants Independence Bowl," *The Associated Press*, November 16 1977.

"Army Says No to Bowl Bids," *The Associated Press*, November 22, 1946.

"Army Says No to Bowl Game Talk," *The Associated Press*, November 15, 1957.

"Army Stalls Way Out of Rose Bowl Game," *United Press*, November 26, 1945.

"Army to Make Announcement on Bid to Bowls," *United Press*, November 21, 1946.

"Army Won't Play in Bowl Game," *The Associated Press*, November 24, 1945.

Bailey, John Wendell. Football through the years at USMA. Box 16, USMA Library: West Point.

"Big Nine and West Coasters Meet Today," *The Associated Press*, November 19, 1946.

Blaik, Earl H. *The 'Red' Blaik Story*. New Rochelle, NY: Arlington House, 1974.

Blaik, Earl H., with Cohane, Tim. *You Have to Pay the Price*. New York: Holt, Rinehart and Winston, 1960.

Bowen, George. "Middie Players Irked at Bowl Bid Refusal," *The Associated Press*, December 1, 1956.

"Bruins, Trojans Voted for Army in Rose Bowl," *The Associated Press*, November 20, 1946.

Bump, Larry. "W. Point Could Halt Colgate Bid," *Democrat and Chronicle*, November 18, 1977.

"Cadets are First Choice as Guest in Orange Bowl," *United Press*, November 19, 1946.

"Cadets get Feeler from Cotton Bowl," *United Press International*, November 11, 1958.

"Cadets May Play in Bowl," *The Associated Press*, November 17, 1945.

"Coach of Cadets Spurns Bowl Bid," *The New York Times*, November 27, 1955.

"Colgate's Bowl Chances Cut Short by Army Overtures?" *The Ithaca Journal*, November 18, 1977.

"Coast Guard Football" Coast Guard Bears. Last accessed on May 2, 2022.
https://www.uscgasports.com.

Green, Russ. "Bowl Fluff in the Air at Service Tilt," *United Press*, November 25, 1955.

Green, Russ. "Midshipmen Upset Army, 27 to 20," *United Press*, November 27, 1954.

Grimsley, Will. "Army Takes Wait and See Stand," *The Associated Press*, November 14, 1967.

Grimsley, Will. "Post Season Bowl Game Pegs Falling in Place," *The Associated Press*, November 4, 1963.

Hobbing, Bob. "Middies Turn Down Cotton Bowl Invite," *The Associated Press*, December 1, 1956.

"Independence Bowl Considers 4 Schools," *The Times Sun*, November 20, 1977.

"Independence Tabs Louisville for Tech," *The Shreveport Times*, November 21, 1977.

"Invitations to Army Accumulate, USMA Officials Unavailable," *United Press*, November 22, 1946.

Kriek, Jim. "Pitt Apparently Never Had a Chance for Cotton Bowl," *Courier Sports*, December 20, 1963.

"Merchant Marine Academy Football" USMMA Football. Last accessed on May 2, 2022. https://www.usmmasports.com.

Mills, Nicolaus. *Every Army Man is With You: The Cadets who Won the 1964 Army-Navy Game, Fought in Vietnam, and Came Home Forever Changed*. Lanham, MD: Rowman & Littlefield, 2015.

"More Bowls Games Set," *The Associated Press*, November 20, 1977.

"Navy Football" Navy Football. Last accessed on May 2, 2022. https://www.navysports.com.

"Navy Takes Cotton Bowl Bid after Rocking Army," *The Associated Press*, November 30, 1957.

"No Bowl Bids for Army Team," *The Associated Press*, November 17, 1967.

"No Bowl Games for Navy unless they Beat Army," *The Associated Press*, November 19, 1957.

"Pacific Coast, Big Nine Leagues Sign Bowl Pact," *The Associated Press*, November 20, 1946.

"Pitt Panthers are Underdogs in Tilt with Cadets Today," *The Associated Press*, November 16, 1968.

"Pitt Stays Possible Choices for Three Grid Bowl Games," *The Associated Press*, November 12, 1957.

"Rose Bowl Game, 1902 Rose Bowl, 1916-1946 Rose Bowls" *Wikipedia*. Last accessed on April 26, 2022. https://www.en.m.wikipedia.org.

"Rose Bowl Urged by Scribes to Invite Army," *The Associated Press*, November 18, 1946.

Roberts, Randy. *A Team for America: The Army-Navy Game that Rallied a Nation at War*. Boston: First Mariner Books, 2012.

"Sugar Bowl Has Big Jackpot But Needs Two Teams," *The Associated Press*, November 23, 1949.

U.S. Congress. House. *Report and Hearings of the Special Committee on Service Academies of the Committee of the Armed Forces*, 90th Congress, 1st and 2nd sessions, 1968-1969.

U.S. Department of Defense. United States Military Academy. *1977 Football Programs*. Sports Information Office: West Point.

West Point Association of Graduates. "Five Superintendents Discuss the History of West Point," *AOG Years of a Century Told*. Last accessed on April 26, 2022. https://www.westpointaog.org.

Weyand, Alexander M. "Football Beginnings at West Point," *Assembly*, October 1955, 8-9.

"Win, Lose or Draw, Army Won't Play in Bowl Game," *The Associated Press*, November 15, 1957.

CHAPTERS 4-5 (1984):

"Army's football team left the first Cherry Bowl with," *United Press International*, December 23, 1984.

"Army fruitful in Cherry Bowl," *Record Journal*, December 24, 1984.

"Army grounds down Michigan State in first Cherry Bowl," *Rome News Tribune*, December 23, 1984.

"Army hits the dusty trail to win," *United Press International*, December 2, 1984.

"Army Marches to Cherry Bowl victory," *Eugene Register Guard*, December 32, 1984.

Atkins, Harry. "Cherry Bowl," *The Associated Press*, December 23, 1984.

Atkins, Harry. "Courageous Sassaman paces Army," *Modesto Bee*, December 23, 1984.

"Black Knights nuke Penn, 48-13," *The Evening News*, October 21, 1984.

Bonnell, Rick. "Most bowl bids in - but SU still out," *Syracuse Herald American*, November 25, 1984.

"Bowl Picture Still Scrambled," *The Associated Press*, November 20, 1984.

"Cadets rip Colgate in opener, 41-15," *The Associated Press*, September 16, 1984.

"Cadets shock Volunteers with 24-24 tie," *The News and Courier*, September 23, 1984.

"Cadets within one victory of clinching winning season," *Newburgh Evening News*, November 15, 1984.

"Cherry Bowl," *The Washington Post*, December 23, 1984.

"Cherry Bowl," *Wikipedia*. Last accessed on February 19, 2022. https://www.en.m.wikipedia.org.

"Cherry Bowl success but not to MSU," *Windsor Star*, December 24, 1984.

Green, Jerry. "Army won as it should: On ground," *The Detroit News*, December 23, 1984.

Henning, Lynn. "Cherries for Cadets," *The Detroit News*, December 23, 1984.

Hotel Thayer. 1984 Cherry Bowl Football Team, *Plaque*, photo received May 31. 2022.

Juliene, Joe. "Army's ground troops roll over Navy," *The Bulletin*, December 2, 1984.

Mariotti, Jay. "Just a bowl of cherries," *The Detroit News*, December 23, 1984.

Michigan State University. Athletic Department. "Cherry Bowl Play-by-play and Statistics. *1984 Michigan State Spartans Football*, 1984.

Morris, Herbert. "An Interview the Coach Jim Young," *Assembly*, March 1985.

"Navy seeking to snap Army wishbone," *Newburgh Evening News*, November 30, 1984.

"New era begins for Army team," *Star News*, December 22, 1984.

"1984-1985 NCAA football bowl games" *Wikipedia*. Last accessed on February 19, 2022. https://www.en.m.wikipedia.org.

"1984 Air Force Falcons football team," *Wikipedia*. Last accessed on January 23, 2022. https://www.en.m.wikipedia.org.

"1984 Army Cadets football team," *Wikipedia*. Last accessed on January 23, 2022. https://www.en.m.wikipedia.org.

"1984 Boston College Eagles football team," *Wikipedia*. Last accessed on January 23, 2022. https://www.en.m.wikipedia.org.

1984 Cherry Bowl. MPG Video, 135 minutes. Televised on December 22, 1984 in Pontiac, Michigan: Mizzou TV Sports.

"1984 Cherry Bowl," *Wikipedia*. Last accessed on February 19, 2022.
https://www.en.m.wikipedia.org.

"1984 Colgate Red Raiders football team," *Wikipedia*. Last accessed on January 23, 2022.
https://www.en.m.wikipedia.org.

"1984 Duke Blue Devils football team," *Wikipedia*. Last accessed on January 23, 2022.
https://www.en.m.wikipedia.org.

"1984 Harvard Crimson football team," *Wikipedia*. Last accessed on January 23, 2022.
https://www.en.m.wikipedia.org.

"1984 Michigan State Spartans football team" *Wikipedia*. Last accessed on January 1, 2022.
https://www.en.m.wikipedia.org.

"1984 Montana Grizzlies football team," *Wikipedia*. Last accessed on January 23, 2022.
https://www.en.m.wikipedia.org.

"1984 Navy Midshipmen football team," *Wikipedia*. Last accessed on January 23, 2022.
https://www.en.m.wikipedia.org.

"1984 Penn Quakers football team," *Wikipedia*. Last accessed on January 23, 2022.
https://www.en.m.wikipedia.org.

"1984 Rutgers Scarlet Knights football team," *Wikipedia*. Last accessed on January 23, 2022.
https://www.en.m.wikipedia.org.

"1984 Syracuse Orangemen football team," *Wikipedia*. Last accessed on January 23, 2022.
https://www.en.m.wikipedia.org.

"1984 Tennessee Volunteers football team," *Wikipedia*. Last accessed on January 23, 2022. https://www.en.m.wikipedia.org.

"1985 Cherry Bowl," *Wikipedia*. Last accessed on February 19, 2022. https://www.en.m.wikipedia.org.

"Old Army game is winning one again," *Pittsburgh Post-Gazette*, November 10, 1984.

"Rutgers Losses Bowl Bid," *The Associated Press*, November 22, 1984.

"Sassaman guides Army past Spartans," *Mid Cities Daily News*, December 23, 1984.

"Sassaman joins Army legends, leads Cadets over Mich. State," *Pittsburgh Post-Gazette*, December 24, 1984.

"Shades of Red Blaik! The Cadets are back," *Pittsburgh Post-Gazette*, October 26, 1984.

Shanahan, Tom. "Army's 1984 Team Secured in West Point History," *GoBlackKnights.com*, November 29, 2012.

Shapiro, Michael. "Japan Crowd Warms Up to Army's Offensive Show," *The New York Times*, November 18, 1984.

Stieg, Bill. "Army's resurgent football program may benefit from national patriotism," *Newburgh Evening News*, November 28, 1984.

"Spartans, Cadets ready for Cherry Bowl clash," *Deseret News*, December 22, 1984.

"Stop boot Army past Air Force," *The Evening News*, November 4, 1984.

The Cherry Bowl, Inc. *Cherry Bowl Program*. Midland, MI: Pendell Printing, 1984.

"Unbeaten Army bombs Harvard," *The Evening News*, October 7, 1984.

U.S. Department of Defense. United States Military Academy. Office of Athletic Communications. *Army Football Guide*. West Point, NY: N.p., 1984.

U.S. Department of Defense. United States Military Academy. Office of Athletic Communications. *Army 1985 Football Annual*. West Point, NY: College Promotions Corporation, 1985.

Van Der Horst, Roger. "New-Look Army Threatens Orange," *Syracuse Herald American*, October 27, 1984.

Vecsey, George. "Army's greatest teams never reached a bowl," *Pittsburgh Post-Gazette*, December 24, 1984.

White Jr., Gordon S. "Army Likely for Cherry Bowl," *The New York Times*, November 20, 1984.

CHAPTERS 6-7 (1985):

"Air Force Rolls Over Army, 45-7," *The Washington Post*. November 10, 1985.

Army-Navy Annual Committee. *The 1985 Army-Navy Annual Official Program*. Philadelphia, PA: N.p., 1985.

"Bowl Picture Taking Shape," *The Associated Press*, November 18, 1985.

Carder, Shiloh. "Best Games and moments in Peach Bowl history," *Yardbarker*, December 11, 2018.

Chick-fil-a Peach Bowl, Communications Department. "*1985 Peach Bowl Game Book*," 1985 Peach Bowl Committee, 1985.

Freitag, Michael. "6 at Yale are Penalized for Prank in Marching Band," *The New York Times*, October 20, 1985.

"History of the Marching Illini," *Marching Illini*. Last accessed on January 24, 2022.
https://www.marchingillini.com.

Hotel Thayer. 1985 Peach Bowl Football Team, *Plaque*, photo received May 31. 2022.

"Illinois Seeking Peach Bowl Bid," *The Associated Press*, November 19, 1985.

Jensen Jr., Michael. "Army an Easy Winner," *The New York Times*, October 13, 1985.

Makrides, Alex. "Top 10 games in Peach Bowl history," *Atlanta Journal-Constitution*, December 25, 2017.

Morris, Herbert. "An Interview the Coach Jim Young," *Assembly*, March 1985.

"1985 Air Force Falcons football team," *Wikipedia*. Last accessed on January 23, 2022.
https://www.en.m.wikipedia.org.

"1985 Army Cadets football team," *Wikipedia*. Last accessed on January 23, 2022.
https://www.en.m.wikipedia.org.

"1985 Boston College Eagles football team," *Wikipedia*. Last accessed on January 23, 2022.
https://www.en.m.wikipedia.org.

"1985 Colgate Red Raiders football team," *Wikipedia*. Last accessed on January 23, 2022.
https://www.en.m.wikipedia.org.

"1985 Holy Cross Crusaders football team," *Wikipedia*. Last accessed on January 23, 2022.
https://www.en.m.wikipedia.org.

"1985 Illinois Fighting Illini football team," *Wikipedia*. Last accessed on January 23, 2022.
https://www.en.m.wikipedia.org.

"1985 Memphis State Tigers football team," *Wikipedia*. Last accessed on January 23, 2022.
https://www.en.m.wikipedia.org.

"1985 Navy Midshipmen football team," *Wikipedia*. Last accessed on January 23, 2022.
https://www.en.m.wikipedia.org.

"1985 NCAA Division 1-A football season," *Wikipedia*. Last accessed on January 23, 2022.
https://www.en.m.wikipedia.org.

"1985 Notre Dame Fighting Irish football team," *Wikipedia*. Last accessed on January 23, 2022.
https://www.en.m.wikipedia.org.

1985 Peach Bowl. MPG Video, 152 minutes. Televised on December 31, 1985 in Atlanta, Georgia: *CBS Sports*.

"1985 Peach Bowl," *Wikipedia*. Last accessed on January 23, 2022.
https://www.en.m.wikipedia.org.

"1985 Penn Quakers football team," *Wikipedia*. Last accessed on January 23, 2022.
https://www.en.m.wikipedia.org.

"1985 Rutgers Scarlet Knights football team," *Wikipedia*. Last accessed on January 23, 2022.
https://www.en.m.wikipedia.org.

"1985 Western Michigan Broncos football team," *Wikipedia*. Last accessed on January 23, 2022.
https://www.en.m.wikipedia.org.

"1985 Yale Bulldogs football team," *Wikipedia*. Last accessed on January 23, 2022.

https://www.en.m.wikipedia.org.

O'Donnell, Michael. "Illinois Expects Peach Bowl Bid," *Chicago Tribune*, November 19, 1985.

"Orange must continue winning for bowl bid," *Syracuse Herald-Journal*, November 5, 1985.

"Peach Bowl," *Wikipedia*. Last accessed on May 11, 2022. https://www.en.m.wikipedia.org.

Peach Bowl. *1985 Peach Bowl Eighteenth Annual Program*, San Francisco, CA: Touchdown Publications, 1985.

Ramsey, David. "Oh, so close: Colgate just misses miracle rally," *The New York Times*, October 27, 1985.

Rollow, Cooper. "McCallum Carries Navy Over Army," *Chicago Tribune*, December 8, 1985.

Sports Associates, Inc. *GamePlan College Football Annual Preview*. Syracuse, NY, 1985.

Trutor, Clayton. "How the Peach Bowl Became One of College Football's Great Games," *SBNation*, December 29, 2020.

U.S. Department of Defense. United States Military Academy. Office of Athletic Communications. *Army Football Guide*. West Point, NY: N.p., 1986.

U.S. Department of Defense. United States Military Academy. Office of Athletic Communications. "Army Football Top Moments: Number 8," *GoArmyWestPoint.com*, October 21, 2015.

U.S. Department of Defense. United States Military Academy. Office of Athletic Communications. *Army 1985 Football Annual*. West Point, NY: College Promotions Corporation, 1985.

U.S. Department of Defense. United States Military Academy. Office of Athletic Communications. *Army 1986 Football*

Annual. West Point, NY: College Promotions Corporation, 1986.

U.S. Department of Defense. United States Military Academy. *1985 Football Programs*. New York, NY: Everest Programs, 1985.

University of Illinois, Athletic Department, "Illinois History," *2021 Illinois Football Record Book*, Champaign, IL: Premier Print Group, 2021.

University of Illinois. Athletic Department. "Peach Bowl Play-by-play and Statistics. *1985 Illinois Fighting Illini Football*, 1985.

Wallace, William N. "Army's Air Attach Stuns Illini," *The New York Times*, January 1, 1986.

Wallace, William N. "Army Crushes Yale by 59-16 to go 4-0," *The New York Times*, October 6, 1985.

Wallace, William N. "Navy Stuns Army in 17-7 Upset," *The New York Times*, December 8, 1985.

Wallace, William N. "Peach Bowl; Army and Illinois: An Offensive Match," *The New York Times*, December 31, 1985.

White Jr., Gordon S. "Army Overcomes Solid Rutgers, 20-16," *The New York Times*, September 22, 1985.

White Jr., Gordon S. "Notre Dame Ends Army Streak, 24-10," *The New York Times*, October 20, 1985.

Yannis, Alex. "Army Rolls Over Western Michigan," *The New York Times*, September 15, 1985.

Zemek, Matt. "The 1985 Peach Bowl: Validation," *CBS Sports*, June 26. 2015.

CHAPTERS 8-9 (1988):

Adelsberger, Bernard J. "Rolling Army takes momentum against touch Alabama team," *Army Times*, December 26, 1988.

"Alabama Crimson Tide football," *Wikipedia*. Last accessed on January 23, 2022. https://www.en.m.wikipedia.org.

"Alabama Wins Sun Bowl," *The Washington Post*, December 25, 1988.

Army-Navy Annual Committee. *The 1988 Army-Navy Annual Official Program*. Philadelphia, PA: N.p., 1985.

"Army fans revel in return to winning ways," *The Associated Press*, November 20, 1988.

"Army not feeling at home in Ireland," *The Associated Press*, November 18, 1988.

"Bama rallies to top Army," *The Associated Press*, December 24, 1988.

"Boston College Upsets Army 38-24 in Ireland," *The Associated Press*, November 20, 1988.

"Bowl secrets are out, but still unofficially," *Kokomo Tribune*, November 13, 1988.

Burleson, Al. "Tide players overcome injury losses for one more bowl game," *Army Times*, December 26, 1988.

Cialini, Joe. "Sun Bowl eyes Lions-Panthers," *United Press International*, November 8, 1988.

"Derrick Thomas," *Wikipedia*. Last accessed on January 23, 2022. https://www.en.m.wikipedia.org.

Hamilton, Nancy. "Sun Bowl Stadium," *Handbook of Texas*, June 23, 2016.

"Irish eyes will be smiling on BC-Army matchup," *The Associated Press*, November 17, 1988.

John Hancock Sun Bowl. *The 54th Annual John Hancock Sun Bowl Program*, San Francisco, CA: Touchdown Publications, 1988.

"Legends of the Sun Bowl: Derrick Thomas 2000," *El Paso Times*, December 31, 2021.

"List of Sun Bowl records set or tied during," *United Press International*, December 24, 1988.

Morris, Herbert. "Coach Jim Young Reviews the 1988 Football Season," *Assembly*, February 1989.

"1986 Army Cadets football team," *Wikipedia*. Last accessed on January 23, 2022.
https://www.en.m.wikipedia.org.

"1987 Army Cadets football team," *Wikipedia*. Last accessed on January 23, 2022.
https://www.en.m.wikipedia.org.

"1988-89 NCAA football bowl games," *Wikipedia*. Last accessed on January 23, 2022.
https://www.en.m.wikipedia.org.

"1988 Air Force Falcons football team," *Wikipedia*. Last accessed on January 23, 2022.
https://www.en.m.wikipedia.org.

"1988 Alabama Crimson Tide football team," *Wikipedia*. Last accessed on January 23, 2022.
https://www.en.m.wikipedia.org.

"1988 All-SEC football team," *Wikipedia*. Last accessed on January 23, 2022.
https://www.en.m.wikipedia.org.

"1988 Army Cadets football team," *Wikipedia*. Last accessed on January 23, 2022.

https://www.en.m.wikipedia.org.

"1988 Boston College Eagles football team," *Wikipedia*. Last accessed on January 23, 2022.
https://www.en.m.wikipedia.org.

"1988 Bucknell Bison football team," *Wikipedia*. Last accessed on January 23, 2022.
https://www.en.m.wikipedia.org.

"1988 College Football All-Americans," *Wikipedia*. Last accessed on January 23, 2022.
https://www.en.m.wikipedia.org.

"1988 Holy Cross Crusaders football team," *Wikipedia*. Last accessed on January 23, 2022.
https://www.en.m.wikipedia.org.

1988 John Hancock Sun Bowl. MPG Video, 188 minutes. Televised on December 24, 1988 in El Paso, Texas: *CBS Sports*.

"1988 Lafayette Leopards football team," *Wikipedia*. Last accessed on January 23, 2022.
https://www.en.m.wikipedia.org.

"1988 Navy Midshipmen football team," *Wikipedia*. Last accessed on January 23, 2022.
https://www.en.m.wikipedia.org.

"1988 NCAA Division 1-A football rankings," *Wikipedia*. Last accessed on January 23, 2022.
https://www.en.m.wikipedia.org.

"1988 NCAA Division 1-A football season," *Wikipedia*. Last accessed on January 23, 2022.
https://www.en.m.wikipedia.org.

"1988 Northwestern Wildcats football team," *Wikipedia*. Last accessed on January 23, 2022.
https://www.en.m.wikipedia.org.

"1988 Rutgers Scarlet Knights football team," *Wikipedia*. Last accessed on January 23, 2022. https://www.en.m.wikipedia.org.

"1988 Sun Bowl," *Wikipedia*. Last accessed on January 23, 2022. https://www.en.m.wikipedia.org.

"1988 Vanderbilt Commodores football team," *Wikipedia*. Last accessed on January 23, 2022. https://www.en.m.wikipedia.org.

"1988 Washington Huskies football team," *Wikipedia*. Last accessed on January 23, 2022. https://www.en.m.wikipedia.org.

"1988 Yale Bulldogs football team," *Wikipedia*. Last accessed on January 23, 2022. https://www.en.m.wikipedia.org.

"Notre Dame agrees to either Fiesta or Orange bowls," *Syracuse Herald-Journal*, November 10, 1988.

"Sun Bowl," *Wikipedia*. Last accessed on January 23, 2022. https://www.en.m.wikipedia.org.

"Sun Bowl (stadium)," *Wikipedia*. Last accessed on January 23, 2022. https://www.en.m.wikipedia.org.

"Sun Bowls eyes Army, too," *The Associated Press*, November 11, 1988.

"Sun Bowl Would Take Syracuse," *Syracuse Herald-Journal*, November 1, 1988.

U.S. Department of Defense. United States Military Academy. Office of Athletic Communications. *Army Football Guide*. West Point, NY: N.p., 1988.

U.S. Department of Defense. United States Military Academy. Office of Athletic Communications. *Army Football Guide*. West Point, NY: N.p., 1989.

U.S. Department of Defense. United States Military Academy. Office of Athletic Communications. *Army 1987 Football Annual*. West Point, NY: College Promotions Corporation, 1987.

U.S. Department of Defense. United States Military Academy. Office of Athletic Communications. *Army 1988 Football Annual*. West Point, NY: College Promotions Corporation, 1988.

U.S. Department of Defense. United States Military Academy. Office of Athletic Communications. *Army 1989 Football Annual*. West Point, NY: College Promotions Corporation, 1988.

University of Alabama. Football Communications. "Game Book," *1988 John Hancock Sun Bowl*, December 24, 1988.

University of Missouri. Athletic Department. "From the Sun Bowl Vault: A History of the Sun Bowl," December 5, 2006.

White Jr., Gordon S. "Tide Edges Cadets in Sun Bowl," *The New York Times*, December 25, 1988.

CHAPTERS 10-11 (1996):

Allen, Teddy. "Band, award to be featured," *The Times*, December 31, 1996.

Anderson, Craig. "Navy sunk by its failure in clutch spots," *The Sunday Capital*, December 9, 1996.

"Army-Navy is a sellout," *The Capital*, October 31, 1996.

"Army comeback can make one feel pretty patriotic," *The Times*, January 1, 1997.

"Army pushes record to 8-0," *The Associated Press*, November 3, 1996.

"Army rally douses Navy," *The Stars and Stripes*, December 8, 1996.

"Army 39, Yale 13," *The Associated Press*, October 6, 1996.

"Army topples Ohio in debut," *The Associated Press*, September 15, 1996.

"Army 27, North Texas 10," *The Associated Press*, September 29, 1996.

"Army ups record to 5-0," *The Associated Press*, October 13. 1996.

"Auburn survives Army's miracle rally, 32-29," *ESPNet Sportszone*, January 1, 1997.

Auburn University. Auburn Athletic Department. Media Relations Office. "*2003 Auburn University Football Media Guide*," Birmingham, AL: EBASCO Printing, 2003.

Auburn University. Auburn Athletic Department. "Play-by-play and game statistics," *1996 Independence Bowl*, December 31, 1996.

Auburn University, Auburn Athletic Department. *The 1996 Auburn Independence Bowl Media Guide*. Birmingham, AL: EBASCO Media, 1996.

"Black Knights head for Shreveport," *Pointer View*, December 23, 1996.

Bounds, Jeff. "Broadcasters get first shot to cover Independence Bowl," *The Times*, December 31, 1996.

"Bowl facts," *Pointer View*, December 23, 1996.

"Bowl looks at Lobos," *The Associated Press*, November 7, 1996.

"Bowl picture confused by championship upsets," *The Sunday Capital*, December 9, 1996.

"Bowling for big, big dollars," *The Associated Press*, November 18, 1996.

Burrows, Mike. "Black Knights just pawns in polls," *Gazette Telegraph*, November 6, 1996.

"Cadets crack Top 25s," *The New York Times*, November 10, 1996.

"Cadets march to 7-0 mark," *The Associated Press*, October 27, 1996.

"Cadets will likely fall from Top 25," *The Times*, January 1, 1997.

Cotton, Anthony and Wang, Gene. "No secret: Navy's bowl-bound," *The Capital*, October 26, 1996.

Feild, Reeves, "Fans cheered one moment, cringed next," *The Times*, January 1, 1997.

Ferrell, Scott. "Good plotlines in the I-Bowl for soap lovers," *The Times*, December 31, 1996.

Ferrell, Scott. "Heartbreaker for Cadets: Corporal punishment, Army's kick to tie Auburn sails wide," *The Times*, January 1, 1997.

Ferrell, Scott. "Only losers were those who didn't attend," *The Times*, January 1, 1997.

Ferrell, Scott. "Will speed kill Army?" *The Times*, December 31, 1996.

Greenstein, Teddy. "No Bowl for Irish," *Chicago Tribune*, December 3, 1996.

Gross, Joe. "Clinton ends presidential streak," *The Sunday Capital*, December 9, 1996.

Gross, Joe. "Time for Navy to do some bowl-searching," *The Capital*, November 25, 1996.

"Haka Bowl," *Wikipedia*. Last accessed on January 23, 2022. https://www.en.m.wikipedia.org.

Hawkins, Stephen. "Auburn survives Army's rally," *The Associated Press*, January 1, 1997.

Herron, Chuck. "Losing big lead evokes bad memories for Auburn," *The Times*, January 1, 1997.

"How Army has fared in previous bowl games," *The Times*, December 31, 1996.

"How Auburn has fared in previous bowl games," *The Times*, December 31, 1996.

"I-Bowl boast a rich history," *The Times*, December 31, 1996.

"Independence Bowl," *Wikipedia*. Last accessed on January 23, 2022. https://www.en.m.wikipedia.org.

"Independence Stadium (Shreveport)," *Wikipedia*. Last accessed on January 23, 2022. https://www.en.m.wikipedia.org.

Kekis, John. "One-man army ends Army's run," *The Stars and Stripes*, November 18, 1996.

Longman, Jere. "Army taking no further questions," *The New York Times*, November 10, 1996.

"McAda sparks Army to victory over Duke," *The Associated Press*, September 22, 1996.

McLain, Jim. "At least Sutton, younger Bowden are getting along," *The Times*, December 31, 1996.

McLain, Jim. "Comeback comes too late," *The Times*, January 1, 1997.

McLain, Jim. "Crawling out from the Hudson," *The Times*, December 31, 1996.

McLain, Jim. "Mr. Up-the middle," *The Times*, December 31, 1996.

Moran, Malcolm. "Cadets surf Green Wave to 6-0 mark," *The New York Times*, October 20, 1996.

Murphy, Mark. "Auburn Aims to Break Army's Wingbone," *Inside the Auburn Tigers*, December 21, 1996.

Murphy, Mark. "Auburn to Meet Army in 1996 Independence Bowl," *Inside the Auburn Tigers*, December 9, 1996.

"1989 Army Cadets football team," *Wikipedia*. Last accessed on January 23, 2022.
https://www.en.m.wikipedia.org.

"1990 Army Cadets football team," *Wikipedia*. Last accessed on January 23, 2022.
https://www.en.m.wikipedia.org.

"1991 Army Cadets football team," *Wikipedia*. Last accessed on January 23, 2022.
https://www.en.m.wikipedia.org.

"1992 Army Cadets football team," *Wikipedia*. Last accessed on January 23, 2022.
https://www.en.m.wikipedia.org.

"1993 Army Cadets football team," *Wikipedia*. Last accessed on January 23, 2022.
https://www.en.m.wikipedia.org.

"1994 Army Cadets football team," *Wikipedia*. Last accessed on January 23, 2022.
https://www.en.m.wikipedia.org.

"1995 Army Cadets football team," *Wikipedia*. Last accessed on January 23, 2022.
https://www.en.m.wikipedia.org.

"1996 Air Force Falcons football team," *Wikipedia*. Last accessed on January 23, 2022. https://www.en.m.wikipedia.org.

"1996 Army Cadets football team," *Wikipedia*. Last accessed on January 23, 2022. https://www.en.m.wikipedia.org.

"1996 Auburn Tigers football team," *Wikipedia*. Last accessed on January 23, 2022. https://www.en.m.wikipedia.org.

"1996 Duke Blue Devils football team," *Wikipedia*. Last accessed on January 23, 2022. https://www.en.m.wikipedia.org.

"1996 Fordham Rams football team," *Wikipedia*. Last accessed on January 23, 2022. https://www.en.m.wikipedia.org.

"1996 Independence Bowl," *Wikipedia*. Last accessed on January 23, 2022. https://www.en.m.wikipedia.org.

"1996 Lafayette Leopards football team," *Wikipedia*. Last accessed on January 23, 2022. https://www.en.m.wikipedia.org.

"1996 Miami Redskins football team," *Wikipedia*. Last accessed on January 23, 2022. https://www.en.m.wikipedia.org.

"1996 Navy Midshipmen football team," *Wikipedia*. Last accessed on January 23, 2022. https://www.en.m.wikipedia.org.

"1996 North Texas Mean Green football team," *Wikipedia*. Last accessed on January 23, 2022. https://www.en.m.wikipedia.org.

"1996 Ohio Bobcats football team," *Wikipedia*. Last accessed on January 23, 2022. https://www.en.m.wikipedia.org.

1996 Poulan Weedeater Independence Bowl. MPG Video, 95 minutes. Televised on December 31, 1996 in Shreveport, Louisiana: *ESPN*.

"1996 Rutgers Scarlet Knights football team," *Wikipedia*. Last accessed on January 23, 2022. https://www.en.m.wikipedia.org.

"1996 Syracuse Orangemen football team," *Wikipedia*. Last accessed on January 23, 2022. https://www.en.m.wikipedia.org.

"1996 Tulane Green Wave football team," *Wikipedia*. Last accessed on January 23, 2022. https://www.en.m.wikipedia.org.

"1996 Yale Bulldogs football team," *Wikipedia*. Last accessed on January 23, 2022. https://www.en.m.wikipedia.org.

"1996 Army Final Statistics," *The Times*, December 31, 1996.

"1996 Auburn Final Statistics," *The Times*, December 31, 1996.

Pasqualoni, Paul. "How do you stop Army?" *The Times*, December 31, 1996.

Price, Stephen D. "Moms and others cheer on their favorite I-Bowl players," *The Times*, January 1, 1997.

Price, Stephen D. "More tailgaters expected than ever before," *The Times*, December 31, 1996.

Prime, John Andrew. "Barksdale opens door for the Army," *The Times*, December 31, 1996.

"Quarterback rattled only by howitzer," *The Times*, January 1, 1997.

Radiance Technologies Independence Bowl. Office of Media and Community Relations. "Game Book," *1996 Poulan Weedeater Independence Bowl*, December 31, 1996.

Radiance Technologies Independence Bowl. Office of Media and Community Relations. "*2018 Independence Bowl Media Guide*," 2018 Walk-On's Independence Bowl, 2018.

Rosenblatt, Richard. "New No. 1 FSU awaits Sugar Bowl opponent," *The Associated Press*, December 2, 1996.

"Running Ronnie," *Pointer View*, December 23, 1996.

Seraile, Brian. "After the Independence Bowl, part on!" *The Times*, December 31, 1996.

"Shreveport Cuisine," *Pointer View*, December 23, 1996.

"Special events," *Pointer View*, December 23, 1996.

Stingley, Alisa. "VFW to receive Bradley award," *The Times*, December 31, 1996.

Thompson, Bob. "Kicker takes the rap," *The Times*, January 1, 1997.

U.S. Department of Defense. United States Military Academy. Office of Athletic Communications. *1996 Army Football Media Guide*. West Point, NY: N.p., 1996.

U.S. Department of Defense. United States Military Academy. Office of Athletic Communications. *No. 24 Army Cadets (10-1) vs. Auburn Tigers (7-4) Game Notes*, December 10, 1988.

Walker, Don. "Auburn pulls rank on Army: Last-chance field goal sails wide for Cadets," *The Times*, January 1, 1997.

Wallace, Robert. "A change in personalities," *The Times*, December 31, 1996.

Wallace, Robert. "Army reaches spotlight: Cadets feature nation's top ground attack," *The Times*, December 31, 1996.

Wallace, Robert. "Auburn fell short of goals," *The Times*, December 31, 1996.

Wallace, Robert. "Pass-happy Tigers set standards," *The Times*, January 1, 1997.

Wallace, Robert. "Tight end has adjusted to life as blocker," *The Times*, December 31, 1996.

"Welcome to Shreveport," *Pointer View*, December 23, 1996.

CHAPTERS 12-13 (2010):

"Army Football Gunning for Bowl Game," *CBS News New York*, August 24, 2010.

Beretta, Bob. "Ellerson announces Class of 2014 football recruits," *Pointer View*, July 1, 2010.

Beretta, Bob. "Gridders hit midway point of spring practice," *Pointer View*, March 4, 2010.

"Casey's Call: College Football - Week 7 Preview," *CBS News New York*, October 15, 2010.

East-West Shrine Game. "Josh McNary Named 2011 Pat Tillman Award Winner," *Press Release*, January 13, 2011.

Kelly, Robert H. "Armed Forces Bowl 2010: Army Tops SMU 16-14 in Dallas," *TexSports Publications*, December 30, 2010.

Military Bowl. "Northrop Grumman, USO Join Forces with Re-Branded Military Bowl in Washington, D.C.," *Press Release*, October 27, 2010.

"Rich Ellerson Signs Two-Year Extension with Army," *CBS Sports New York*, December 7, 2010.

"SMU Mustangs football," *Wikipedia*. Last accessed on March 12, 2022.
https://www.en.m.wikipedia.org.

Southern Methodist University. Athletic Public Relations Office. *Post-Game Notes*, December 30, 2010. Last accessed on March 12, 2022.
https://www.smumustangs.com.

Southern Methodist University. Athletic Public Relations Office. *2010 SMU Football Media Guide*, Dallas, TX: N.p., 2021.

Southern Methodist University. Athletic Public Relations Office. *2021 SMU Football Media Guide*, Dallas, TX: N.p., 2010.

Texas Christian University. *TCU Student Media*. Renovation makes stadium louder, August 16, 2010. Last accessed on March 12, 2022.
https://www.tcu360.com.

"1997 Army Cadets football team," *Wikipedia*. Last accessed on January 23, 2022.
https://www.en.m.wikipedia.org.

"1998 Army Cadets football team," *Wikipedia*. Last accessed on January 23, 2022.
https://www.en.m.wikipedia.org.

"1999 Army Black Knights football team," *Wikipedia*. Last accessed on January 23, 2022.
https://www.en.m.wikipedia.org.

"2000 Army Black Knights football team," *Wikipedia*. Last accessed on January 23, 2022.
https://www.en.m.wikipedia.org.

"2001 Army Black Knights football team," *Wikipedia*. Last accessed on January 23, 2022.
https://www.en.m.wikipedia.org.

"2002 Army Black Knights football team," *Wikipedia*. Last accessed on January 23, 2022. https://www.en.m.wikipedia.org.

"2003 Army Black Knights football team," *Wikipedia*. Last accessed on January 23, 2022. https://www.en.m.wikipedia.org.

"2004 Army Black Knights football team," *Wikipedia*. Last accessed on January 23, 2022. https://www.en.m.wikipedia.org.

"2005 Army Black Knights football team," *Wikipedia*. Last accessed on January 23, 2022. https://www.en.m.wikipedia.org.

"2006 Army Black Knights football team," *Wikipedia*. Last accessed on January 23, 2022. https://www.en.m.wikipedia.org.

"2007 Army Black Knights football team," *Wikipedia*. Last accessed on January 23, 2022. https://www.en.m.wikipedia.org.

"2008 Army Black Knights football team," *Wikipedia*. Last accessed on January 23, 2022. https://www.en.m.wikipedia.org.

"2009 Army Black Knights football team," *Wikipedia*. Last accessed on January 23, 2022. https://www.en.m.wikipedia.org.

"2010 Air Force Falcons football team," *Wikipedia*. Last accessed on March 15, 2022. https://www.en.m.wikipedia.org.

"2010 Armed Forces Bowl," *Wikipedia*. Last accessed on January 23, 2022. https://www.en.m.wikipedia.org.

"2010 Army Black Knights football team," *Wikipedia*. Last accessed on January 23, 2022. https://www.en.m.wikipedia.org.

"2010 BCS Profiles: Independent FBS Schools," *Bleacher Report*, July 23, 2010.

2010 Bell Helicopter Armed Forces Bowl. *More than a Bowl Game Program*. Elmont, NY: University Sports Publications, 2010.

2010 Bell Helicopter Armed Forces Bowl. MPG Video, 123 minutes. Televised on December 30, 2010 in Dallas, Texas: *ESPN*.

2010 Bell Helicopter Armed Forces Bowl. *2010 Game Book*, Fort Worth TX: N.p., 2010.

"2010 Duke Blue Devils football team," *Wikipedia*. Last accessed on March 15, 2022. https://www.en.m.wikipedia.org.

"2010 Eastern Michigan Eagles football team," *Wikipedia*. Last accessed on March 15, 2022. https://www.en.m.wikipedia.org.

"2010 Hawaii Warriors football team," *Wikipedia*. Last accessed on March 15, 2022. https://www.en.m.wikipedia.org.

"2010 Kent State Golden Flashes football team," *Wikipedia*. Last accessed on March 15, 2022. https://www.en.m.wikipedia.org.

"2010 Navy Midshipmen football team," *Wikipedia*. Last accessed on March 15, 2022. https://www.en.m.wikipedia.org.

"2010 North Texas Mean Green football team," *Wikipedia*. Last accessed on March 15, 2022. https://www.en.m.wikipedia.org.

"2010 Notre Dame Fighting Irish football team," *Wikipedia*. Last accessed on March 15, 2022.
https://www.en.m.wikipedia.org.

"2010 Rutgers Scarlet Knights football team," *Wikipedia*. Last accessed on March 15, 2022.
https://www.en.m.wikipedia.org.

"2010 SMU Mustangs football team," *Wikipedia*. Last accessed on January 23, 2022.
https://www.en.m.wikipedia.org.

"2010 Temple Owls football team," *Wikipedia*. Last accessed on March 15, 2022.
https://www.en.m.wikipedia.org.

"2010 Tulane Green Wave football team," *Wikipedia*. Last accessed on March 15, 2022.
https://www.en.m.wikipedia.org.

"2010 VMI Keydets football team," *Wikipedia*. Last accessed on March 15, 2022.
https://www.en.m.wikipedia.org.

"2011 East-West Shrine Game," *Wikipedia*. Last accessed on March 13, 2022.
https://www.en.m.wikipedia.org.

U.S. Department of Defense. United States Military Academy. Office of Athletic Communications. *Air Force Game Sold Out*, October 22, 2010. Last accessed on March 11, 2022.
https://www.goarmywestpoint.com.

U.S. Department of Defense. United States Military Academy. Office of Athletic Communications. *Army, Bell Helicopter Armed Forces Bowl Announce Partnership*, April 16, 2010. Last accessed on March 11, 2022.
https://www.goarmywestpoint.com.

U.S. Department of Defense. United States Military Academy. Office of Athletic Communications. *Army Accepts Bell*

Helicopter Armed Forces Bowl, November 30, 2010. Last accessed on March 11, 2022.
https://www.goarmywestpoint.com.

U.S. Department of Defense. United States Military Academy. Office of Athletic Communications. *Army Agrees to Extend Contract of Rich Ellerson*, December 7, 2010. Last accessed on March 11, 2022.
https://www.goarmywestpoint.com.

U.S. Department of Defense. United States Military Academy. Office of Athletic Communications. *Army Defensive End Named Lott Trophy Quarterfinalist*, October 21, 2010. Last accessed on March 11, 2022.
https://www.goarmywestpoint.com.

U.S. Department of Defense. United States Military Academy. Office of Athletic Communications. *Army Duo Honored by CFPA*, October 4, 2010. Last accessed on March 11, 2022.
https://www.goarmywestpoint.com.

U.S. Department of Defense. United States Military Academy. Office of Athletic Communications. *Army Duo Named Academic All-American*, November 23, 2010. Last accessed on March 11, 2022.
https://www.goarmywestpoint.com.

U.S. Department of Defense. United States Military Academy. Office of Athletic Communications. *Army Football Names 2010 Captains*, October 26, 2010. Last accessed on March 11, 2022.
https://www.goarmywestpoint.com.

U.S. Department of Defense. United States Military Academy. Office of Athletic Communications. *Army Highlights CBS College Sports Programming*, July 1, 2010. Last accessed on March 11, 2022.
https://www.goarmywestpoint.com.

U.S. Department of Defense. United States Military Academy. Office of Athletic Communications. *Army Home Game*

Kickoff Times Set for Noon, March 26, 2010. Last accessed on March 11, 2022.
https://www.goarmywestpoint.com.

U.S. Department of Defense. United States Military Academy. Office of Athletic Communications. *Army Now Bowl Eligible for First Time since 1996,* November 13, 2010. Last accessed on March 11, 2022.
https://www.goarmywestpoint.com.

U.S. Department of Defense. United States Military Academy. Office of Athletic Communications. *Army Sells Out Armed Forces Bowl Ticket Allotment,* December 28, 2010. Last accessed on March 11, 2022.
https://www.goarmywestpoint.com.

U.S. Department of Defense. United States Military Academy. Office of Athletic Communications. *Army Signs Backup Bowl Agreement,* October 26, 2010. Last accessed on March 11, 2022.
https://www.goarmywestpoint.com.

U.S. Department of Defense. United States Military Academy. Office of Athletic Communications. *Army Spring Football Game - Gold 42, Black 35,* March 27, 2010. Last accessed on March 11, 2022.
https://www.goarmywestpoint.com.

U.S. Department of Defense. United States Military Academy. Office of Athletic Communications. *Army Steps into National Spotlight,* October 14, 2010. Last accessed on March 11, 2022.
https://www.goarmywestpoint.com.

U.S. Department of Defense. United States Military Academy. Office of Athletic Communications. *Army to Face SMU in Bell Helicopter Armed Forces Bowl,* December 5, 2010. Last accessed on March 11, 2022.
https://www.goarmywestpoint.com.

U.S. Department of Defense. United States Military Academy. Office of Athletic Communications. *Army Unveils New Football Uniforms*, August 9, 2010. Last accessed on March 11, 2022.
https://www.goarmywestpoint.com.

U.S. Department of Defense. United States Military Academy. Office of Athletic Communications. *Big Play Highlights Saturday Football Scrimmage*, August 14, 2010. Last accessed on March 11, 2022.
https://www.goarmywestpoint.com.

U.S. Department of Defense. United States Military Academy. Office of Athletic Communications. *Black Knights hit Field for First Day of Spring Practice*, February 17, 2010. Last accessed on March 11, 2022.
https://www.goarmywestpoint.com.

U.S. Department of Defense. United States Military Academy. Office of Athletic Communications. *Black Knights Hold Mock Game at Michie Stadium*, August 30, 2010. Last accessed on March 11, 2022.
https://www.goarmywestpoint.com.

U.S. Department of Defense. United States Military Academy. Office of Athletic Communications. *Black Knights Hold Second Spring Scrimmage*, March 6, 2010. Last accessed on March 11, 2022.
https://www.goarmywestpoint.com.

U.S. Department of Defense. United States Military Academy. Office of Athletic Communications. *Black Knights Open Preseason Camp Monday*, August 1, 2010. Last accessed on March 11, 2022.
https://www.goarmywestpoint.com.

U.S. Department of Defense. United States Military Academy. Office of Athletic Communications. *Bowl Blog #1 - Welcome to Fort Worth*, December 26, 2010. Last accessed on March 11, 2022.

https://www.goarmywestpoint.com.

U.S. Department of Defense. United States Military Academy. Office of Athletic Communications. *Carlton Named Honorable Mention CFPA Kicker of the Week*, November 8, 2010. Last accessed on March 11, 2022.
https://www.goarmywestpoint.com.

U.S. Department of Defense. United States Military Academy. Office of Athletic Communications. *Ellerson Named Coach of the Year Finalist*, December 13, 2010. Last accessed on March 11, 2022.
https://www.goarmywestpoint.com.

U.S. Department of Defense. United States Military Academy. Office of Athletic Communications. *Erzinger Earns CFPA Honorable Mention*, October 18, 2010. Last accessed on March 11, 2022.
https://www.goarmywestpoint.com.

U.S. Department of Defense. United States Military Academy. Office of Athletic Communications. *Football Players Visit Cook Children's Hospital*, December 28, 2010. Last accessed on March 11, 2022.
https://www.goarmywestpoint.com.

U.S. Department of Defense. United States Military Academy. Office of Athletic Communications. *Football Team Welcomes Home Heroes*, December 28, 2010. Last accessed on March 11, 2022.
https://www.goarmywestpoint.com.

U.S. Department of Defense. United States Military Academy. Office of Athletic Communications. Game Notes, Post-Game Notes, Post-Game Quotes, Game Recap, and Game Statistics for each game during 2010 Army Football Season; and Season Statistics. Last accessed on February 28, 2022.
https://www.goarmywestpoint.com.

U.S. Department of Defense. United States Military Academy. Office of Athletic Communications. *Hassin Earns Two*

Weekly Honors, November 1, 2010. Last accessed on March 11, 2022.
https://www.goarmywestpoint.com.

U.S. Department of Defense. United States Military Academy. Office of Athletic Communications. *Homme Named Semifinalist for NFF Award*, September 30, 2010. Last accessed on March 11, 2022.
https://www.goarmywestpoint.com.

U.S. Department of Defense. United States Military Academy. Office of Athletic Communications. *McNary Adds Another Preseason Honor*, June 9, 2010. Last accessed on March 11, 2022.
https://www.goarmywestpoint.com.

U.S. Department of Defense. United States Military Academy. Office of Athletic Communications. *McNary Honored by College Football Performance Award*, September 13, 2020. Last accessed on March 11, 2022.
https://www.goarmywestpoint.com.

U.S. Department of Defense. United States Military Academy. Office of Athletic Communications. *McNary Named Finalist for Burlsworth Trophy*, December 3, 2020. Last accessed on March 11, 2022.
https://www.goarmywestpoint.com.

U.S. Department of Defense. United States Military Academy. Office of Athletic Communications. *McNary Named Midseason All-American*, October 20, 2010. Last accessed on March 11, 2022.
https://www.goarmywestpoint.com.

U.S. Department of Defense. United States Military Academy. Office of Athletic Communications. *McNary Named to Lott Trophy Watch List*, April 15, 2010. Last accessed on March 11, 2022.
https://www.goarmywestpoint.com.

U.S. Department of Defense. United States Military Academy. Office of Athletic Communications. *McNary One to Watch for Lombardi Award*, August 27, 2010. Last accessed on March 11, 2022.

https://www.goarmywestpoint.com.

U.S. Department of Defense. United States Military Academy. Office of Athletic Communications. *2009 Army Football Media Guide*. West Point, NY: N.p., 2009.

U.S. Department of Defense. United States Military Academy. Office of Athletic Communications. 2010 Armed Forces Bowl Champions, December 31, 2010. Last accessed on March 11, 2022.
https://www.goarmywestpoint.com.

U.S. Department of Defense. United States Military Academy. Office of Athletic Communications. *2010 Army Football Media Guide*. West Point, NY: N.p., 2010.

U.S. Department of Defense. United States Military Academy. Office of Athletic Communications. *2011 Army Football Media Guide*. West Point, NY: N.p., 2011.

Acknowledgements

I would like to thank the many folks that have encouraged me in this effort, especially the unyielding support of my beautiful bride and lifelong partner, Hilary.

Many of the members of my USMA Class of 1978 continue to support my crazy efforts of writing about Army Football - thanks to my brothers and sister.

Hopefully the athletic administrative will become more supportive in the future. Meanwhile, I would like to thank their historian Mady Salvani for her continued support.

Thanks to the wp.org organization, and the many class and other moderators. This provides many West Point graduates and friends with breaking and informative news that you just cannot find elsewhere. Please continue to support this organization.

My appreciation to a number of university athletic departments and bowl committees for providing information on the first four Army bowl games, such as Payton Holcombe (University of Alabama), Josh Maxson (University of Alabama), Kirk Sampson (Auburn University), Kent William Brown (University of Illinois), Benjamin Phlegar (Michigan State University), Scott Swegan (Stanford University), Matt Garvey (Peach Bowl Committee), and Erik Evenson (Independence Bowl Committee). Sure hope to meet you Erik at the 2022 Independence Bowl this December. Last but not the least, thanks to Kaitlyn R. of the Thayer Hotel staff on information on the bowl plaques.

THE END

Another book by Mike Belter, available as either a free eBook or you may buy it as a paperback. **Operation Black September: The 1977 Army Football Team**. The 1977 Army Football Team was the most successful team at West Point during the 1970s. The team won the Commander-in-Chief's Trophy by beating both Navy and Air Force and was offered a bowl bid. Players were united by their two Co-Captains (Chuck D'Amico and Leamon Hall), and this led to the only winning Army Football team between the 1972-1984 seasons. Key to the season was Operation Black September, when on a dark night in September before the 1977 season began, the starters gathered in the middle of the field at Michie Stadium, pledged to do their best for the team and each other, and each cut their right thumbs and placed their bloody fingerprint on a football (they called it the Blood Ball). Follow these Army Cadets through a tough season playing the eventual national champion and the previous season's national champion, plus nine other opponents to a winning record of 7-4-0, the best season since 1968 and something Army would not repeat until 1984.

www.ingramcontent.com/pod-product-compliance
Lightning Source LLC
LaVergne TN
LVHW051540070426
835507LV00021B/2344